Actions of Their Own to Learn

TRANSGRESSIONS: CULTURAL STUDIES AND EDUCATION

Series Editor

Shirley R. Steinberg, *Werklund School of Education, University of Calgary, Canada*

Founding Editor

Joe L. Kincheloe (1950–2008) *The Paulo and Nita Freire International Project for Critical Pedagogy*

Editorial Board

Rochelle Brock, *University of North Carolina, Greensboro, USA*
Annette Coburn, *University of the West of Scotland, UK*
Kenneth Fasching-Varner, *Louisiana State University, USA*
Luis Huerta-Charles, *New Mexico State University, USA*
Christine Quail, *McMaster University, Canada*
Jackie Seidel, *University of Calgary, Canada*
Cathryn Teasley, *University of A Coruña, Spain*
Sandra Vega, *IPEC Instituto de Pedagogía Crítica, Mexico*
Mark Vicars, *Victoria University, Queensland, Australia*

This book series is dedicated to the radical love and actions of Paulo Freire, Jesus "Pato" Gomez, and Joe L. Kincheloe.

TRANSGRESSIONS: CULTURAL STUDIES AND EDUCATION

Cultural studies provides an analytical toolbox for both making sense of educational practice and extending the insights of educational professionals into their labors. In this context *Transgressions: Cultural Studies and Education* provides a collection of books in the domain that specify this assertion. Crafted for an audience of teachers, teacher educators, scholars and students of cultural studies and others interested in cultural studies and pedagogy, the series documents both the possibilities of and the controversies surrounding the intersection of cultural studies and education. The editors and the authors of this series do not assume that the interaction of cultural studies and education devalues other types of knowledge and analytical forms. Rather the intersection of these knowledge disciplines offers a rejuvenating, optimistic, and positive perspective on education and educational institutions. Some might describe its contribution as democratic, emancipatory, and transformative. The editors and authors maintain that cultural studies helps free educators from sterile, monolithic analyses that have for too long undermined efforts to think of educational practices by providing other words, new languages, and fresh metaphors. Operating in an interdisciplinary cosmos, *Transgressions: Cultural Studies and Education* is dedicated to exploring the ways cultural studies enhances the study and practice of education. With this in mind the series focuses in a non-exclusive way on popular culture as well as other dimensions of cultural studies including social theory, social justice and positionality, cultural dimensions of technological innovation, new media and media literacy, new forms of oppression emerging in an electronic hyperreality, and postcolonial global concerns. With these concerns in mind cultural studies scholars often argue that the realm of popular culture is the most powerful educational force in contemporary culture. Indeed, in the twenty-first century this pedagogical dynamic is sweeping through the entire world. Educators, they believe, must understand these emerging realities in order to gain an important voice in the pedagogical conversation.

Without an understanding of cultural pedagogy's (education that takes place outside of formal schooling) role in the shaping of individual identity – youth identity in particular – the role educators play in the lives of their students will continue to fade. Why do so many of our students feel that life is incomprehensible and devoid of meaning? What does it mean, teachers wonder, when young people are unable to describe their moods, their affective affiliation to the society around them. Meanings provided young people by mainstream institutions often do little to help them deal with their affective complexity, their difficulty negotiating the rift between meaning and affect. School knowledge and educational expectations seem as anachronistic as a ditto machine, not that learning ways of rational thought and making sense of the world are unimportant.

But school knowledge and educational expectations often have little to offer students about making sense of the way they feel, the way their affective lives are shaped. In no way do we argue that analysis of the production of youth in an electronic mediated world demands some "touchy-feely" educational superficiality. What is needed in this context is a rigorous analysis of the interrelationship between pedagogy, popular culture, meaning making, and youth subjectivity. In an era marked by youth depression, violence, and suicide such insights become extremely important, even life saving. Pessimism about the future is the common sense of many contemporary youth with its concomitant feeling that no one can make a difference.

If affective production can be shaped to reflect these perspectives, then it can be reshaped to lay the groundwork for optimism, passionate commitment, and transformative educational and political activity. In these ways cultural studies adds a dimension to the work of education unfilled by any other sub-discipline. This is what *Transgressions: Cultural Studies and Education* seeks to produce – literature on these issues that makes a difference. It seeks to publish studies that help those who work with young people, those individuals involved in the disciplines that study children and youth, and young people themselves improve their lives in these bizarre times.

Actions of Their Own to Learn

Studies in Knowing, Acting, and Being

Edited by

Bonnie Shapiro
University of Calgary, Canada

BRILL
SENSE

LEIDEN | BOSTON

The Library of Congress Cataloging-in-Publication Data is available online at http://catalog.loc.gov

ISBN: 978-94-6351-198-8 (paperback)
ISBN: 978-94-6351-199-5 (hardback)
ISBN: 978-94-6351-200-8 (e-book)

All chapters in this book have undergone peer review.

Copyright 2018 by Koninklijke Brill NV, Leiden, The Netherlands.

Koninklijke Brill NV incorporates the imprints Brill, Brill Hes & De Graaf, Brill Nijhoff, Brill Rodopi, Brill Sense and Hotei Publishing.

All rights reserved. No part of this publication may be reproduced, translated, stored in a retrieval system, or transmitted in any form or by any means, electronic, mechanical, photocopying, recording or otherwise, without prior written permission from the publisher.

Authorization to photocopy items for internal or personal use is granted by Koninklijke Brill NV provided that the appropriate fees are paid directly to The Copyright Clearance Center, 222 Rosewood Drive, Suite 910, Danvers, MA 01923, USA. Fees are subject to change.

This book is printed on acid-free paper and produced in a sustainable manner.

TABLE OF CONTENTS

Part I: Agency, Personal Meaning, Action, and Activism in Research and Learning

1. Action to Learn as a Form of Knowledge ... 3
   Bonnie Shapiro

2. Activism, Action and Becoming: Taking Action to Learn What It Means to Embrace an Activist/Agentic Research Identity ... 17
   Paul Hart and Catherine Hart

3. Walking My Talk: Taking Action to Learn/Relearn/Unlearn towards Engaged Pedagogy ... 41
   Peta White

4. Transforming Park Education as a Transformed Park Educator ... 59
   Don Carruthers Den Hoed

Part II: Actions of Their Own to Learn in Knowledge Building Communities

5. Taking Actions to Learn as Part of a Classroom Collective ... 87
   Jo Towers and Lyndon C. Martin

6. Taking Action to Learn by Asking One's Own Questions in a Physics Course for Prospective Teachers ... 105
   Emily Hanke van Zee

7. Primary School Students' Constructions of Help-Seeking: A Resource for the Design of Learning Environments ... 123
   Bonnie Shapiro

8. The School That Listens: Freedom to Learn without Labels ... 143
   Alison Peacock

9. Understanding and Supporting Professionals' Own Efforts to Learn in Online Health Disciplines Courses ... 159
   Sherri Melrose

TABLE OF CONTENTS

Part III: Participative Research, Teaching, and Learning: Disrupting Social and Political Discourses

10. Student-Led Learning for 'Altruistic' Socio-Political Actions   177
    J. Lawrence Bencze

11. Learning to Engage in Social Action Using Photovoice: A Participatory Action Engagement to Transform Learning   199
    Kathleen C. Sitter

12. Adapting Photovoice in the Classroom: Guiding Students in the Creation of a Photovoice Project   215
    Kathleen C. Sitter

13. A New Paradigm for Teaching, Leading and Learning in Participatory Learning Environments   225
    Eugene G. Kowch

14. Designing Support for Active Participation in Learning and Research   253
    Bonnie Shapiro

About the Contributors   271

PART I

AGENCY, PERSONAL MEANING, ACTION, AND ACTIVISM IN RESEARCH AND LEARNING

BONNIE SHAPIRO

1. ACTION TO LEARN AS A FORM OF KNOWLEDGE

HOW DO HUMAN BEINGS CREATE MEANING FOR THEMSELVES?

What does it mean to take actions of one's own to learn? In this volume we present research and writing from a diverse range of professional research contexts that uncover some of the ways human beings take actions of their own to create meaning. We present research and descriptions of practice that contribute fresh, new understandings of the complex, dynamic processes involved when human beings take action to build new knowledge. Taking action to learn refers to the activities learners engage in within formal and informal learning settings. It also refers to the actions researchers take during the process of building new knowledge as they pose questions about the world and design new ways to collect and analyse information to answer those questions.

Traditionally, the process of building new knowledge has been viewed as a solely cognitive, intellectual engagement occurring only in the mind. Our work asserts that a conception of what it means to learn must be framed as part of a larger process of building understanding that involves more than the mind. To learn in this way is to engage in a quest to understand that is much like engaging in research. Understanding the ways learners and researchers engage in building knowledge is freshly conceptualized in this volume to include aspects of the whole human being that have been excluded. We offer new conceptions of knowledge-building that include understandings of the ways learners and researchers experience and make sense of the world through capacities that include their own deep interests and concerns, actions, thoughts, and feelings that involve the body as well as the mind.

Social cognitive theorist Albert Bandura (2001) writes that the essence of humanness is the capacity to exercise control over the nature and quality of one's life:

> Among the mechanisms of personal agency, none are more central or pervasive than people's beliefs in their capability to exercise some measure of control over their functioning and over environmental events. (Bandura, 2001, p. 10)

Human beings are agents of the experiences in their lives, acting in dynamic ways as they engage with environment. This is the foundational perspective underlying new conceptions of cognition that assert that knowing and learning are inseparable from the actions taken by the individual to learn (Masciotra, Roth, & Morel, 2007; Thompson, 2007; Varela, Thompson, & Rosch, 1991). To understand the experience

B. Shapiro (Ed.), Actions of Their Own to Learn, 3–15.
© 2018 Koninklijke Brill NV. All rights reserved.

of knowing, doing and being as inseparable is to recognize that the knower's actions and the knower's environment exist in a dynamic and synergetic relationship.

The dramatic pace of changing social, environmental and political realities demands a continual rethinking of what we must know in order to live meaningfully and well, prompting new debates about how learning, teaching and research should be (re)conceptualized. One argument contends that attention should focus on defining which content knowledge is of greatest importance. While establishing *what* to learn is important, in this volume we give high status to the importance of new studies and thinking that help understand the ways human beings learn *how* to build new knowledge.

As agents of action, learners can also become self-aware examiners of their own functioning, able to play a part in their own self-development, adaptation, and self-renewal (Bandura, 2001). Experiences that offer opportunities to actively participate in learning help build participants' positive self image as a successful agent of action in learning. Knowledge, actions to learn, sense of identity and research/learning environments are therefore dynamically interwoven. When learners have the opportunity to understand and reflect on their own natural approaches to learning, they are better able to consider trying new approaches and actions that lead to greater success. The quest to seek new knowledge finds participants often working simultaneously as researchers, teachers and learners. The actions, thoughts and feelings involved in efforts to seek new understandings can be seen as resources that may support or interfere with the process of knowledge-building.

In this volume we present stories of our professional work and our mutual pursuits to gain understanding of features of our own and others' actions to learn. Taking action to learn is conceptualized broadly here as constituting the thoughts, feelings and activities involved during participation in knowledge-building processes. This volume is organized around three contexts: (1) Researchers and learners seeking agency and personal meaning, (2) Research on learners' active engagements in learning with others, and (3) The creation and design of environments that support taking action to learn.

Our chapters are guided by a range of theoretical frameworks that seek to understand learning as knowing, acting and being. A constructivist world-view is at the foundation of many chapter discussions. It sees the development of new understanding as a process of engagement with new ideas mediated through prior ideas and experiences, resulting in the construction of new mental representations. Emerging enactivist world-view perspectives add additional dimensions that give high status to the kinds of actions human beings take as they build new understandings. It is through both types of these types of engagements – intellectual and action/doing, that individuals also develop views about their capabilities and strengths as learning beings. In this book, we recognize the emergence of new understandings and the development of learner identity by recognizing the ways knowing, acting, and being are interwoven in the process of learning. We conceptualize learner engagement in *Actions of Their Own to Learn*, as itself, *a vital form of knowledge*. In order to develop and support this knowledge, it must be more fully understood.

STUDYING ACTIONS TO LEARN AS A FORM OF KNOWLEDGE: WHAT CHIILDREN BRING TO LIGHT

As editor, my conceptualization of this volume emerges from longstanding interests in personal meaning and agency in learning (Shapiro, 1994, 2011, 2014a, 2014b, 2015, 2016). A number of years ago, I developed a study to understand the ways children engage in knowledge-building as they learn concepts in science (Shapiro, 1994, 2011). The ways students make their own efforts to learn had long been an area of interest in my work as a classroom teacher and science teacher educator. I 'embedded' in a grade five classroom over a three-month period. Fully welcomed by students and staff, I sat every day with a delightful group of 11–12 year old children to understand how they took actions of their own to learn while engaged in studies of the science topic *light*. A primary focus in research on children's learning in science at the time was devoted to building representations of children's ideas about science concepts typically taught in the school program. Piaget's work to understand children's ideas about a range of topics was highly regarded at that time (Piaget, 1971). His research engaged children in clinical interviews, usually conducted outside of the classroom settings, in an effort to represent learner ideas about phenomena. This highly influential work inspired the beginning of a huge volume of research studies, conference presentations and international seminars and curriculum development (Novak, 1987; Pfundt & Duit, 1991). Piaget's foundational work identified students' most commonly held ideas about a range of natural phenomena and began to describe patterns in some of the ways learner conceptions deviated from accepted understandings. In science learning, the primary goal of much of the work that followed was to move students from the "wrong" ideas they held about a topic, referred to as *misconceptions*, to scientifically correct ideas. As I explored this fascinating line of inquiry, I began to question some of its assumptions. In some studies, descriptions of learner ideas seemed to miss some of the very thoughtful ways children were thinking as they expressed their ideas. Some conference presentations on learner conceptions seemed to trivialize, even at times ridicule, children's ideas. While assisting students to move towards the most scientifically correct ideas seemed a worthy goal, I felt that something was missing in the research literature. Learners' thinking processes and the ways they were connected to active efforts to learn were not being given valued consideration. In an effort to move away from a sole focus on mental constructions of knowledge, I created a study to document the actions learners were taking to learn as well as their thoughts and feelings as they engaged in knowledge-building. The primary goal was to contribute deeper understanding of the wholeness of learners' experiences as they built new knowledge in the classroom setting. The intentions were to give high importance to the variety of ways learners moved through their learning world, to document their feelings about learning science and how their learning experiences affected development of a *sense of identity* as learners of science. The project challenged a sole focus on identifying learners' incorrect ideas in science by presenting case report descriptions of the interplay between cognition, action and the environment as learners contributed to their own knowledge development in real learning settings.

The ideas about knowledge-building are rooted in the ways we conceptualize the nature of mind in the complex and dynamic processes involved in coming to know. A constructivist worldview presents learning as a process in which human beings are actively involved in the mental constructions of ideas using prior knowledge and experiences as a foundation. One of the first constructivist theoreticians, psychologist George Kelly, explained that we use personal constructs to organize and engage with new ideas (Kelly, 1969). A personal construct is essentially a linguistic structure used as a template to "straddle the unfamiliar with the familiar." Kelly's work has been effectively used to help individuals learn to change their thinking in a variety of psychological and educational contexts. He suggested the metaphor, "the person as a form of motion," to emphasize the dynamic changing nature of knowledge-building. Changing ideas and actions are accomplished by helping the individual recognize the ways they use their own constructs to build understanding and as a vehicle to help them consider new constructs and ways of behaving. In educational settings, this suggests the value of building language-rich environments to assist learners in the process of modifying their understandings. In this active process, new knowledge emerges as do new understandings of self, sense of identity and being. The primary assumption of a constructivist perspective is that individuals build their own meanings for events and experiences. Its dominant focus in the literature has been to describe the ways learners use prior ideas to build new mental constructions (Shapiro, 1994, 2011). In this study I attempted to add new dimensions to explain the ways children learn concepts in science by showing the ways children's active efforts to engage in their learning world contribute to learning new concepts in science, and their own understandings of themselves as learners.

Six children were involved in the foundational study, three girls and three boys. Two were identified by their teacher as high achievers and showed a very high level of emotional adjustment within and outside the setting. Two were achieving at an average level and with a normal level of emotional adjustment. Two were struggling with their schoolwork and with personal and social emotional issues both inside and outside the classroom. Video and observational records documented daily actions and conversations in the classroom as they moved through their individual and group learning. I spoke with students regularly to learn how they experienced and described new developing understandings as well as actions and feelings in the learning settings that had been constructed for them. Instructors guide students using instructional goals and objectives. At the same time, I discovered the many ways each individual takes actions based on their own personal interests and purposes.

The remarkable insight that emerged through study with individual students was that each child demonstrated their own unique approach to being in, and learning about, their world. I found that each child in the study displayed a unique 'personal orientation to learning' that had pattern and coherence and revealed an approach to meaning-making that was stable over the considerable length of time

I spent in the classroom. The research revealed how children engaged in natural and spontaneous actions as they moved through their learning world. Each person showed a unique way of taking action to learn. Each student's actions also had an observable impact on fellow students' learning activities and on the classroom teacher's actions as well. The students' actions revealed a blend of their own meaning-making goals and the instructional goals of their teacher. The discovery of these patterns showed the ways learners engaged in actions of their own as a resource for understanding their world. I began to conceptualize these actions as a form of knowledge children were using as a resource for learning. Each person employed their own actions as a resource that was used to 'live their questions' about the world. Each person's actions influenced their developing sense of identity as a science learner. The case reports show the ways that each child's unique *approach to learning* affected their ultimate acquisition of scientific content knowledge (Shapiro, 1994, 2011). While each story provided vital insights, the story of the efforts of one of the more mystifying children in the study, Melody, is presented here as an example of how one research participant uniquely transformed my thinking as a researcher.

Like all of the children in the study, Melody's *actions of her own to learn* in the world of the classroom were a unique mix of the goals of her teacher, the curriculum, and her own goals and interests in the classroom. Interviews with Melody showed that she was aware of some of her own meaning- making approaches in action. She was aware of some of the challenges for her in school, telling me "I have some difficulty sometimes in school. I'm in the lower reading group, and in math, and a lot of the time, I don't know or understand what I am supposed to do. Mr. Ryan doesn't help me sometimes." Melody did not appear to be aware of aspects of the pattern of her actions to learn in the classroom that led her teacher to constantly redirect and reprimand her. She frequently mentioned to me that she almost never understood the purpose of a lesson task or what it was that she was supposed to be doing. Although she felt it was her teacher's responsibility to make sure she understood what to do, never once did I observe her asking him for help in order to clarify the instructions or how to work with the materials. Her natural pattern was to engage with members of her study group to learn what to do and often to learn what the correct answers were. She quickly identified the students in the larger classroom who were most likely to have correct responses and took action to learn what they were thinking and doing. Her profound interest in the social lives of others, and in conversing with them about what they were thinking meant that she was frequently absent from her study group. Often I would find her out of her seat looking at what other groups in the class were doing and talking about. Melody possessed an amazing ability to state the ideas that were emerging in several of the study groups in the classroom. The highly developed social skills that got her into trouble daily, served as a powerful resource for learning in the classroom world. She attained a considerable grasp of some of the most difficult science content at the end of the unit evidenced by work on the summative evaluation materials and in personal interviews with her. At the same time, these powerfully effective actions that helped her learn were causing her to be regularly reprimanded by the teacher for "not doing what she was supposed to be doing." Melody's behaviour was often also highly annoying to fellow students during the lessons. Instead of clarifying and attending to the tasks set by the teacher, Melody would regularly play with the science equipment, using it to explore or test out ideas completely unrelated to the lesson. When doing so, she would often successfully draw all of the children in her study group away from accomplishing the tasks on the worksheet, engaging them with her own personal line of inquiry. She regularly spoke to me about her love of science because of all the beautiful things "you get to look at." In small group work she often drew the attention of fellow students to the aesthetic features of materials. In the example below, the children are working on an activity with a light source called "Bend that Beam":

[Melody reaches over to move the light source around]

Martin:	Get outa here Melody!
Melody:	I was trying to fix it, Martin. Let me use your magnifier.
Martin:	No. Get outa here. We're trying to do the activity.
Melody:	I just want to use if for a minute. You're supposed to share.

[Melody moves the beaker around to create a new effect]

Martin:	Hey don't! Hey, that's not what we're supposed to do, Melody. Get outa here!
Melody:	I was just fixing it. Oh, oh, look Yasmin, look inside the light source. OOoooooh! Neat! Wow, look!
Yasmin:	Neat eh? [All of the group members now gather around the light source]
Melody:	It looks like a pretty little house in there. And it looks just like grass down there.
Yasmin:	Hey, look. It looks like you can see a little school in there.
Steven:	It looks like peat moss.
Martin:	Oh, it's weird. It's all sorts of little silver things. [Martin reaches down into the light source] Oh, ouch! Hey! There, boy, is that hot! Man, I burned my finger.
Yasmin:	Yeah. My hand is way out here and it's hot.

[Martin returns to the worksheet]

Martin:	Okay. Steven. Let's draw this. There. I drew mine. [Martin manipulates the light source] Hey! Look what it does when you move the light beams!

[Despite the movement of the group back to the task at hand, Melody continues to look down into the light source. Martin covers part of the top to alter the angle of the beams pasting through the beaker, one of the required lesson tasks, then moves the light box away from her]

Melody: Don't! Oooooh. It looks like a bug.
Martin: Whaaaaaat?! [Loudly] Who cares? Go away Melody. Get outa here. Do what you're supposed to do. Okay, okay, what's this word, Steve?
Yasmin: Particular dummo. You're supposed to see where it crosses and put it on the sheet.

(Shapiro, 1994, p. 118)

Melody was drawn to the aesthetic features of the materials, such as "the pretty way the light box looks when staring straight down at it." Though this interest moved her away from the goals of the science lesson, another aspect of the way she took action to pursue her interests had a more positive impact on her learning. Because of her deep interest in the social life of school and social interactions, Melody showed remarkable awareness of scientific meanings that were emerging in small groups in the classroom. What she did not seem to be aware of was the way that her unique, personal approaches ran counter to the expectations for performance in her classroom.

I presented case reports documenting the activities of each child in the study group to deepen understanding of learners' ways of being engaged in their learning. Lave (1988) referred to such descriptions as "displays or performances of knowing in action." My purpose was to build understanding of the impact of actions to learn on knowing and sense of identity as learners. I learned from all of the children, and uniquely from Melody, that it was *because of*, not *despite* her habit of distractedly playing with the equipment, looking for the beauty in her world and socializing, that she was grasping ideas. Melody's own unique approach to take actions to learn allowed her to put some of the main ideas of the lesson together without ever reading the directions on class worksheets or trying to figure out on her own what needed to be done. She grasped many science ideas in this way. Unfortunately, because of her ongoing awareness that she usually did not know what to do in her lessons, she developed an extremely poor sense of herself as a successful learner of science.

There is a tendency in school settings to reinforce particular learning orientations or ways of taking action to learn, over others. Students who work quietly and sequentially are typically rewarded with good grades and accolades from their teachers, parents and guardians. They require less time and challenge for a teacher who must deal with a large number of students. It is sometimes challenging to work with a child who makes large, and sometimes loud leaps of insight. Melody was confounding to her teacher whose primarily interaction with her was to redirect her to "stop what she was doing and do what she was supposed to be doing." Because of this, he did not have an opportunity to observe the profound impact she was having on fellow students and ultimately, the ways that she was grasping concepts that many others did not.

As Maturana and Varela (1987) so powerfully first elucidated, human beings learn by moving through the world they inhabit. They are transformed by experiences as they take actions of their own to learn in the world. At the same time, learners transform the world as they take action in it, as noted in the emerging enactivist perspectives literature (Masciotra, Roth, & Morel, 2007). To understand how to best guide and support *learning about how to learn* we must first value the ways human beings naturally and spontaneously take actions of their own to learn as they build knowledge. The action each individual takes is unique, revealing a pattern of behaviour that has structure and coherence (Shapiro, 1994, 2011). The pattern of natural, spontaneous actions may not necessarily be apparent to the person who is acting. The pattern of actions represents a repertoire of skills used as resources to learn about and move through the world. This personal repertoire of skills is used in the complex process of building knowledge in formal, organized learning settings where traditionally, knowledge outcomes are pre-determined. This repertoire of skills is also used in other kinds of knowledge-building settings where individuals make spontaneous choices as they learn, often based on unexpected challenges and issues that emerge as part of the process of solving a problem. Depending on the ways that individuals take actions of their own to learn, they may find the learning experience and the design of the learning setting highly compatible with their own personal approach to learning. In this case, they often experience a strong affirmation and *sense of identity as a successful knowledge builder.* If their personal actions and approaches to learning are not accepted or supported within the learning environment, as was the case for Melody, the learner may experience frustration and may cause instructor frustration. Melody clearly developed a poor sense of identity as a learner. She consistently saw herself as failing as a knowledge builder. Melody was not aware of her own pattern of behaviour when learning or the importance of taking responsibility for her own actions to learn. I followed the children for many years into junior high school, high school and college or university, and into their adult lives, For most of the participants in the study group, the patterns appearing in the early grades persisted, and this was true for Melody. With others, due to institutional interventions, or life circumstances, these patterns changed (Shapiro, 1994).

As mentioned, my thinking as a researcher about the ways children were learning was deeply influenced by the patterns I identified in the ways the children took actions to learn. The reflexive nature of this type of long-term research also demonstrated the importance of considering the influence of the researcher on the participants. The children discovered that I had been a classroom teacher for a number of years before I began research work in their classroom. One day they asked if I would sometime teach them while visiting in the classroom. I resisted at first, as this was not part of the research agreement arranged with their teacher. I was also concerned that doing so could potentially influence or interfere with my work as researcher. When an actual movement developed to recruit me, cheerfully supported by their teacher, I finally accepted the invitation, realizing that it was an excellent opportunity to gain deeper insight into their ways of learning and knowing from a teaching perspective.

ACTION TO LEARN AS A FORM OF KNOWLEDGE

I created a lesson to help students learn to use a heuristic tool, a concept map, to organize some of the ideas about light that they were learning. I began the discussion by saying, 'As you all know, I am not only a researcher in your classroom looking at the ways you are learning ideas here, but I am also a teacher. As a teacher, it is my responsibility to teach in the best way I can, and you know that when you are a student, it is your responsibility to make every effort to learn well. I'm going to share with you today something that you can do to be a better student, that is, to better take up *your* responsibility to be a better learner.'

I was astounded by the initial response of the students. There was such excitement in the room about this new idea that they might actually be able to learn to take actions that would *enhance their own personal learning efforts*!! I will never forget the looks of excited interest on their bright, shining faces. Clearly, the idea that there might be actions they could take *to become even better learners* was entirely new to them. I believe that the reason the children listened and responded with such enthusiasm was in large part due to their recognition of the ways I had been so carefully and respectfully listening to them in the effort to uncover the nature of their efforts to learn. I continued to have contact with the children throughout their junior high and high school years as I now that they are adults, I continue to learn about their ideas about the meaning of science learning in their lives.

THE CHAPTERS IN OUR VOLUME: STUDYING ACTIONS OF THEIR OWN TO LEARN AS A FORM OF KNOWLEDGE

As I pursued this work further, I learned about the journeys and diverse efforts of outstanding colleagues who are also engaged in work to understand how learners and researchers work as agents of action in their own efforts to learn. I invited them to contribute to this volume by addressing the overarching question, "What does it mean to take actions of one's own to learn?" Each chapter presents an interpretation of this question through research and reflection as the authors describe their own unique research and teaching/practice contexts. The chapters are organized into three sections.

Section One: Agency, Personal Meaning, Action and Activism in Research Lays the Groundwork for Understanding Agency in Meaning-Making

Following this introductory chapter, *Paul Hart and Catherine Hart* present an exploration of the meaning of activism-action-and-becoming in environmental education research. Their discussion challenges researchers to take action to become critically engaged in (re)conceptualizing the meaning of research work in environmental education. The authors argue that researchers, as knowledge builders, must take action to understand the emerging values of the communities they study. Hart and Hart discuss what it means for researchers to be affected by and engage with the values of the communities they research. They recommend resources to help researchers consider the ways they may embrace activist, agentic identities in their work.

Australian environmental educator *Peta White* was amazed to find that a carbon footprint calculator revealed her own footprint to be far larger than she, an environmental educator, would ever have predicted. She describes the design of an autoethnographic study that allowed her to take actions of her own to learn how she might change some living habits in order to reduce her carbon footprint. The experience with her methodological approach and the new knowledge understandings she gained are presented as the foundation for the creation of curriculum resources to help her own teacher preparation students learn to take their own actions to reduce their carbon footprints. *Don Carruthers den Hoed* describes his use of a transformational theory of knowledge-building as a resource for rethinking his work as a Provincial Parks educator. Don reflects on the circumstances that inspired changes in his role as designer of educational experiences in provincial parks. His thoughtful model provides a framework for thinking about learning in informal settings, and in application to the development of resources to guide visitors to become active rather than passive participants in parks learning experiences.

Section Two: Actions of Their Own to Learn in Knowledge-Building Communities

Chapters in this section provide new insight into the ways that taking actions to learn are achieved by individual learners are also dependent on the emergence of meanings that are developed in community with others.

Mathematics educators *Jo Towers and Lyndon Martin* employ an enactivist perspective to examine the ways learners take action as members of a mathematics learning community. They describe a setting wonderfully orchestrated by a skilled classroom teacher who creates structures that engage students in improvisational and collective actions to learn as they solve complex problems in mathematics. They show how students learn individually and also take action with others to build communal knowledge about the social world.

Physics teacher educator *Emily Hanke van Zee* describes work with prospective teachers in her inquiry-based physics course where she helps students develop the skills needed to ask their own questions about science phenomena studied in class. Student teachers make their own decisions about *what* to study, and *how* to pursue studies of physics phenomena. They share the results of their work with their classroom community of student teacher colleagues. They create resources to be used in formal school based learning settings. The also invite family members and friends to participate as learners with the curriculum experiences as well.

Science teacher educator, and editor of this volume, *Bonnie Shapiro*, employs constructivist and enactivist perspectives, to document elementary school students' efforts to seek help when needed while engaged in learning with others in science study groups. The help-seeking approaches they use are seen as displays of the skill repertoires learners draw on that reveal their ideas about how to act, and who to engage with when they do not understand what to do next in learning. This research suggests ways classroom settings can be organized in ways that provide better support for learners' own efforts to seek help in learning.

Education administrator *Dame Alison Peacock* shows how listening in authentic ways to children's ideas and concerns about their learning informs her award-winning work to create a culture of success in a school where both students and teachers once struggled (Peacock, 2010). Dame Peacock shares how she learned along with staff and students that a focus on building trust became the essential foundation that helped both teachers and students develop the confidence needed to see themselves as collaborators, rather than competitors in learning and teaching. This insight, created a new "culture of self-regulation" in the school, where all participants recognized themselves as leaders in their own personal quests to learn and as leaders in the support of the learning of one another.

Nurse educator, *Sherri Melrose* presents case reports of adult learners in the health professions, to show the ways a university conceptualizes the creation of structures of adult online learning environments that recognize and support learner autonomy for those studying courses in the health professions. She explores the ways learning experiences are designed with understandings of the unique ways that mature learners must often overcome significant challenges involved as they learn to take actions of their own to learn.

Section Three: Design for Participative Research, Teaching, and Learning: Disrupting Social and Political Discourses

The chapters in this section present practical and theoretical resources to help create environments for original, self-directed knowledge-building activities. Authors present their views about the ways educational structures must be re-organized to support the efforts of learners to take their own actions to learn. They show how new structures must often challenge and disrupt traditional ways of organizing knowledge and learning environments.

Science educator *Lawrence Bencze* presents the story of his lifelong work to support and study inquiry teaching approaches that promote knowledge-building and dissemination activities, where students are in full control of decisions about how their scientific inquiries will proceed. His recent research and teaching activities guide students to take "altruistic" learning actions of their own to identify, based on a social justice perspective, science and environmental issues of critical importance in the world. His work addresses the challenges of new, activist engagements in science education, noting that as students take actions of their own to learn, they may arrive at conclusions that do not necessarily align with those of mainstream professional scientists and/or engineers, thereby informing and at the same time, challenging current scientific, social and political knowledge structures.

Social work educator *Kathleen Sitter* employs photovoice, a participatory visual media approach that brings people together to help them address social justice and human rights issues together. Collectively they learn to take actions of their own to present concerns that have not yet been heard by those who have the power to respond. Participants engage in a structured research process using film and photographs as pedagogical tools to articulate and share with others aspects of a story or issue that is of common concern. In this way, they learn to take action to build awareness and engage in political action. Kathleen writes, "I have found that it is in the midst of these pedagogical spaces where critical moments of consciousness occur and where individuals also become active participants in transformational learning." (Sitter, this volume) She presents two chapters in this volume, one building the theoretical foundations of the photovoice approach by exploring its roots in visual media and social change theory. In the second chapter she presents practical considerations and an example of a photovoice project developed by her students.

Educational leadership professor *Eugene Kowch* describes the kinds of administrative approaches needed to build and sustain participative teaching and learning practices that create opportunities for students *and their teachers* to take greater actions of their own to learn. For educators to be successful, Eugene argues that they must be empowered to open up pedagogical spaces by shifting to an information age paradigm. He explores the elements and features of this new paradigm approach and suggests practical suggestions for more collaborative and co-created settings.

A RESOURCE TO GUIDE ONGOING RESEARCH AND THINKING

Through presentations of research and descriptions of practice in this volume we strive to present insights to understand how human beings take actions of their own to build knowledge. This volume is designed to serve as a resource to help identify the kinds of conditions needed to guide and support self-directed efforts. Each contribution offers a unique theoretical approach to understand the complex, dynamic processes involved as human beings engage in personal and social action as they participate in knowledge-building activities. Our chapters explore theoretical foundations and practices that support individual and collective meaning-making in a wide range of contexts. Central to this perspective on the study of learning, is a valuing of accounts of the lived experience of cognition. Included here are stories of the authors' unique uses of theory and the presentation of research findings. They are also the stories of the authors' personal journeys to find new frameworks to position and guide their work. Each chapter of the book, is rooted in the conviction of the importance of the view that the self-directed nature of learning must take a more central place in the understanding of the processes of knowledge acquisition. We offer new theoretical orientations and suggestions to inspire more participative research and greater support for individual and collective meaning-making. It is our hope that this volume provides guidance for researchers and educators involved in the creation of new learning and research environments that help others acquire the freedom, confidence and support they need to learn to more effectively take actions of their own to learn in all aspects of their lives.

REFERENCES

Bandura, A. (2001). Social cognitive theory: An agentic perspective. *Annual Review of Psychology, 52*(1), 1–26.
Kelly, G. (1969). *A theory of personality: The psychology of personal constructs.* New York, NY: W. W. Norton.
Lave, J. (1988). *Cognition in practice.* Campbridge, MA: Harvard University Press.
Masciotra, D., Roth, W.-M., & Morel, D. (2007). *Enaction: Toward a zen mind in learning and teaching.* Rotterdam, The Netherlands: Sense Publishers.
Maturana, H. R., & Varela, F. J. (1987). *The tree of knowledge: The biological roots of human understanding.* Boston, MA: Shambala.
Novak, J. (1987). *Proceedings of the second international seminar on misconceptions and educational strategies in science and mathematics.* Ithaca, NY: Cornell University.
Peacock, A. (2010). The Cambridge primary review: A voice for the future. *Forum, 52*(3), 373–380. Retrieved from http://wroxhamtla.org.uk/wpcontent/themes/striking/resources/research/articles/The_Cambridge_Primary_Review_a_voice_for_the_future.pdf
Pfundt, H., & Duit, R. (Eds.). (1991). *Bibliography: Students' alternative frameworks and science education* (3rd ed.). Kiel: IPN-Kiel.
Piaget, J. (1971). *The construction of reality in the child.* New York, NY: Ballantine Books.
Shapiro, B. (1994). *What children bring to light: A constructivist perspective on children's learning in science.* New York, NY: Teachers College Press.
Shapiro, B. (2011). Towards a transforming constructivism: Understanding learners' meanings and messages of learning environments. *Journal of Educational Thought, 45*(2), 165–202.
Shapiro, B. (2014a, July 24–27). *Personal constructions of STEM learning.* First Congress on the Construction of Personal Meaning, The Constructivist Psychology Network, Coast Plaza Hotel, Vancouver.
Shapiro, B. (2014b). Engaging novice teachers in semiotic inquiry: Considering the environmental messages of school learning settings. *Cultural Studies in Science Education, 9*(4), 809–824.
Shapiro, B. (2015). Structures that teach: Using a semiotic framework to study the environmental messages of learning settings. *Journal of Eco-Thinking, 1*, 1–15.
Shapiro, B. (2016, January 31–February 2). *Children's constructions of help-seeking in learning: A resource for the design of science learning experiences.* Presentation to the 28th Annual Ethnographic & Qualitative and AABSS Research Conference and Pre-Conference Workshops, Organized by University of Las Vegas College of Education, Las Vegas, NV.
Thompson, E. (2007). *Mind in life: Biology, phenomenology and the sciences of mind.* Cambridge, MA: Harvard University Press.
Varela, F. J., Thompson, E., & Rosch, E. (1991). *The embodied mind.* Cambridge, MA: MIT Press.

Bonnie Shapiro
Werklund School of Education
University of Calgary, Canada

PAUL HART AND CATHERINE HART

2. ACTIVISM, ACTION AND BECOMING

Taking Action to Learn What It Means to Embrace an Activist/Agentic Research Identity

INTRODUCTION: RESEARCHING AS LEARNING AND BECOMING

In this chapter we explore how root concepts of activism-action-and-becoming in research challenge researchers to take action to learn to become critically and newly engaged in ways that question and reconceptualize research work in environmental education (EE). We explore possibilities for learning as processes of inquiry using examples from the field of EE research and hope that our discussion will serve as a guide others who wish to explore this path in EE research. First, we have wondered how researchers in EE are working to resolve what Wright and McInnis (1975) historically described as "the worldview issue" as grounding for a socially critical mandate. We discuss what it might mean for researchers to learn to become more critically engaged in academic activism not only in ways that open up the breadth of an expanding research field but more importantly in transforming the depth of our own consciousness. We consider disruption as crucial in questions about the nature and quality of social science and educational research as well as purposes and practices of EE research.

Historically, movements for change in thinking that challenge dominant discourses of "progress" in societies have been disciplined or marginalized (Burrell & Morgan, 1979). This portrayal of "philosophical perspectives" provides insight for those interested in learning how to construct arguments that clarify what is driving change and resistance at levels of discourse in thought. Within the field of EE Robottom and Hart (1993) and Fien (1993) used similar heuristics as framings in theory, at the level of worldviews, to characterize shifts in thinking required to address the international goals of EE as a field struggling to find a places within the educational discourses of "progress." Our focus in this chapter is on related dimensions of research that exemplify attempts to understand the rethinking and learning that emerged as EE challenged orthodoxy within a rapidly evolving politics of social and educational enquiry.

Gough (1987) summarized this change in thinking about educational practices and experiences in terms of new epistemological and ecological paradigms. Fien's (1993) discussion of worldview differences contrasted the dominant social paradigm and a new environmental paradigm. And, Stevenson (1987) characterized forms of knowledge underlying the pedagogical process and teachers' curriculum as a kind of objectivist-subjectivist split which underpinned the quantitative-qualitative shift in educational research. Robottom and Hart (1993) then portrayed this issue as a debate requiring engagement across a range of positivist, interpretivist and critical perspectives as ontologically and epistemologically contested and methodologically engaged. The point was not to seek accommodation but to learn to value their differences in thinking within, against and beyond these historically situated forms of thought, and to recognize what they both reveal and conceal in the present. Rather than adopt a compatibilist voice for paradigmatic accommodation, the argument was for social accommodation at a meta-paradigmatic level. Researcher learning across multiple perspectives seemed crucial for conceptualizing educational research that could address educational problems irrespective of viewpoint. At the time it seemed to us that, despite incongruencies with traditional positivist forms of EE inquiry, engaging rather than ignoring the debate was necessary given the evolution of thinking in the broad fields of social science and education.

Now, over twenty years later, it would be difficult to ignore the onto-epistemological shifts that frame educational research. This chapter explores how roots of activism-action-and-becoming in EE research challenge researchers to become critically re-engaged in learning how to continually question and reconceptualize research work. We do this by actively challenging older methodologies and methods as ways of opening ourselves to ongoing spaces and places of generative problem solving and mapping new approaches that can address complexities of human-more-than-human issues. We begin this process using mappings as heuristics or learning devices for framing research possibilities and for generating pathways across assemblages that help us make sense of intra-actions among research processes. We define "researching" as "coming to know," that is, as learning, with implications for researcher identity or subjectivity. If learning is viewed as becoming, then learning to do research differently implicates an onto-epistemic struggle. For example, learning framed within EE worldviews could be seen as collaborative, participatory, critical and inquiry-based within relational onto-epistemic positionings that could become transformative. A worldview rooted in change sees EE researchers as activist researchers who are open to critical, perhaps disruptive, mobile views on movement within qualitative research methodologies and methods. As Lather (2007) says, moving against tendencies to settle in to various dogmas and reductionism, methodologies of "getting lost" operate at the intersection of research theory and politics.

Thinking of EE researchers' tendencies toward becoming activist, it seems reasonable to look for connections between those inclined toward troubling our taken-for-granted ways of coming to know the world and those who engage in research activism through approaches to inquiry, such as poststructural and new materialist, that disrupt more traditional approaches with notions of collaborative purposeful transformation of research with potential to shift worldviews. And because educational research and social research are evolving, and in the process becoming more complex and inclusive, it seems appropriate to explore promising pathways of change. We see potential in framings and mappings that implicate theory across several levels of thinking, from onto-epistemic, as informed across theoretical perspectives (e.g., feminist, indigenous) to emerging methodological multiplicities that provide praxis for fieldwork methods.

CONCEPTUAL RESOURCES FOR ACTIVITIST INQUIRY

A common foundation for new socio-environmental approaches in EE, that are often participatory and action-oriented, is relational ontology. Social phenomena are viewed as embedded and co-constructed within situated contexts in contrast to essentialist notions of subject-object where learning, or coming to know, is viewed in terms of individual cognition. The reductionist metaphor is replaced with a co-evolutionary metaphor—complementarity of organism and environment. Within this framing, ontology and epistemology are interconnected with implications for research in conceptualizing and studying the social world, including how we view self-identity, knowledge and human-more-than-human relations. This onto-epistemic positioning underlies research directions in several fields including social and discursive psychology, cultural geography, science studies (Latour, 2005) and literary studies (e.g., Masny & Cole, 2012) and emerging research in education. Reductionist coding strategies are no longer assumed to transcend the intimate complexities of lived experiences. Earlier forms of qualitative methodologies (e.g., ethnography, phenomenology) based on interpretivist/constructivist theory have been repositioned within inter-relational/interactional framings where researchers and participants co-construct accounts of experiences. These experiences are described as intra-actions, both discursive and embodied, in constant dialogue in relation to the world.

Within the context of EE research, these shifts have potential to expand relational onto-epistemic framings toward an "activist" emphasis on human action, one that posits learning as an active endeavor in social relations that extend to nonhuman worlds. In other words, the research focus shifts to explore active engagement with the world as a core reality of learning and coming to know. Researching finds a theory base in purposeful collaborative transformation as agentive grounding for learning. Active engagement with researching agents acting in the world forms the basis for many new and emerging approaches to social and educational research. For example, a common foundation of socio-material (and socio-cultural) approaches to inquiry extends relational ways of being and knowing toward projects that collaboratively transform the world—an activist stance that assumes people can come to know themselves by engaging the moral-ethical (ideological) dimensions of activity itself (Stetsenko, 2008). In terms of educational and social research, activist researchers, often with commitments to social and environmental justice, are disrupting their own qualitative inquiries toward emergent innovative approaches. The inherent complexity in tracing these activities warrants mapping researcher positions at meta-theoretical levels from onto-epistemic to methodological. In so doing we see ourselves reconstituting the potential for making sense of the fragmentation of novel approaches that conceptualize and study nature-cultures, context, social interaction, language and discourse and for exploring connections between learning, educational theory and practice.

EXPLORING RESEARCH ACTIVISTS' ENGAGEMENT IN EDUCATIONAL RESEARCH

Addressing complexity in recent changes in qualitative research suggests the need for theory that can address questions beyond normalized, narrative-based, highly interpreted stories and simplistic notions of representation. This means going outside EE research to explore diverse approaches to social and educational research more broadly. Within a context of academic activism educational researchers now view their task within, against and beyond inherited concepts and methodologies. Many researchers critically question research process issues in ways that open up discussion of research theory-praxis. For example, Gough's (2010) notion of rhizomatic play uses maps of networks that shake the arborescence of the research tree by destabilizing taken-for-granted assumptions about what counts as evidence and as knowledge. Here, our process for generating action in EE research begins with framings as mapping ways of playing with linkages across levels of research thought from worldview to fieldwork. In essence, we are mapping changes to framings of the field of qualitative inquiry as a kind of genealogy of change moving through positivist interpretivist, critical, poststructural and new materialist research positions. Our focus is on the movement from relational to transformative-activist, onto-epistemic positioning as relevant to EE (i.e., social and environmental justice) purposes.

What appears to be happening in social and educational research journals is active resistance to simplistic "quick" qualitative research as well as a need for more depth of theoretical grounding. The complexity of human and beyond-human issues implicates a need for theoretical grounding at all levels of thought from theory to fieldwork praxis. In order to make sense of the complexities of thinking with inquiry across onto-epistemic, theoretical perspectives, methodologies and methods, we used representations of inquiry based in Crotty (1998), in combination with framings by Lather and St. Pierre (Lather, 2006) in several iterations, most recently illustrated in Table 2.1.

We have adapted and extended these mappings and have constructed diffractively our own mapping of qualitative inquiry emerging from challenges to represent the rapid evolution of thinking in qualitative and post-qualitative research.

In each case, this work is viewed as experiential and emergent, (Davies, 2014) presenting "concepts for thinking" about processes of inquiry. The purpose is to make

RESEARCH PERSPECTIVES

ONTO-EPISTEMIC GROUNDINGS
Realist-Objectivist   Materialist/Embodied   Constructivist/Subjectivist   Relational   Constructionist

THEORETICAL PERSPECTIVES
•Arts-based   •Feminist   •Queer Theory GLBTQ(O)   •Endarkened   •Indigenous/Decolonizing   •Postcolonial   •Cultural Studies
Interpretivist   Critical Theory (Relationalist)   Poststructural (Postmodernism)
Social Theories (Symbolic Interactionism)

METHODOLOGIES
Empiricist   Grounded Theory   Ethnography   Phenomenology   Narrative Inquiry   Action Research   Deconstruction

Quantitative
Experimental
Mixed Methods

- Critical
- Institutional
- Reflexive
- Performative
- Visual
- Autoethnographic
- Self Study

- Hermeneutical
- Transcendental
- Existential
- Critical
- Ethnomethodology
- Philosophical Inquiry

- Auto/Biography
- Life History
- Oral History
- Critical
- Discursive Psychology
- Sociolinguistics
- Urban Sociology

- Participatory (PAR)
- Critical
- Collaborative
- Social and Cultural Geography

- (Critical) Discourse Analysis
- Foucauldian Analysis
- Counternarrative

METHODS   •Experimental/Quantitative   •Fieldwork   •Observation   •Interview   •Focus Group/Collaborative
•Case Study   •Narrative/Converstion/Content-Concept/Document Analysis   •Performance   •Emerging Methods

REPRESENTATION   •Simple Linear Text   •Multi-layered text   •Stories   •Poetic   •Visual   •Hypertext   •Numerical

Figure 2.1. Research perspectives

Table 2.1. Revised paradigm chart (Lather, 2006, p. 37)

Predict	Understand	Emancipate	Brk Deconstruct	Next?
*Positivist Mixed methods	*Interpretive Naturalistic	*Critical Neo-Marxist	Poststructural Postmodern	Neo-positivism
	Constructivist Phenomenological	< Feminist > Critical race theory Praxis-oriented Freirian participatory < action research	Queer theory < Discourse analysis	
	Ethnographic			
	Symbolic/ interaction		Postcolonial	Post-theory
			Post-Fordism	Neo-pragmatism
	Interpretive mixed methods		Post-humanist	Citizen inquiry
			Post-critical	Participatory/ dialogic Policy analysis
		Gay and lesbian theory		
			Postparadigmatic diaspora (John Caputo)	
		Critical ethnography	Post everything (Fred Erickson)	Post-post

evident entangled structures of changing and contingent worldviews as manifest in research theory and practice. What emerges from working with these concepts simultaneously at several levels of thought is a means to disrupt lazy thinking and to open pathways across activism, action and becoming.

Each heuristic provides inter-relational conceptual connections that allow researchers to take up ways of thinking with, against and beyond theory. If we keep notions of active learning in mind, then certain concepts may become onto-generative, offering both patterns of becoming for researchers and working assemblages for experimental approaches to inquiry. Jackson and Mazzei (2012), for example, used concepts such as performativity (from Butler [see Davies, 2008]) and intra-action (from Barad, 2008) to try to make sense of early experiences of first-generation female academics. Such approaches create openings for making sense of qualitative research data as narrative across multiple perspectives. For these researchers, theoretical application of particular concepts has led to design and process experiments resulting in methodological reconceptualization, grounded in learning theory, that is within, against and beyond interpretivism and representation within qualitative inquiry. Jackson and Mazzei (2012) moved beyond conventional qualitative data analysis, reductionist coding and transparent narratives to disrupt research strategies and engage complexities of social life. This researcher-as-activist stance is part of a movement to disrupt hegemonic tendencies in traditional qualitative research in favour of irruption of transgressive data (St. Pierre, 1997a). Although many special issues of qualitative research journals illustrate diverse and heterogeneous theoretical stances, these are only beginning to penetrate research in areas such as science and environmental education (e.g., Koro-Ljungberg & MacLure, 2013).

Researcher positioning that recognizes the limits of received practices of "data" collection and "analysis," and actively works the limits, conceptually and methodologically, offers a new political ontology of concepts as methods, as ways of thinking beyond signification and subjectification, beyond becoming inside discourse, beyond particular representation of truths that might be conceptualized in many ways. Here we focus on one way of "thinking with complexity" using combinations of concepts as generative of activist approaches to learning how to inquire in Masny's (2012) conceptual sense-making of multiple literacies theory (MLT). We could not locate a relevant example from EE research.

Masny's (2012) use of certain concepts in relation to the research assemblage provides a way to explore theory-practice connections concerning how discourse, text resonance and embodied sensations and becoming (i.e., ontological subjectification) relate to one another. Drawing on the figuration of the rhizome to think conceptually about research, Masny's (2012) assemblage can be used as a lens (see Figure 2.2) that crosses theory and practice as well as the lived (actual) embodied experience and what goes on in thought (the virtual). Worldviews, conceived in the virtual (mind), are "actualized" according to relational contexts. Masny's (2012) focus is on concepts such as "environmental" literacy which, once created, become a territory subject (as environmental literacy was) to deterritorialization. Undoing a territory (e.g., teacher and students critically engaging environmental literacy) implies a process of learning but in the process "becoming" which goes to worldview. In the interaction becoming is in the virtual but in the activist classroom it becomes actualized and may imply change in action.

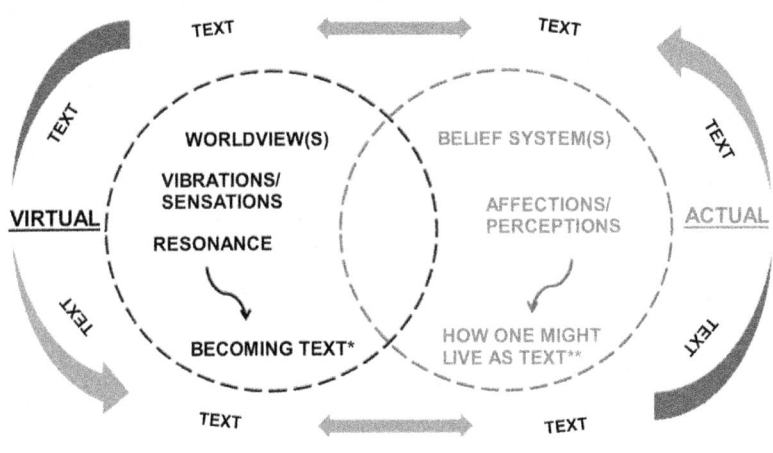

*Lines of Flight/ Deterritorialization
**Territorialization

Figure 2.2. Experiential emergent mappings as concepts for thinking about research processes (from Masny, 2012, p. 114)

Learning, as a function of discourse and prediscursive experience, actualized to a particular context in space and time as an open system of beliefs, predisposes a reading of the world and self that connects with how one might live. Thus environmental experiences may deterritorialize previous experiences setting off transformation of thought and action. Consider Austrian violinist Andre Rieu's disruption of the concept "symphony," as territory/discourse in the actual which deterritorializes the virtual, that is, in never being able to think "symphony" in the same way again. Thus, environmental literacy as a construct may disrupt ways of becoming in the world as research literacies disrupt ways of doing research (i.e., research discourses)—as Cynthia Dillard (2006) says, when the music changes, so should the dance.

Masny's (2012) multi-conceptual analysis of MLT involved multiple levels of thought from worldview to research methods and although discourse-focused, accommodated new materialist conceptions of embodiment in actualizing effects of discourse of thought and praxis. Thus, disruptions or deterritorializations of inquiry are always already disruptive yet productive in deepening thinking concerning complexities of human thought and action. As Alaimo (2010) indicates, if nature is to "matter" then we need to continue to work with new concepts to disrupt taken-for-granted assumptions in our EE inquiries with more conscious focus on changing worldviews as more complex onto-generic thinking devices capable of merging activism action and becoming (see, for example, Pearce, Kidd, Patterson, & Hanley, 2012). We need to do this by continually disrupting the politics of inquiry.

DISRUPTING EE RESEARCH: TAKING AN ACTIVIST ACADEMIC INQUIRY STANCE IN ENVIRONMENTAL EDUCATION RESEARCH

Reconceptualizing EE research can be construed heuristically as a complex assemblage into which new concepts are introduced in order to disrupt traditional concepts such as environmental literacy. In this chapter, following Masny (2012), we have begun to map the process of working with concepts using heuristics or framing devices to illustrate how the research process can evolve—as mappings or cartographies that become more complex. We make sense of the complexity using examples of work from researchers already actively engaging in continuing debates within education research that seem to apply to EE research. They are working within concepts that create different paths for thinking about EE and environmental literacy. They intend to provoke us as inquirers to think creatively and differently and to openly search for possibilities. We focus here, specifically, on mapping concepts for research in order to push thinking beyond what is taken for granted— what Deleuze calls "virtual"—so that we see the territory of our inquiries differently and perhaps make an actual difference that may translate into different forms of EE research praxis to see what it could produce.

Somewhat parallel to Masny and Cole's (2012) mappings of becoming literate with respect to pedagogy, we see the need to create mappings of becoming literate in research methodologies and methods, grounded in ontology and epistemology, as representative of competent qualitative scholarship. We identify with Masny's application of Deleuzian thinking primarily because it allows a move away from textual models of culture/discourse and towards ethics, affect and politics of embodiment and living systems that resonate with new materialist thinking, and, as Barad (2007) indicates, with environment (i.e., beyond the anthropocene).

However, with reference to the processes of EE research, a focus on becoming literate is not enough anymore. Focusing on the research process is an opportunity for concept creation. Problem-becoming concepts are generative-disruptive of, for example, the territory of environmental literacy or place-based education, or EE itself. Concerned about how empiricist systems of inquiry explore problems as closed hierarchical systems (arborescent tracings), Deleuze and Guattari (1987) proposed rhizomatic mappings beyond the traces—researching beyond existing framings. They emphasize the importance of researcher transformations within research experiences as identity forming (i.e., becoming), as a way to do research differently and do different research to see what is produced. EE research draws from different theoretical frameworks—positivist, constructive/interpretivist, critical, poststructural, new materialist, posthuman—across many theoretical perspectives—feminist, postcolonial, GLTBQ(O), indigenous, arts-based and more—as theoretical bases for multiple methodologies and methods are each theorized and diverse in their own right. It follows that applications of qualitative methods such as interviewing require grounding in methodological and theoretical terms (see Roulston, 2010). The expanding array of perspectives is complex (see Figure 2.2).

At issue for EE researchers is that each onto-epistemic and theory-into-research-method perspective is always already in conceptual de- and re-territorialization. Knowing the territory becomes a base for active de/re-territorialization and engages diverse theoretical bases for academic activism from framing research questions to positioning researcher selves. Theoretical naivety is a subject of critique in qualitative inquiry and is used to establish credibility/plausibility of methodological grounding. An extensive research literature, in an expanding array of new journals, contests research processes within both old 'mutated' evidence-based methods as well as newer but ill-conceived "simplistic" qualitative inquiries. Academic activist inquiry takes a pro-active engaged stance to the challenges of theory-process issues, keeping interchange open across emerging approaches. For example, Hickey-Moody and Haworth (2009) characterize learning-based research in terms of "good citizens" (as rule based), "nomads" (as independent) and "smiths" who excel at disrupting dominant discourses of educational research. Along with Semetsky (2009) and Masny (2012) these concepts raise questions concerning what can count as activist inquiry and how this might relate to "becoming" research active or actualized as part of an inquirer's worldview. It would seem that becoming an activist researcher means learning to work within, as well as breaking away from, existing research structures/discourses using frameworks, mappings and concepts-in-relation for thinking critically about what and how we are doing research. The following examples explore activist forms of inquiry as actualized in ways that allow for disruption of beliefs, affections, texts and discourse, each as ways of learning to learn differently through research applications.

Exploring activist researchers' engagement in educational research, in terms of how it functions and what it produces, is usefully introduced in Jackson and Mazzei's (2012) *Thinking with Theory*. The authors' intent is to create ways of thinking philosophically and methodologically together within and against simplistic interpretivism. Drawing on six poststructural theorists (Derrida, Spivak, Foucault, Butler, Deleuze, & Barad) they read the same interview data across specific theoretical concepts such as performativity, power/knowledge and desire, one from each theorist. The point was that these multiple conceptual perspectives permitted more complex readings of the "data," recognized as partial, incomplete and always in a process of restorying. Jackson and Mazzei's (2012) disruption is not in rejecting qualitative research methods but in actively questioning what we mean by "analysis", "data", "voice", "narrative", and "representation", what we as researchers ask of data, what we think we hear and our ability to think differently with data.

Jackson and Mazzei (2012) put new concepts to work as onto-generic devices that are generative, keep meaning on the move and may disrupt the theory-practice binary.

This kind of methodological reconceptualization is what many activist researchers such Colebrook (2012), Barad (2007), and Koro-Ljungberg (2016) offer as design experiments, as ways of exposing dominant socio-cultural discourses as ontological signatures of identity/subjectivity/becoming that mark the terrain or territory. Perhaps working concepts such as these can be seen as devices of "seeing"—as onto-generative devices for diffracting what we think (as we see) long enough to think again. In the absence of comprehensive understanding of the philosophical positions of many theorists, perhaps these ideas concerning conceptual analysis can provide reasonably coherent access for application in research studies. When this conceptual base is set within the context of meta-frames (such as the heuristics displayed above), EE researchers gain some reasonable grounding in application of onto-epistemics, crucial to establishing researcher credibility. Brown, Carducci and Kuby (2014) embrace a wide array of methodological framings, calling attention to new ways of knowing-becoming. They elaborate on a need for healthy disruption of theory and practice, research roles and relationships, collection and analysis of "data," representing and disseminating research findings, moving beyond rigid onto-epistemic boundaries and assumptive frameworks. Disrupting "becomes" part of researcher identity considering how research emerges from the researcher's personal biography and lived experience and how their worldview implicates everything from conceptualization of research problems to (re)presentation of findings.

"WORKING THE RUINS" OF RELATIONALITY AND RESPONSIBILITY: NEW VOCABULARIES

In these examples re-thinking research methodologically and philosophically together is a challenging but necessary to attempt to address the complexities of social life and more-than-human existence. Arguably, qualitative inquiry work is always already interrupted or disrupted by, if not criticalist then poststructuralist, admonitions to address issues of interpretation and representation. St. Pierre and Pillow's (2000) idea of "working the ruins" has been used to open up questions about qualitative research values, including somewhat taken-for-granted beliefs in research associated with progress and identity as humanist forms of truth and reality. "Working the ruins" opened doors for different kinds of research—more participatory, uncertain and partial—and a linguistic turn where language assumed more importance, as did subjectivity.

MacLure (2011) used this figuration of "ruins" to argue for new forms of relationality and responsibility that value complexity, sustained engagements, entanglements and interferences; that actually have the force to be sensitive to differences and particularities; to be dangerous enough to pierce common sense (taken-for-granted values) and to become more materially engaged with affects and embodiments. While "working the ruins" was a methodological project of change (St. Pierre & Pillow, 2000), to escape gravity (i.e., dominant discourses, interpretive mastery, narrative coherence) seems to require more folding, deviating and material intensities that move people beneath the surface. As MacLure (2011) says, it is now necessary to work infra-empirically, beneath the surface and even beyond human—beyond the linguistic turn in poststructural theorizing—because of its emphasis on a discursive constitutive force of discourse and culture at the expense of matter and nature. Similarly, Jones and Jenkins (2008) reject the ethical indifference of interpretivism in favour of a more ethically engaged approach to Indigenous discourse capable of bringing forth new material realities. Somewhat parallel applications of newer post-empiricist approaches to chaos theory, quantum mechanics and neuroscience may be found in a number of new materialist and socio-materialist forms of cultural-historical activity theory, actor-network theory and complexity theory (see Fenwick, Edwards, & Sawchuk, 2011; Law, 2008).

Vocabularies of post-humanism and, more recently, nonhuman entanglements emerge from authors interested in transforming materialities of education from "matters of fact" to matters of "concern" in search of openings for change. These authors raise critical questions through a kind of materiality of critique that extends the boundaries of linguistic discursity (from poststructuralism) (see Latour, 2005). For example, Postma (2012) intersects ANT with Butler's (1990) performativity, the ontological politics of Mol (1999) and the agental realism of Barad (2007). This socio-material re-conception of critique-as-inquiry engages concepts from each theorist in aid of practical real-world issues. However, rather than take such concepts as foundational categories, they are engaged relationally, as Masny (2012) does in engaging multiple literacies and as we suggest as a way of re-engaging with environmental literacies. However, what is needed more in EE research are methodologies and methods that recognize and trace and map the struggles, negotiations and accommodations whose effects constitute what happens in the field, including conferences and organizations that in turn implicate what happens in EE texts and contexts. Materialities also include what happens to students, teachers, learning activities and spaces and what counts as knowledge, pedagogy, curriculum and so forth.

Following this line of reasoning, EE, from a socio-material perspective, is viewed as emerging from these various forms of association—sociocultural, sociopolitical, socio-environmental—as assembled and only "becoming" possible in the enactment. Thus, rather than abstract or theoretical, concepts are used to intervene and even to disrupt (environmental) educational issues to reframe how we might interact and engage them (Fenwick & Edwards, 2010). EE is now characterized by a complex of themes (including national standards in the USA), approaches to research, and theoretical interests. Plurality and maturation are represented by handbooks (Stevenson et al., 2013) and special issues (see, for example, Reid, 2016). If we think forward, yet draw genealogically from several orientations to EE, we may gain perspective on how the field has evolved. However, human-nonhuman issues remain problematic as phenomena to be explored and studied. What seems evident in recent research interests is a shift in focus from issues defined as personal and social to questions of hybrid assemblages of bodies, desires, ideas, symbols and materials that are always active and reconstituting themselves. The story, however, is just beginning. Socio-material approaches now reside among/beside many other emerging methodologies as ways to conceptually explore and interrupt or disrupt not only material enactments of discourses-practices but approaches to inquiry itself. In the next section of the chapter, we introduce what we think are strategic imaginings, where issues with existing qualitative methods have drawn reaction, usually for good reason, despite their popularity in introductory or generic texts, by making visible issue ranging from methodology to the microdynamics of qualitative inquiry.

THE POLITICS OF EMERGENCE: IMAGINING POSSIBILITIES

Beyond the framings and mappings presented, it seems prudent in this space to focus on the evolution of thinking in qualitative inquiry that might be deemed activities of inquiry with minor deviation as necessary. The challenge is to illustrate changing theoretical framings from dynamic perspectives as diverse as postcritical, postcolonial and many other "posts," as destabilized forms that create new spaces for dialogue and debate. Directions seem more important than comprehensive coverage and the stuff of handbooks. Our focus is on certain turning points in creating more activist opportunities for learning.

In the endpiece to the compendium *What makes education environmental?* entitled "The end of naiveté" Noel McInnis and Don Albrecht (1975) state that the greatest obstacle to making EE successful is the worldview that programs people to see themselves as "distinct from" rather than "distinct within" the dynamics of natural processes. The promise of EE, then and now, lies in facilitating the emergence of a more inclusive, more than human, worldview. And as James Swan (1975) says, in the same volume, the great revolution will come from the inside out. Arguably, EE researchers have always, more or less, been activist about not only the environment but also the kinds of inquiry conducive, ultimately, to worldview change. And so, arguably, they have been inclined to become somewhat critical researchers interested in, for example, new ethics of *The World Conservation Strategy* (IUCN/UNEP/WWF, 1980) and socially critical curriculum that encourages community actions as forms of political participation in more ecologically sustainable societies. They have endorsed school experiences that involved critical thinking and problem solving intended to promote social and environmental change (see Stevenson, 1987) as well as a socially critical orientation to educational and social inquiry (Robottom & Hart, 1993).

When Robottom and Hart (1993) challenged the field of EE to engage the debates in educational research, arguing that critical participatory forms of inquiry were more congruent with the socially critical goals of EE than traditional quantitative-based research, resistance was palpable and political. Ensuing discussion and debate implicated an onto-epistemic shift from dominant realist-empiricist theory toward narrative and relational grounding for a variety of participatory, practice-based and action-based inquiry. Implicated was a social dimension of learning as part of a deeper relational onto-epistemology compatible with an expanding array of qualitative methodologies and methods. This reconceptualization of what could count as legitimate social and educational research was characterized by valuing the meanings and perspectives of learners in terms of their increasing consciousness of their values and ultimately their worldview. For researchers, social learning involved the expansion of ideas concerning the value of the social-relational participatory construction of knowledge (as learning) (see, for example, Wals, 2007).

Conceding educational and EE research as multi-paradigmatic implies the valuing of different perspectives, assuming that knowledge (learning) is a social construction of communities of inquirers (from classrooms to communities) operating from a variety of perspectives. Clearly EE and EE research in social critical forms challenges traditional research, standard pedagogy and patterns of curriculum development and professional development of teachers to take action to learn. Palmer's (1998) and subsequent reviews (Hart & Nolan, 1999; Rickinson, 2000) of theory and practice concerning EE and EE research report evidence of gradual change, particularly in the broadening of thinking concerning research paradigms, following feminist and general educational and social research. However, the problem of a lag in uptake in more specialized areas such as EE research becomes increasingly complex as changes in educational inquiry continue to accelerate. In the final section of the chapter, we focus on areas of change in social research process that optimistically might appeal to the more activist nature of inquiry within EE research.

One way to show the proliferation of literature informing research and learning about research and learning is to note special issues of widely consulted journals that explore theories and practices of inquiry. For example, *Qualitative Inquiry, 18*(9), "Problematizing Methodological Simplicity in Qualitative Research"; *Qualitative Research, 9*(5), "Qualitative Research and Methodological Innovation"; *Educational Philosophy and Theory, 40*(1), "Complexity Theory and the Philosophy of Education; *Pedagogy, Culture and Society, 12*(3), "Space, Identity and Education." What began in the 1990s with the legitimation of qualitative research approaches has morphed into something quite remarkable, in theory and in practice, requiring education faculty specialists in qualitative research methodologies and methods. We focus first on levels of theory, beginning with onto-epistemic (i.e., seeing/knowing), where many papers reconsider founding ontologies. For example, Lenz Taguchi (2013), in reconsidering the relationship between processes of producing knowledge and processes of being-becoming (i.e., learning), explored researchers' taken-for-granted assumptions of themselves as rational and self-reflexive in their need to interpret and represent participants. Resisting the role of the researcher, as one who interprets and learns and knows, required collaborative self-critique and a certain deterritorializing of habits of thinking and doing analysis. St. Pierre (2011b) wonders if it was ever possible to stay within such a subject-dependent ontology and a researcher-as-knower epistemology (as habitual ways of thinking about researcher positioning)? The point is that most introductory texts in qualitative research represent qualitative methodology as divorced from epistemology. Seriously questioning this representation of thought (and learning) constitutes a major onto-epistemic shift toward notions of knowing-being-learning beyond human rational self-reflexive mindwork. Such a shift can be considered activist in the ontological sense of making possible new and other meanings of matter and discourse in becoming "researcher."

Dolphijn and van Tuin (2012) have conceptualized new materialism beyond older forms of critical resistance to realist and social constructionist positions. Relevant to EE research, human agents, matter and discourse are seen as intra-acting within complex networks (e.g., in socio-relational approaches to complexity, ANT and CHAT). Human and nonhuman intentionality and agency, where discursive-material and nature-cultures are seriously considered, push dualisms and differences to the limit (Braidotti, 2012). Coming to know (i.e., learning) takes place on a two-way track between matter and discourse that includes historical sets of material conditions that are effects of material-discourse and nature-culture intra-actions. Interpreted meanings evolve as investigation of forces (discursive and material) as mutually implicated and co-productive in these relations. Rather than tracing what emerges in the process of analysis to a root origin or essence (themes, categories, patterns), we look for connections in the joint researcher-participant assemblage which is capable of decentering assumed practices of thinking. Interpreting and analyzing is the hard, collaborative relational work of participants and researchers requiring a research ontology that is mutually constitutive, multiple, generous and performative.

EE RESEARCH? CONSIDER ARTS-BASED A/R/TOGRAPHY

The point is, that the older interpretivist style of thinking about the role/position of the qualitative researcher (having empiricist reductionist tendencies) has been supplanted by more complex and complicated thinking about researcher-collaborator positioning using new concepts/metaphors such as rhizome and assemblage as the unit of sense making instead of the dominant researcher "I." This movement signals a shifting researcher identity (Lenz Taguchi, 2012) and could be illustrated with examples from any major methodological perspective. We have chosen an example from a relatively recent research focus on visual methodologies/methods with associations in arts-based research. Visual approaches, beyond textual modes, are already somewhat disruptive of basic qualitative approaches and provide much scope for creativity in thinking within and against common tendencies of interpretivist reduction strategies. Visual approaches are part of a larger theoretical framing of qualitative studies that focus on the senses for thinking through research questions. Examples of such theorizing are found in Pink's (2012) *Advances in Visual Methodology* in Leavy's (2015) version of *Method Meets Art* as well as the *Handbook of Arts-Based Research* (Knowles & Cole, 2008). In describing the philosophical grounding of arts-based inquiry, Leavy (2015) characterizes a paradigm based in aesthetic knowing which is capable of disrupting assumptions of ordinary learning and actively engaging.

Founded on legacies of theoretical formations from feminist poststructuralism and other post-and critically informed social-justice movements, whose onto-epistemic claims bare directly on methodologically based applications of method, emergent arts-based researchers pride themselves on exploring old research questions in new ways. Their purpose is to "jar" researchers into thinking research differently, seeing and thinking differently, and ultimately as they learn to be more holistic, evocative, provocative, to challenge dominant discourses, unsettle politics and taken-for-granted assumptions, and to be more participatory and useful. Pelias' (2004) arts-based texts are methodological calls that create new ways of thinking about research practices, engage new tools/concepts and create new ways of knowing and being with new representational and performative forms from a/r/tographics to visual, creating new research spaces among knowing, doing and making. Visual methodologies as they emerge and become more conceptually coherent may serve as a vehicle for ideology or discursive critique. The visual plays a large role in crossing binaries of race, class, gender, culture that carries transformative power resisting social stereotyping, confronting dominant views and accessing hidden dimensions of social life through photovoice, collage and many forms of photos or videos, often taken or selected by participants. One would hope for as much in renewed approaches to EE research.

With historical roots in visual anthropology and sociology, visual methodologies and methods provide one means of de-emphasizing text and creating openings to complexity and performativity as embodiment of inquiry (Rose, 2005). From photo elicitation in interviewing to photo blogs, newer approaches attempt to accommodate weakness in earlier methods. As Crang (2010) indicates, a variety of visual methods were almost killed off before they were born because of assumptions of detachment and objectification, bound to issues of representation. Since that time, participatory visual images have been used to enable participants to represent themselves; narrating their lives and partial interpretation; reducing colonial optics; engaging cultural sensitivities; and offering transgressive learning by confronting the limits of representation. As Crang (2010) says, it is not about abandoning the visual and seeking other senses but recasting the methods by more deeply engaging theory as related both to methodological grounding and onto-epistemic grounding—carefully disentangling the relationships of vision, knowing and becoming. So, while aesthetic manipulation of images is probably more likely than words, what researchers make of whatever they observe will be affected by their theoretical frames, their worldview. What we also need are concepts that open possibilities for seeing human subjectivities as emergent within relational fields (Hultman & Lenz Taguchi, 2010) where nonhuman matters are equally at play.

The point of interest for this chapter is found in ways that visual methodologies and methods can enhance possibilities of disrupting the role of the researcher as "producer of knowledge" in the research process. It is not hard to see how, in arts-based research, methods are always already impacted by onto-epistemics of researchers' ways of being and seeing. We can see consequences for EE research if educational researchers challenge anthropocentric analysis by engaging concepts that decenter the researcher. In questioning the perceptual style and habits of seeing by looking for the force of the material environment, the kinds of experiences that constitute the child's becomings in a natural setting, for example, we may begin to "see" differently. The difference, says Dillard (2000), is like walking with and without a camera. Seeing with a camera is about analyzing and verbalizing. But there are ways of seeing that involve letting go, returning to our senses. It is less like seeing than being where experience itself is considered to be a constitutive force with methodological and ethical consequences for research.

Once again, however, there is more to this than meets the "I." Pourchier and Holbrook (2014) characterize a/r/tography as a disruptive methodology—a living inquiry that requires researchers to learn to "let go" of the ruins of research-as-usual (St. Pierre & Pillow, 2000). They take the stance that good research means developing spaces for counter-narratives and counter-theories that disrupt realist tales of conventional qualitative research as well as counter-criteria with onto-epistemic and educative authority. We believe that a/r/tography is a way of conceptualizing what others, including St. Pierre (1997b), identify as transgressive data that are outside tidy categories and not usually accounted for in qualitative educational research. Like St. Pierre, we wonder if transgressive thinking might shift ways of knowing and being (i.e., worldviews).

As Karen Barad (2007) sees it, feminist poststructural educational research has problematized humanistic notions of the child as autonomous and detached from environment. A relational materialist focus moves researchers beyond contextual and situational centredness of the anthropocentric ways of seeing-being which further opens up inquiry by decentering visual imaging (of, say children) as a relationship between material environment and social discourse—intra-actively. Neither is ontologically or epistemologically prior. Understanding learning from different ontologies/epistemologies (ways of being [seeing] and knowing) implicates how we construct our inquiries as intra-activist or not—how one engages methodology and method. As Springgay, Irwin, and Kind (2008) say, a/r/tography constructs researching-as-knowing as a complication, recognizing that meaning making as learning can be disruptive of identities, roles and understandings. Enacting a/r/tography is relational, in line with complexity theories of learning as a participation in the co-evolution of knower-known that transforms both (see also Davis, Sumara, & Luce-Kapler, 2000).

RESPONSIBLE ACTIVISM: THE NECESSIYT OF CONCEPTUAL REGROUNDING

How can we think about the consequences of our research if we understand learning and becoming with worldview in mind (Lenz Taguchi, 2010)? Embracing research as activism means conceptualizing researcher as primary instrument at every stage of the inquiry process. Subjectivity, positionality and meaning making of the researcher profoundly shape research methods, and thus data and findings. Researchers thus have responsibilities for articulating their perspective on the learner in the world whether represented or part of a collaborative construction of meaning or as entangled becomings. In other words, conceptual foundations of research methodology and method are crucial. An example of the ways these worldviews are differently conceptualized can be seen in an analysis of interview methods. For example, Roulston (2010) characterizes a typology of conceptions of approaches that resonate with onto-epistemic assumptions underlying research study design. She articulates theoretical frames for six conceptualizations that range from neo-positivist assumptions of participants' representations of their authentic selves, to interactive/participatory and deconstructionist conceptions where relational, empathic, ethical, performative and transformative possibilities are engaged. When embracing an activist research agenda issues of onto-epistemic divergences are manifest in processes of being/becoming in participant and research subjectivities.

Activist methods address simplistic uses of the interview as a methodological technique. For example, Kuntz and Presnell (2012) approach the research process as a wholly engaged encounter, an embodied act of tactical intervention, as an "intraview", as an integrative way of knowing and becoming. Employing strategies that organize time and spaces of experience as material modifications of process, different conceptualizations of interview engage power differently and intervene diffractively in the onto-epistemics of place and structure more consciously—shifting the logic underlying taken-for-granted assumptions concerning 'interview' and 'intraview.' The concept of *intraview* works at understanding the embodied and emplaced nature of the interaction as a kind of becoming with knowing.

It seems to us to be an activist stance toward their research when Kuntz and Presnall (2012) question how they might re-conceive the interview beyond representational assumptions of knowing subjects and objective observers, beyond the production of humanist subjects and the power epistemology of the disembodied spectator "I" (see also, St. Pierre, 2011a). It seems clearly activist when they reveal systems of logic that dominate the patterned processes of meaning making that reproduce social structures rather than attend to the intra-active social, discursive and material process of subjectification. It seems activist to re-figure the traditional interview as a tactic of the intraview which explores the intersection between knowing and becoming as multi-directional intractions among language and embodiment—knowing and becoming beyond the conventional—as an event, a becoming within embodied experience.

Such performative, agential work illustrates the point of this chapter in not only the Baradian (2008) linking of material and discursive epistemology with embodiment and emplacement in relational ontology. Researchers as activist agents means engaging research within processes of becoming, that is, engaging actively within the encounter as relation rather than the transcript as representational. Interpretation becomes description of intra-action as spoken, material and affective expression of doing and emotion. Sarah Pink's (2009) work on sensory ethnography, in resituating the interview as a constitutive event, recognizes such research events as processes of emplacement, embodiment and sense making as collaborative events requiring, among other things, diffractive seeing, peripheral vision, whole-body listening and nomadic or mobile thinking (Kuntz & Presnell, 2012).

An upshot of much of the critique of interview method is a concern about rendering the embodied interaction into transcript language that fails to capture the dynamism and creative force of the materialities of interaction. In other words, researchers are now asking what it might mean to inquire within, against and beyond representation. MacLure (2011) argues for interactional methods that can engage research in ways that reduce the mediation of reality through language. Acknowledging that poststructural research has attempted to unsettle the foundations of discourse, the structures of academic language and codes of mediation, activist researchers recognize that we simply cannot dress up interpretation; we can't mask intact subjects or orchestrated voices of material realities of participants that are displaced by research in ways that undermine prospects of socio-political change. These ideas resonate with foundations of EE research as disruptive of the fascination with the status quo in research and praxis. Interviews become intraviews—conversations where the embodiments of interaction are made visible, including emotion-silences-gestures and visuals that render language possible as revealed in our ways of "seeing by being" with people. This has been called an "orthopedics of affect." Rather than abandoning linguistic forms of representation, we learn how to work its ruins, to mobilize the material (embodied), in spite of its uncertainties. It has also been characterized as post-qualitative arguments that reject the ethical indifference of interpretivism. There are also resonances with indigenous research discourse and new feminist materialism writings that find reductionism simplistic and offensive for many reasons.

BECOMING ACTIVIST: LEARNING HOW?

In this chapter, focused on activist-inspired notions of learning in environment-related education, we seem to have come full circle. We can recognize activist researchers and environmental educators as generally critical of the status quo in worldview and in academic inquiry. With Postma (2012), we acknowledge that our notions of "becoming critical" have moved beyond an historical base in critical theory. With MacLure (2010, 2011) and others, we recognize that qualitative inquiry has moved interactively beyond discursive in new material and affective intensities in ways that no longer privilege human interpretation and representation. And with Alaimo (2010) we acknowledge that if nature is to matter we need more complex understandings of how in fact nature matters more and more. All of this can be read into St. Pierre's (2011a) question: How might we live and think differently if we conceived (and inquired) of the world differently? And so, we have focused on *How* activist researchers can themselves be considered activist in terms of changing their research processes in ways that implicate all levels of thinking—with, against, beyond—theory. And this journey may be read within and beyond the onto-epistemics of EE research which is really about how we come to be and know—in other words, how we learn in different ways.

We believe it to be the case, as MacLure (2011) says, that theory has not had enough of a chance to proliferate, in its most recent entanglements with material complexities of the real world. Issues remain as theory has evolved into more recent post-qualitative engagements and has become more disruptive. We see some promise in recent attempts to escape naïve interpretivism and the presumption of narrative coherence, and to get beyond discourse, as Ringrose (2011) says, to explore how we might re-invent our relationship with the empirical in new ways. We see potential, for example, in materialist critiques of representation which has what MacLure (2010) describes as radical implications for qualitative inquiry and the associated confounding of interpretation, in particular against simplistic reduction of narrative complexity. We see creative possibilities in emerging methodologies and methods that are onto-epistemically conscious, transgressive and transformative in terms of application of new field methods beyond interviewing, and what can count for "analysis" or as "data" (Koro-Ljungberg & MacLure, 2013). As Lenz Taguchi (2012) argues, considering how matter and meaning can be viewed as mutually constituted in interview data implies a reconceptualization of thinking beyond interpretation of research. Both researcher and participant are encouraged to engage to undertake research where mutual entailment of discourse and matter is explored. In such a relationship neither discursive practices nor material phenomena are considered ontologically or epistemologically prior. Neither can be explained in terms of the other. They must be mutually articulated as a complexity that may include nonhuman and the material environment in a co-existent relationship (Barad, 1999, pp. 7–8).

The problem now resides in how to actually do research that can accommodate matter and meaning—the actual and the virtual, in Masny's (2012) terms. Possibilities include kinds of diffractive analysis (after, Barad, 2007) where attention to what is going on physically and mentally within an intra-view process is integrated into text-based researcher accounts of "becoming-with," or in Alaimo's (2010) terms, transcorporeal engagements with data.

Great promise obtains, we think, if, as inquirers, we begin to more consciously associate research and participant becomings within a mutual learning process that understands learning and becoming from an onto-epistemic worldview. Intra-actions between discourses (as human mindwork) and embodiment of human and nonhuman come to matter as interconnections with ethical responsibilities, political engagements and transgressive possibilities. Such interconnections require post-critical explorations of worldview as openings for new ways of learning/knowing/doing research that implicate more complex engagement within/against/beyond research methodologies (see Koro-Ljungberg, 2012; Koro-Ljungberg, Carlson, Tesar, & Anderson, 2015). We are interested in how researchers and participants can learn to grow within, against and beyond uncertainty and how this works to generate methodologies as always becoming (Koro-Ljungberg, 2012) in new and creative ways that resist simplification.

With respect to EE research, it is encouraging to see how new materialist researchers engage in studies beyond human. Lenz Taguchi (2010) addresses learning and becoming within non-hierarchical or "flattened" systems of mutual interrelationship between humans (as organism) and environments. Barad (2007) characterizes the dissolved relationships between being and learning as onto-epistemic—the view that the material world acts upon human thinking as much as our own human thinking does. Discourse, it seems, is produced as much through embodied natural experience as it is through cultural-based perception. And habits of learning and pedagogy are tied to material and discursive conditions. They have agency in the construction of knowledge. Now, more than at any other time, we seem to have attended to the theory base in research, but not yet to the conceptual foundations of research (i.e., worldview). In other words, as environmental educators remind us, humans cannot put themselves apart from and above the rest of the world. We cannot ignore our interdependence with other organisms and matter.

The force of learning and knowing as onto-epistemic comes within and beyond the learner, in intra-actions taking place as embodied connections to things as well as in discursive minds! For activist educational researchers and for EE researchers, there appear to be choices within a growing body of diverse scholarship which crosses diverse theoretical stances. We argue that there is a pressing need for theories and concepts of environmental sustainability which can approach discursive constitutedness as well as prediscursive dimensions of embodiment and transcorporeal relations (see Lykke, 2010). In ways somewhat parallel to Hekman's (2008) story for an ontology for feminism, we see environmental sustainability, and with it EE, at a crossroads. Integrating different bodies of theoretical work from social sciences, we see an onto-epistemic turn toward integration of the discursive (virtual) and the material (actual). We see this integration as a shift away from how people write (Ingold, 2008) the world to how their worlds are formed through continual embodied processes of engagement, sensing, encountering and intra-action (Roe & Greenhough, 2014).

As EE researchers continue to develop conceptual resources to engage as agents taking an activist stance toward educational inquiry, we might aim to become more theoretically active, critically and creatively. We believe that we will benefit from inquiries focused on human and nonhuman ways people have come to construct themselves materially and discursively, that is, intra-actively. We need to continue to articulate how activist researchers construct their research selves in order to perform their work beyond representation/interpretation as they translate their theoretical arguments philosophically, morally and ethically, into research praxis. We argue for change in EE learning processes in terms of how learner-as-researcher engages the world as assemblages of humans (i.e., materialities and immaterialities—such as emotions and beliefs) and nonhumans learning to live together. From our vantage point in mid-2016, we can say that we are working actively to construct methodological resources and skills to undertake research that takes both discursive and material engagement, as well as creativeness of social research, seriously (after Thrift, 2000). We hope that the conceptual resources, ideas and practical suggestions that we have presented that ground our work in this direction are useful to others who are moving activism into EE research itself.

REFERENCES

Alaimo, S. (2010). *Bodily natures: Science, environment, and the material self.* Bloomington, IN: Indiana University Press.
Barad, K. (1999). Agential realism: Feminist interventions in understanding scientific practices. In M. Biagioli (Ed.), *The science studies reader* (pp. 1–11). New York, NY: Routledge.
Barad, K. (2007). *Meeting the universe halfway: Quantum physics and the entanglement of matter and meaning.* Durham, NC: Duke University Press.
Barad, K. (2008). Posthumanist performativity: Toward an understanding of how matter comes to matter. In S. Alaimo & S. Hekman (Eds.), *Material feminisms* (pp. 120–154). Bloomington, IN: Indiana University Press.
Braidotti, R. (2012). Interview with Rosi Braidotti. In R. Dolphijn & I. van der Tuin (Eds.), *New materialism: Interviews & cartographies* (pp. 19–37). Ann Arbor, MI: Open Humanities Press.
Briggs, C. (2007). Anthropology, interviewing, and communicability in contemporary society. *Current Anthropology, 48*(4), 551–580.
Brown, R., Carducci, R., & Kuby, C. (Eds.). (2014). *Disrupting qualitative inquiry: Possibilities and tensions in educational research.* New York, NY: Peter Lang.
Burrell, G., & Morgan, G. (1979). *Sociological paradigms and organizational analysis.* London: Heinemann.
Butler, J. (1990). *Gender trouble: Feminism and the subversion of identity.* New York, NY: Routledge.
Colebrook, C. (2012). Foreward: The multiple, the letter, and the theorist. In D. Masny & D. Cole (Eds.), *Mapping multiple literacies: An introduction to Deleuzian literacy studies* (pp. vii–xii). London: Continuum.
Crang, M. (2010). Visual methods and methodologies. In D. Delyser, H. Steve, A. Stuart, C. Mike, & M. Linda (Eds.), *The Sage handbook of qualitative geography.* Los Angeles, CA: Sage Publications.
Crotty, M. (1998). *The foundations of social research: Meaning and perspective in the research process.* Thousand Oaks, CA: Sage Publications.
Davies, B. (Ed.). (2008). *Judith Butler in conversation: Analyzing the texts and talk of everyday life.* New York, NY: Routledge.
Davies, B. (2014). Reading anger in early childhood intra-actions: A diffractive analysis. *Qualitative Inquiry, 20*(6), 734–741.
Davis, B., Sumara, D., & Luce-Kapler, R. (2000). *Engaging minds: Learning and teaching in a complex world.* Mahwah, NJ: Lawrence Erlbaum.
Deleuze, G., & Guattari, F. (1987). *A thousand plateaus: Capitalism and schizophrenia* (B. Massumi, Trans.). Minneapolis, MN: University of Minnesota Press.
Dillard, A. (2000). *Pilgrim at tinker creek.* New York, NY: Harper Perennial. (first published 1974)
Dillard, C. (2006). When the music changes, so should the dance: Cultural and spiritual considerations in paradigm 'proliferation.' *International Journal of Qualitative Studies in Education, 19*(1), 59–76.
Dolphijn, R., & van der Tuin, I. (2012). *New materialism: Interviews & cartographies.* Ann Arbor, MI: Open Humanities Press.
Fenwick, T., & Edwards, R. (2010). *Actor-network theory and education.* London: Routledge.
Fenwick, T., Edwards, R., & Sawchuk, P. (2011). *Emerging approaches to educational research: Tracing the socio-material.* London: Routledge.
Fien, J. (1993). *Education for the environment: Critical curriculum theorizing and environmental education.* Geelong: Deakin University Press.
Gough, N. (1987). Learning with environments: Towards an ecological paradigm for education. In I. Robottom (Ed.), *Environmental education: Practice and possibility* (pp. 49–68). Geelong: Deakin University Press.
Gough, N. (2010). Performing imaginative inquiry: Narrative experiments and rhizosemiotic play. In T. Nielsen, R. Fitzgerald, & M. Fettes (Eds.), *Imagination in educational theory and practice: A many-sided vision* (pp. 42–60). Tyne: Cambridge Scholars.
Hammersley, M. (2003). Recent radical criticism of interview studies: Any implications for the sociology of education. *British Journal of Sociology of Education, 24*(1), 119–126.

Hart, P., & Nolan, K. (1999). A critical analysis of research in environmental education. *Studies in Science Education, 34*(1), 1–69.
Hekman, S. (2008). Constructing the ballast: An ontology for feminism. In S. Alaimo & S. Hekman (Eds.), *Material feminisms* (pp. 95–119). Bloomington, IN: Indiana University Press.
Hickey-Moody, A., & Haworth, R. (2009). Affective literacies. In D. Masny & D. Cole (Eds.), *Multiple literacies theory: A Deleuzian perspective* (pp. 79–92). Rotterdam, The Netherlands: Sense Publishers.
Holstein, J., & Gubrium, J. (2004). The active interview. In D. Silverman (Ed.), *Qualitative research: Theory, method and practice* (2nd ed., pp. 140–161). London: Sage Publications.
Hultman, K., & Lenz, T. H. (2010). Challenging anthropocentric analysis of visual data: A relational materialist methodological approach to educational research. *International Journal of Qualitative Studies in Education, 23*(5), 525–542. doi:10.1080/09518398.2010.500628
Ingold, T. (2008). Anthropology is not ethnography: Radcliffe-Brown lecture in social anthropology. *Proceedings of the British Academy, 154*, 69–92.
IUCN/UNEP/WWF. (1980). *World conservation strategy*. Gland: IUCN.
Jackson, A., & Mazzei, L. (2012). *Thinking with theory in qualitative research: Viewing data across multiple perspectives*. New York, NY: Routledge.
Jones, A., & Jenkins, K. (2008). Indigenous discourse and "the material": A post-interpretivist argument. *International Review of Qualitative Research, 1*(2), 125–144.
Knowles, G., & Cole, A. (Eds.). (2008). *Handbook of the arts in qualitative research*. Thousand Oaks, CA: Sage Publications.
Koro-Ljungberg, M. (2012). Researchers of the world, create! *Qualitative Inquiry, 18*(9), 808–818.
Koro-Ljungberg, M. (2016). *Reconceptualizing qualitative research: Methodologies without methodology*. Thousand Oaks, CA: Sage Publications.
Koro-Ljungberg, M., & MacLure, M. (2013). Provocations, re-un-visions, death, and other possibilities of "data." *Cultural Studies <–> Critical Methodologies, 13*(4), 219–222.
Koro-Ljungberg, M., Carlson, D., Tesar, M., & Anderson, K. (2015). Methodology brut: Philosophy, ecstatic thinking, and some other (unfinished) things. *Qualitative Inquiry, 21*(7), 612–619.
Kuntz, A., & Presnall, M. (2012). Wandering the tactical: From interview to intraview. *Qualitative Inquiry, 18*(9), 732–744.
Lather, P. (2006). Paradigm proliferation as a good thing to think with: Teaching research in education as a wild profusion. *International Journal of Qualitative Studies in Education, 19*(1), 35–58.
Lather, P. (2007). *Getting lost*. Albany, NY: SUNY Press.
Latour, B. (2005). *Re-assembling the social: An introduction to actor network theory*. London: Oxford University Press.
Law, J. (2008). Actor-network theory and material semiotics. In B. Turner (Ed.), *The new Blackwell companion to social theory* (3rd ed., pp. 141–158). Oxford: Blackwell.
Leavy, P. (2015). *Method meets art: Arts-based research practice* (2nd ed.). New York, NY: Guilford.
Lenz, T. H. (2010). *Going beyond the theory/practice divide in early childhood education*. London: Routledge.
Lenz, T. H. (2012). A diffractive and Deleuzian approach to analyzing interview-data. *Journal of Feminist Theory, 13*(3), 265–281.
Lenz, T. H. (2013). Images of thinking in feminist materialism: Ontological divergences and the production of researcher subjectivities. *International Journal of Qualitative Studies in Education, 26*(6), 706–716.
Lykke, N. (2010). Taking turns. *NORA—Nordic Journal of Feminist and Gender Research, 18*(2), 131–136.
MacLure, M. (2010). The offence of theory. *Journal of Education Policy, 25*(2), 277–286.
MacLure, M. (2011). Qualitative inquiry: Where are the ruins? *Qualitative Inquiry, 17*(10), 997–1005.
Masny, D. (2012). Multiple literacies theory: Discourse, sensation, resonance and becoming. *Discourse: Studies in the Cultural Politics of Education, 33*(1), 113–128.
Masny, D., & Cole, D. (2009). *Multiple literacies theory: A Deleuzian perspective*. Rotterdam, The Netherlands: Sense Publishers.
Masny, D., & Cole, D. (2012). *Mapping multiple literacies: An introduction to Deleuzian literacy studies*. London: Continuum.

McInnis, N., & Albrecht, D. (Eds.). (1975). *What makes education environmental?* Louisville, KY: Data Courier.
Merriam, S. (2009). *Qualitative research: A guide to design and implementation.* San Francisco, CA: Wiley.
Mol, A. (1999). Ontological politics: A word and some questions. In J. Law & J. Hassard (Eds.), *Actor-network theory, and after* (pp. 74–89). Oxford: Blackwell.
Palmer, J. (1998). *Environmental education in the 21st century: Theory, practice, progress and promise.* London: Routledge.
Pearce, C., Kidd, D., Patterson, R., & Hanley, U. (2012). The politics of becoming… making time… *Qualitative Inquiry, 18*(5), 418–426.
Pelias, R. (2004). *A methodology of the heart: Evoking academic and daily life.* Walnut Creek, CA: AltaMira.
Pink, S. (2009). *Doing sensory ethnography.* Thousand Oaks, CA: Sage Publications.
Pink, S. (2012). *Advances in visual methodology.* London: Sage Publications.
Postma, D. (2012). Education as sociomaterial critique. *Pedagogy, Culture & Society, 20*(1), 136–156.
Potter, J., & Hepburn, A. (2005). Qualitative interviews in psychology: Problems and possibilities. *Qualitative Research in Psychology, 2,* 175–196.
Pouchier, N., & Holbrook, T. (2014). Always already inquiry: A/r/tography as a disruptive methodology. In C. Kuby, R. Carducci, & R. Nicole (Eds.), *Disrupting qualitative inquiry: Possibilities and tension in educational research* (pp. 109–128). New York, NY: Peter Lang.
Reid, A. (2016). Researchers are experienced readers: On recognition, aspiration and obligation. *Environmental Education Research, 22*(3), 422–431.
Rickinson, M. (2000). Special issue: Learners and learning in environmental education: A critical review of evidence. *Environmental Education Research, 7*(3), 208–318.
Ringrose, J. (2011). Beyond discourse: Using Deleuze and Guattari's schizoanalysis to explore affective assemblages, heterosexually striated space, and lines of flight online and at school. *Educational Philosophy and Theory, 43*(6), 598–618.
Robottom, I., & Hart, P. (1993). *Research in environmental education: Engaging the debate.* Geelong: Deakin University Press.
Roe, E., & Greenhough, B. (2014). Experimental partnering: Interpreting improvisatory habits in the research field. *International Journal of Social Research Methodology, 17*(1), 45–57.
Rose, G. (2005). *Visual methodologies: An introduction to the interpretation of visual materials.* Thousand Oaks, CA: Sage Publications.
Roulston, K. (2010). Considering quality in qualitative interviewing. *Qualitative Research, 10*(2), 199–228.
Scheurich, J. (1995). A postmodernist critique of research interviewing. *International Journal of Qualitative Studies in Education, 8*(3), 239–252.
Semetsky, I. (2009). Deleuze pure and applied becoming ethical: Transversing towards ecoliteracy. In D. Masny & D. Cole (Eds.), *Multiple literacies theory: A Deleuzian perspective* (pp. 93–104). Rotterdam, The Netherlands: Sense Publishers.
Springgray, S., Irwin, R., & Kind, S. (Eds.). (2008). A/r/tographers and living inquiry. In G. Knowles & A. Cole (Eds.), *Handbook of the arts in qualitative research* (pp. 83–92). Thousand Oaks, CA: Sage Publications.
St. Pierre, E. (1997a). Guest editorial: An introduction to figurations—a poststructural practice of inquiry. *International Journal of Qualitative Studies in Education, 10*(3), 279–284.
St. Pierre, E. (1997b). Methodology in the fold and the irruption of transgressive data. *International Journal of Qualitative Studies in Education, 10*(2), 175–189.
St. Pierre, E. (2011a). Post qualitative research: The critique and the coming after. In N. Denzin & Y. Lincoln (Eds.), *The Sage handbook of qualitative* research (4th ed., pp. 611–625). London: Sage Publications.
St. Pierre, E. (2011b). Refusing human being in humanist qualitative inquiry. In N. Denzin & M. Giardina (Eds.), *Qualitative inquiry and global crisis* (pp. 40–55). Walnut Creek, CA: Left Coast Press.
St. Pierre, E., & Pillow, W. (2000). *Working the ruins: Feminist poststructural theory and methods in education.* New York, NY: Routledge.
Stetsenko, A. (2008). From relational ontology to transformative activist stance on development and learning: Expanding Vygotsky's (CHAT) project. *Cultural Studies of Science Education, 3*(2), 471–491.

Stevenson, R. (1987). Schooling and environmental education: Contradictions in purpose and practice. In I. Robottom (Ed.), *Environmental education: Practice and possibility* (pp. 69–82). Geelong: Deakin University Press.

Stevenson, R., Brody, M., Dillon, J., & Wals, A. (Eds.). (2013). *International handbook of research on environmental education*. New York, NY: Routledge.

Swan, J. (1975). Forerunners of environmental education. In N. McInnis & D. Albrecht (Eds.), *What makes education environmental?* Louisville, KY: Data Courier.

Thrift, N. (2000). Dead or alive? In I. Cook, D. Crouch, S. Naylor, & J. Ryan (Eds.), *Cultural turns/ geographical turns: Perspectives on cultural geography* (pp. 1–6). Harlow: Prentice Hall.

Wals, A. (Ed.). (2007). *Social learning towards a sustainable world*. Wageningen: Wageningen Academic.

Wright, I., & McInnis, N. (1975). The end of naiveté. In N. McInnis & D. Albrecht (Eds.), *What makes education environmental?* (pp. 452–456). Louisville, KY: Data Courier.

Paul Hart
Faculty of Education
University of Regina, Canada

Catherine Hart
Faculty of Education
University of Regina, Canada

PETA WHITE

3. WALKING MY TALK

Taking Action to Learn/Relearn/Unlearn towards Engaged Pedagogy

INTRODUCTION

I tell you this to break your heart, by which I mean only that it break open and never close again to the rest of the world. (Oliver, 2005, p. 54)

We exist in a time where social pressure and desire to conform encourages us to live in excess and wastefully (Leonard, 2010), yet we are seeing increasingly unstable climatic events (Gore, 2011). For example, we are hearing reports from many scientists that suggest that we can, and should, be making changes in how we live (Gilding, 2011). We are past the place of hiding in denial regarding the need for change (Gore, 2011). "We must accept the world as we know it is going to change" (McKibben, 2010, p. 176), yet finding ways to engage others in social/cultural change towards living more sustainably is challenging.

As a teacher educator, I have asked the question, 'how might I model action and change to help my students learn how to take action to make changes in their own lives'? The following chapter offers a glimpse into my five-year journey to answer this question. It is a small example of the evolving decision making processes I have implemented in an attempt to bring change to personal living practices, the ways I have embraced new discourses that support sustainable living, and my efforts to translate this experience into teacher education curriculum and learning. This work has meant focussing on the development of my own personal living educational theory (Whitehead, 1989). And I have attempted to build this work into what I call 'engaged pedagogy.' This has become my activism in/through education and an effort to 'walk my talk.' I begin by presenting the details of this personal journey, with journal entries followed by a discussion of the many helpful new educational and ecological discourses that have become resources to ground new thinking about my role as activist and model for my students.

MY JOURNEY INTO ACTION LEARNING/RELEARNING/UNLEARNING

There is no passion to be found playing small in settling for a life that is less than the one you are capable of living. (Mandela)

My Journey Began with a Shocking Realisation

It was the revelation that my personal living choices resulted in me not walking my talk as an environmental educator that initiated my embodied research journey. I realised that if change begins within, I needed to work to begin that change.

> Here I am, having recently moved to Canada to study environmental education, and I have an ecological footprint of 16.4 hectares. Oh, the irony! Oh, the embarrassment! And it's not just the literal interpretation that is so devastating, it is the implied reality that comes from realising that not everyone can live like me and I feel almost gratitude that this is the case… this is what I mean by reality – what a horribly privileged feeling! How can I possibly hold my head up in any educational situation and profess to know anything about environmental education when, right now, I embody the problem, and I am certainly not living the solution. This needs to change; I need to change how I practice living if I am to practice environmental education with any dignity, self-respect, and intentionality. (Journal 1, 3rd October, 2005)

I learned about the ecological footprint analysis when I first used an ecological footprint calculator. Ecological footprint analysis is a tool that can help translate sustainability concerns into public action – it is both analytical and educational. "It accounts for the flow of energy and matter to and from any defined economy and converts these into the corresponding land/water area requirements from nature to support these flows" (Wackernagel & Rees, 1996, p. 3). The ecological footprint calculation is a tool that prompts a quantifiable measurement of how living practices have a real cost to the environment. It is a tool that facilitates comparison to how other individuals, events, or organisations might also impact the environment. While this tool is not without issues. For example it doesn't account easily for the cost to the environment of the infrastructure involved with our western ways of living, yet it does provide useful information to make comparisons. I found within it ideas that suggested how I might continue to change my practices to reduce my ecological footprint even further.

> I read about the creation of the calculation (Wackernagel & Rees, 1996) and was impressed with its logic and relevance. As I investigated the ecological footprint concept, I found it to be a treasure trove of ideas and possibilities for future action. Each question of the calculation offers many opportunities to (re) consider my current living practices in such a way that I might lower my total hectare (land/water) use. I found a local online calculator (Royal Saskatchewan Museum) that facilitated a quantified measurement while prompting and generating ideas for continued improvement. The beauty of using a locally generated calculator was that the factors relating to city infrastructure and governance were already accounted for. My data would be corrected for living in Regina. (Journal 1, 11th November, 2005)

The Royal Saskatchewan Museum (1999) Ecological Footprint Calculator allowed me to compare my results with other Canadians and people living in other parts of the world, which was useful when considering the implications of my privileged existence and the injustices experienced by others not immersed within my worldview, societal discourses, and western paradigms. However, over time I have come to understand that the living practices I changed most significantly are those made acceptable by western discourse. I make no claim to abstract these living practices towards societies not privileged with such excess and access to resources. This is an important consideration, and one that must be made very clearly when presenting my lived experience. This work is socially bounded.

Through using the Ecological Footprint Calculator my results were presented in ways that visually represented the magnitude and implications of my current living decisions and choices.

- The choices I make everyday affect every other living being. When used with honesty, this tool demonstrates how every decision I make has a result or an impact on others (human and more than-human).
- The ecological footprint calculation makes the implications of my daily living choices more visible and obvious.

All those times when we are home alone, and no-one is looking, we decide to finally clear the hallway by putting all the recycling into the garbage, or to drive the car instead of catching the bus, or to leave the lights on in rooms we have just vacated. These are choices. They are not always made out of convenience. Sometimes it's wilful; however, sometimes it is unconscious. It is our personal responsibility to think through these choices and to make better ones with the bigger (environment included) picture in mind. There is no easy way out of the situation (environmental devastation and/or social collapse) we are in. We are being socially constructed to let others do the hard work for us. In fact, the definition of 'convenience' is paying other people to do it for you. (Journal 2, 19th February, 2006)

I (Re)Learned How to Practice Living: Taking Action to Learn/relearn/unlearn

I proposed that with some strategic changes to my living practices I could lower my ecological footprint and respectfully present myself as an intentional environmental educator who walked her talk, took her own advice, and could offer personalised experiences in and around how to make sustainable living choices. I set a goal.

An ecological Footprint of 16.4 hectares is unacceptable, given my chosen profession and philosophical position. While there are obvious reasons for this high hectare use (travelling from Australia to Canada), some changes are required in my living practices so that I am walking my talk and can become the intentional environmental educator I want to be. I aim to reduce my footprint so that if everyone lived like me, while valuing the greatest amount of biodiversity, we could all live on our one planet. I will make changes to my living practices until I achieve a stable ecological footprint of 1.8 hectares (at this point in time with this current world population). I give myself permission and time to explore and embody these changes, ensuring that they become integral to my lifestyle choices. I will also look for the discourses that allow and disallow such practice, considering agency and positioning. I want to feel the rub of the dominant discourses as I come up against them. (Journal 1, 12th October, 2005)

My journey was quite an intense experience and often I felt as though I was Alice, disappearing down a self-generated rabbit hole. Unpacking my decisions and becoming confident in my choices took time and embodied experience. It was only as I put my whole body into this research that significant changes occurred. It took time to raise my awareness regarding how to change, and then to work out how to embody that change in an ongoing manner.

Figure 3.1 offers a graphic representation of how my ecological footprint reduced from 16.4 hectares in July 2005 to 1.8 hectares in July 2009. The higher results coincide with a lot of air travel as I chose to visit Australia once every two years – to spend Christmas with my family. I was careful in my calculations to measure successfully embodied changes to my practice, not just anticipated or desired change. My results now hover around 2–3 hectares, depending upon my transport choices as these choices are the most variable and environmentally costly.

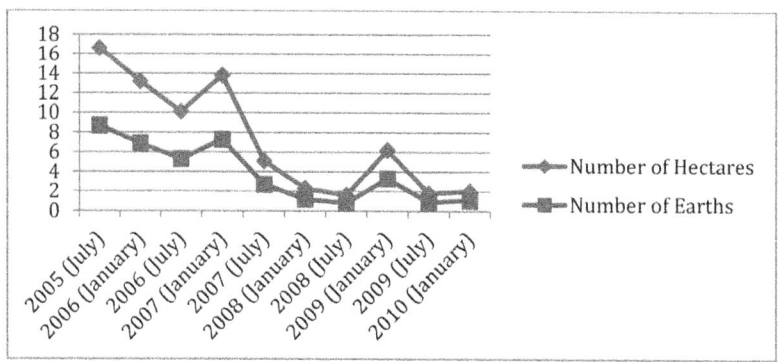

Figure 3.1. A graphic representation of my ecological footprint analysis from July 2005 through to January 2010. The top line illustrates the actual hectare result while the bottom line is the calculated number of earths required if everyone lived like me

It took some time for me to begin to unravel my (co)constructed notions of what it meant to live as a thirty something woman in our society. Once I began to develop awareness of the possibilities I actively looked for new insights through exploring new educational and ecological discourses. I was surprised about how restricted in practice and thought I have been and how freeing and enlivening my new living practices were becoming. After three years of constant consideration I became more aware, passionate, knowledgeable, and determined; however, I'm surprised it took so long!

Figure 3.2 offers a visual representation of some of the changes I implemented in my daily life. The ecological footprint calculator gave me some ideas for areas in which I could take action, and others seemed to be obvious. It helped me to keep reading and talking and working on developing further ideas and testing the discourses around what it means to live more sustainably. I decided to select from a wide range of specific areas of action and challenge that I synthesised into the following headings: transport, energy conservation, water consumption, clothing, housing, consumerism, shopping, food, waste management, personal and cleaning products and others. The full details of what changed related to my personal context yet some details are helpful as they offer some examples of the depth and breadth of action I attempted:

Following are some reflections about these actions in several areas.

- *Transport*: I reduced my air travel, which was challenging as my family and friends live in a different country (opposite side of the world), so I made a commitment to only go home for Christmas every second year. I also reconsidered travel within my current continent, choosing alternatives to air transit whenever possible. I took the train across half of the US, I loaned my car so that one car was servicing two people, and I eventually sold it, choosing to manage my transport in other ways. These included a bike when feasible (not in winter for me), walking (possible though more difficult in winter), and public transport. Often my best choice was to not travel, and this took some effort to get my head around. As Westerners, we have become so accepting of travel, it feels like our right. If I couldn't find safe passage there and back I would just not go. I enjoyed feeling the discourses at play, especially when my friends were frustrated with my choices. Their comments and encouragements voiced many of the dominant discourses and allowed me to feel disciplining discourses in action.
- *Clothing*: I learned how to shop for and wear second hand clothes, even shoes. I limited the amount of clothes I owned, returning any unnecessary items to a second hand shop. I attempted to streamline my choices producing a versatile 'classic' wardrobe rather than a selection of rapidly outdating fashions. I also valued spending time to mend my clothes and took extra care in laundering them so that most items experienced an elongated lifetime. I decided not to purchase clothes that were not made from natural fibres or that were processed in environmentally damaging ways (like bleached cotton). I considered where an item was manufactured and attempted to buy locally produced clothes.
- *Housing*: I rented rooms close to the university area, house sat, and moved into residence on campus before purchasing an apartment just across the road from campus. These decisions meant that I utilised high-density living and limited

the need for transport. Owning my own home meant that I could implement many energy and water saving strategies. It also meant that I could challenge myself to furnish a home without resorting to purchasing new items. I found garage sales very useful in providing well priced, quality items. I also found that I didn't really require much additional furniture, challenging another social discourse. My belongings grew, however, filling the available space, if I wasn't vigilant.
- *Consumerism*: I lived to the quote "every cent you spend is a vote for the kind of environment you want to live in" (no reference). This kept me out of Dollar Stores and Walmart. I became very conscious of the items I purchased, becoming aware of the implications of the choices I was making. I considered where I was shopping and who had been involved in the production of the goods. I valued the environmental impact of each stage of production. I took time to learn about the processes that products underwent, and grew increasingly concerned at the international transit that many products experience before finding their way to the shop. I learned how to find alternatives to products that didn't live up to my ethics. I learned to live without, and liked it. I was determined to become un-tied to stuff (Journal 5, 20th September 2009).

A Focus on Food: Three Opportunities to Get It Closer to 'Right' Each Day!

My favourite environmental issues are those that relate to how we choose to manage our health and, more specifically, food consumption. Food and health are interrelated and have become areas where we often seek others' advice, opinion, and products looking for that golden bullet, fast fix, and cure all. Food and health are wonderful areas where personal challenges to embrace a more sustainable living practice can be rewarding and relatively easy to undertake.

I enjoyed one wonderful Canadian summer immersing myself in food: Reading, viewing, gardening, preserving, re-considering, and constantly inquiring. These are some of the activities of learning to become responsible for my own food. I studied the food systems of western society, especially in North America, which have become corporatised where priority is given to economic growth rather than consumer health. Documentaries such as Food Inc. (Kenner, 2008) demonstrate some of the problems and present the issues in a clear, easy to comprehend, medium. Additionally, Pollan (2006) has written extensively on how to reconsider our food choices from McDonald's to growing and gathering our own foods. Kingsolver (2007) moved her entire family to a location where they could begin to live without the corporatised food system. They learned to grow and prepare their own food and consume local products. I found this inspirational and, in my own way, began to emulate the journey towards taking responsibility, working towards practicing greater sustainability, and finding healthier ways of nourishing myself.

Health care, as it relates to food, can be as easy as reading and understanding the ingredients in the products we choose. Many products that we eat and apply to our bodies are neither good for us nor safe for consumption. I understand the trust and unquestioned belief in our system that suggests we wouldn't be able to make the purchase if it wasn't safe, yet, as it turns out, the safeguards that should protect the consumer are not in place as we might hope and they really don't deserves our trust. As consumers we should investigate these issues and make our own *informed* decisions. Additionally, many of the processes that our food goes through before it gets to us are alarming and could result in serious health issues. This includes: pesticide use and excessive artificial fertilising, packaging, canning, high heat extrusion, transportation around the world, and often back again, waxing, and preserving, with a special mention for genetic engineering.

I have changed the way I feed myself. I only shop around the edges of the supermarket, if I go there at all, preferring local food markets or organic shops. I support the local Farmers' Market, preferring to buy from people with whom I have relationships. I make most of my food from scratch having sourced local providers. I have even grown much of my own food and preserved it where I can: dehydrating, canning, and freezing vegetables. However, living in a place that is frozen for over half the year has increased these challenges. And, as a consequence, I have learned about sprouting where I can produce my own fresh, local nutrients throughout the year. I refuse to purchase strawberries year round as they are a seasonal fruit, I don't eat bananas as they are not grown on this continent, and I won't eat beef that isn't locally grown, grass-fed in pasture and locally processed.

Many of these choices cost me time and energy and, occasionally, more money. Yet they offer so much more: increased nutrients leading to a better value, better health, exercise, clear choices with most of the implications revealed, and a significantly increased level of responsibility for my food consumption and personal and environmental health. I have learned a lot about food and food preparation and I enjoy the connections I've made with local producers. I am proud of the efforts I have made towards becoming a more responsible and sustainable consumer.

And Where Am I Now?

During my study period I managed to work my way down to living with an ecological footprint of 1.8 hectares. If everyone lived like this way, we could all live on our one planet. I continue to measure my ecological footprint every six months, acknowledging that sometimes my choices result in higher than desired analyses while at other times it remains low. I have purchased a car now, and yes, it hurts to have to increase my footprint calculation; however it was necessary given a change in my circumstance and I can see a time in the future when I will be able to revert to non-car ownership. I own an apartment that brings the benefit of ensuring that some of my living practices reduce my impact; however other challenges are created

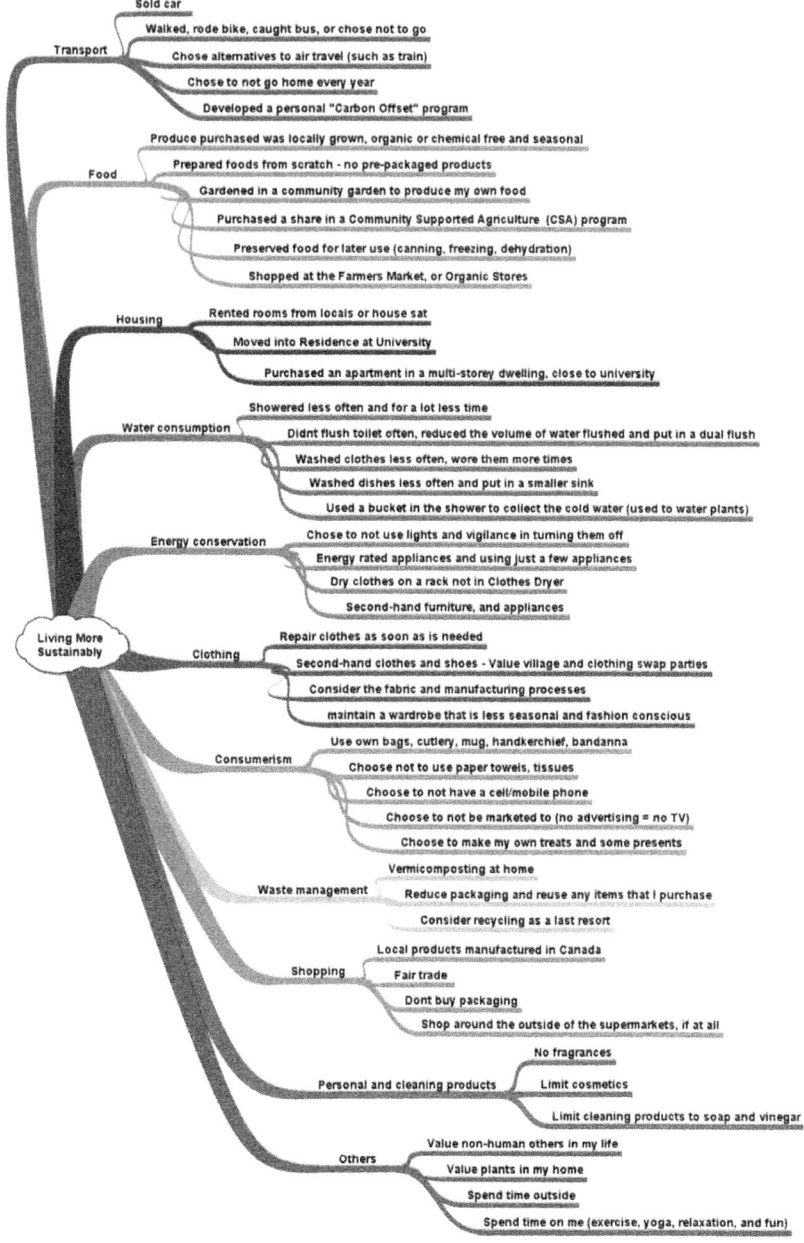

Figure 3.2. A visual representation of the issues addressed and actions taken to reduce my ecological footprint to become an intentional practitioner learning to live more sustainably in western society

through this choice. It is okay to measure impacts and implications of my choices, to be aware of them, and to consciously change my mind, if deemed necessary. I find ways to live with less that result in making me feel that I actually live with more: greater consciousness and consideration, better health, and a deeper connection to my community, my ecosystems, and my body.

I continue to use humour to cope with many situations. I enjoy a good laugh at myself... regularly. I try to not get wrapped up in the craziness of my efforts and I try to keep it real. These challenges are useful... the disruptions are beneficial to me as they ground me in practices that provide a platform for how I want to be as an educator. I feel that I live with an intentionality that affords me a position of familiarity and knowledge that brings power, experience, and story to my educational practices. I have great passion for this work as it keeps me healthy, happy, connected, informed, challenged, in community, and alive.

RECOGNISING MY ROLE AS ACTIVIST

Another world is not only possible, she is on her way. On a quiet day, I can hear her breathing. (Roy, 2003, p. 112)

Activism has been defined as the doctrine or practice that emphasises direct vigorous action especially in support or opposition to one side of a controversial issue (Activism, n.d.). Gerum (2007) stated that activism was "being the change, actively leading a life that reflects the kind of world you want to live in, and it's about creating action beyond yourself and acting as an agent of change" (p. 193). Thus, activism is about embodying change as well as enabling others to see the need for undertaking their own change processes. Schugurensky (2007) offered the following statement at a conference titled "Educational activism: social justice in classrooms, schools and communities" held at the Ontario Institute for Studies in Education, Toronto, Canada in November 2007.

Activism is any intentional action, individual or collective, to make a better world. By a better world I mean a world where all human beings can develop their full potential, a world that is more democratic, just, peaceful, sustainable and enjoyable than the world that we have today. I am aware that there is another type of activism, one that moves in the opposite direction, that is, towards a world characterized by more unequal distribution of wealth and opportunities, violence, oppressive relations, war, poverty, pollution, discrimination, and so forth. (p. 1)

While playing with possibilities here, Schugurensky exemplifies a critical theory of uptake of discourses. While some might choose to take "activism" up as an alternative view of the dominant discourse (environmentalism perhaps), others choose the dominant view itself (such as capitalist consumerism); however, often this choice to follow the dominant discourses are not acknowledged as intentional choices as they are the socially acceptable choices.

Activism, or active and engaged citizenship, can be working towards establishing different dominant discourses around a variety of issues. These issues might include:

> Tackling large public issues, local problems, improving livability, reducing conflict, bridging towards stronger democracy, rekindling a sense of community, alternative pathways to better health, and increasing social capital. (Dobson, 2003, p. 4)

And regardless of the different types and scopes of activism, a common feature is that often these activities are beyond what is expected from us in our daily lives; activism is something that we do because we believe in the goodness of the cause, usually on a voluntary basis.

Renowned educational activist, hooks (1994) states,

> [m]y commitment to engaged pedagogy is an expression of political activism. Given that our educational institutions are so deeply invested in a banking system, teachers are more rewarded when we do not teach against the grain. The choice to work against the grain, to challenge the status quo, often has negative consequences. And that is part of what makes that choice one that is not politically neutral. (hooks, 1994, p. 203)

hooks (1994) further describes how her pedagogical philosophies were designed and tested and how she practices with the aim of being critical and political, thereby creating opportunities for transformation of her students and herself, as she continues to learn with her students. She also demonstrates personal agency as she makes the decision to "teach against the grain" (hooks, 1994, p. 203).

Intentionality, or choice, is integral to activist practice. Taking time to explore alternative discourses, to come to know the implications of one choice over another, and making thoughtful value judgments as to which is more appropriate is the basis of activism, as this intentionality precedes any action. In this way activism may be an appropriate method employed to expose and explore problems in dominant discourses.

Kumashiro (2004) suggests that activists:

> … work to change laws and policies by lobbying legislators or staging protests, they teach others to break through the glass ceilings or challenge discriminatory employment or housing or healthcare practices, and they organize community or school groups for political action. And as they teach us to become dissatisfied and uncomfortable with the norms of society, they ask us to examine why we have already become uncomfortable with the "queers" of society. (Kumashiro, 2004, p. 45)

He goes on to liken activism to teacher education, which mirrors my feelings regarding the opportunity (and responsibility) provided through transformative education and critical engaged pedagogies towards supporting social/cultural change towards a more sustainable society. The choice to practice transformative education is activism and an example of personal/political agency.

EDUCATION WITH A CRITICAL TURN: MODELLING CRITICAL ENGAGED PEDAGOGY AND CURRICULUM PRACTICE

Critical theories offer the potential of emancipation through the critique of systems of domination or dependence, thus being critical is being political (Ellsworth, 2005; Kincheloe, 2008; Shor, 1992; 1999; Stronach & MacLure, 1997). The employment of critical theory demands that the researcher considers her self-production and construction and how this process shapes how she (co) constructs her world. It is in the practice of critical theory that forms of self-reflection are gainfully engaged as the practitioner is in a constant state of becoming. And in particular, as a teacher educator, this grounding allows me to offer a transformative education that is critical in nature and that works at the level of ontology, epistemology, and axiology. Working with these new insights is one way to bring about social/cultural change: transformation via education for myself, my students, my students' future students, and our communities. The teacher is an artist, but being an artist does not mean that he or she can make the profile or shape the students. What the educator does in teaching is to make it possible for the students to become themselves (Horton & Freire, 1990). The following exploration will consider critical possibilities in transformational education, or as Taylor (2009) calls it "teaching for change" (p. 3). Undergirding this work with transformational education and the desire to teach for change are critical engaged pedagogies.

Helping My Students Understand the Meaning and Value of Critically Engaged Pedagogy

Critical pedagogies are those that engage us in thinking and actively working to understand and participate in different, new, and challenging ways: to think, as an action, about the issues that confront us. The content of such praxis can be varied. I ask students to challenge themselves, through action, to change an aspect of how they currently live towards a more sustainable practice. Based on my own experiences undertaking such critical work, I can model ways that I challenged myself, sharing my stories.

Pedagogy can be described as "the production and transmission of knowledge, the construction of subjectivity, and the learning of values and beliefs" (Kincheloe, McLaren, & Steinberg, 1997, p. xiii). Pedagogy can refer "to knowledge as a thing made [as well as] knowledge as in the making" (Ellsworth, 2005, p. 1). Therefore, the experiences of the learner during "the means and conditions, the environmental and events of knowledge in the making" (Ellsworth, 2005, p. 1) are open to exploration. And, as such, pedagogy can be (re)considered

... as the impetus behind the particular movements, sensations, and affects of bodies/mind/brains in the midst of learning, and it explores the embodied experiences that pedagogy elicits and plays host to: experiences of being radically in relation to one's self, to others, and to the world. (Ellsworth, 2005, p. 2)

The state of becoming is constantly (re)informed by the simultaneous experience of what is becoming while learning and what is learned while becoming. "Pedagogy, like painting, sculpture, or music, can be magical in its artful manipulation of inner ways of knowing into a mutually transforming relation with outer events, selves, objects, and ideas" (Ellsworth, 2005, p. 7).

Being critical implies a central goal of "becom[ing] more skeptical toward commonly accepted truisms" (Burbules & Berk, 1999, p. 45). Skepticism is useful when "our beliefs remain unexamined, [as] we are not free; we act without thinking about why we act, and thus do not exercise control over our own destinies" (Burbules & Berk, 1999, p. 46). Learning to challenge commonly and socially accepted 'truisms' leads to self-sufficiency, and "a self-sufficient person is a liberated person... free from the unwarranted and undesirable control of unjustified beliefs" (Siegel, 1988, p. 58). Critical pedagogy, therefore, "illuminates the relationship among knowledge, authority, and power" (Giroux, 1994, p. 30).

The purpose of critical pedagogy is to engage learners in the act of what Freire calls *conscientizacao*, which has been defined as "learning to perceive social, political, and economic contradictions, and to take action against the oppressive elements of reality" (Freire, 1970/1995, p. 17). Gruenewald (2008) suggests, "critical pedagogies are needed to challenge the assumptions, practices, and outcomes taken for granted in dominant culture and in conventional education" (Gruenewald, 2008, p. 308). Bowers' (1997, 2001) critique offers that critical pedagogy often betrays a sweeping disinterest in the fact that human culture has been, is, and always will be, nested in ecological systems. He suggests that the discourses of ecological systems are often lost as mechanistic and modernist views are privileged.

hooks (2010) reminds us that "thinking is an action" (p. 7) as it is "where visions of theory and praxis come together" (p. 7). The action of thinking is something that can (and has) become undervalued and under-utilised in our classrooms and so taking time to teach thinking skills and to engage students in the thinking processes becomes important to successful practice leading to social/cultural change. I suggest that hooks 'engaged pedagogy' can be considered as the practice of 'critical pedagogy.' "Engaged pedagogy emphasizes mutual participation because it is the movement of ideas, exchanged by everyone, that forges a meaningful working relationship between everyone in the classroom" (hooks, 2010, p. 21). The importance of having a unique voice and independent thought, where all contributions are 'worthy' and every student is encouraged to participate in the learning process in the ways that they feel most comfortable is the integrity of engaged pedagogy, hooks (2010) says. "To educate for freedom, then, we have to challenge and change the way everyone thinks about pedagogical process. This is especially true for students" (hooks, 1994, p. 144).

SO WHAT? PERSONAL CHANGE THROUGH AUTOETHNOGRAPHY

"Who are you?" said the Caterpillar. This was not an encouraging opening for a conversation. Alice replied, rather shyly, "I – I hardly know, Sir, just at present – at least I know who I was when I got up the morning, but I think I must have been changed several times since then." (Carroll, 2004, p. 55)

Personal change, as investigated through autoethnography, and framed theoretically through critical poststructural ecofeminist activism, happened. I learned how to be critically engaged with my personal living choices, successfully lowering my impact on the environment while remaining within my culture. I decreased my ecological footprint, I refined my decision making strategy, I gained knowledge, changed my practice, and occasionally this influenced others to change as well.

My research inspired a metamorphosis of my practice: personally and professionally. I believe I have become a better educator, researcher, and activist as a result of the critical consideration and reflexive practice undertaken. Self-focused research has enabled me to change, my students to experience transformational education that may have changed them, and, I want to believe, leads to changes in society. Through embodiment and doing, as well as theorising and thinking, I have come to know differently. Dewey (1929) suggested that theory must be accompanied with doing and making (p. 281) and this action orientated research undertook embodied practice to reveal not only an experience about what it felt like to change, but also to establish a model of what change could be like for others. Thus, Cuomo's (1998) "thoughtful practice" (p. 143) was evoked as choices were carefully considered and then modelled for others' consideration.

The *so what?* of this research is that these changes matter as they become a new way of being for me, inspire others to consider undertaking change, and begin to change the discourses around what is possible. I have heard and felt the dominant discourses as they rub against my intentions for a different, more sustainable practice. Seeing, hearing, and feeling the dominant discourses has been as important as finding ways to struggle against them, encouraging others to look beyond the socially constructed ways of being. Walking my talk has enabled a different way of seeing, being, doing and thinking with others and has resulted in what feels like a meaningful continuation of change, or critical reflexivity.

An Activism of Hope and Hopefulness

I explore options and challenge my (co)constructed notions continually. I practice making change in my life by doing the small things: many of the small things. I recycle and reuse and, better yet, I reduce and re-think. I use less water and energy and produce less waste. I look for alternatives to air transit and take these options when they make sense and I choose to travel less often than I have. I buy second hand clothes when I really need them. I eat locally and seasonally, forming relationships with food producers. I live close to where I work in a multi-story apartment building, reducing my need for ground transport. These small changes are relatively easy steps to put into practice. It is the cumulative action of these small changes that results in me feeling like I am making a difference and generating discourses of change. These small changes give me a sense of achievement and I choose to celebrate each as a success. I feel hopeful about my changing practice, increasing awareness of discourses, and the influence I provide to change the discourses and, ultimately, others' practice.

I feel great about the time and energy I have put into critiquing my living practices; however it's the ability to hear, see, and feel the discourses as they rub against my new found understandings that is most interesting. As I take the time to explain some of my choices to vendors at the Farmers' Market or in other places I consume, I hope that my opinion might sway their practices a little. I encourage my friends to reconsider some of their practices. I challenge my students to take on their own personal challenges. But mostly, I listen and feel as the dominant discourses wash over me with their disciplining comments or actions or through permission giving advertisements and marketing strategies intending to maintain the excessively consuming ways of western society.

I believe that many are challenged by my discourse and practice around becoming more sustainable. I have been told that my presence makes people behave or feel differently about their practice and choices. I don't actively attempt to generate these feelings (usually of guilt I assume) but I am curious when they are expressed. I wonder at the reasons these people use for not practicing more sustainability if they can simply choose not to because there is no pressure to do so. Perhaps mandating change would be effective? It seems to be working well for Sweden. Ultimately, I'm reminded that it's just desire and active choice that changes practice towards becoming more sustainable.

When offering a presentation to a group of students undertaking environmental activism in their class recently, I was asked if I ever felt anger at the constant application of dominant discourses that are wasteful and perpetuate overconsumption. Upon reflection on this great question I realised that I don't. I have considerable patience as my practice is about how I can change. I'm not able to change others, however I can prompt, suggest, and offer the possibility of other ways of being and doing. Change begins within and as Gandhi's lifework and writing suggests, you must be the change that you wish to see in the world. I strive to follow this mandate, hoping to influence others along the way by changing the discourses around what is possible and acceptable.

I often receive critique of this work that suggests that these small personal changes don't make any effective impact on the footprint of my society. I can see that the impacts of my changes are small in comparison to the changes large corporations need to make. However, changes to how I choose to live are the ONLY changes I can make. My practices impact larger corporations as I choose not to purchase their products and services and to be vocal about it. I use my dollars as a vote for the kind of environment I want to live in. I feel empowered through this critically reflexive practice. I am changing my impact and I am attempting to influence and encourage others' to do the same.

I feel hopeful as my changing practice becomes easier and more ingrained in my body. I no longer have to use my decision making process as often, although I need to remain aware of the implications of each choice. I'm getting better at becoming more aware. The choices I want to make are easier to embody now. Perhaps the item I want is easier to find because it's more available, or the ingredients have changed, or I am used to doing things a different way, or going without. Not eating bananas while living in Canada is now ok and I can begin new challenges (such as, not eating chocolate because that too is not produced on this continent. I know where to look for the kind of shampoo I am prepared to use. I have developed deeper awareness of the numbers on the stickers on my fruit and the ingredients in products.

I feel hopeful when I hear others talk about the changes they are taking on. Leonard (2010) offers great cause for positivity. I have had the pleasure of working with this activist twice now and each time she delivers a keynote address that generates hope and inspiration. Through greater awareness of the implications of our choices Leonard's audiences are becoming more sustainable in their practices. I know this because I am one of them and my colleagues and friends confide in me their own challenges and successes as a result of their interactions with these ideas. As Kingsolver reminds us:

> The arc of history is longer than human vision. It bends. We abolished slavery, we granted universal suffrage. We have done hard things before. And every time it took a terrible fight between people who could not imagine changing the rules, and those who said, "We already did. We have made the world new." The hardest part will be to convince yourself of the possibilities, and hang on. If you run out of hope at the end of the day, to rise in the morning and put it on again with your shoes. Hope is the only reason you won't give in, burn what's left of the ship and go down with it. The ship of your natural life and your children's only shot. (Kingsolver, 2008, para. 17)

Finally, I remind myself that language matters. We are not participating in an environmental crisis. We are deeply involved in a social crisis. The false naming of these crises allows for a lack of recognition as to the underlying practices that generate such varied issues and consequences. Humans have misunderstood our place in the Earth systems and we are overstepping our bounds causing damage to others' and the systems themselves. Yet, I reflect that in some ways a crisis is good! Change comes with education, mandate, or crisis. Education works for some, sometimes. Mandating change takes considerable effort, requires policing, and has been a successful strategy in some cases. However, social crisis will come (and in many cases is here already) and almost inevitably with some major devastating catastrophe the over population and excessive consumption will end. I don't like this idea; it will come as a shock and with certain pain and distress, and I hope my friends and family are the ones who make it through. However I also believe that if we can't control ourselves and become aware of our place within our Earth systems then catastrophic social crisis will make us change.

Things will change... there is always change... change brings equilibrium. Ecosystems, for example, are in constant states of flux as they work to establish equilibrium. I suggest that the pendulum has swung as far out as it can and it is time for it to swing back in and western society will have little choice but to change. Peak oil is a concept that has been with us for a while and drives some change. What if we are now at peak humanity? Managing population pressure is a difficult concept. Yet, as with each social/environmental issue, it is one that each individual can take a stand on and make personal choices to practice with critical consciousness. I am reminded of the quote by Buckminster Fuller "You never change things by fighting the existing reality. To change something, build a new model that makes the existing model obsolete."

Klein's (2014) book "This Changes Everything; Capitalism vs. The Climate" suggests that the real issue at hand is the prevailing economic system and a constant demand for growth. She suggests that the challenge is not to focus on doing things that reduce the effect of climate change, but that we work out how to engage in a different set of ground rules with our economic system. I think Leonard (2010) describes how a linear system is just not going to work in a finite system in her "Story of Stuff" video. In her 2013 video "The Story of Solutions" she even suggests how we can see it differently. This kind of thinking is what we need: Solutions activism that generates hope and possible ways forward.

I choose to see the social crisis as an opportunity for hope and hopefulness. "What we are looking for is empowerment of a particularly deep kind: the enablement of being – or even better, of becoming. For we humans are nothing if not human becomings, always in the process of change" (Fisher, 2006, p. 46). Learning how to live sustainably was where I began in this work. I want to re-name the work to learning to 'live critically.' Change is constant in our society. New ideas and trends take hold each day. So, to be clear, it is not unbounded change that I'm after, it is specifically related to: resource consciousness, limiting energy, water, and waste production, learning to respect all beings and to know and live as part of the Earth systems. I want western society to become critical about our place in the Earth systems; acting as if we are a part of this system, not owner/manager of all systems, is imperative to our survival. I feel as though I have achieved steps towards practicing this way and I know others' are acting similarly.

BEST WISHES FOR A SUSTAINABLE FUTURE!

Finding words to clarify my worldview, as well as others' that share elements of my worldview was inspirational and resulted in me finding my community. In this community I discovered strategies and ideas regarding practices and ways to articulate and theorise. For example, I learned to unpack the complexity, develop an awareness of my assumptions (Cuomo, 1998) and the discourses from which they came, look for synergies rather than difference (Robinson, 2009) and to consider Earth as a complex system rather than discrete parts that can be completely knowable (Meadows, 2008). Appreciating the intricate and interwoven nature of these systems and my small part within them holds me accountable for my every action. I now have a solid platform upon which I can walk my talk when practicing/performing environmental education/educator. I have been transformed through an educational strategy. I embodied these changes and learned to feel the impact of discourses. I have become and continue to become critically reflexive when choosing the possible implications of my choices. And as a result of this personal change my ability to teach others has changed.

REFERENCES

Bowers, C. A. (1997). *The culture of denial: Why the environmental movement needs a strategy for reforming universities and public schools*. Albany, NY: State University of New York Press.
Bowers, C. A. (2001). *Educating for eco-justice and community*. Athens, GA: The University of Georgia Press.
Burbules, N. C., & Berk, R. (1999). Critical thinking and critical pedagogy: Relations, differences, and limits. In T. S. Popkewitz & L. Fendler (Eds.), *Critical theories in education: Changing terrains of knowledge and politics* (pp. 45–76). New York, NY: Routledge.
Carroll, L. (2004). *Alice's adventures in Wonderland* (Special ed.). New York, NY: Barns and Noble Incorporated.
Cuomo, C. J. (1998). *Feminism and ecological communities: An ethic of flourishing*. London: Routledge.
Dewey, J. (1929). *Quest for certainty*. New York, NY: Minton, Balch and Company.
Dobson, C. (2003). *The troublemakers teaparty: A manual for effective citizen action*. Gabriola Island: New Society Publishers.
Ellsworth, E. (2005). *Places of learning: Media, architecture, pedagogy*. New York, NY: Routledge Falmer.
Fisher, F. (2006). *Response ability: Environment, health and everyday transcendence*. Melbourne: Vista.
Freire, P. (1995). *Pedagogy of the oppressed*. New York, NY: Continuum. (Original work published 1970)
Gerum, N. (2007). Finding the "I" in action: Defining activism to include me. In S. Cullis-Suzuki, K. Frederickson, A. Kayssi, C. Mackenzie, & D. A. Cohen (Eds.), *Notes from Canada's young activists: A generation stands up for change* (pp. 189–198). Vancouver: GreysStone Books.
Gilding, P. (2011). *The great disruption: How the climate crisis will transform the global economy*. London: Bloomsbury Publishing.
Giroux, H. A. (1994). Toward a pedagogy of critical thinking. In K. S. Walters (Ed.), *Re-thinking reason: New perspectives in critical thinking* (pp. 200–201). Albany, NY: SUNY Press.
Gore, A. (2011, September 15). *The climate reality project*. Retrieved from http://climaterealityproject.org/
Gruenewald, D. A. (2008). The best of both worlds: A critical pedagogy of place. *Environmental Education Research, 14*(3), 308–324.
hooks, b. (1994). *Teaching to transgress: Education as the practice of freedom*. New York, NY: Routledge.

hooks, b. (2010). *Teaching critical thinking: Practical wisdom*. New York, NY: Routledge.
Horton, M., & Freire, P. (1990). *We make the road by walking: Conversations on education and social change*. Philadelphia, PA: Temple University Press.
Kenner, R. (2008). *Food inc*. Beverly Hills, CA: Participant Media.
Kincheloe, J. L. (2008). *Critical pedagogies* (2nd ed.). New York, NY: Peter Lang.
Kincheloe, J. L., McLaren, P., & Steinberg, S. R. (1997). Series editors' forward. In H. A. Giroux (Ed.), *Pedagogy and politics of hope: Theory, culture, and schooling* (pp. ix–xiv). Boulder, CO: Westview Press.
Kingsolver, B. (2007). *Animal, vegetable, miracle: A year of food life*. New York, NY: Harper Perennial.
Kingsolver, B. (2008, May 11). *How to be hopeful*. Durham, NC: Duke University Commencement Ceremony. Retrieved from http://www.dailygood.org/more.php?n=5140
Klein, N. (2014). *This changes everything: Capitalism vs. the climate*. New York, NY: Simon & Schuster.
Kumashiro, K. K. (2004). *Against common sense: Teaching and learning towards social justice*. New York, NY: Routledge Falmer.
Leonard, A. (2007). *The story of stuff*. Retrieved from http://storyofstuff.org/movies/
Leonard, A. (2010). *The story of stuff: How our obsession with stuff is trashing the planet, our communities, and our health – and a vision for change*. New York, NY: Free Press.
Leonard, A. (2013). *The story of solutions*. Retrieved from http://storyofstuff.org/movies/
Meadows, D. H. (2008). *Thinking in systems: A primer*. White River Junction, VT: Chelsea Green Publishing.
McKibben, W. (2010). Something braver than trying to save the world. In K. D. Moore & M. P. Nelson (Eds.), *Moral ground: Ethical action for a planet in peril* (pp. 174–177). San Antonio, TX: Trinity University Press.
Oliver, M. (2005). *New and selected poems* (Vol. 2). Boston, MA: Beacon Press.
Pollan, M. (2006). *The omnivores dilemma: A natural history of four meals*. New York, NY: Penguin Books.
Robinson, K. (2009). *The element: How finding your passion changes everything*. London: Penguin.
Roy, A. (2003). *War talk*. Cambridge, MA: South End Press.
Royal Saskatchewan Museum. (1999). *Ecological footprints*. Retrieved from http://www.royalsaskmuseum.ca/gallery/life_sciences/footprint_mx_2005.swf
Schugurensky, D. (2007, November 24). *Education in activism, and activism in education*. Presentation at Educational activism: Social justice in Classrooms, Schools and Communities, Ontario Institute of Studies in Education, University of Toronto, Toronto.
Shor, I. (1992). *Empowering education: Critical Teaching for social change*. Chicago, IL: The University of Chicago Press.
Shor, I. (1999). *Critical literacy in action: Writing words, changing worlds*. Portsmouth: Boynton/Cook.
Siegel, H. (1988). *Educating reason: Rationality, critical thinking, and education*. New York, NY: Routledge.
Stronach, I., & MacLure, M. (1997). *Educational research undone: The postmodern embrace*. Buckingham: Open University Press.
Taylor, E. W. (2009). Fostering transformational learning. In J. Mezirow & E. W. Taylor (Eds.), *Transforming learning in practice: Insights from community, workplace, and higher education* (pp. 3–18). San Francisco, CA: Jossey-Bass.
Wackernagel, M., & Rees, W. (1996). *Our ecological footprint: Reducing human impact on the earth*. Gabriola Island: New Society Publishers.
Whitehead, J. (1989). Creating a living educational theory from questions of the kind, 'How do I improve my practice?' *Cambridge Journal of Education, 19*(1), 41–52.

Peta White
School of Education
Deakin University, Australia

DON CARRUTHERS DEN HOED

4. TRANSFORMING PARK EDUCATION AS A TRANSFORMED PARK EDUCATOR

INTRODUCTION

In this chapter, I describe experiences in my career as a programmer and supervisor with a Canadian park agency, and now as a graduate student scholar, that have inspired me to rethink and transform the work of park education to help park visitors experience a dramatically new form of engagement with natural settings. In recent years, I have collaborated with colleagues to re-invent and re-conceptualize our work., This has involved implementing an inclusive model for park-based experiences that transforms a view of visitors from mere users of parks to empowered partners in learning about a shared natural, social and cultural landscape. The story of this shift began when, at the age of sixteen, I began working in the field of interpretation and education in parks and protected areas along the eastern slopes of the Rocky Mountains. Whether answering questions at a visitor centre about where to hike, delivering guided hikes about river ecology, or presenting musical theatre programs about wetland ecosystems, my job was to extoll the virtues of nature on behalf of nature. I was told early in my career that people have enough opportunities to speak for themselves, but that nature has no voice. I sang songs and pointed out natural features to show visitors that wildlife is exciting, funny, and important. I dressed as a beaver and danced about aquatic ecology in hopes that a single program would help campers become stewards of the environment and supporters of parks. Though I still lead programs that aim to connect people with nature and outdoor recreation, I no longer have the same certainty that I could, or even should, be the human voice of nature.

I received that first paycheque from a provincial parks agency twenty-five years ago, and remain with the same agency to this day, now the Head of Inclusion and Public Engagement in the busiest region of my province. My first day of work was spent responding to inquiries at a visitor counter about trails and suggesting experiences to have during their trip. Over the next decade, most days were spent developing or delivering public education and interpretive programs to campers, tourist, and in schools. The following decade was dedicated to outreach and, eventually, a role championing a province-wide inclusion plan that built on my Masters Degree in Education. Today, my work focuses on policy development and planning for a wide range of programs; from marketing and information to public and formal education, and from community and partner relations to inclusion and social research. While I began this career on the front lines of connecting people to nature, I only recently realized the impact I was having behind the scenes, changing the way people connect to nature by changing the framework of park educational programs we deliver and the culture of the agency I work for. I have also recently realized how far-removed I have become from conversations at a visitor centre and programs in the forest.

After two and a half decades, I have found myself questioning what the trade-off is between doing park education (or any education) and supporting those who do park education. Further, over my career, my perspective has shifted and driven me to pursue the integration of social and ecological aspects within park education—wildlife can be valuable to people who don't camp or visit parks at all, and the benefits of inclusion in a shared recreational experience is as meaningful as helping people appreciate the role of beavers. I have encountered people who were silently excluded, and nature that yelled above the din. I learned that the voices of nature and people are the same voice, and in neither case should I try to own that voice.

In this chapter, I will frame and present some key moments or realizations I had in my career as a park educator in order to share approaches and concepts that I feel make parks an ideal setting for transformative learning (TL). I also hope to illustrate my own transformational journey, and finally attempt to reconcile the trade-offs and new perspectives mentioned above with a new, transformational model for park education.

FINDING TRANSFORMATIONAL LEARNING

In early stages of my career, my focus was on developing innovative, direct approaches to how parks engage the public and facilitate learning experiences, especially through outreach and residency programs. As I gained exposure to both diverse and (conspicuously) homogeneous audiences—the former being exciting, the latter disquieting—I felt called to take action to ensure that the people with opportunities to lead and participate in park education didn't all look, walk, talk, and think the same as I do. I found the theory and principles of transformative learning to be an excellent resource to build ideas and programs to address this call to take action.

My initial efforts and early graduate studies focused on the inclusion of persons with disabilities in parks, and the key outcome was the creation of a vanguard jurisdiction-wide inclusion plan for persons with disabilities in parks and wilderness areas. As I reflected on my graduate work and the changes sparked by the inclusion plan, it became clear that exploring inclusion in nature and parks offered compelling links to transformative learning as a field. I am now engaged in deeply reflective study of my work and my calling through a transdisciplinary doctoral studies program. This graduate work not only studies and challenges the core premises of parks and the values they claim to represent, it has driven much of the thinking I applied to an internal reorganization and revitalization of the program I lead. Where my staff were once focused on one-way *service to visitors*—generally isolated in their information, interpretive, or environmental education specializations—they are now fully supported as an integrated team of practitioners who *engage the public* along a continuum of experiences. The shared vision of the team is to support park-based experiences that transform people from mere *users* of parks to empowered *partners* in a shared natural, social, and cultural landscape.

Finally, I am engaged in a transformational personal reflection process that this chapter parallels. Writing this overview has churned up once-still waters and unblocked a flow that was growing stagnant. Once happy presenting entertaining and educational programs about nature to visitors in a park, I am now at a critical turning point in my career where I must decide whether to stay in program coordination, move into a management role, or leave the park agency that has employed me for a quarter-century and pursue work in an academic institution or elsewhere.

Looking at Parks Differently

As a conservation-oriented person, I often question the point of promoting the protection of isolated pockets of land (parks) or entertaining campers and recreational user in support of tourism (park education) when an environmental crisis is threatening the status quo of civilization in the industrial west. The symptoms are frightening: climate change, loss of biodiversity, melting glaciers and ice caps, sprawl of non-living landscapes, pollution, and so on (McKibben, 2010; Orr, 2004; O'Sullivan, 2008; Suzuki, 2009). Massive change is inevitable, prompting McKibben (2010) to suggest we accept and adapt to a new, permanently altered earth. O'Sullivan (2008), blames our consumptive industrial society, stating that "we are damaging the carrying capacity of the Earth in irreversible ways so as to threaten the very existence of life as we know it" (p. 28). Can parks play a role in resolving our relationship with nature, and in sparking the sort of transformative learning experiences that will require? Or is protecting discrete postage stamps of nature as parks simply exacerbating the problem Selby (2000) identifies as "a direct outcome of the dominant western mechanistic worldview with its foundations in 17thand 18th-century scientific notions of separation and domination" (p. 88)? Other scholars echo this indictment of the dualism between us/it, mind/matter, or humans/nature (Evernden, 1993; Knapp, 2005; McKibben, 2010; Orr, 2004; Plumwood, 1993), and Suzuki (2003) states that the "sense of being an intimate part of nature has been shattered over the past few centuries" (p. 1). If we are to adapt to—or *survive* in any manner—the ecological crisis we must reunite with the natural world. Parks are protected more than most other patches of nature, but they share the same air, water, soil, and species. Is setting a park aside a reinforcement of the aforementioned dualism? After decades of work in parks and protected areas, I was beginning to wonder if parks and nature were at best estranged, at worst incompatible.

Even if parks truly do serve their intended conservation purpose—and that question will not be resolved in this chapter—they represent the same kind of public institution as schools or universities. In Alberta, parks have a legislative role to play in conservation, recreation, and education (Province of Alberta, 2005). This is both an opportunity to foster transformative learning, especially among adult and public learners, but it may also be an indication that parks are currently part of the problem described above.

Proposing a 'Different Kind' of Educational Framework for Learning in Parks

Orr (2004) holds educational institutions directly accountable for fostering destructive values and beliefs, and states "more of the same kind of education can only make things worse" (p. 27). The literature backs this up, suggesting: Western educational institutions produce graduates with job readiness but no critical or independent thought (Jones, 2009); Education leads students to accept politicized "assumptions about power, reality, morality, and the formulations of knowledge" (McWhinney & Markos, 2003, p. 20); Graduates may be mature intellectually, but stunted in terms of other intelligences, such as emotion, intuition, and spirit (Ferrer, Romero, & Albareda, 2006). Finally, stubborn institutions will not change their "unidirectional, hierarchical, and essentially reproductive approach to teaching. Most professors are still there to 'profess', while most students are still there to 'absorb it all.' 'Content' is still organized in disciplinary ways both in research and in education (Wals, 2010, p. 381). The intent here is not to seem anti-education, but rather to propose, like Orr, that we need a different kind of education. Gruenewald (2004) describes the ideal model as "able to negotiate the complex ecological interactions between science, politics, and culture, between social and ecological systems, and their impact on human and nonhuman life" (p. 94). I believe building this model can happen through transformative learning in parks, and have experienced educational programs in parks that support the model Orr describes.

Stargazing with Strangers

In one early experience, after delivering my twice-weekly musical theatre program on astronomy that aimed to get people to spend time outside at night and experience nature after the sun goes down, I invited interested campers to join me in the dark parking lot to learn about some basic constellations and maybe see some bats or flying squirrels.

Expecting a handful of first-time campers, I was astonished that each time I presented the program, dozens of families—new and longstanding visitors alike—would remain and patiently wait for me to pack up and turn off the lights. They had simply never learned about the night sky. Each clear night, I was part of a group of strangers laying on our backs in a pitch black parking lot in the middle of nowhere, sometimes for hours on end. When the breeze was warm, they would listen to my stories of constellations, then share their own stories and experiences of being out at night. Often, discussion turned to traditional First Nations inhabitants of the place— what life was like "back then"—and it was obvious that not only the local First

Nations, but their knowledge and culture, were underrepresented in my work and in the experience of the visitors to those late-night sessions. And in a reflection of Orr's interactive model of learning, it was the case almost every night that at least one person in the group was far more knowledgeable than I was on some relevant topic—a notable star or satellite, the warm pavement, the weather, or the flying mammals, and they would take the reins to create a unique learning experience that I clearly remember years later.

The program was never repeated, as my supervisors at the time felt astronomy was too detached a topic, incapable of linking to the desired positive public behaviours we wanted in parks. I was told we wanted people to stop leaving out their garbage and that stars have nothing to do with protecting bear habitat. Had I known then what I know now, I would have argued back and explained that people joined me in the parking lot because they wanted to learn about stars, not parks. I would have explained that the shared, unstructured experience was an opportune time to foster deep conversations about their place and role in that landscape.

In retrospect, this is the kind of experience that helped show me that learning experiences in nature are capable of changing people and doing more than indoctrinating. Regardless of the topic, spending hours observing the world with strangers does something that no program or lesson plan can.

LEARNING FOR CHANGE – TRANSFORMATIVE LEARNING IN PARKS

Transformative learning (TL) originated with Mezirow in the 1970s, and has been revised and expanded into a broad array of literature and practices (Kucukaydin & Cranton, 2013; Taylor, 2008). In essence, TL is about teaching for change, as it "transforms problematic frames of reference—sets of fixed assumptions and expectations (habits of mind, meaning perspectives, and mindsets)—to make them more inclusive, discriminating, open, reflective, and emotionally able to change" (Mezirow & Taylor, 2009, p. 22). This is the kind of learning required for people to move past problematic, dominant paradigms that lead us to believe we are separate from the world. If parks are committed to fostering stewardship then they should aim at this kind of teaching for change. Mezirow's basic theory calls upon six interdependent core elements:

- individual experience
- critical reflection
- dialogue
- holistic orientation
- appreciation for context, and
- authentic relationships

These elements represent a radically different approach than the top-down, political, disciplined educational processes dominating education today (Mezirow & Taylor, 2009). I believe, and hope to show, that parks can offer each of these elements.

Park education—or, broadly, learning experiences in natural settings—are highly suited to the first core element of *individual experiences*, or the combination of prior experiences with learning. From the often cited definition of interpretation as "first-hand involvement with an object, artifact, landscape or site" (Interpretation Canada, 1976), park education is about helping people experience something, and it is this element that is best served by traditional visitor services models for park programming.

However, despite my profound experience stargazing with strangers, my early career taught me that park education often focuses exclusively on the experience, potentially missing the other elements. When my work began to focus on the inclusion of individuals with disabilities, I witnessed first-hand the importance of integrating the entire suite of interdependent core elements. Combining visitor experience, or *individual experiences*, with the other five six core elements can result in lead to the kind of "learning for change" that serves as the foundation for Transformative Learning (Taylor, 2009, p. 4).

The Adaptive Challenge

The 2008 Adaptive Challenge was a weekend-long program that brought persons with disabilities, caregivers, and volunteers together in a Rocky Mountain park. The *individual experiences* of each participant ranged from first-time back to nature since a life-changing accident to frequent hikers who never considered barriers or persons with disability, rather, they just wanted to volunteer for something. The *learning experience* to facilitate various forms of adaptive outdoor recreation was shared, but each participant offered a unique "pedagogical entry point" (Lange, 2004; in Taylor, 2009, p. 6).

The *critical reflection* element of the adaptive challenge offered each of three forms of reflection described by Taylor (2009). Participants reflected on the *content* (e.g., the time spent in nature, the exertion of climbing a mountain or paddling, or the challenge of meeting new people in unfamiliar places), the *process* (e.g., receiving the benefit of adaptive experiences, providing the service of adaptive experiences, or receiving the benefit of providing services, such as able-bodied people who felt they had previously taken their abilities for granted), and the *premise* (e.g., the critical reflection of the purpose of the event itself as about inclusive community-building and not simply recreation in nature) (p. 7).

From the moment the event began, it was clear that the Adaptive Challenge was unique among typical park education programs. Notably, the event concluded with a group debrief that met the criteria of an effective *dialogue* – or social interaction to validate the experience among participants. This shared meaning-making was emotional and relational, and supported people who needed assurance that they weren't alone in feeling that the weekend had changed them.

Perhaps not surprisingly, the event also met the needs of offering an *holistic orientation* to learning. While most park programs I had previously developed were built on a foundation of facts and empirical research about natural history themes, the Adaptive Challenge and other inclusion programs made room for *affective* and *relational* knowing. Traditionally, park programs were framed by identifying audience types and placing them along a fairly linear scale of support for park messages, called the stewardship scale (Husby, 2005, p. 9). This new program, focused on the inclusion of persons with disabilities, muddied the waters by providing a space for the entire person—the spiritual and intuitive, the emotional and the social—and in many cases their caregivers and support groups. Though my programming experience had previously sought to entertain people through humour and laughter mixed with facts and information, inclusion programs were more often than not successful when the mix was heavy on introspection, prayer, and tears.

The adaptive recreation program in parks also fulfilled the requirement of *awareness of context* in fostering transformative learning. While most programs simply invite campers to attend and having them show up, but not knowing much about them beyond a generic audience profile, adaptive recreation programs involved meeting people, understanding their requirements and capabilities, and in some cases even picking them up from group care facilities or drop-in shelters. Overcoming barriers to participation is the focus of the program, yet the experience hardly impacts the barriers people with disabilities face in daily living. Nonetheless, over the course of the Adaptive Challenge it became clear that the opportunity to feel included, empowered, and connected to nature was an important respite from the struggle for to curb cuts, income assistance, and accessible transit. As one participant shared after the 2008 event,

> When one has been pushed to the periphery, 'benched,' pushed aside, ignored, and told they better sit out, it is beyond comprehension that there would be a time when you could try things without criticism, with goodhearted competition, and with acceptance. (Buhl, in Alberta Parks, 2008, p. 28)

Finally, the role of *authentic relationships* was a unique and eye-opening aspect of my experiences in adaptive programming. While personal engagement was required to plan for accommodations, food, and adaptive approaches to the experience, the depth of connection with participants was truly unexpected. Though I am still friends today with individuals who joined the program, one person stands out: Jayne saw a poster promoting an exciting opportunity to join a parks program for a trip into nature, something that was not a regular part of her life. Her parents were worried it was a scam, and she was reluctant to head to the mountains with some stranger in a uniform; she wondered if it was all legitimate. At Jayne's request, we met for coffee and I answered the many questions she asked about the program. I also answered questions about me—more than I would usually answer with my own staff, and certainly more than I would share with an audience at a typical parks program. Her open sharing of fear, previous disappointments, hopes and personal situation was touching and real. It made me rethink the approach to inclusive programming, as well as my entire approach to education. Jayne had a great time, became a leader of the adaptive recreation movement in Alberta, and is a regular volunteer at several parks in her city.

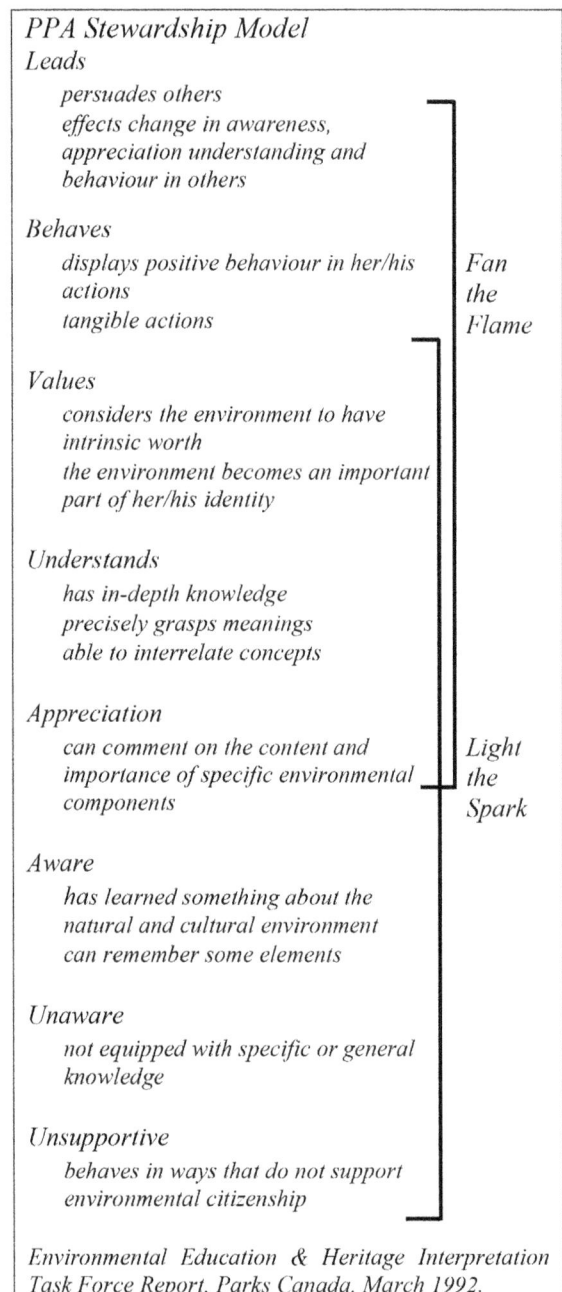

Figure 4.1. Stewardship scale model

INSPIRATION TO CHANGE MY APPROACH – FROM BUMS IN SEATS TO IMPACT

The adaptive programming outlined showed that my approach to park education needed to change, and had immense transformative potential. As I scanned the non-adaptive, non-inclusive programs I was currently running, I realized our model for a stewardship scale and our tools for measuring success were inadequate.

The Existing Model for Park Education

Prior to 2012, the programs I ran built upon on the Parks and Protected Areas stewardship scale, developed in 2005 by Husby, and based on earlier models by Parks Canada (Husby, 2005, p. 9) (Figure 4.1). Regardless of the level of stewardship at which programs aimed, the metric used was the number of people participating, often referred to as "bums in seats." The progression from "light the spark" to "fan the flames" assumed that audiences would increase their stewardship simply by exposure to more programs – little consideration was given to barriers to moving up the scale or individual circumstances that may affect engagement. The model focuses on environmental behaviours, but not social ones, and it places unsupportive people at the bottom, presuming that someone can be *unsupportive* of something they are not *aware* of. Further, though Husby qualified that learning is not a linear progression from "unsupportive" to "leads" (Husby, p. 9), as the model might imply, it has in my experience been interpreted and applied as linear and prescriptive.

A New Model for Park Education

After realizing the potential of inclusion to challenge this linear approach to park education programming, I challenged my organization with the creation of a *continuum of public engagement* (Figure 4.2). The key difference is that the continuum focuses on the interests of the learners (park visitors) and recognizes their desire to make choices in learning, an idea that I now see as complementary to ideas that form the foundation of transformative learning.

- This continuum of engagement differs from the stewardship model in four key ways in its approach to thinking about park visitor learning:
- The continuum allows people to travel up and down the scale from *discovering* parks/park values to *enjoying, valuing,* and *stewarding,* not based on the ability of a program to target a particular audience type, but rather based on the barriers and abilities an individual may bring to the engagement.
- The continuum differentiates between programs with a broad reach, designed for mass exposure to large numbers of people, and those with a small reach, designed to reach more targeted, individualized audiences.
- The continuum differentiates between depth of engagement, from transactional, measured by experience satisfaction, and relational, measured by stewardship actions.

- The continuum includes unengaged and disengaged people, to reflect that some people are not involved in interactions with park education (potential stewards), and some people hold complementary values but do not choose to engage with park education (latent stewards).

The continuum was introduced as part of the *Alberta Parks Inclusion Plan: Everyone Belongs Outside.* Though I felt it served a wide range of park education and engagement programs, the focus on inclusion meant the model was formally introduced to the organization without much resistance from anyone used to the stewardship model.

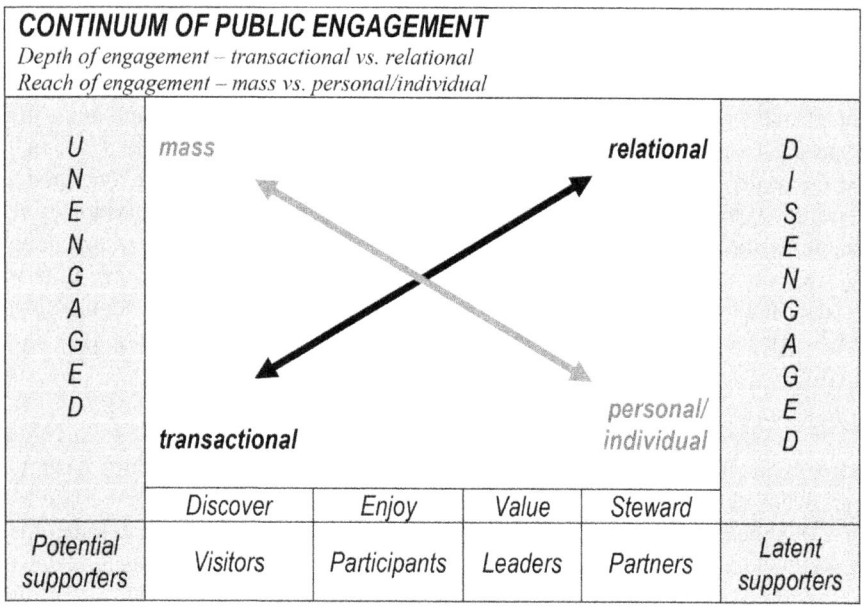

Figure 4.2. Continuum of public engagement

Based on a new way of conceptualizing and recognizing visitors' own efforts to learn, the continuum of engagement offers a practical new framework for how we implement and measure the impact of park education programs. It suggests a rethinking of the purposes of park education ranging from marketing and promotions to public and formal education to volunteer and partner support, and always with room to consider inclusion and removal of barriers. The continuum reflects my own growing understanding of the transformative potential in parks and sparked an interest to know more about transformative learning. It also confirmed my own growing discomfort with the way things had always been done, and inevitably resulted in a transformative process that would shape my work for nearly a decade.

REFLECTING ON MY OWN ACTIONS TO LEARN: A TRANSFORMATIVE PROCESS

A personal engagement with Mezirow's theory is based on what he refers to as a ten-phase process for learning. The phases are:

1. Disorienting dilemma
2. Self-examination
3. A critical self-assessment of assumptions
4. Recognition of a connection between one's discontent and the process of transformation
5. Exploration of options for new roles, relationships and action
6. Planning a course of action
7. Acquiring knowledge and skills for implementing one's plan
8. Provisional trying on of new roles
9. Building competence and self-confidence in new roles and relationships
10. A reintegration into one's life on the basis of conditions dictated by one's perspective (Mezirow, 1994, p. 224).

I Was a Singing, Dancing Beaver until I Licked a Bear Skull: My Personal Transformative Process

Deep reflection upon one key experience that eventually motivated me to host the Adaptive Challenge may provide a useful illustration of these eleven steps. Ultimately this process led to the creation of a Provincial Inclusion Plan which I proposed to my professional community:

1. I had a *disorienting dilemma* when two autistic boys licked a grizzly bear skull during a school program. They were part of a Special Education classroom – Room 11. The school principal had suggested I exclude Room 11 from my in-class presentations, explaining that they "wouldn't get anything out of it." Having the time in my schedule, I said I'd make a stop to see the special education kids, but wouldn't do much more then let the kids see the artifacts I had brought. When the children lined up and dutifully came forward to feel the grizzly bear skull—carefully cleaned and prepared for demonstration—two twin autistic boys leaned in, and each licked the skull. No other child in that school, or in any classroom I visited, knows what a grizzly bear skull tastes like. That night, I licked it myself. Tastes like talc.
2. I *self-examined* and realized that my teaching methods were overwhelmingly visual, auditory, and tactile, rarely smell or taste-based. I also identified a personal sense of largesse that troubled me – I included this group of children out of a sense of nobility, but in fact they were the ones challenging and helping me learn. My own privilege became apparent, as even my work with parks was a result of where I lived, the education I had been provided, the support from my family, and my abilities to access parks and do the work I do.

3. I *critically assessed my assumptions* about my role as a park educator and the mandate of my organization and found them incongruous, especially regarding inclusion of different abilities and perspectives within our approach to learning. Even the goals of the park education program seemed dominated by facts and reluctant to speak of feelings. In speaking to colleagues in environmental education, I learned that they often booked school field programs where certain students would be left at the school, left on the bus, or left at home rather than disrupt field programs with their special needs.
4. I *recognized* that while parks were seeking relevance among people who faced no barriers, and had no reason *not* to visit nature than simply taking the experience for granted, many more people faced barriers to experiencing nature just once in their lifetime and would be happy to just be invited outside to play.
5. I *explored options* for creating an environmental education program that would be accessible for students with different abilities. In a conversation with the Premier's Council on the Status of Persons with Disabilities, I was challenged to think more broadly than a single program to promote access, and to instead consider the systemic problem of inclusion from basic experiences such as connecting to nature. As I left that meeting, I was shaking. I called my wife and told her that I had found my calling.
6. I *planned a course of action*. Already a graduate student pursuing a Masters degree in education related to land trusts and conservancies, I changed my focus completely to examine the inclusion of persons with disabilities in parks and wilderness experiences.
7. I *acquired knowledge and skills* through my graduate studies, and I shared experiences in nature with people with disabilities. I gained new perspectives on a landscape I had long seen in only one particular way, and I gained a new appreciation for what it meant to identify as a person with a disability. I learned about adaptive recreation equipment and the challenge of simply getting around the city, let alone a wilderness setting.
8. I *provisionally tried out new roles*, such as initiating the adaptive recreation program described earlier. I entered discourse as a provocateur and challenged assumptions about who parks should serve, and have switched from a visitor services approach to a public engagement approach, going so far as to rename the program I run from the former to the latter. I worked (and continue to work) to *renegotiate relationships* among my colleagues as I push for more inclusive and empowering approaches to serving the public, whether or not they face barriers to visiting parks. In some cases these relationships are uncomfortable and threaten the privilege, or at least comfort, of people who have long taken the stance that parks are a free and accessible public service, despite my experience to the contrary. I am also *negotiating new relationships* with surrounding communities, so when issues of inclusion and quality of life are discussed, parks are invited to the table.

9. I am still *building competence* and *confidence* in new roles as I find myself uncomfortable speaking on behalf of "others" from my own position of privilege and with the bulk of my experience coming from within a classic park education background.
10. I am already *reintegrating into my life* based on this new perspective. Having moved into a leadership role, I have tried to be a change maker and made decisions to reduce programming for mainstream groups who already enjoy easy access to parks—RV campers, for example—and have redirected these resources toward dedicated inclusion programs that hire and serve people with personal experience of disability and exclusion.

These changes took place over several years, and were never experienced in isolation from other things affecting my life, but I hope this deconstruction helps show how from my perspective, my growth and personal development was sparked by the single *disorienting dilemma* of the two boys licking the skull when I expected them to touch it. As I will show later in this chapter, additional and simultaneous transformative learning experiences are deeply affecting me and challenging what I do, even with the positive addition of inclusion as a core program mandate.

TRANSFORMATIVE LEARNING BEYOND MEZIROW AND A CRITIQUE OF TL

The Transformative Literature field is generative, filled with many case studies, publications, journals and conferences build on the basic premise to help people grow, develop, and live authentic lives. Though my experience as a park educator is primarily framed in Mezirow's original theory, I think it stands as transformative when placed up against other perspectives. For example, Kovan & Dirkx' (2003) study of TL in environmental activists validates the importance of *critically reflective discourse.* Walter (2013) traces the role of TL in the lives of scientist-environmentalists and affirms the importance of single or cumulative *experiences* in self-development. In order to make sense of this substantial body of work, several scholars have developed lenses or typologies of TL. For example, Taylor (2008) distinguishes a) *psychocritical* perspectives (i.e., Mezirow) which promote the critical examination of individual frames of experience, b) *psychoanalytic* views, in which learners develop a deeper understanding of their individual responsibility and inner self, c) *psychodevelopmental* views where learners continue to grow and develop new ways of making meaning through a variety of holistic relationships, and d) *social emancipatory* views, where learners reflect and act to transform the world for equity (pp. 7–8). In addition to these four primary views on transformative learning, Taylor also presents four recent additions to the field, *neurobiological, race-centric, cultural-spiritual,* and *planetary*, though they are essentially presented as things to watch for in the future.

The first three approaches revolve around the Jungian notion of *individuation*, "the *process* by which we become aware of who we are as different from others"

(Cranton & Roy, 2003, p. 91, italics in original). By contrast, the fourth view focuses on *conscientization*, or "consciousness raising" and is "as much about social change as personal transformation, where individual and social transformation are inherently linked" (Merizow & Taylor, 2009, p. 5). Unlike the first three individualistic views, *conscientization* makes room to consider the role of others (ideally both human and non-human) in developing self, and is best suited to tackle critical socioecological issues. In my personal journey as an educator, I have found personal ways in which these four lenses fit my decade-long transformative experience in parks.

- *Psychocritical*: I notice my program audiences, stakeholders, and colleagues are homogeneous, mostly male, and able-bodied. I am reframing my view of parks and park experiences to acknowledge them as places of privilege and exclusion.
- *Psychoanalytical*: I take ownership of the privileges that allow me to work in the field of park education and realize that ignoring that privilege is contrary to my sense of self, and would simply perpetuate the homogeneity that dominated park education.
- *Psychodevelopmental*: I disengage from professional colleagues and institutional models for programming and seek new approaches from academia and non-traditional fields of practice (e.g., adventure therapy, health/wellness, religious organizations).
- *Conscientization*: I try to place myself into a role as a catalyst for inclusion, seeking and sharing through research and knowledge translation the voices of persons with disabilities, newcomers, youth, and indigenous communities within my organization and in public park programming. I question how I can have the greatest impact in creating opportunities for people to connect with, and learn from, nature.

While other scholars rally to this idea of different typologies of TL (e.g., Furman & Gruenewald, 2004; Lange, 2004), O'Sullivan (1999) is often cited for his broad integrated transformative vision that includes "the larger creative processes of the greater earth community and universe" (in Gunnlaugson, 2005, p. 348). O'Sullivan (2001) challenges the imperialistic and western scientific view guilty of dismissing mythic interpretations and non-scientific points of view as primitive. In considering the challenges of this century, O'Sullivan (2008) asserts "transformative learning involves a massive change in consciousness that could bring about a new order of social justice and ecological balance" (p. 30). Any TL park education developed with O'Sullivan in mind could become an exciting opportunity to gain creative insight into non-human and cosmological relationships and dimensions. It would also embrace the kinds of conversations that occurred under the stars after my interpretive program, and open doors to more education about, with, and by traditional indigenous communities within parks.

The original theory of transformative learning has been, and will continue to be critiqued and clarified (Kucakaydin & Cranton, 2013), and there is more to understand about the mechanisms that make TL work (Mezirow & Taylor, 2009). Park education is not immune to these doubts. For example, within the modern educational institutions there are challenges to practice, such as the time required for meaningful process, rigid institutional requirements, potential effects on other learners, and the personal commitment required of teachers (Taylor, 2008). At a theoretical level, TL has been critiqued for overlooking context and the relationship between individual and social change, and for reinforcing rational ways of knowing—though Mezirow concedes intuition could be substituted for critical reflection (Walter, 2013).

Some studies have added to or revised the core elements, though not in such as way as to erode the main theory. For example, Cranton (2004) explores *authenticity* in fostering the emergence of the self (p. 97) and Lange (2004) introduces the concept of *restoration* of participants' foundational ethics, rather than *disruption*. Gunnlaugson (2007) presents a model of *generative dialogue* as a tool for co-creating learning, and Dyson (2010) similarly explores the role of the teacher and the value of a *person-centered* learning approach. Dirkx (2012) highlights *self-formation* as informed by a fuller range of the human psyche. And Walter (2013) argues that the *disorienting dilemma* can be effectively replaced with a *culmination of gradual processes*. Exploring each of these valuable features of TL individually is beyond the scope of this chapter, but I have found them valuable to add to my toolbox of 'Park Education for Change.'

"Perhaps There is No Such Thing as Transformative Learning"

One critique that is often singled out and I feel warrants discussion is Newman's (2012) blunt suggestion that "perhaps there is no such thing as transformative learning; perhaps there is just good learning" (p. 37), followed by examples of that good learning: someone learning to weld to become gainfully employed in a shipyard, a homeless woman learning to navigate the legal system to avoid unjust custody, and a young mother learning to bathe her baby (p. 52). These examples are precisely *why* we need radical approaches to transforming the way people see themselves in the world, and not just more of the same kind of education. The welder could be making transnational oil tankers or be grossly consumptive; the homeless woman could be evading compassionate care *or* personal responsibilities; and the young mother could be excellent at bathing her child, but struggling with postpartum depression. Similarly, park education that is not transformative could simply reinforce the human/nature dualism that persists in so many of the ecological challenges described earlier.

Yet, Newman is touching a nerve. Dirx (2012) admits that some examples of transformative learning are simply skill development, and park education often focuses on basic skills like learning flower names or safely hiking in the backcountry. The crisis of our time calls for no less than O'Sullivan's self-forming, consciousness-raising growth. As Orr (2004) implores, we "encourage young people to find jobs before they find a decent calling. A career is a job, a way to earn one's keep [...] a calling has to do with one's larger purpose, personhood, deepest values, and the gift one wishes to give the world" (p. 22). Simply put, just pursuing *good* learning is not good enough. Transformative learning should inspire the welder to build windmills, the homeless woman to find meaning in her self and community, the mother to know her calling, which may *or may not* be giving baths, and the visitor in a park to deeply feel, value, and act to protect their connection to nature.

THE SOCIOECOLOGICAL GOALS OF TRANSFORMATIVE LEARNING IN PARKS

The more exposure I gained to diverse communities and inclusive experiences, the more difficult it became to separate connection with nature from connection to one another. The inclusion plan I helped create was titled *everyone belongs outside*, and the emphasis on *belong* was meant to reference the sense of social connection that permeated so many of the inclusive programs. More than creating additional audiences for typical park programs, inclusion was creating new kinds of park experiences that depended on these new, diverse, participants.

Sauer (2007) suggests that after the first earth day, *environmentalism* became overly biological in focus and acted to "separate human from natural ecology" (p. 8). Similarly, Evernden (1993) traces *ecology* from its idealist, holistic beginnings, to what today has become an "anti-mystical biological specialty" (p. 6). It may seem obvious to suggest the goal of transformative learning for our purposes in Parks education is "*environmentalism*" or "*ecology.*" Similarly, the progression of someone working to achieve on the stewardship scale, or on the "steward" portion of the continuum of engagement suggest the idea of people who share ecological values with parks. However, these concepts are situated in disciplined, empirical, dualistic frameworks and may be unfit for the socioecological task at hand. I believe that the continuum of engagement works because it included the discovery, enjoyment, valuing, and stewardship of social *and* ecological experiences.

Transformative Parks?

The research and thinking that I have engaged in has convinced me of the value of applying transformative learning concepts in my own work, and led me to ask the question, 'Could the global system of parks cultivate the socioecological values needed for sustainability through transformative learning?' While parks are not formal educational institutions (possibly to their advantage) they have a long history in interpretation, non-formal mediated experiences designed to elicit wonder and draw out meaning (Hvengaard, Shultis, & Butler, 2009). Park interpretation offers knowledgeable facilitators who could help learners move toward integrated meaning (Lange, 2004). Further, parks should have no trouble fulfilling the core elements set out by Mezirow (*experience, critical reflection, dialogue, holistic orientation, appreciation for context,* and *authentic relationships*). And finally, as I have introduced my peers to transformative learning concepts, I have seen evidence that parks can foster transformative learning rooted in *conscientization*. This is most clear in my current personal journey, which I will describe in detail at the conclusion of this chapter.

Though this is promising, and many park education programs are collaborative and inclusive, parks overall are still rooted in preservationist and dualist ideals (Clarke, Fluker, & Risby, 2008; Evernden, 1993). Parks often cite ecological integrity as the basis of their understanding of natural system. However, Clark, Fluker, and Risby (2008) suggest the current model is *wilderness-normative*, which reinforces the rational dualism problematized earlier in this chapter and reflects a "pristine state of nature that does not include humans" (p. 154). If, as I posed, the global system of parks could cultivate the socioecological values needed for sustainability through transformative learning, they would need to foster specific values that reflect Leopold's original land ethic (1949) and

> ...the existence of an ecological conscience, and this in turn reflects a conviction of individual responsibility for the health of the land. Health is the capacity of the land for self-renewal. Conservation [or stewardship] is our effort to understand and preserve this capacity. (p. 220)

Values for Transformative Parks

The key to this is moving from parks as places with boundaries and unreal experiences to parks as catalysts for new, authentic relationships with the natural world. It should be easy for current managers to accept, considering that "as all good ecologists understand, relationships are essential to the functioning of healthy ecosystems" (Neves-Graca in Brockington, 2004, p. 198). I believe parks can support relationships that cultivate five distinct values, presented below as a series of hypothetical applications in park education:

1. *Transpersonal Integration*
   The more optimal transpersonal collaborative model of ecological integrity identified by Manuel-Navarette (2003; in Clarke et al., 2008) "recognizes interdependence of individuals with surrounding social and ecological systems" (p. 154). This ideology would foster the dignity of non-human others and human-others everywhere, and would surpass deep ecology by avoiding the domination of egoic self-creation (Fox, 1990, p. 197). Someone who values transpersonal collaboration will be open to non-anthropocentric action on a planetary scale.

   Actions for Transpersonal Integration: Parks educators would facilitate understanding beyond a visit, the visitor, or the view by including concepts of integral ecology (Esbjörn-Hargens & Zimmerman, 2009), presenting and respecting the landscapes of matter, life, mind and spirit and connecting these landscapes to experience, behavior, culture, and systems.

2. *Authentic Experience of Learning in Nature*
   As Louv (2011) explains, "Young, old, or in between, we can reap extraordinary benefits by connecting—or reconnecting—to nature" (p. 5). These benefits occur

within a variety of dimensions, such as the mind, body, spirit, and shadow (Wilber et al., 2012). Intimate connection with nature is essential for countering the apathy and disconnection felt by many people on the planet (Pyle, 2003), as well as for fostering behaviours that heal nature in return. However, some natural experiences are not authentic. As DeLuca and Demo (2001) state, "wilderness is not a fact but a political achievement" (p. 555) Cultivating the ability to tell the difference, and to avoid the consumptive resourcism driven by hyperreal experiences, is essential to meaningful stewardship of the real, not of the simulated. Someone who values authentic experience of nature will be willing to work for the natural and wild, not just the aesthetically pleasing and shallow.

Actions for authentic experience of nature: Parks already facilitate opportunities for inclusive experiences, but must reveal the truth of the natural settings. Aplet's (1998) model of practice places wilderness along a continuum of freedom with control on one axis, and naturalness on the other. Every natural setting along this continuum is authentic in some way, but this can only lead to stewardship if people are made aware of their assumptions about the authenticity of a place.

3. *Transformation*

As explored throughout this chapter, the dominant social paradigm is distancing people from learning and being in nature and leading to destructive behaviours worldwide. O'Sullivan (2008) leads the way in encouraging creativity and "a massive change in consciousness that could bring about a new order of social justice and ecological balance" (p. 30). Education and conservation institutions that are entrenched in the dominant culture are rooted in power and must be reinvented (Freyfogle, 2006; Orr, 2004). The transformative mandate for land stewardship is to

…reconcile the scientific approaches of ecology and economics with the ethics and spiritual perspective of traditional societies, lest we fall prey to the kind of anthropocentric thinking that has been the bane of the traditional ecological paradigm that dominated the last Century. (Harmon & Putney, 2003, p. 40)

Someone who values transformation will be open to action that is authentic, thoughtful, and creative.

Actions for transformation: Parks could move beyond shallow experiences and foster O'Sullivan's consciousness raising ecological balance through disorienting dilemmas—experience of a lifetime, and continual exposure, a lifetime of experiences. Park managers and supporters are the first who must first transform. The first step may be bluntly sharing the peril the planet, and park, are facing.

4. *(Re)Inhabiting Place*

While the goal of sustainability must be global, value for the local is essential to fostering a sense of place (Hay, 2005; McKibben, 2010). Local also refers to time, and the sense of being bound to seasons and the cycles of the land (Leopold, 1949). Though the sustainability called for in the introduction of this chapter is global, as Dowie (2009) explains, "the dozens of successful models in place on every continent prove that community-initiated and managed conservation can work" (p. 268). Rather than prevent indigenous and local communities from connecting with their sacred landscapes, they should be reunited. At the same time, our urbanized society should try to (re)unite with nature and overcome the dualism and detachment in which we live help people inhabit both city and country, simultaneously. Someone who values Inhabiting Place will be moved to action based on a land ethic and will be grounded in the rhythm and stories of multiple places as home.

Actions for (Re)Inhabiting Place: Parks must work toward more collaborative or community managed landscapes with diverse, local, and indigenous communities (Dowie, 2009). Parks can also bridge rural and urban divides through nearby nature sites, service projects, as well as by helping people develop attachment to nature as their "home" through ecotherapy and by placing themselves in the environment.

5. *Stewardship as a Responsibility*

Ecuador offers a remarkable, and fairly unique recognition of the intrinsic value of nature, by recently granting constitutional rights to nature, stating:

Nature or Pachamama, where life is reproduced and exists, has the right to exist, persist, maintain and regenerate its vital cycles, structure, functions and its processes in evolution. (Ecuador in Charman, 2008, p. 131)

This same spirit of intrinsic rights should be extended and the obligation it implies should be practiced among all human-others and non-human others. As Shiva (2004) puts it, "separation of rights and responsibility is at the root of ecological devastation, and gender and class inequality (p. 12). A person who values stewardship as a responsibility will be moved to action because it is the right thing to do.

Actions for Stewardship as a Responsibility: The Ecuador model is a good place to start, and parks can at least ensure the rights of nature within their land bases. Volunteer programs should also shift from service *to* park agencies to service *with* park agencies, or even service with nature. The public should be empowered as a collaborator and co-creator of the health of parks through all their actions.

Reimagining Parks as Relationships

The world is changing and will continue to change. It is unrealistic to think that parks and protected areas can stay the same forever. Chape, Spalding, and Jenkins (2008) explain that global change "will not only place more pressure on the world's protected areas, but also bring their role into sharper focus" (p. 158). The global protected areas network offers a ready-made system to cultivate the stewardship values listed above, but only if they adapt and transcend their current, compromised model. The question I am personally faced with is whether I can adapt alongside an agency that has guided my professional and educational path for the majority of my adult life.

FINAL REFLECTIONS: TRANSFORMATIVE HOMECOMING

Twenty-five years ago, I thought I should work for parks because I was an environmentalist. Now I recognize that parks are not *authentic* representations of wild nature (Birch, 1990). This is evident in the long-standing tension between parks and indigenous people (Dearden & Langdon, 2009), which not only challenges the *authenticity* of the place, but also the *context*. Further, many of the *experiences* in parks are insulated as *disorienting dilemmas*, such as the buffer of cultivated campgrounds, public safety services, or conversely, barriers that may prevent *cumulative ongoing experiences*. Finally, parks contain all the same institutional challenges faced by schools: time, resources, and disciplinary mandates. If we can resolve these issues, parks can foster incredible transformative experiences, and possibly just in time. Plumwood (1993) is clear: "The master culture must now make its long-overdue homecoming to the earth. This is no longer simply a matter of justice, but now also a matter of survival" (p. 6). Perhaps a park can be where that transformative homecoming takes place—or perhaps the homecoming requires parks to have no boundaries and extend to where people return after their visit to connect with nature. If my own work extends to the world beyond parks, where my agency has little mandate, then how do I fit?

My Ongoing Transformative Experience

To imagine how transformative learning in park might look in my work, I will again visit Mezirow's phases through my current *ongoing transformative experience*, an extension of the first illustration of a single *disorienting dilemma*. It is this process that I alluded to in the beginning of this chapter that is leading me to question my future career path, and indeed my future role in parks.

In twenty-plus years working for parks, my *ongoing experience* has been to increasingly notice people, including colleagues, taking their access to nature for granted. At the same time, as I participated in more inclusive programs, I have increasingly experienced openly spiritual gratitude and respect for nature from marginalized groups. This built on the original transformative experience above, but is also a unique experience.

1. I *self-examined* and felt shame for spending so much energy facilitating experiences for people who took nature for granted, and not effecting change. I questioned my calling and sought answers within my faith and my family.
2. I *critically assessed my assumptions* about my role as a park educator and the mandate of my organization, and found them incongruous, especially regarding inclusion, social change, and research.

3. I *recognized* a community that held similar discontent, and built relationships with allies. My manager (an ally) supported my pursuit of a PhD to generate deeper conversation. My immediate colleagues, many of whom had participated in inclusion programs with me, supported the restructuring of our Visitor Services program into a broader Public Engagement program. This change would allowed us to maintain traditional park programs while building our capacity for relational, transformative, deep engagement with more diverse individuals.
4. I *explored options* for graduate school, its impact on my career and family, and how I could make it happen. I challenged the model of a Stewardship Scale and developed the previously mentioned continuum of engagement model that has taken root in inclusion, but not in other areas of park education practice.
5. I *planned a course of action* to take educational leave and pursue a degree in interdisciplinary studies while building support within parks for social research. I took on a higher-level role within my work that allowed me to dedicate park resources to inclusion, community and partner support, research, and evaluation.
6. I am *acquiring knowledge and skills* through the PhD process, as well as through experience in higher levels of responsibility. Some of this knowledge and skill development has been a parallel disorienting experience, as my personal values and beliefs were disrupted and in some cases shattered and rebuilt.
7. I *provisionally try out new roles*, such as initiating social research projects and acting within parks as a park *researcher*, not a park *educator*. I enter discourse as a provocateur and challenge assumptions about how parks should measure their impact and success, even if that means questioning the value of parks altogether. I must *renegotiate relationships* among my colleagues as I grow in ways that disrupt our shared values, and am *negotiating new relationships* with academics and inclusion-oriented people as an academic practitioner.
8. I am still *building competence* and *confidence* in new roles as I learn through process, reflection and as grow from relationships. I am wrapping up the restructuring of the public engagement section and moving on to a maintenance role. However, I am still uncertain (and possibly experiencing another disorienting dilemma) as the multiple roles mentioned above may be unsustainable, and the end of the restructuring process marks the end of a clear professional mandate. Further, questioning my work at the fundamental levels implied by the required, aspirational, values described in previous section feels, at times, like the proverbial cartoon character sawing off the branch holding him up.

I am already *reintegrating into my life* on the basis of conditions dictated by this new perspective. I am reviewing my role based on the new organizational structure so I can work within the continuum of engagement, rather than the stewardship scale. I am considering the pursuit of management roles with parks that may offer more responsibly and opportunity, though may also increase the distance between me and the transformative learning processes that matter so much to me. And I am examining ways to complete my PhD and maintain my academic interests as part of my work, and if I cannot then I will seek a role as an academic or instructor.

Clearly I Am Unsettled

I applied for a management position, and I interviewed. It was a challenging process that clarified that my choice only superficially lies between working for nature, working for parks, or working for a park agency. On the drive home from the interview – and from picking up my son from a day with his grandparents – there were northern lights in the sky. I stopped the car, turned off the lights, and shared what I knew about the aurora and listened to his observations and wonder about the shimmering sky. Like laying in the parking lot with strangers, and like finding a sense of belonging on an adaptive trip, I now know that the choice is about the kind of relationships I want to have, and the kind of person I want to be. I know I want to be connected with nature.

Reconnecting people to nature is a top priority in adapting to the current environmental crisis, it should be the top priority for parks, and it is a top priority for my own work to be meaningful. O'Sullivan's (2003) call to "embrace the larger earth community where humans are a part of a more complete system making up the fabric of life" (p. 330) is the perfect call-to-arms for parks worldwide. As a place, parks can only fail or succeed in preserving themselves. As a relationship and a catalyst, parks can contribute to healing the earth. As a living being, I can be connected and whole whatever I do.

REFERENCES

Alberta Parks. (2008). *Push to open: The adaptive Kananaskis challenge*. Retrieved from http://albertaparks.ca/media/1812977/pushtoopen_sml.pdf

Alberta Parks. (2012). *Everyone belongs outside: Alberta Parks inclusion plan*. Retrieved from http://www.albertaparks.ca/inclusion

Aplet, G. H. (1998). On the nature of wildness: Exploring what wilderness really protects. *Denv. UL Rev., 76*, 347.

Birch, T. H. (1990). The incarceration of wildness: Wilderness areas as prisons. *Environmental Ethics, 12*(1), 3–26.

Brockington, D., Duffy, R., & Igoe, J. (2008). *Nature unbound: Conservation, capitalism, and the future of protected areas* (Kindle ed.). London: Earthscan. Retrieved from Amazon.ca

Chape, S., Spalding, M., & Jenkins, M. (2008). *The world's protected areas: Status, values and prospects in the 21st century*. Berkeley, CA: University of California Press.

Charman, M. (2008). Ecuador first to grant nature constitutional rights. *Capitalism Nature Socialism, 19*(4), 131–133.

Clarke, D. A., Fluker, S., & Risby, L. (2008). Deconstructing ecological integrity policy in Canadian national parks. In K. S. Hanna, D. A. Clarke, & S. Slocombe (Eds.), *Transforming parks and protected areas: Policy and governance in a changing world* (Kindle ed., pp. 154–168). New York, NY: Routledge. Retrieved from Amazon.ca

Cole, D. N., & Yung, L. (2010). *Beyond naturalness: Rethinking park and wilderness stewardship in an era of rapid change*. Washington, DC: Island Press.

Cranton, P. (2004). Developing authenticity as a transformative process. *Journal of Transformative Education, 2*(4), 276–293. doi:10.1177/1541344604267898

Cranton, P., & Roy, M. (2003). When the bottom falls out of the bucket: Toward a holistic perspective on transformative learning. *Journal of Transformative Education, 1*(2), 86–98. doi:10.1177/1541344603001002002

Dearden, P., & Langdon, S. (2009). Aboriginal peoples and national parks. In P. Dearden & R. Rollins (Eds.), *Parks and protected areas in Canada: Planning and management* (pp. 373–402). Don Mills: Oxford University Press.

DeLuca, K. M., & Demo, A. T. (2000). Imaging nature: Watkins, Yosemite, and the birth of environmentalism. *Critical Studies in Media Communication, 17*(3), 241–260.

Dirkx, J. M. (2012). Self-formation and transformative learning: A response to "calling transformative learning into question: Some mutinous thoughts," by Michael Newman. *Adult Education Quarterly, 62*(4), 399–405. doi:10.1177/0741713612455642

Dowie, M. (2009). *Conservation refugees: The hundred-year conflict between global conservation and native peoples.* Cambridge, MA: MIT Press.

Dyson, M. (2010). What might a person-centred model of teacher education look like in the 21st century? The transformism model of teacher education. *Journal of Transformative Education, 8*(1), 3–21. doi:10.1177/1541344611406949

Esbjörn-Hargens, S., & Zimmerman, M. E. (2009). *Integral ecology: Uniting multiple perspectives on the natural world.* Boston, MA: Integral Books.

Evernden, L. L. N. (1993). *The natural alien: Humankind and environment.* Toronto: University of Toronto Press.

Ferrer, J., Romero, M., & Albareda, R. (2006). The four seasons of integral education: A participatory proposal. *ReVision: A Journal of Consciousness and Transformation, 29*(2), 11–23.

Fox, W. (1990). *Toward a transpersonal ecology: Developing new foundations for environmentalism.* Boston, MA: Shambhala.

Freyfogle, E. T. (2006). *Why conservation is failing and how it can regain ground.* New Haven, CT: Yale University Press.

Furman, G. C., & Gruenewald, D. A. (2004). Expanding the landscape of social justice: A critical ecological analysis. *Educational Administration Quarterly, 40*(1), 47–76. doi:10.1177/0013161X03259142

Gruenewald, D. A. (2004). A foucauldian analysis of environmental education: Toward the socioecological challenge of the earth charter. *Curriculum Inquiry, 34*(1), 71–107.

Gunnlaugson, O. (2005). Toward integrally informed theories of transformative learning. *Journal of Transformative Education, 3*(4), 331–353. doi:10.1177/1541344605278671

Gunnlaugson, O. (2007). Shedding light on the underlying forms of transformative learning theory: Introducing three distinct categories of consciousness. *Journal of Transformative Education, 5*(2), 134–151. doi:10.1177/1541344607303526

Harmon, D., & Putney, A. D. (2003). *The full value of parks: From economics to the intangible.* Lanham, MD: Rowman & Littlefield Pub Inc.

Hay, R. (2005). Becoming ecosynchronous, part 1: The root causes of our unsustainable way of life. *Sustainable Development, 13*(5), 311–325.

Husby, W. (2005). Towards stewardship. *Interpscan, 31*(1), 8–16.

Hvengaard, G. T., Shultis, J., & Butler, J. R. (2009). The role of interpretation. In P. Dearden & R. Rollins (Eds.), *Parks and protected areas in Canada: Planning and management* (pp. 202–235). Don Mills: Oxford University Press.

Interpretation Canada. (1976). *Our work defined.* Retrieved from http://www.interpscan.ca/our-work-defined

Jones, P. (2009). Teaching for change in social work: A discipline-based argument for the use of transformative approaches to teaching and learning. *Journal of Transformative Education, 7*(1), 8–25. doi:10.1177/1541344609338053

Knapp, C. (2005). The "i-thou" relationship, place-based education, and Aldo Leopold. *Journal of Experiential Education, 27*(3), 277–285.

Kovan, J. T., & Dirkx, J. M. (2003). Being called awake: The role of transformative learning in the lives of environmental activists. *Adult Education Quarterly, 53*(2), 99–118. doi:10.1177/0741713602238906

Kucukaydin, I., & Cranton, P. (2013). Critically questioning the discourse of transformative learning theory. *Adult Education Quarterly, 63*(1), 43–56. doi:10.1177/0741713612439090

Lange, E. A. (2004). Transformative and restorative learning: A vital dialectic for sustainable societies. *Adult Education Quarterly, 54*(2), 121–139. doi:10.1177/0741713603260276

Leopold, A. (1949). *A sand county almanac and sketches here and there*. London: Oxford University Press.

Louv, R. (2011). *The nature principle: Reconnecting with life in a virtual age*. New York, NY: Algonquin Books.

McKibben, B. (2010). *Eaarth: Making life on a tough new planet*. Toronto: Knopf Canada.

McWhinney, W., & Markos, L. (2003). Transformative education: Across the threshold. *Journal of Transformative Education, 1*(1), 16–37. doi:10.1177/1541344603252098

Merriam, B. (2004). The role of cognitive development in Mezirow's transformational learning theory. *Adult Education Quarterly, 55*(1), 60–68. doi:10.1177/074171360426889

Mezirow, J. (1994). Understanding transformation theory. *Adult Education Quarterly, 44*(4), 222–232. doi:10.1177/074171369404400403

Mezirow, J., & Taylor, E. W. (2009). *Transformative learning in practice: Insights from community, workplace, and higher education* (Kindle ed.). San Francisco, CA: Jossey-Bass. Retrieved from Amazon.ca

Newman, M. (2012). Calling transformative learning into question: Some mutinous thoughts. *Adult Education Quarterly, 62*(1), 36–55. doi:10.1177/0741713610392768

Orr, D. W. (2004). *Earth in mind: On education, environment, and the human prospect*. Washington, DC: Island Press.

O'Sullivan, E. (1999). *Transformative learning: Educational vision for the 21st century*. London: Zed Books.

O'Sullivan, E. (2001). Beyond globalization: Visioning transformative education within a politics of hope. *Review of Education, Pedagogy, and Cultural Studies, 23*(3), 317–333. doi:10.1080/1071441010230305

O'Sullivan, E. (2008). Finding our way in the great work. *Journal of Transformative Education, 6*(1), 27–32. doi:10.1177/1541344608316960

Plumwood, V. (1993). *Feminism and the mastery of nature* (Kindle ed.). London: Routledge. Retrieved from http://Amazon.ca

Province of Alberta. (2014). *Provincial parks act*. Edmonton: Queens Printer. Retrieved from http://www.qp.alberta.ca/documents/Acts/P35.pdf

Pyle, R. M. (2003). Nature matrix: Reconnecting people and nature. *Oryx, 37*(2), 206–214. doi:10.1017/S0030605303000383

Sauer, P. (2007). Reinhabiting environmentalism. In B. Lopez (Ed.), *The future of nature: Writing on human ecology* (pp. 5–13). Minneapolis, MN: Milkweed.

Selby, D. (2000). A darker shade of green: The importance of ecological thinking in global education and school reform. *Theory Into Practice, 39*(2), 88–96.

Shiva, V. (2004). Earth democracy: Creating living economies, living democracies, living cultures. *South Asian Popular Culture, 2*(1), 5–18.

Shultis, J. (1995). Improving the wilderness: Common factors in creating national parks and equivalent reserves during the nineteenth century. *Forest & Conservation History, 39*(3), 121–129.

Shultis, J., & More, T. (2011). American and Canadian national park agency responses to declining visitation. *Journal of Leisure Research, 43*(1), 110–132.

Suzuki, D. (2003). *The David Suzuki reader: A lifetime of ideas from a leading activist and thinker*. Vancouver: Greystone.

Suzuki, D. (2009). *The big picture: Reflections on science, humanity, and a quickly changing planet*. Vancouver: Greystone

Taylor, E. W. (2000). Fostering Mezirow's transformative learning theory in the adult education classroom: A critical review. *CJSAERCEE, 14*(2).

Taylor, E. W. (2008). Transformative learning theory. *New Directions for Adult and Continuing Education, 2008*(119), 5–15.

Wals, A. E. (2010). Mirroring, gestaltswitching and transformative social learning: Stepping stones for developing sustainability competence. *International Journal of Sustainability in Higher Education, 11*(4), 380–390. doi:10.1108/14676371011077595

Walter, P. (2013). Dead wolves, dead birds, and dead trees: Catalysts for transformative learning in the making of scientist-environmentalists. *Adult Education Quarterly, 63*(1), 24–42. doi:10.1177/0741713611426348

Wilber, K., Patten, T., Leonard, A., & Morelli, M. (2012). *Integral life practice: A 21st-century blueprint for physical health, emotional balance, mental clarity, and spiritual awakening.* Boston, MA: Integral Books.

Zimmerman, M. E. (2002). Deep ecology, ecoactivism, and human evolution. *ReVision, 24*(4), 40–45.

Don Carruthers Den Hoed
Interdisciplinary Graduate Program
University of Calgary, Canada

PART II

ACTIONS OF THEIR OWN TO LEARN IN KNOWLEDGE BUILDING COMMUNITIES

JO TOWERS AND LYNDON C. MARTIN

5. TAKING ACTIONS TO LEARN AS PART OF A CLASSROOM COLLECTIVE

INTRODUCTION

This chapter describes the actions taken to learn by a group of high school students during mathematics lessons in a Canadian school. The examples we offer are representative of the collective learning environment collaboratively created by the mathematics teacher and her students and we use them to show how a classroom collective can work to foster meaningful learning and to analyse what it might mean to learn, and to learn to act, within such a context.

UNDERSTANDING CLASSROOM COLLECTIVES

We will begin by explaining what we mean by a 'classroom collective.' Despite the fact that we gather bodies together to learn in schools, many of our current schooling structures draw on the Cartesian ideal of the self as solitary, coherent, and independent of context. The ideal knower in this frame, and hence the focus of most research and scholarship concerning learning, is the autonomous individual. In our work over the last 20 years, however, we have deliberately looked beyond a focus on the individual in an attempt to theorize and understand the collective as a learning unit.

In interpreting the basic idea of a collective we draw on enactivism, a theory of cognition that views human knowing and meaning-making as processes that are understood and theorized from a biological standpoint (Proulx, Simmt, & Towers, 2009). As Maturana and Varela (1992) note, species and environment co-adapt to each other, meaning that each influences the other, a process they refer to as *structural coupling* (Maturana & Varela, 1992). Within an enactivist perspective on classroom processes, then, learning is seen as reciprocal activity—the teacher brings forth a world of significance with the learners (Kieren, 1995; Maturana & Varela, 1992). The teacher is a fundamental part of the learners' processes (Proulx, 2010), and a "full participant in the emerging cognitive structure of the learning unit" (Towers & Martin, 2009, p. 47). However, while enactivist thought helps to emphasize the critical role of the teacher as a trigger, it cannot be assumed that the responsibility to learn rests solely within the learner(s) and simply needs to be 'facilitated.'

> It is in the *interaction* between the learner and environment that learning happens, not 'because of' the learning environment (including the teacher) or [the actions of] the learner him/herself. Simplistic interpretations of cause and effect in teaching and learning are therefore problematized in an enactivist interpretation. (Towers, Martin, & Heater, 2013, p. 425)

The starting point, then, for understanding classrooms as collectives is the severing of an attachment to the individual and a commitment to understanding what constitutes learning in groups.

LEARNING IN GROUPS

While much of the school-based research on learning in groups focuses on small-group activity within the context of the larger classroom group, a significant section of this discussion considers the classroom group as the unit of study (e.g., Jones & Tanner, 2002; Nathan & Knuth, 2003). Analysis of discourse in such classrooms consistently points to the significance of shared authority for learning in the classroom (e.g., Forman & Ansell, 2002; Ju & Kwon, 2007). For example, borrowing from Lehrer, Schauble, Carpenter, and Penner's (2000) work, Forman and Ansell (2002) note that,

> students' meaningful activities with material objects and mathematical objects need to take precedence over their dependence on the intellectual authority of teachers and texts. Instead of memorizing and applying information from authorities, students need to conjecture and experiment. In addition, they need to address each other's argumentative positions…to advance argumentative claims. (p. 257)

Forman and Ansell (2002) also note that in sharing authority for learning, teachers must learn to solicit arguments from students rather than always presenting arguments themselves, and students must learn to provide explanations and to evaluate their classmates' arguments. Additionally, both teachers and students must learn to value and legitimate student explanations within the classroom discourse. Similarly, Ju, and Kwon (2007) note the importance of the teacher valuing student justifications and argumentation, and inviting more than one way of knowing. Where this kind of shared authority is authentically practiced, such as in the classroom we describe in this chapter, learning is recognised to be emergent and "collectively determined" (Sawyer, 2004, p. 13). In our own work we have studied extensively the ways in which learning occurs when students truly value one another's contributions and re-work and build on these contributions. In a process we have termed *improvisational coaction* (borrowing from theoretical studies of improvisational processes in theatre and jazz) (Martin & Towers, 2009), we have documented the emergent structures that allow for students' improvisational actions (to learn).

> Improvisational coacting...is a process through which mathematical ideas and actions, initially stemming from an individual learner, become taken up, built upon, developed, reworked and elaborated by others, and thus emerge as shared understandings for and across the group, rather than remaining located within any one individual. (Martin & Towers, 2009, p. 4)

In later examples we show how, through this kind of improvisational coaction, students can take actions as a collective in a mathematics classroom.

METHODS

Data Collection

The study on which these ideas are based was designed to explore the nature of *collective mathematical understanding*—acts of mathematical understanding that can not simply be located in the minds or actions of any one individual but instead emerge from the interplay of ideas of individuals as these become woven together in shared action (Martin & Towers, 2009, 2015; Martin, Towers, & Pirie, 2006). In particular we were interested in (1) exploring the classroom conditions within which collective mathematical understanding might emerge—including group characteristics, task structures, and teacher role and (2) determining how collective mathematical understanding relates to and enhances personal mathematical understanding. Data were collected in two classrooms in one high school in a large Canadian city. Mathematics lessons were videorecorded (with two cameras in each classroom) daily for several weeks at the beginning of the semester with a follow-up period of 5 daily lessons at the end of the semester, copies of student work and the teachers' planning notes were collected, field notes were recorded daily during data collection periods, and initial planning meetings with the participant teacher were also videorecorded. For the purposes of this chapter we focus on data collected in one Grade 10 classroom.

Data Analysis

Data analysis proceeded through an adaptation of the approach proposed by Powell, Francisco, and Maher (2003). The first stage of analysis involved becoming familiar with the sessions in full, viewing the lessons in their entirety to get a sense of their content without imposing a specific analytical lens. In the second stage, the video data were described through writing brief, time-coded descriptions of each video's content. In Stage Three the data (video recordings, time-coded notes, supplementary materials) were reviewed to identify "critical events" with regard to our objectives. Thus, we identified instances where collective growing understanding could be observed. Stage Four involved examining these critical events to identify and construct a series of emerging narratives about the data. This perspective on the role of students in taking actions of their own to learn is developed from one such narrative.

FINDINGS

We have detailed the structures and norms of the particular classroom on which we focus here quite extensively in another publication (Towers, Martin, & Heater, 2013). Below, we summarize relevant parts of that description with particular foci on the role of students in the collective and the conditions necessary for the students to learn, and then we present three examples. The first features a small group of students and is taken from a lesson towards the end of the semester in which the class has been asked to prove the veracity of a particular geometrical relationship. We use this example to explore the actions taken by the students to learn mathematics in this collective context as well as to explore the ways in which the teacher intervenes in the learning process. The second example is taken from an episode in which the teacher discovers that the students are missing a crucial mathematical technique that she expected they would know. We use this example to show how the teacher ensures that students are still required to take actions of their own to learn, even at moments when, in other classrooms, they might expect to be shown the steps of a procedure. The third example is taken from an episode in which the teacher speaks directly with the whole class about reviewing their learning. We use this example to show how the teacher shapes how students can learn to act and learn to learn in this context.

Classroom Structures and Processes

Our focus classroom, which is small for the 35+ students populating this Grade 10 class, is arranged conventionally with single-student desks in rows facing the front of the classroom. Whiteboards cover three walls of the room. The teacher, Sharon, is an experienced teacher but only in her second year teaching in this particular school. Sharon's mathematics lessons always begin with random assignment of seating. Students participate good-humouredly throughout the semester in ever more creative daily strategies to vary the seating plan. Students show no reluctance to work with any other member of the class, which we find interesting given the social stratifications and gender norms that typically operate in high schools.

> [While] work sometimes begins with the teacher writing a problem on the board…sometimes students are expected to continue working on a problem from the previous day despite now [working] with new group members. Most days, the students are…encouraged to get out of their desks to work on the many whiteboards… They jostle for position, some students writing on the board, others offering suggestions about what to write or draw. Students often add to one another's drawings, or erase all or parts of a drawing someone else has created. No one objects to such 'interference' [and all amendments are

taken as friendly]... Work on the whiteboards [which is visible at all times for others to see] is treated as public property and belongs to the group... Students in this classroom move constantly. They participate in a discussion here, move off to add something to a drawing over there, listen in on another group as they pass by (sometimes contributing but just as often not), pass on an idea they've just heard about, and sometimes (but not always) return to the group where they started... Disagreements about mathematical processes and solutions erupt and are resolved, usually without recourse to asking the teacher to intervene....From time to time, students are asked to return to their seats. They might be assigned some practice questions to reinforce a concept that has emerged in the problem-solving, or be asked to make their own notes on their findings...or participate in a whole-class discussion as a new topic is introduced or as a particularly thorny problem is explored. Sharon...shows great curiosity about every detail of the mathematizing... When she sees an incorrect solution emerging in one area of the classroom, she rarely acts immediately to redirect the group, trusting the collective and giving students time to self-correct... She actively engages in *doing* mathematics at the whiteboards, not simply checking the students' mathematics, because the nature of the problems she sets means that there are always new avenues to explore and student approaches that are novel to her. (Towers, Martin, & Heater, 2013, pp. 427–428)

Taking Actions to Learn

In the following excerpt, we attempt to give a sense of the flow of events and contributions that ultimately lead students to a solution of a particular problem. We do this through a narrative description of events rather than through the presentation of extensive excerpts of transcript interspersed with analysis of specific speech acts. We have purposely chosen, in order to be able to describe events without the aid of the video, an episode in which the action can be described by reference to just a small number of central characters, in which there are not too many comings and goings, and in which the teacher makes a brief appearance. In much of our data there is more movement of group members, more obvious "importing" of ideas from students from further away than just the two neighbouring groups, and often a disappearance of the original small-group members altogether as the groups fluidly dissipate and reform elsewhere. While such episodes could be said to also 'represent' the data— in fact, they may be more representative of the data we gathered—such events are extremely difficult to describe on paper and would likely make for frustrating reading. We therefore elected to choose a somewhat less complex example for the purposes of clarity in this medium.

On the particular day we have chosen to describe, the topic of study was geometry. The class was asked to prove that angle AOB is twice angle ACB (see Figure 5.1).

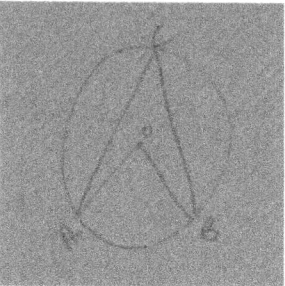

Figure 5.1. Sharon's diagram

Three students, Simon, Cerys, and Leah, who were seated together for the brief introductory remarks from the teacher, move to a section of the whiteboard to begin work. All around the room, other groups are working on the same problem on other sections of whiteboard. All work is visible for others to see. Cerys draws the figure onto the whiteboard, however her diagram shows point C as vertically above O (Figure 5.2), which the teacher's did not (see Figure 5.1).

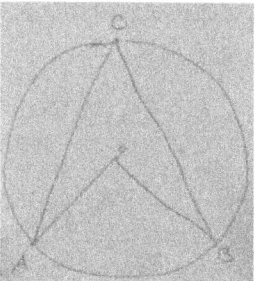

Figure 5.2. Cerys' diagram

Cerys and Leah begin talking about which line segments on the diagram are equal and which angles are equal. For the moment, Simon remains a step behind the two girls and watches their progress. Cerys and Leah add a dotted line to the diagram (AB) and establish that AO=BO and that angles OAB and OBA are equal to one another. They propose that angles CAO and CBO are also equal, but quickly dismiss this claim, recognizing that "no, they're not necessarily [equal]." Cerys adds various lines and several annotations indicating perpendicularity and equivalence (see Figure 5.3).

For several seconds the group seems stuck and Leah steps away from the board. Cerys draws Simon into the conversation and they have a brief discussion about angles that might be equivalent, then a student from a neighbouring group to the left leans over to point at the diagram—noting that point C is not necessarily vertically above the centre, O. Cerys insists that "it doesn't really matter" but the intervener

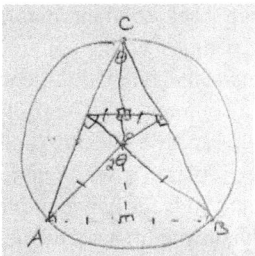

Figure 5.3. Annotated diagram

insists that it does. Seconds later a second student from the same neighbouring group leans over and says, "Wait, this makes no sense." Pointing to all the line segments that Cerys has marked with a dash, she adds, "You're saying that all these lines are equal." Cerys adds a second dash to some and a second and third dash to others to differentiate and the students all laugh. Leah takes the pen from Cerys and immediately launches into a new problem-solving effort. She draws an excerpt of the diagram, emphasizing the arc length AB and proposing that an approach might be made by considering this length (Figure 5.4). This seems provocative for the group and Simon adapts the figure to use the line segment AB rather than the arc AB and "flipping" the triangle to create a duplicate (Figure 5.5).

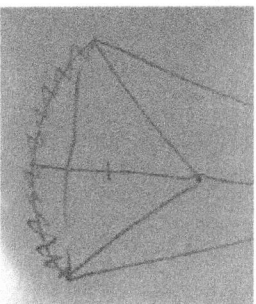

Figure 5.4. Leah's diagram

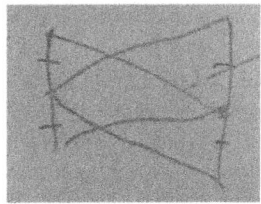

Figure 5.5. Simon's diagram

Simon then refers his group back to their diagram (Figure 5.3) and begins discussing what these inverted triangles would look like in situ and what equivalence relationships would be apparent. At this point, a student from the neighbouring group at the right intervenes to make a comment which is not picked up by the microphone but which prompts Leah to say "Oh, oh, oh!" in an excited manner, and she now erases the whole diagram (Figure 5.3), replaces it with one in which point C is clearly not vertically above the centre, O, and adds further annotations (Figure 5.6). Meanwhile, Simon now begins working with the members of the neighbouring group to the right. They create a separate diagram and begin to annotate it (Figure 5.7).

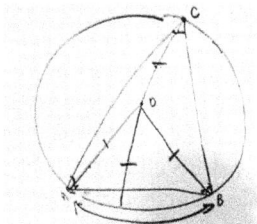

Figure 5.6. Leah's diagram

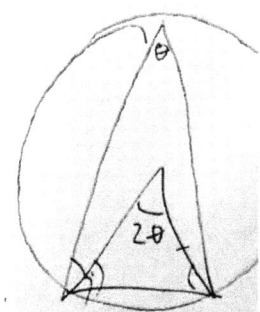

Figure 5.7. Simon's diagram

At this point (approximately 20 minutes into the problem-solving process) Sharon asks the class to pause in their work and offers them the opportunity to see the way she solved the problem. She stresses that there are many ways to prove the relationship and hers would be only one way and that they could continue with their work afterwards, but the offer is met with vehement protests. Students call out "I want to prove it" and "I want to figure this out." Cerys adds, "I want to solve it, though." Sharon acknowledges the will of the group and gives them more time. Nevertheless, the break seems to signal a moment for refocusing and Simon asks Cerys and Leah to consider the approach his new group has taken. He erases the diagram he has been working on with his new group and re-draws it, larger in scale, so both groups can see.

Cerys and Leah engage, Cerys challenging some of Simon's proposals for angle equivalencies and Leah challenging the fact that Simon is still drawing the figure as though C were vertically above the centre and therefore making some (erroneous) assumptions based on this. After a few moments, Cerys and Leah turn back to their diagram (Figure 5.6) and continue work, but their focus now seems to be on angle relationships rather than lengths of line segments, although they do not seem to have a systematic way of notating angles—some they mark with an arc, some they assign a letter, some they give a symbol such as a small dot. Meanwhile, Simon calls the teacher over to ask a question and while Sharon is nearby she glances over at Cerys and Leah's diagram and suggests that they consistently use small letters to denote angles. They re-annotate their diagram. The teacher then asks the students to identify symbolically the angles at O and they add further annotations (Figure 5.8).

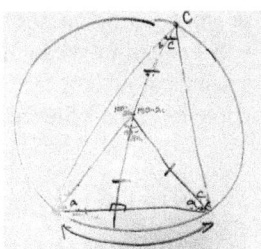

Figure 5.8. Final diagram

Cerys and Leah now begin a proof, starting by expressing the 360 degree angle at O. They continue by simplifying the expression. With one further intervention from the teacher (who points out that an expression they create during this simplifying process (90-a) is exactly half of an expression representing one of the angles of interest (angle AOB, which is labelled 180-2a), they are able to effect the final line of their proof.

We see in this extract many examples of students taking actions of their own to learn. To begin, we note the students were highly active rather than passive in their learning. Conditions for learning were carefully orchestrated such that the environment was structured by the teacher to make space for students' creativity in engagement and for their diverse ways of knowing and learning. For example, the random groupings, that changed from day to day, afforded many opportunities for students to engage and re-engage with others and provided the mechanism for collective actions and understandings. Students were called upon to articulate their own understandings while coacting to accommodate those of others. The changing group structures meant that each student was responsible for carrying forward knowledge from one group to another and from one day to the next, and for developing the capacity to blend their understandings with other perspectives.

A second feature of the environment that is critical to understanding how students took actions of their own to learn is the consistent use of whiteboards as a "thinking space." All work in this classroom was public, and so students learned to take responsibility for what they wrote or drew on the whiteboards, as such material was constantly available for scrutiny, questioning, and challenge. This is not to say that such material became fixed because it was public. On the contrary, students in this classroom learned that knowledge is mutable and open to interrogation and can be seen from multiple points of view, and, as such, mathematical work was frequently erased or revised as new(er) understandings came into play.

A third way in which this example offers insights into the actions that students (can) take to learn is through an examination of the help-giving behavior that we observed. In the above example we see that help-giving by peers in this classroom is (1) often not invited, but gifted anyway, (2) taken as a friendly amendment to the mathematics, not as a "correction," and certainly not as a critique of the person or group whose mathematics is amended or questioned, and (3) listened to with hermeneutic intent—always with an ear to what might possibly be true about what is being offered, even if it seems at odds with the current mathematical path. In this way, groups serve as a foil for each other and as an internal verification mechanism.

Learning to Take Actions to Learn

The self-reliance that is evident in students' actions in the above example does not, of course, simply happen. Many high school students have been conditioned by their school experiences to be passive learners and to expect to be shown every detail of the content to be learned and every step of the procedures to be followed. In contrast, Sharon had high expectations for student agency throughout the semester. The two examples we offer in this section show how Sharon carefully scaffolded challenge in her classroom such that students *needed* to be active in order to learn.

The first of these two examples occurred approximately six weeks into the semester. The class had been working on determining the factors of polynomial expressions and Sharon noticed that many students were factoring using long division. She queried whether they knew how to do synthetic division. Some students made tentative noises in the affirmative but it seemed to be clear to Sharon that some students did not know this technique and others may have only partially remembered or understood it from previous years. The following interaction ensued:

Sharon: So now for us to be able to factor and decide if something's a factor it would be a lot easier if we could do something other than long division every single time, wouldn't it?
Students: Yes.

TAKING ACTIONS TO LEARN AS PART OF A CLASSROOM COLLECTIVE

Sharon: So you understand how long division works. There's a bit of a shortcut. It's called synthetic division. I am not going to tell you how to do it, I want you to take a look at this and see if you can recognise what I'm doing. [*Walks to whiteboard*] Alright. Some of you have seen this before. Now, there's a couple of ways to do this, this is how I do it.

Sharon then proceeded, in silence, to work through the synthetic division for $(2x^3 + 3x^2 - x + 4)$ divided by $(x + 1)$. See Figure 5.9.

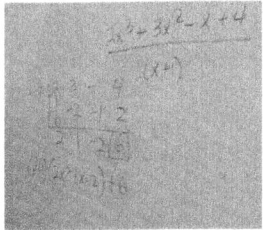

Figure 5.9. Synthetic division

Sharon: OK. Take a look. Write it down. Because I'm going to give you a [new] question and you're going to go to the board and see if you can figure out the pattern and what's going on....[*Pause*] Get it down and we're moving to the boards. See if you can figure out the pattern. What happened there?

Sharon now writes a new problem for the students to solve on the board using synthetic division $[(2x^4 - 3x^3 + x^2 - x + 7)$ divided by $(x - 2)]$. They move to the whiteboards and begin working. The groups we observed proceeded in much the same way—one student began laying out the solution, using the same synthetic division framework offered by the teacher, with other group members watching the unfolding mathematics and intervening in the process to question a step, change a value, or discuss what should happen next. In one group, a student who had used the procedure before confidently began working through the problem. She erroneously, though, chose −2 rather than +2 as the initial root. Her group members, both of whom were meeting this procedure for the first time, watched for a while as she explained the first few steps and then participated in generating the last few elements of the division. Cerys, who we met earlier, was one of the group members who hadn't met the procedure before and as they put the final touches to their procedure she glanced around the room and seemed to notice something about other groups' solutions. She says, "Wait, no, you guys, this is wrong, this is wrong, because this [pointing to the −2 they have used as one of the roots] is not the root." The other group members quickly acknowledge the amendment and, without further explanation from Cerys

97

about what the root should be and why, the student wielding the marker changes the sign on the root and they re-work their entire solution. Here, then, we see the significance of the public nature of the work. Our focus group here do not copy the neighbouring solutions, but those solutions provide an internal check on the reasoning of the collective as a whole. In this sense, the entire classroom participates in generating knowledge about synthetic division. We note, also, that it is not the student in the small group who initially brought the most knowledge about this piece of mathematics who was able to correct their mis-step but, rather, one of the students who had not met the procedure before. This shows that Sharon is justified in the trust she has that the students have enough familiarity with the long division algorithm that they will be able to engage with a new division method. The public nature of the work invites collective action and serves to constrain erroneous solutions. At this point, Sharon offers one more problem, which the class solves quickly and confidently, and says nothing more about synthetic division. She does not pause to review the steps of the synthetic division method. She is confident that the class, as a collective, can self-moderate and accommodate the new technique into its repertoire and that she can move on, without comment or explanation of the technique, to the next task.

In the next classroom excerpt, we show how the students learned to be active in documenting their learning. We do this by carefully examining how the teacher treated "note-taking" as a mechanism for learning. In traditional high school mathematics classrooms, notes are often provided by the teacher and copied down by the students. In this classroom, however, as we noted earlier, the teacher rarely provides a worked example (and never, during our data collection period, provided notes for students) and so the question of how students made notes, and about what, drew our attention. The following extract is taken from a lesson in which Sharon asked the students to make their own notes for the topics that the class had been working on in previous lessons. She begins by emphasizing that how students put together their review notes is going to be entirely up to them, and then writes three key ideas on the board—function, solving equations, and inequalities.

Sharon: In your function, what is it about a function? What are the things we talked about? I am open to anybody. When we talk about functions in general, what did we look at?
Student: Graphs.
Student: Max and min.
Sharon: I heard it. Say it louder....
Student: Graphs.
Sharon: Alright, then. Graphs. [*Adds "graphs" to the board. See Figure 5.10*] We looked at graphs of some functions and there were some important things that we have to know. Does it have max and min values and how are they determined? [*Adds "max/min" to the board*] And you need to know or confirm if it has absolute or relative or

	both. [*Adds "absolute/relative" to board*] OK? What else do we need to be able to figure out from the graph?
Student:	Range and domain.
Sharon:	Domain and range. [*Adds "domain + range" to the board*] And what affects the domain and range....OK. What else on graphs did we do, did we talk about?
Student:	X and y.
Sharon:	Ah-ha. Intercepts. OK [*Writes "intercepts" on board*]
Student:	Symmetry.
Sharon:	Symmetry. [*Adds to "symmetry" to the board*] Does it have it? Is it possible? [*Adds "possible" to the board*] And what kind?
Student:	Point and line.
Sharon:	Yep. Point and line symmetry we talked about. [*Adds "point/line" to the board*] Sometimes it's possible but not always there. Sometimes it's always there. OK. So that was the graphs. What else in functions did we look at? Being able to recognise a polynomial from its graph, and?
Student:	Equations.
Sharon:	Equations [*Circles "solving equations" on the board*] So, the different forms of the equations and how they work. How you can determine the equation from the graph and vice versa. [*Pause*] [*Writes "forms" on board*] Solving equations. Each one of them was different so I guess you just need to have your own key steps [*Writes "key steps" on board*]. What's a super duper duper important part whenever you get a solution?
Student:	Check it.
Sharon:	[*Writes "check" on board*]... And then inequalities. [*Circles the word "Inequalities" on board*] How to work with inequalities. OK, so however you decide to set it up—it can be a chart, it can be a web, it can be, you know, section cards, I don't care—but all of this needs to show up so that when you're going to study and review, it's there. You might want to include definitions, examples, graphs, questions you need answered, anything....OK? Now, get any clarifying questions taken care of. Are we OK?
Students:	Mmm-hmmm.
Sharon:	...OK. Have fun. Get started.

In the above extract we are able to see that Sharon took care to ensure that students were pointed to the key pieces of mathematics that she knew they would have encountered in her classroom, but she did not make notes for the students, nor did she specify precisely how they should document the ideas. In addition, her advice about note-taking privileges the big ideas of the topics, not particular techniques or procedures. For example, she notes that the students should pay attention to how

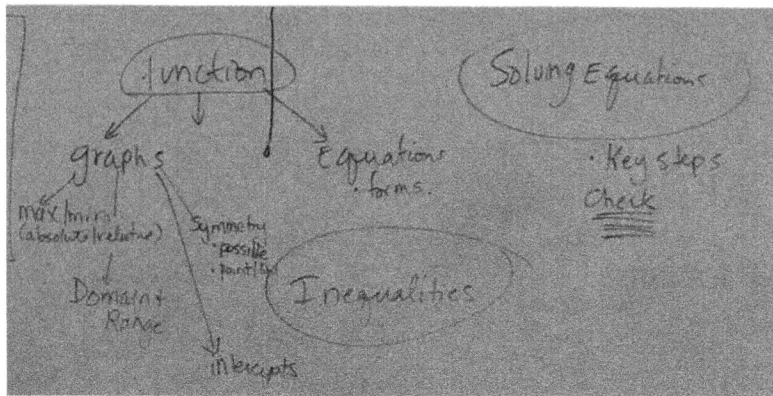

Figure 5.10. Structuring note-taking

maximum and minimum values are determined, and to what affects the domain and range of a graph. Her advice about notes on inequalities is even more restrained—students should simply know "how to work with inequalities." Interestingly, she encourages students to include in their notes "questions [they] need answered." Students therefore learn that note-taking is a learning event, one in which they need to ask as well as answer their own queries about topics.

DISCUSSION

The above examples reveal several aspects of a classroom that operates as a collective, where each member is responsible to all other members, where work is public and shared, and where the teacher is a fundamental part of the learning environment and brings forth a world of (mathematical) significance with the learners (Kieren, 1995; Maturana & Varela, 1992). As we can see from the first example we offered, this positioning of the teacher shifts his/her role away from being sole arbiter of mathematical truth or "corrector" of mistakes, and leaves him/her free to engage in *doing* mathematics *with* the students, something that Sharon did daily and with relish. The active help-giving behaviour of the students that was evident in the first example also transformed the help-giving behaviour of the teacher so that, as we described above, help-giving by the teacher that is perceived as simply "telling" students how to solve the problem is soundly rejected, but the students accept the teacher's help-giving when it engages the specific mathematizing at play (e.g., Sharon's suggestion to be consistent in labeling angles, and her pointing to the significant relationship between two algebraic expressions—90-a and 180-2a).

Our second example shows that students cannot simply be abandoned to the mathematics and expected to take actions of their own to learn in the absence of a support structure that helps them learn *how* to take actions of their own in learning mathematics. In our example, Sharon was careful to expose the students to a new mathematical technique in the context of a method with which they were already familiar (long division) and a problem that they had already solved by this familiar method. She also knew that there was sufficient knowledge already in the group that together they could reason through the new method and make sense of it but that this required the students to take actions of their own to learn. Taking action, in this sense, did not mean students listening while the teacher explained the new technique, it meant encountering just the right amount of mystery set within the context of known material (the known long division method and the known solution to the particular problem) so that action was possible. Such positioning is what Sawyer (2003), drawing on the work of Csíkszentmihályi, refers to as orchestrating for *group flow*—creating conditions such that "the skills of the [group members] are perfectly matched to the challenges of the task" (p. 40). In other words, this carefully scaffolded task meant that together—as a whole group—the students had the necessary tools to learn the synthetic division technique while simultaneously solving a new problem. The lack of fuss, questions, and consternation when Sharon moved on to the next task reveals that these highly active and engaged learners were quickly comfortable with the technique and ready to apply it to new problems.

The third example offers a glimpse into an aspect of high school students' learning that is under-researched—the practice of note-taking. Often, high school classrooms are structured around the very act of note-taking—the teacher reviews the previous day's homework, demonstrates the new technique for the day, which students carefully copy down in their notes, and then students practice the technique, often using textbook exercises. In the classroom we describe here, though, classroom activities are more fluid and there is rarely a structured example worked through by the teacher that students might copy down. Hence, the question of what students ought to 'note'—what counts as noteworthy in this space—is a matter of negotiation. As we can see from the third example, the teacher uses this indeterminacy as a moment for teaching, helping students to learn *how* they should learn from what transpires in the class. Several times we noted students using their agency—taking actions of their own to learn—by discussing with peers what should constitute the content of their notes for a particular topic. Hence, content was reviewed naturally and organically (and continually) rather than artificially as (only) a summing up exercise before moving to a new topic. The question of what was worthy of learning therefore became *part of* the learning event.

CONCLUSION

In examining the phenomenon of students taking actions of their own to learn as part of a collective, we have drawn attention to the critical role of the teacher in setting up an environment in which taking actions to learn is not only helpful but *required* in order to participate in unfolding understandings. We also note, though, that not just any kind of action is desirable in this context. The actions students take are improvisational coactions—actions in which ideas, although they might initially stem from an individual learner, "become taken up, built upon, developed, reworked and elaborated by others, and thus emerge as shared understandings for and across the group" (Martin & Towers, 2009, p. 4). Students did not arrive in this setting already knowing how to work in this way—they learned to participate through immersion in the context and they gradually took responsibility for their own learning. "Instead of memorizing and applying information from authorities" (Forman & Ansell, 2002, p. 257), students "learned to address each other's argumentative positions…[and] to advance argumentative claims" (p. 257). Hence, in this environment, learning was collectively determined (Sawyer, 2004) and the class as a whole (including the teacher) became "the body that learns" (Towers, 2011).

ACKNOWLEDGMENTS

We gratefully acknowledge the support of the Social Sciences and Humanities Research Council of Canada (SSHRC), Grant # 435-2009-383. SSHRC exercised no oversight in the design of the research, the collection, analysis, and interpretation of data, or the writing of this report.

REFERENCES

Forman, E. A., & Ansell, E. (2002). Orchestrating the multiple voices and inscriptions of a mathematics classroom. *Journal of the Learning Sciences, 11*(2–3), 251–254.

Jones, S., & Tanner, H. (2002). Teachers' interpretations of effective whole class interactive teaching in secondary mathematics classrooms. *Educational Studies, 28*(3), 265–274.

Ju, M.-K., & Kwon, O. N. (2007). Ways of talking and ways of positioning: Students' beliefs in an inquiry-oriented differential equations class. *Journal of Mathematical Behavior, 26*(3), 267–280.

Kieren, T. E. (1995, June). *Teaching mathematics (in-the-middle): Enactivist views on learning and teaching mathematics.* Paper presented at the Queens/Gage Canadian National Mathematics Leadership Conference, Queens University, Kingston.

Lehrer, R., Schauble, L., Carpenter, S., & Penner, D. (2000). The inter-related development of inscriptions and conceptual understanding. In P. Cobb, E. Yackel, & K. McClain (Eds.), *Symbolizing and communicating in mathematics classrooms* (pp. 325–360). Mahwah, NJ: Lawrence Erlbaum Associates, Inc.

Martin, L. C., & Towers, J. (2009). Improvisational coactions and the growth of collective mathematical understanding. *Research in Mathematics Education, 11*(1), 1–20.

Martin, L. C., & Towers, J. (2015). Growing mathematical understanding through collective image making, collective image having, and collective property noticing. *Educational Studies in Mathematics, 88*(1), 3–18. doi:10.1007/s10649-014-9552-4

Martin, L. C., Towers, J., & Pirie, S. E. B. (2006). Collective mathematical understanding as improvisation. *Mathematical Thinking and Learning, 8*(2), 149–183.

Maturana, H. R., & Varela, F. J. (1992). *The tree of knowledge: The biological roots of human understanding* (2nd Rev. ed.). Boston, MA: Shambhala Press.

Nathan, M. J., & Knuth, E. J. (2003). A study of whole classroom mathematical discourse and teacher change. *Cognition and Instruction, 21*(2), 175–207.

Powell, A., Francisco, J., & Maher, C. (2003). An analytical model for studying the development of learners' mathematical ideas and reasoning using videotape data. *Journal of Mathematical Behavior, 22*(4), 405–435.

Proulx, J. (2010). Is "facilitator" the right word? And on what grounds? Some reflections and theorizations. *Complicity: An International Journal of Complexity and Education, 7*(2), 52–65.

Proulx, J., Simmt, E., & Towers, J. (2009). The enactivist theory of cognition and mathematics education research: Issues of the past, current questions and future directions. In M. Tzekaki, M. Kaldrimidou, & H. Sakonidis (Eds.), *Proceedings of the 33rd annual meeting of the international group for the psychology of mathematics education* (Vol. 1, pp. 249–252). Thessaloniki: PME.

Sawyer, R. K. (2003). *Group creativity: Music, theater, collaboration.* Mahwah, NJ: Lawrence Erlbaum.

Sawyer, R. K. (2004). Creative teaching: Collaborative discussion as disciplined improvisation. *Educational Researcher, 33*(2), 12–20.

Towers, J. (2011, May). *The class as a body that learns: Theoretical and methodological issues.* Invited presentation at the Doyal-Nelson Symposium, The biology of cognition and its implications for curriculum and pedagogy, University of Alberta, Edmonton.

Towers, J., & Martin, L. C. (2009). The emergence of a 'better' idea: Preservice teachers' growing understanding of mathematics for teaching. *For the Learning of Mathematics, 29*(3), 44–48.

Towers, J., Martin, L. C., & Heater, B. (2013). Teaching and learning mathematics in the collective. *Journal of Mathematical Behavior, 32*(3), 424–433.

Jo Towers
Werklund School of Education
University of Calgary, Canada

Lyndon C. Martin
Faculty of Education
York University, Canada

EMILY HANKE VAN ZEE

6. TAKING ACTION TO LEARN BY ASKING ONE'S OWN QUESTIONS IN A PHYSICS COURSE FOR PROSPECTIVE TEACHERS

This entire class is based off asking questions and it has helped me learn because of our small group work. We are looking at questions we find to be interesting and that makes it easier to want to learn and be engaged with the topic.
(Student response to anonymous survey about physics, 111)

How can a teacher create opportunities for students to generate and explore their own questions? This narrative describes my journey in designing and teaching an inquiry-based physics course for prospective teachers. My intent has been to create a learning environment within which small groups of students feel comfortable in taking action to learn by discussing their own ideas and in making choices about how and what to explore about the physical phenomena that we are investigating. The quote above suggests my efforts worked, at least for this student.

The purpose of this chapter is to make explicit ways that I attempt to nurture student questioning in this course. Two questions frame the discussion: What have I learned about questioning practices through my teaching experiences and research? How have I used those understandings in engaging students in generating and exploring their own questions?

First I briefly review literature about the nature of student questioning and summarize findings from my research on questioning in precollege classrooms. Next I discuss my approach to researching my own teaching practices and students' learning. After describing the physics course, I then present several ways in which I have fostered student questioning. These include welcoming student questions during class sessions, eliciting student questions within homework assignments, and creating field experiences in which students assume roles as teachers to begin learning how to foster such student questioning themselves. I conclude the chapter with reflections about ways to foster student questioning.

EXPLORING THE NATURE OF STUDENT QUESTIONING

The dearth of student questioning during instruction has been a persistent problem. About a hundred years ago, for example, Dewey (1916) noted:

> No one has ever explained why children are so full of questions outside of the school (so that they pester grown-up persons if they get any encouragement), and the conspicuous absence of display of curiosity about the subject matter of school lessons.... (p. 183)

Dewey also suggested a remedy:

> ...where children are engaged in doing things and in discussing what arises in the course of their doing, it is found...that children's inquiries are spontaneous and numerous, and the proposals of solution advanced, varied, and ingenious. (p. 183)

Dewey's insight into the importance of engaging students "in doing things and in discussing what arises in the course of their doing" (p. 183) anticipated the current emphasis on engaging students in active explorations (NGSS Lead States, 2013) and in interactive discourse practices in science classrooms (Kelly, 2007).

Lemke (1990) analyzed several discourse structures through which science teachers typically discourage their students' engagement in learning science by dominating what is said and done. He also suggested alternative practices, such as "organize more class time for student questions, student individual and group reports, true dialogue, cross-discussion, and small group work" (p. 168).

Several teachers have documented such learning experiences at the elementary level. Doris (1991), for example, illustrated many ways to nurture children's curiosity. Gallas (1995) recorded and interpreted enthusiastic questioning when young children were offered opportunities to talk about what they thought about a topic and why they thought that. Pearce (1999) described many ways to engage fifth grade students in their own investigations. The students' explorations culminated in a "Kids Inquiry Conference" in which the children discussed their findings with one another, like scientists at a conference, rather than competing in front of adult judges at a science fair.

Chin and Osborne (2008) considered roles student questions may play in both learning and teaching science. Questions that emerge can help teachers diagnose students' ideas, indicate the level of student thinking, enhance the curriculum, and contribute to a teacher's growth in conceptual and pedagogical expertise. Barriers to student questioning include teachers' perceptions of time and curriculum constraints, knowledge level, a view of teaching as transmission of information, and discomfort with open-ended discourse practices. Students may also avoid asking questions for social, cultural and personal reasons.

Explicit attention to formulating questions sometimes occurs during literacy instruction; students may then transfer these skills to science contexts (Shapiro, 1994, p. 194). Students also can be taught to generate better researchable questions (Cuccio-Schirripa & Steiner, 2000; Shapiro, 1996, 2015; Sharkawy, 2010). In addition, explicit instruction about questioning strategies can help students talk about science with one another (Chin & Osborne, 2010; Iwasyk, 1997; Rothstein & Santana, 2011).

In the US, the recently released *A Framework for K-12 Science Education* (National Research Council, 2012) and *Next Generation Science Standards* (NGSS Lead States, 2013) identify eight science and engineering practices that students should learn how to use when learning science. The first is "asking questions and defining problems."

As discussed next, my interest in engaging students in asking their own questions has emerged from my teaching experiences and research program.

EMERGENCE OF MY INTEREST IN GUIDING STUDENTS TO TAKE ACTIONS OF THEIR OWN TO LEARN THROUGH QUESTIONING

Like many teachers, I began teaching science based on my own experiences: My students sat at desks lined up in rows while I stood in front and told them what I thought they ought to know.

Later I learned a different way, as an instructor in special physics programs for minority students and teachers (McDermott, 1990, 2006). These served as sites for developing the *Physics by Inquiry* curriculum (McDermott & The Physics Education Group, 1996). In these programs, students worked in small groups while staff circulated among the tables. It was here that I learned how to listen closely to what students were saying to one another and to ask questions or make comments only as needed. As lead instructor eventually, I mentored new staff members, who often struggled to respond to student questions by asking questions that prompt the next step in thinking rather than by telling answers, a "dilemma of teaching" that others have documented (e.g., Volkmann & Zgagacz, 2004, pp. 595–598).

For my postdoctoral research project, I collaborated with a high school teacher, Jim Minstrell, who engaged his students in many thoughtful discussions while conducting his own research on physics learning (Minstrell, 1982, 1992, 2000). Together we explored how he used questioning to guide student thinking (van Zee & Minstrell, 1997a, 1997b). As shown in the appendix, I created a visual way to represent questions and comments that he, as the class teacher, and his students made during a discussion. Minstrell described many of his questions as *reflective tosses*. He envisioned catching the meaning of a student's prior utterance and tossing responsibility for thinking back to the student, for example, "What do you mean by [the term] 'average' here?" (van Zee & Minstrell, 1997, p. 235). He asked such questions to make meanings clear, to explore various points of view in a neutral manner, and to help students monitor the discussion and their own thinking.

In addition, I explored ways to encourage students to take actions to learn by asking their own questions during science lessons facilitated by experienced teachers (van Zee, Iwasyk, Kurose, Simpson, & Wild, 2001). We found that students asked questions when we invited them to do so, they made multiple observations over long time periods, they felt comfortable trying to understand one another's thinking, and they were collaborating with one another in small groups.

I also analyzed an extended student-generated inquiry discussion about the moon in my seminar for undergraduate students interested in teaching high school science or mathematics (van Zee, 2000). A key aspect was not only waiting for students to speak (Rowe, 1986; Tobin, 1987), but also enacting what I called *attentive silence* (listening closely to each student speaker) and *reticence* (refraining from responding with my own interpretation of what was being said).

A colleague, David Hammer, and I invited experienced teachers to focus on the science in what the children said and did while talking about phenomena in open-ended ways (Hammer & van Zee, 2006). During summer institutes, participating teachers worked in small groups, asking questions of one another in their roles as student inquirers. Their questions were similar to those Minstrell asked as a teacher during guided inquiry discussions (van Zee, Hammer, Bell, Peters, & Roy, 2005).

These experiences formed the perspective underlying my approach to designing the physics course for prospective teachers. As discussed next, I have documented ways in which I try to extend and encourage student questioning in my courses.

AN INTERPRETATIVE RESEARCH APPROACH

In order to document what happens in the physics course, I conduct a form of research known as *teacher research* (Cochran-Smith & Lytle, 1993; Roberts, Bove, & van Zee, 2007; Roth, 2007). Teacher research involves constructing a detailed account of one's own teaching practices and students' learning. With Institutional Review Board approved forms, I ask consent from my students to collect data in my courses while teaching. These data include video recordings of class sessions and copies of student writings, drawings, and responses on anonymous questionnaires. Data also include my reflections about my intentions and experiences in designing and teaching the course.

This form of research is also referred to as the scholarship of teaching and learning (Shulman, 2004), self-study (Loughran, 2007), and practitioner research (Zeichner & Noffke, 2001). The narrative presented here builds upon my earlier studies conducted with support from the Spencer Foundation Practitioner Research program (van Zee, 2000; van Zee, Lay, & Roberts, 2003), Carnegie Academy for the Scholarship of Teaching and Learning (Roberts, Bove, & van Zee, 2007), and the National Science Foundation (Hammer & van Zee, 2006; van Zee, Hammer, Bell, Peters, & Roy, 2005; van Zee, Iwasyk, Kurose, Simpson, & Wild, 2001; van Zee et al., 2013a, 2013b).

Because my perceptions and philosophical commitments can bias accounts of my own teaching practices and students' learning, I do not attempt to develop generalizations that apply across multiple contexts. Instead my intent is to provide information and explicit examples that others may find useful in their own settings.

TAKING ACTION TO LEARN BY ASKING ONE'S OWN QUESTIONS IN A PHYSICS COURSE

THE PHYSICS COURSE

I have collaborated with the chair of the physics department and a professor of literacy to design a physics course for prospective elementary and middle school teachers that integrates science and literacy learning (van Zee, Jansen, Winograd, Crowl, & Devitt, 2013a, 2013b). In designing this course, I have drawn upon materials that emphasize active engagement of students in exploring physical phenomena (American Association of Physics Teachers, 2001; McDermott & Physics Education Group, 1996; Robinson, Goldberg, & Otero, 2012; Rutherford, Holton, & Watson, 1971; Ukens, Hein, Johnson, & Layman, 2004). In teaching the course, I have attempted to encourage students to take action to learn by asking their own questions about the phenomena we are exploring.

The physics course meets in a laboratory for 2.5 hour sessions, twice a week, for ten weeks. My students are prospective teachers, primarily female undergraduates majoring in health and human sciences. We restrict entry to those who have completed at least one of three required mathematics courses for students who plan to apply to enter our elementary teacher education program later in their studies. Peer instructors, who are graduates of the course, assist me both in teaching physics and in helping students understand and come to appreciate our inquiry-based instructional approach.

During the course, we engage the students in explorations of the nature of light phenomena, thermal phenomena, influence of light and thermal phenomena on local weather and global climate change, and the nature of astronomical phenomena within the Sun/Earth/Moon system (i.e., phases of the moon and Earth's seasons). Each unit begins with identification of resources (Hammer, 2000) such as students' initial ideas, development of powerful ideas based on evidence, use of these powerful ideas to construct explanations of intriguing phenomena, development of mathematical representations, and use of these representations to estimate a quantity of interest (van Zee, 2015).

Below I describe ways I structure class sessions, homework assignments, and field experiences to foster student questioning, with evidence consisting of quotes from students' responses. A course wiki provides detailed examples of these activities at http://physics.oregonstate.edu/coursewikis/ph111

FOSTERING STUDENT QUESTIONING DURING CLASS SESSIONS

The primary way I foster the development of questioning skills is to structure class activities so that students can express their own ideas and ask questions about what interests them. As discussed below, the first major course activity on Day 1 engages students in identifying questioning as important in fostering learning. Most activities throughout the course include opportunities for small groups to generate and explore their own questions. Every session ends with students reflecting upon what they have just learned and are still wondering.

Engaging Students in Identifying Questioning as Important in Fostering Learning

My intent on the first day of class is to provide opportunities for students to identify explicitly, and to experience for themselves, ways to foster science learning (van Zee & Roberts, 2001). During the opening activity, students draw pictures of themselves learning science, at some time in their lives, inside or outside of school, when they enjoyed the process. They introduce themselves to the whole group by describing these positive science-learning experiences and reflecting upon aspects that had fostered their learning. (For details, click on *Instructional Strategies* on the course wiki, next on *Aspects that Foster Science Learning;* to see a video clip, click on *Day-by-Day Summary, Fall 2009, Day 1, Sharing Science Experiences.*) Generally the students articulate some version of being actively engaged, asking questions, and exploring in small groups. For example:

Class List of Aspects That Have Fostered Science Learning:

Group work, understandable, discussion, asking questions, fun, entertaining, interactive, exciting, surprising, choice, visual, field trips, exploration, and suspense. (Physics 111, list generated by students on Day 1)

We decorate the walls with their drawings and list. I often refer to this list, particularly when students seem puzzled by my expectation that they generate and explore their own questions within the topic that we are investigating.

Generating and Exploring Students' Own Questions in Small Groups

Later in the first day's session, we put immediately into practice the expectation that students will be generating and exploring their own questions. After initial demonstrations and discussions about light, each small group gets their own lamp, barrier, meter stick, and screen with an open-ended prompt: "What can you find out about light and shadows with this equipment?"

My peer instructors and I circulate among the groups and offer encouragement with gentle guidance as needed. Members of each small group generate a question they want to explore and record their question and findings on a large white board. The small groups then present their results to the whole group. (For details, click on *Day-by-Day Summary* on the course wiki, next on *Fall 2009,* then on *Day 1* and finally on *Light Exploration.*) For homework, I give students pieces of cardboard and suggest they invite friends or family members to explore light and shadow phenomena with them in a similar open-ended way. (For further details about "friends and family" assignments, see, Crowl, Devitt, Jansen, van Zee, and Winograd, 2013, and the section on field experiences below.)

On Day 2, the small groups again generate their own questions within the context of the next step in our exploration of light phenomena, making and using pinhole cameras. Most are surprised to see an upside down projection of a light bulb when looking at a lamp through a pinhole camera. (For details, click on *Activities* on the course wiki, next on *Light,* then on *Pinhole Phenomena.*) For homework, the students engage friends or family members in exploring pinhole phenomena. The students also reflect on the week's experiences by making and supporting claims about ways to foster science learning. They use a "claim with support by evidence" format that I model in the instructions. A student wrote:

Claim: Allowing students to conduct their own experiments fosters science learning

Evidence: In class on Tuesday we experimented with light and shadows by moving the barrier around the table and observing the different shadows it produced…Later that day, my roommate and I looked at the shadows from a pair of sunglasses, which led to the discovery that the more translucent an object, the lighter the shadow will be. On Thursday, we experimented with pinhole cameras. Although we did not discover the reasoning by ourselves behind the upside down projection, our experiments ruled out several variables. For example, we looked at the light bulb with and without the tube and wax paper. Finally, my Mom and I experimented with the shape of the pinhole and found that a square pinhole produced the same projection as the original circle. (Physics 111 student, Homework 1)

The students post their reflections on our electronic bulletin board to share their evolving understandings about ways to foster science learning.

Reflecting and Articulating Questions Near the End of Each Class

We end each class with a practice adapted from John Layman's physics course at the University of Maryland, sharing reflections about what each learned that day and is still wondering. During Day 3, for example, we use pinhole phenomena to estimate the sun's diameter. (For details, click on *Day-by-Day Summary* on the course wiki, next on *Fall 2009,* then on *Day 3,* and finally on *Diameter of the Sun* and *Reflections.*) A student stated that she learned "How to determine how big the sun was using the pinhole phenomena" and wondered "How accurate are our estimates of the sun's size?" Another student wondered "Can this concept be applied to the moon?" Articulating such questions and listening to others' ponderings may prompt students to continue investigating outside of class. This feedback also sometimes influences my instructional plans for the next session.

FOSTERING STUDENT QUESTIONING WITHIN HOMEWORK ASSIGNMENTS

The homework assignments provide several contexts for encouraging students to take action to learn by asking their own questions. As discussed below, these include having small groups generate and design on-going investigations on which they report as part of the weekly homework assignment. We also undertake whole group explorations based on questions of interest that emerge from these small group reports. In addition, I ask students to generate questions in their reflective writings based on course readings and other assignments. Near the end of the term, they formulate, research, and report on emerging issues and topics of interest.

Generating and Designing On-Going Small Group Investigations

In addition to open-ended explorations within one class period, members of each small group also generate and explore a question that involves making observations outside of class. On the first sunny day, for example, we go outside to start sky journals where students will be recording daily observations of the sun and the moon. After a few days, small groups generate questions they can answer by observing the moon over the next two weeks. (For details, click on *Activities* on the course wiki, next on *Sun/Earth/Moon System Phenomena*, and then on *Sky Journals* under Week 1 and *Generating Questions about the Sun and Moon* under Week 2.) One student wrote on her first homework assignment:

> Our group decided to ask the question, "How does time change the moon's position in the sky?" To do this each of us will record the moon's placement in the sky at a specific time for 10 days. Since there are four of us we will record the moon's placement in the sky every hour from 7 pm to 10 pm….My role in this is to record the moon at 8 pm….

On her second homework assignment a week later she wrote:

> We observed that the time does in fact change the placement of the moon. From 7–10 pm we noticed the moon moves up from East to West. This supported our first claim that the moon does move with time… However, we noticed that the moon has changed placement at the same time every evening. Our first day at 8 pm we noticed the moon was up in the East of the sky. By the end of our experiment we noticed that at 8 pm the moon was way lower and hardly seen… (She included photos of her sky journal pages as evidence to support her claims.) (Physics 111 student, Homework 1 and 2)

This group found that they had to adjust their design because, by the second week of observations, the moon had not yet risen by 7 pm, a time they had assigned themselves for making observations. As course instructor, I chose not to intervene in their plans. I thought it important to let them experience not seeing the moon as they had anticipated and having to modify their procedure accordingly.

Building Whole Group Explorations upon Small Group Reports

Usually at least one of the groups makes the intriguing paradoxical observation that the moon appears to move east to west, like the sun, over several hours but west to east over several days (van Zee, 2000). Once this puzzling behavior emerges from the small group reports, we document it with trips outside when the moon and sun are both visible during class on subsequent days. Understanding why this puzzling behavior seems to occur becomes a highlight of our discussions. Within a later homework, students summarize their growing understandings that the apparent east to west daily motion of both the sun and the moon is due to our view from a rotating earth whereas the west to east motion of the moon observed over several days is due to the moon's actual motion in revolving around the earth. This is an example of students generating an anticipated specific question as well as generating through direct personal engagement and observation, intriguing issues and observations that become of interest to explore.

Generating Questions within Reading Reflections and Other Assignments

The weekly readings include articles written by teachers reflecting upon their experiences teaching science through inquiry (e.g., Hogan, 2007; Iwasyk, 1997; Kurose, 2000; Roberts, 1999). I ask students to develop strategies for integrating science and literacy learning as they read. (For details, click on *Instructional Strategies* on the course wiki, next on *Literacy,* and then on *Reading Strategies* and *Science Journal Articles.*) These strategies include asking oneself questions before, during, and after reading each article (Devitt, 2010; van Zee et al., 2013a, 2013b). For example, while reading a first grade teacher's chapter about using motion detectors to teach how to write sequential directions (Hogan, 2007), a student wondered, "what new, exciting, technologies will be available when I have my own classroom?" I also ask students to propose questions about each topic we have explored. They post these on our discussion board to help study for examinations.

Formulating, Researching, and Reporting on One's Own Question of Interest

Toward the end of the course, we explore the influence of light and thermal phenomena on global climate change, with an emphasis on understanding the greenhouse effect and physical causes of rising sea levels (van Zee, Roberts, & Grobart, 2016). This includes students reporting something they find interesting on university, state, national, and international websites about climate change. They also formulate their own questions about global climate change and identify, use, and critique relevant internet resources to craft a report of their findings (For details, click on *Activities* on the course wiki and next on *Climate Change*).

FOSTERING STUDENT QUESTIONING DURING FIELD EXPERIENCES

There are several ways that I create opportunities during field experiences for the students to gain experience in fostering questioning to enhance learning. As discussed below, approaches include enticing others, such as friends or family members, to ask questions while exploring physical phenomena together. I also ask students to create children's books that foster open-ended conversations. In addition, the students engage children in asking questions during field experiences.

Enticing Others to Ask Questions during 'Friends and Family' Assignments

One way to give students experience in fostering questioning during open-ended explorations is through homework assignments in which they engage friends or family members, preferably of the age they want to teach, in learning what they themselves have just learned in class (Crowl, Devitt, Jansen, van Zee, & Winograd, 2013). After exploring light and thermal phenomena, for example, we consider the influence of thermal conductivity, specific heat, and reflectivity in developing explanations for why one often experiences hot sand, cool water, sea breezes, and clouds forming in the sky during an afternoon at the beach. A student reflected:

> I shared my knowledge about sea breezes with my roommate…She wondered why when the warm moist air was rising, it did not take form of a white cloud. She then proceeded to ask about what a cloud really was and why on sunny days they were white and on rainy days they were grey. Together we started forming questions like "What happens when the sand cools off at night?" "What happens to the warm moist air once it becomes a cloud?" and "What does it mean when there are no clouds in the afternoon?"…I value the way… (we) were able to ask and answer each other's questions. I was really happy that my roommate felt comfortable enough to really challenge my understanding of sea breezes. If she did not understand a concept, she would ask questions until she understood…So it was really nice to have her poke and pry at what I understood. (Physics 111 student, friend/family homework assignment)

This student was learning to talk and write about science in a non-threatening context as well as to listen closely to what a science learner was saying and asking.

Creating a Children's Book Fostering Open-Ended Conversations

One homework assignment includes creating a children's book that could help children participate in open-end conversations about science. One student created a book that opened with "When you spend a day at the beach, what kinds of things do you notice?" (Eby, 2015). As shown in Figure 6.1, she also created engaging diagrams to illustrate her text:

> What does the sand feel like? Is it warm? What if you dig your toes down a little further?
>
> What about the water? Why do you think the water feels much colder than the sand? Isn't the sun shining on both of them?

Subsequent pages engage the reader in developing an explanation. The students try out their children's books with friends or family members, preferably of the age

TAKING ACTION TO LEARN BY ASKING ONE'S OWN QUESTIONS IN A PHYSICS COURSE

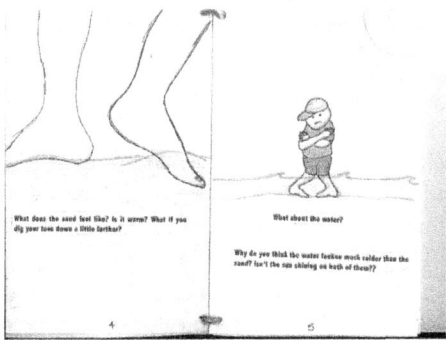

Figure 6.1. Page of children's book created by Physics 111 student

they want to teach, as well as with children during a "Discovery Day" session at the university. These sharing times provide opportunities to learn to listen closely to what learners are saying and to respond in ways that encourage further thinking and questioning.

Designing and Implementing Opportunities for Children to Ask Questions

During our university's Discovery Day for local schools, my students offer experiences using light sensors, temperature probes, and motion detectors connected to computers. In one set of activities, children can switch temperature probes between cups of hot and cold water, for example, while watching a computer drawing graphs of temperature versus time. A student wrote:

> During Discovery Day, I was at the temperature probes station and one boy asked, before I had time to ask him myself, "what would happen if we put the cold one into the hot one?" I was impressed that he (wanted to) explore that wondering on his own. So I asked him what he thought might happen. He was not sure so I narrowed it down a bit and asked what he thought the blue line on the graph would do, will it go up or down? He said up so I let him explore to find out. The boy got excited and said "wow!" when he saw his prediction come true…I learned how to foster their exploration in learning more about their questions themselves…. (Physics 111 student, reflection on Discovery Days)

Asking students to write about such experiences signals the importance of learning both about science content and also effective approaches to science pedagogy.

Students also participate in a field trip to a local elementary school to work with a small group of children to explore phenomena similar to what they have themselves explored in class. In preparation, each student designs a 5E lesson plan that includes components titled Engage, Explore, Explain, Elaborate, Evaluate (Bybee, 2014). One student described teaching children using two temperature probes and a computer interface as follows:

> I chose to offer my students a chance to generate ideas of what they already know about hot and cold thermal phenomena and then develop an experiment for them to each follow through. Each student had the opportunity to form their own hypothesis and explore with the thermal probes; while a single student would implement their chosen experiment and watch the graph, the other two students and I would help them by pouring water as needed or pressing the buttons on the computer so that the student who had developed the plan could focus on their observations. We discussed openly any disagreements about what might happen and/or any results that did or did not match our predictions. Towards the end of our time together, we discussed and wrote down the most interesting things we learned. (Physics 111 student, field trip teaching description)

As part of the final assessment, students design another 5E lesson plan to teach an aspect of the topic of climate change for the age group they are hoping to teach.

STUDENTS' REFLECTIONS ON LEARNING TO ASK AND USE QUESTIONS IN TEACHING AND LEARNING

Reflection on pedagogical issues occurs throughout the course. As discussed above under class sessions, we close each class with a group reflection where each student comments upon "what was learned?" and "what still wondering?" Homework assignments include weekly reflections on the readings, most of which include examples of practicing teachers' writing about their experiences using inquiry-based instructional approaches. As discussed below, I also ask each small group to generate and explore a question about teaching and learning science in the context of their field trip to the elementary school. Students also respond to anonymous surveys in the middle of the course and during the last session.

Generating and Exploring Pedagogical Questions about Science Teaching and Learning

While preparing for our trip to the elementary school, small groups generate questions about instructional issues to explore while teaching. A student reported:

> My group's question before we went into the classroom was "What is the balance between explaining and letting students explore on their own?"…I think that it is important to let kids explore on their own, and if they need some direction or assistance then asking them questions is a good way to teach them without actually giving them an answer. It allows them to continue exploring

with a little more guidance. An example of this was when we first started and a little girl said, "How did it do that?" and the other students got excited and started telling her excitedly. I realized that I did not really need to worry about explaining because they would figure it out from experimenting more, and they had their peers to help them.... (Physics 111 student, field trip reflection)

During the next class session, small groups talk about their questions and their experiences of working with children, record some aspect of their inquiry on a large whiteboard, and present their question and findings to the whole group for discussion.

Reflecting upon Learning and Teaching Science through Inquiry

On an anonymous online survey, I ask about ways, if any, the course is modeling learning about the cross cutting concepts specified in the new standards for teaching science in the United States. These cross cutting concepts include: patterns, cause and effect, scale, proportion, and quantity, systems and systems models, energy and matter, structure and function, stability and change (NGSS Lead States, 2013). A student wrote:

The most important to me is cause and effect because we observe what is happening first, which allows us to wonder and come up with our own idea of why that is happening. Then we are able to put it into experiments where we try different things to learn the effects of why it occurred. (Physics 111 student, online survey response)

On an anonymous survey at the end of the course, a student reported an increased interest in science and wrote,

Science has always been more challenging for me and therefore pretty boring. This class made me feel excited to learn again.

Another student indicated an increased intention to teach science through inquiry and wrote,

This class showed me how important it is to actively explore science concepts.

INSTRUCTOR REFLECTION

What have I learned through designing and teaching an inquiry-based physics course that encourages students to take action to learn by asking questions of their own? I recognize the importance of engaging students both "in doing things and in discussing what arises in the course of their doing" (Dewey, 1916, p. 183). Focusing like Dewey on "doing things" has meant involving students in inquiries broadly defined by myself as the instructor with opportunities for small groups to generate and explore their *own* questions within those contexts. "Doing things" also has included having students reflect on stories written by experienced teachers about teaching science through inquiry as well as involving students in planning and teaching science this way themselves during various field experiences.

The "discussing what arises in the course of their doing" aspect emphasized by Dewey has taken many forms in my course. I have guided students to ask and answer questions during small group conversations, large group discussions, and through talking about science with friends and family members at home, with individual children during Discovery Day at the university, and with small groups of children at a local elementary school. Here the emphasis has been on students asking questions that help clarify and communicate their ideas, develop explanations, and interpret what others are saying and doing.

My students have asked questions in multiple contexts for multiple purposes, similar to those reported by Chin and Osborne (2008) in their review. The students all entered the course knowing something about the moon, for example, but expressed puzzlement and wonderment as they observed that the moon seems to move east to west across the sky during several hours but west to east over several days. I encouraged them to formulate their own questions to explore within the context of our investigations in class. In their reflections at the end of each class session, they often expressed wonderings in which they made connections among related ideas. They reported many questions friends and family asked to clarify meanings and propose explanations during explorations at home and often referred to their own questions that emerged as they deepened their understanding through these conversations. As the instructor, I both valued and felt challenged by the questions my students asked. Questions I anticipated provided insights into where the students were in their thinking. Those that surprised me deepened my own understanding and often prompted me to modify my plans, particularly questions they expressed during our "what learned?", "what still wondering" reflections at the end of class.

What am I still wondering about? Like the students quoted above, I ponder the balance between "explaining and letting students explore on their own." How can I continue ensuring adequate 'time to play' while choosing to add new topics? I take seriously anonymous suggestions for improvement such as, "I think it would be helpful to have fewer or shorter activities during class. This would allow us to naturally come to conclusions rather than be rushed into them or given the answer," a comment I attribute directly to my having added new activities and discussions about weather and climate change without sufficient cutting of existing material. I also am contemplating suggestions gleaned from the professional literature for teaching new ways to formulate high quality questions. The main question that I continue to pose for myself is: Which way and how should I incorporate such guidance within our current practices?

This chapter is designed to describe and share my ongoing efforts in an evolving process of designing, trying, and pondering structures that facilitate helping students' learn to engage in questions of their own to make choices and develop strategies for their own learning. My hope is that others will find such examples inspiring and hopefully, useful in their own settings.

REFERENCES

American Association of Physics Teachers. (2001). *Powerful ideas in physical science*. College Park, MD: American Association of Physics Teachers.

Bybee, R. (2014). The BSCS 5E instructional model: Personal reflections and contemporary implications. *Science and Children, 51*(8), 10–13.

Chin, C., & Osborne, J. (2008). Students' questions: A potential resource for teaching and learning science. *Studies in Science Education, 44*(1), 1–39. doi:10.1080/03057260701828101

Chin, C., & Osborne, J. (2010). Students' questions and discursive interaction: Their impact on argumentation during collaborative group discussions in science. *Journal of Research in Science Teaching, 47*(7), 883–908. doi:10.1002/tea.20385

Cochran-Smith, M., & Lytle, S. (1993). *Inside outside: Teacher research and knowledge*. New York, NY: Teachers College Press.

Crowl, M., Devitt, A., Jansen, H., van Zee, E., & Winograd, K. (2013). Encouraging prospective teachers to engage friends and family in exploring physical phenomena. *Journal of Science Teacher Education, 24*(1), 93–110. doi:10.1007/s10972-012-9310-3

Cuccio-Schirripa, S., & Steiner, H. E. (2000). Enhancement and analysis of science question level for middle school students. *Journal of Research in Science Teaching, 37*(2), 210–224.

Devitt, A. (2010). *Implementing science notebooks and reading strategies in a physics course for prospective elementary and middle school teachers*. Master's Project, Oregon State University, Corvallis, OR.

Dewey, J. (1916). *Democracy and education*. New York, NY: Macmillian.

Doris, E. (1991). *Doing what scientists do: Children learn to investigate their world*. Portsmouth, NH: Heinemann.

Eby, B. (2015). *A day at the beach*. Unpublished manuscript.

Gallas, K. (1995). *Talking their way into science: Hearing children's questions and theories, responding with curricula*. New York, NY: Teachers College Press.

Hammer, D. (2000). Student resources for learning introductory physics. *American Journal of Physics, 68*(S1), S52–S59.

Hammer, D., & van Zee, E. H. (Eds.). (2006). *Seeing the science in children's thinking: Case studies of student inquiry in physical science*. Portsmouth, NH: Heinemann.

Hogan, K. (2007). How can playing with a motion detector help children learn to write clear sequential directions? In D. Roberts, C. Bove, & E. van Zee (Eds.), *Teacher research: Stories of learning and growing* (pp. 2–9). Arlington, VA: National Science Teachers Association Press.

Iwasyk, M. (1997). Kids questioning kids: "Experts" sharing. *Science and Children, 35*(1), 42–46.

Kelly, G. J. (2007). Discourse in science classrooms. In S. Abell & N. Lederman (Eds.), *Handbook of research on science education* (pp. 443–470). New York, NY: Routledge.

Kurose, A. (2000). Eyes on science: Asking questions about the moon on the playground, in class, and at home. In J. Minstrell & E. van Zee (Eds.), *Inquiring into inquiry learning and teaching in science* (pp. 139–147). Washington, DC: American Association for the Advancement of Science. Retrieved from http://www.aaas.org/programs/education/about_ehr/pubs/inquiry.shtml

Lemke, J. (1990). *Talking science: Language, learning, and values*. Westport, CT: Ablex.

Loughran, J. (2007.) Researching teacher education practices: Responding to the challenges, demands, and expectations of self-study. *Journal of Teacher Education, 58*(1), 12–20.

McDermott, L. C. (1990). A perspective on teacher preparation in physics and other sciences: The need for special science courses for teachers. *American Journal of Physics, 58*(8), 734–742.

McDermott, L. C. (2006). Preparing K-12 teachers in physics: Insights from history, experience, and research. *American Journal of Physics, 74*(9), 758–762.

McDermott, L. C., & The Physics Education Group. (1996). *Physics by inquiry*. New York, NY: John Wiley & Sons.

Mehan, H. (1979). *Learning lessons: Social organization in the classroom*. Cambridge, MA: Harvard University Press.

Minstrell, J. (1982). Explaining the "at rest" condition of an object. *The Physics Teacher, 20*(1), 10–14.

Minstrell, J. (1992). Facets of students' knowledge and relevant instruction. In R. Duit, F. Goldberg, & H. Niedderer (Eds.), *Research in physics learning: Theoretical issues and empirical studies* (pp. 110–128). Kiel: IPN.

Minstrell, J. (2000). Implications for teaching and learning inquiry: A summary. In J. Minstrell & E. van Zee (Eds.), *Inquiring into inquiry learning and teaching in science* (pp. 471–496). Washington, DC: American Association for the Advancement of Science. Retrieved from http://www.aaas.org/report/inquiring-inquiry-learning-and-teaching-science

National Research Council. (1996). *National science education standards*. Washington, DC: National Academies Press. Retrieved from http://www.nap.edu/openbook.php?isbn=0309053269

National Research Council. (2012). *A framework for K-12 science education: Practices, crosscutting concepts, and core ideas*. Washington, DC: National Academies Press. Retrieved from http://www.nap.edu/openbook.php?record_id=13165

NGSS Lead States. (2013). *Next generation science standards: For states, by states*. Washington, DC: National Academies Press. Retrieved from http://www.nextgenscience.org

Pearce, C. (1999). *Nurturing inquiry: Real science for the elementary classroom*. Portsmouth, NH: Heinemann.

Roberts, D. (1999). The sky's the limit: Parents and first-grade students observe the sky. *Science and Children, 37*(1), 33–37.

Roberts, D., Bove, C., & van Zee, E. H. (Eds.). (2007). *Teacher research: Stories of learning and growing*. Arlington, VA: National Science Teachers Association.

Robinson, S., Goldberg, F., & Otero, V. (2012). *Physics and everyday thinking*. Mount Kisco, NY: It's About Time, Inc.

Roth, K. (2007). Teachers as researchers. In S. Abell & N. Lederman (Eds.), *Handbook of research on science education* (pp. 1203–1260). New York, NY: Routledge.

Rothstein, D., & Santana, L. (2011). Teaching students to ask their own questions: One small change can yield big results. *Harvard Education Letter, 27*(5), 1–2.

Rowe, M. B. (1986). Wait time: Slowing down may be a way of speeding up! *Journal of Teacher Education, 37*(1), 43–50.

Rutherford, F. J., Holton, G., & Watson, F. G. (1971). *Project physics*. New York, NY: Holt, Rinehart, & Winston.

Shapiro, B. (1994). *What children bring to light: A constructivist perspective on children's learning in science*. New York, NY: Teachers College Press.

Shapiro, B. (1996). A case study of change in elementary science student teacher thinking during an independent investigation in science: Learning about "the face of science that does not yet know." *Science Education, 80*(5), 535–560.

Shapiro, B. (2015). Questioning for teaching and learning in science. In R. Gunstone (Ed.), *Encyclopedia of science education*. Dordrecht: Springer. doi:10.1007/978-94-007-6165-0_205-2

Sharkawy, A. (2010). A quest to improve helping students learn how to pose investigable questions. *Science and Children, 48*(4), 32–35.

Shulman, L. (2004). *Teaching as community property: Essays on higher education*. San Francisco, CA: Jossey-Bass.

Tobin, K. (1987). The role of wait time in higher cognitive learning. *Review of Educational Research, 57*(1), 69–95.

Ukens, L., Hein, W. W., Johnson, P. A., & Layman, J. (2004). Powerful ideas in physical science. *Journal of College Science Teaching, 33*(7), 38–41.

van Zee, E. H. (2000). Analysis of a student-generated inquiry discussion. *International Journal of Science Education, 22*(2), 115–142.

van Zee, E. H. (2015). *Physics 111 course wiki*. Retrieved from http://physics.oregonstate.edu/coursewikis/ph111

van Zee, E. H., & Minstrell, J. (1997a). Reflective discourse: Developing shared understandings in a high school physics classroom. *International Journal of Science Education, 19*(2), 209–228.

van Zee, E. H., & Minstrell, J. (1997b). Using questioning to guide student thinking. *The Journal of the Learning Sciences, 6*, 229–271.

van Zee, E. H., & Roberts, D. (2001). Using pedagogical inquiries as a basis for learning to teach: Prospective teachers' perceptions of positive science learning experiences. *Science Education, 85*(6), 733–757.

van Zee, E. H., Iwasyk, M., Kurose, A., Simpson, D., & Wild, J. (2001). Student & teacher questioning during conversations about science. *Journal of Research in Science Teaching, 38*(2), 159–190.

van Zee, E. H., Lay, D., & Roberts, D. (2003). Fostering collaborative inquiries by prospective and practicing elementary and middle school teachers. *Science Education, 87*(4), 588–612.

van Zee, E. H., Hammer, D., Bell, M., Roy, P., & Peter, J. (2005). Learning and teaching science as inquiry: A case study of elementary school teachers' investigations of light. *Science Education, 89*(6), 1007–1042.

van Zee, E. H., Jansen, H., Winograd, K., Crowl, M., & Devitt, A. (2013a). Fostering scientific thinking by prospective teachers in a course that integrates physics and literacy learning. *Journal of College Science Teaching, 42*(5), 29–35.

van Zee, E. H., Jansen, H., Winograd, K., Crowl, M., & Devitt, A. (2013b). Integrating physics and literacy learning in a physics course for prospective elementary and middle school teachers. *Journal of Science Teacher Education, 24*(3), 665–691. doi:10.1007/s10972-012-9323-y

van Zee, E. H., Roberts, D., & Grobart, E. (2016). Ways to include climate change in courses for teachers. *Journal of College Science Teaching, 45*(3), 28–33.

Volkmann, M. J., & Zgagacz, M. (2004). Learning to teach physics through inquiry: The lived experience of a graduate teaching assistant. *Journal of Research in Science Teaching, 41*(6), 584–602.

Zeichner, K. M., & Noffke, S. E. (2001). Practitioner research. In V. Richardson (Ed.), *Handbook of research on teaching* (pp. 298–330). Washington, DC: American Educational Research Association.

Emily Hanke van Zee
Department of Physics
Oregon State University, USA

APPENDIX

For my postdoctoral research project, I collaborated with a high school teacher, Jim Minstrell, in exploring how he used questioning to guide student thinking (van Zee & Minstrell, 1997a, 1997b). As shown below, I created a visual way to represent questions and comments that he, as the class teacher, and his students made during a discussion. On large pieces of poster paper, I drew vertical rectangles to record questions, their form (noted above each question) and function (noted below the question). I also drew horizontal rectangles whose lengths represented the duration of student comments.

Figure 6.2 represents a typical teacher-dominated discourse pattern known as a series of IREs (Mehan, 1979). An IRE is a teacher *I*nitiated question, short student *R*esponse, followed by a teacher *E*valuation and typically, the next teacher question.

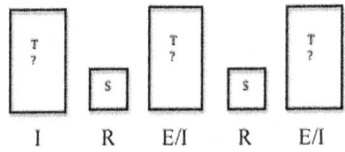

Figure 6.2. Visual representation of a series of IREs, read left to right

The vertical rectangles represent a series of teacher questions as well as their forms and functions. The short horizontal rectangles represent brief student responses. This representation conveys visually the constraint that IREs impose on students responding with extended explanations and/or questions.

What I was attempting to document through studying Minstrell's teaching was a different pattern that I was observing, instances in which the teacher's questions prompted elaborated student responses as shown in Figure 6.3. Minstrell described many of his questions as *reflective tosses*. He envisioned catching the meaning of a student's prior utterance and tossing responsibility for thinking back to the student, for example, "What do you mean by [the term] 'average' here?" (van Zee & Minstrell, 1997, p. 235). He asked such questions to make meanings clear, to explore various points of view in a neutral manner, and to help students monitor the discussion and their own thinking

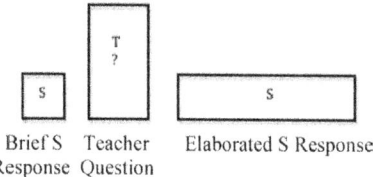

Figure 6.3. Visual representation of a teacher question (vertical rectangle) that prompted an elaborated student response (long horizontal rectangle)

This representation conveys visually the open opportunity that such teacher questions provide for a student to respond with an extended statement of what he or she is thinking. Such a discourse structure puts other students in the conversationally appropriate position to take action to learn by asking a question as shown in Figure 6.4.

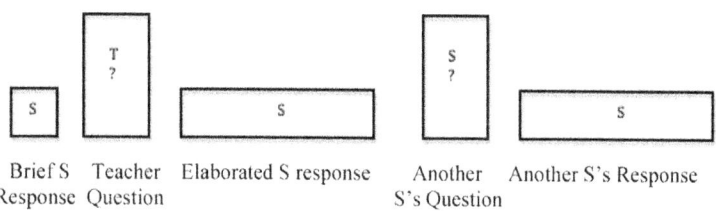

Figure 6.4. Visual representation of a teacher question (left vertical rectangle) that initiates a student-generated inquiry discussion with students both asking (right vertical rectangle) and answering questions (long horizontal rectangles)

In this pattern, I noted that if the teacher stayed quiet and waited, another student might risk asking a question. Then other students might be inspired to take action to learn by responding with their own additional ideas and subsequent questions.

BONNIE SHAPIRO

7. PRIMARY SCHOOL STUDENTS' CONSTRUCTIONS OF HELP-SEEKING

A Resource for the Design of Learning Environments

Observation in a grade 3–4 classroom during a STEM construction activity:

The children have collected materials for group work on building a tower. Alin approaches her teacher at the front of the class.

    Aline: Ms. M., I am not quite sure what it is we are supposed to do now. What, um…which items we are…

    Ms. M.:   Weren't you listening? I just explained. Go back to your group now and ask what it is you are to do.

INTRODUCTION – WHAT IS THE STUDENT ASKING FOR?

This report on research emerges from ongoing studies of the ways children take actions of their own to learn by seeking help when needed school settings. During interviews with teachers about individual children's learning there is sometimes irritation expressed regarding students' ways of asking for help and the need to take time to answer their questions. In one interview a teacher described a child who appeared to ask questions at inappropriate times and constantly. Work with students has led me to consider if perhaps educators might usefully ask the question, 'What is it that the student is really asking for?' and 'Can we help students learn to ask for help in the most effective ways?' Deborah Britzman (2004) has said, "We need to create spaces where learners are able to put into words what their worries are."

Over many years I have conducted longitudinal studies to understand personal engagement factors and features of learning environments that give insight into why some students seem to readily grasp science concepts that others struggle to understand (Shapiro, 1994). One striking observation during this time was that while some students seem regularly ask for help when needed in learning, many avoid requesting assistance. In some classrooms there are rules about how to ask for help, but in most, there is uncertainty about when to ask and how. Students cannot predict what will happen when they muster the courage needed to ask for help, and their requests are met with a wide range of responses from teachers and fellow students.

This chapter describes the use of a research approach designed to include young children's own language and thinking to understand the ideas and concerns that influence their decisions to take action to ask for help. The research is built on the assumption that by understanding the ways that children think about seeking help when needed in learning, educators will be better able to design environments that encourage and support learners' own help-seeking efforts. It is designed to gain new insights in the best ways to help students by creating new institutional structures to help them learn.

RESEARCH ON HELP-SEEKING IN LEARNING ENVIRONMENTS

Educators, researchers and psychologists of learning have agreed that one of the most important skills children develop to facilitate their own learning is the ability to seek appropriate help when needed from others (Alevin, Stahl, Schworm, Fischer, & Wallace, 2003; Gardner, 2007; Karabenick, 1998; Meichenbaum & Biemiller, 1998; Shapiro, 2008). Although taking action to secure help when needed may seem to involve simply making a simple request for assistance, the act of seeking help engages students in the use of a complex repertoire of linguistic skills, social abilities and capacities that must be developed. For many students, seeking help is an act fraught with worry about the difficulty and risks associated with it, and it is an act to be avoided (Ryan, Pintrich, & Midgley, 2001). The child's first ideas about seeking help when needed are provided by their most significant role models very early in life. The child observes the ways adults or others in their lives decide if and how to ask for help. They observe their ways of determining when to ask, use of language, body language and gestures, comfort level, timing of the request, who is approached and who is avoided. And they also observe the frustrations and successes in the effort to access assistance when needed. The child's observations of their models' attitudes and orientations to seeking help suggest to them how to know when one needs help, how and when safe it is ask for help, who to seek help from, how to most effectively frame a request for help, whether or not to persist in seeking help when needed and how to follow up once help is given or not given. These observations are used to build powerful frameworks and a model for acting when experiencing difficulty throughout the child's life. But children also construct meaning about seeking help using resources available through social interactions and understandings acquired through engagement in learning environments that have been constructed for them. From a semiotic interpretive perspective, they read the actions of others and learn to use this knowledge as a resource that is based on observations of those close to them interwoven with traditions and practices with the family, the community and learning settings (Shapiro, 1998; Shapiro & Kirby, 1998).

PERSONAL CONSTRUCT THEORY AS A FOUNDATION TO RESEARCH CONSTRUCTIONS OF SEEKING HELP WHEN LEARNING

George Kelly's Personal Construct Theory (PCT), (1963, 2003) provides a particularly useful theoretical foundation and data gathering tools to engage in research on children's meaning making. PCT stresses the importance of understanding the ways human beings construct meaning about the events in their lives, not simply their reactions to events. Meaning making is not only a personal matter. It is mediated by language, through engagement in social settings and through the interpretation of social and cultural values and institutional structures, making this particularly valuable in understanding learning in school settings. The use of language (Halliday, 1978; Lemke, 2003) and the sign and signification systems in learning environments (Danesi, 2007; Shapiro, 1998, 2008, 2014) are among the most significant communication vehicles of cultural traditions used and perpetuated by learners and educators. The research was conducted "*in action*" during a unit of study in a grade three/four split classroom in order to observe and describe children's actions to seek help while learning, but also to engage them in discussions to learn how they described the thinking that guided their actions.

Three key research strategies were used in the study based on the theoretical foundations of Personal Construct Theory: (1) Classroom observations and records of classroom conversations as students worked in groups of three and four on the Technology design task, "Building a Tower"; (2) Interviews with children using the online collaborative data-gathering tool, WEBGRID III to organize and represent Repertory Grid interview data; and (3) Additional personal conversations with participants and their teachers to learn about classroom experiences, ideas about learning and views about seeking help in learning. The Repertory Grid interview is a powerful technique emerging from Personal Construct Theory that allows the representation and exploration of an individual's idea constructions, language and views about a study topic. Details of the steps and procedures involved in the grid interview are described in the section below.

THE RESEARCH APPROACH

Over a four-week period, classroom observations of six students, ongoing conversations and the Repertory Grid Interviews were recorded and analysed to allow representation of the thoughts, feelings and strategies of student engagement in the tower building activity. Three of the student case reports and display grids are presented in this chapter using Webgrid III. Webgrid III is an online data collection and analysis tool used with the individual children in the study to generate personal constructs and as a resource to engage in conversation. Webgrid III can be used to organize data into Grid Displays. It also generates representations of participant knowledge using cluster analysis. In the present research, Repertory Grid interviews reveal the linguistic categories that each individual uses as a resource to understand and engage in the task of seeking help.

Repertory Grid technique, developed by George Kelly (1963) has been used extensively in a wide range of social science research settings. The procedure first involves creating a list of Elements or topics. In this study the list of topics features the kinds of help-seeking activities children typically engage in, in the school setting. Participants assist with the generation of Elements with the researcher to assure that

Element items are stated using children's own language. The 9 Elements generated were: (1) Watch the other kids to find out what to do; (2) Ask the teacher for help; (3) Figure out what to do on my own; (4) Ask a friend for help; (5) Ask another student who usually knows what to do; (6) Look in a book for help; (7) Ask my parent or guardian; (8) Re-read the directions on the worksheet or board to figure out what to do; and (9) Do nothing. The list of Elements is entered into the Webgrid program, which then randomly presented three Elements for review. A procedure is followed to generate personal constructs: Each participant is asked to indicate which two Elements they consider to be similar in some way, and different from the third. For example, Student A was given these three Elements: *(2) Ask the teacher for help*, *(4) Ask a friend for help*, and *(1) Watch the other kids to find out what to do*. Student A grouped Elements 4 and 1 and said that both items involve, "Getting ideas from my friends," while Element 2 is different because it involves, "Just getting help directly from the teacher." The elicitation procedure continues with randomly generated sets of Elements and the organization and production of personal constructs by participants. In this way, individuals' own linguistic structures describing their ideas about help-seeking and help-giving are captured. These structures are called constructs. In the application of Repertory Grid in the present research, the interviews with students were developed as a collaborative conversation and involved discussion between participants and researchers about the topic of study, the learning activity students were involved with at the time and ideas about help-seeking and help-giving. Use of the Repertory Grid allows for clarification of ideas, first, as the initial grid generating activity proceeds and then, during the construct elicitation process. Use of the technique allows a representation of each individual's ideas using their own language structures to describe experience. Grids may also be compared to show similarities and differences among individuals or groups. Each single grid can be usefully further analysed for content and structure. The visual grids that are generated are useful in comparing individual and group structures and importantly, for engaging in discussions with both students and teachers about their meaning.

Six children were followed and interviewed in the research and case reports were constructed for each child. Case reports for three students are presented in this chapter. Marie, Shenai, and Alan. During 10 class sessions devoted to the tower design and building activity, observational data, conversations, and Repertory Grid conversations were recorded and analysed. The group of six students included three boys and three girls and was based on teacher and student self reports. It represented a range of students experiencing high, average and low academic achievement levels. The students demonstrated a range of high, average and low help-seeking skills, and a range of confidence levels as reported by their teacher. A range of levels of interest in science learning was also expressed by students themselves. The reports presented in this chapter summarize and discuss the constructs of Marie, Shenai, and Alan. Information in each individual is presented along with self-reports and teacher reports of student achievement and views on their help-seeking abilities. Marie is considered to be achieving at a high academic level with high help-seeking skills. Shenai demonstrated achievement at a low academic level and demonstrates low help-seeking skills. Alan is considered to be working at a high academic level and demonstrates high help-seeking skills. Summary reports describe in-class observations and accompany each students' display grid and knowledge constructions in order to discuss individual student goals and ideas about help-seeking while they were learning.

The science curriculum program structure used in this setting is based on provincial government guidelines and includes within each grade level, five topics of study. Topics are balanced to include physical science, chemical science, and biology. Within There is also an instructional focus each set of five topics per grade level, one focuses on *problem solving through technology*. The classroom was a large split grade 3/4 class taught by Ms. Bea, Ms. Chin and a teaching assistant. During the set of lessons and activities observed, all students were engaged with the grade three technology topic, *Building with a variety of materials*. The teachers also integrated a building activity into the lessons using second topic from the grade three program titled, *Testing materials and designs*. These topics were combined because of the potential for planning activities to lead to student engagement in inquiry as students tested materials and made decisions about which kinds of materials might be best suited to construct a tower structure. In the "building activity," students used and tested a range of materials, shapes and thicknesses to find out what makes a structure strong and stable and to find out how much material is needed to build to design specifications. In the testing materials portion of the activity, students engaged in an inquiry to learn which shapes and structures are particularly strong. The teachers indicated that they had noted so many parallels between the two topics in the curriculum that they began to see them as one unit of study. During the first session, students worked in groups with a variety of different materials to learn about their relative strength of the materials and ease of use in building the tower. Students shared their experiences and discussed their structures at the end of the session. In the second session, students were given the task of working in groups to build a tall, at least 30 cm, stable tower structure that would hold a hard-boiled egg placed at the top for 30 seconds or longer. Students worked with a variety of materials and were asked to make decisions about which materials worked best. During the sessions 4–6, all student groups worked with only one type of material decided by the entire class. They chose plastic straws. An interesting feature of Ms. Bea's instructions to the students during the fourth session involved guidance and foreshadowing to develop one of the learning objectives of the "testing materials" unit. She suggested that students could employ more methods for making a structure stronger and more stable, by, for example, but adding or joining parts to form triangles. As the teacher explained the task to students, she showed students two rectangles and three triangles made from straws. "We are going to use different shapes in our tower designs," she says. "Look at these shapes. These might be some shapes that we use. You can make any kinds of shapes you wish. Sometimes it may make the tower stronger if you put together shapes, like this… [She demonstrates using two triangles, then three, to show how strong several shapes

127

together can be]." The large number of tasks required of students were: to understand the verbally stated purposes of the activities; organize into activity groups; work with one another to gather the correct type and amount of material to work with; read task instructions; engage with fellow students in the activity challenge; assess the group's success and task achievement; compare their tower with the designs produced by other groups; engage in whole class discussions about the overall achievement of assigned tasks; and follow instructions to dismantle and store materials.

CASE REPORTS AND REPERTORY GRID ANALYSES

In the pages that follow, display grids are shown to demonstrate some of the features and insights of grid representations of constructs. The three individuals selected for discussion and comparison below demonstrated different ideas about seeking help that are shown in their individual grid display. Each grid display is accompanied by observational and interview data including teacher observations, students' own self reports and researcher observations.

Marie

Marie was 9 years old and in Grade 3 at the time of the research. Classroom observations and conversations with Marie and her teacher reveal a remarkable social presence and confidence in the classroom. She regularly engages in conversation with her peers, both getting and giving help, yet she rarely asks her teacher for assistance. She is identified by her teacher as an average to high achiever (Table 7.1) with an average interest in science, the subject matter in this case, and with average to high help-seeking skills. Her teacher rates her as average to high in self-confidence in learning and with high acceptance among her peers and high in social skills. Marie identifies herself as an average achiever academically with average interest in science. Marie's mother is an elementary school teacher. Marie comments that she spends time in her mother's classroom and plans to become a teacher. She says that she likes the way her mother works with the children in her class. The opportunity to consider learning through the lens of her mother's role appeared to have given Marie an unusual depth of insight into the teacher's role in learning and her view of herself as learner.

Table 7.1. Marie, female, grade 3, age: 9 years, 1 month

	Teacher observations	Student self report
Academic achievement:	Average-High	Average
Interest in science:	Average	Average
Help-seeking skills:	Average-High	
Self-confidence:	Average-High	
Peer acceptance/social skills:	High	

Researcher/Observations/Themes

Strong social presence; asks peers for help and regularly gives help to peers, often observing the need for help in others, but rarely asks for help from the teacher.

```
DISPLAY: Marie
Domain: Personal Constructs
Context: Help-seeking behavior, 9 elements, 6 constructs
```

	Construct A	Ratings	Construct B
	No risk	3 1 1 5 1 1 1 1 5	Risk of being laughed at
	Will know the answer and will help you	2 3 4 2 2 1 1 3 5	Not really sure that there will BE help
	Allowed – it is OK	1 1 1 1 3 1 1 5	Not allowed
	Using your own mind	4 4 1 4 4 5 3 1 4	Not really trying to discover the answer on your own
Progressing – testing your brain. Know what you need to know to go on		4 2 1 5 4 2 3 1 5	Not progressing. Not learning, sitting playing, getting in trouble
Doing your share. Trying and doing your part in group		4 5 1 2 4 1 1 1 5	Not doing your share. Not trying & you have to report to your group

```
                              9. Do nothing
                           8. Re-read the directions on the worksheet or board to figure out what to do
                         7. Ask my parent or guardian for help
                       6. Look in a book for help
                     5. Ask another student who usually knows what to do
                   4. Ask a friend for help
                 3. Figure out on my own what to do
               2. Ask the teacher for help
             1. Watch the other kids to find out what to do
```

Figure 7.1. Marie, display grid

Marie's Display Grid (Figure 7.1)

Marie shows a very extensive range of thinking and constructs about help-seeking. The elaboration of constructs shows that she draws on many different ideas associated with ideas about how to seek help. She showed in her work with the grid how she thinks about taking responsibility to give help as a member of a learning community. Marie's language and constructs show an intensive and primary interest in considering how she is perceived in the classroom when seeking assistance.

The number and range of distinctions in Marie's constructs demonstrates her concern about being humiliated, *Risk of being laughed at* when asking for help. She shows that although she ranks as "none to minimal" (ranked 1), her construct, *Risk of being laughed at* when assessing "Element 2. Ask the teacher for help," she indicates that there is great potential risk when asking a friend for help (ranked 5). As Marie was observed to rarely ask the teacher for assistance, all of the rankings for "Element 2. Ask the teacher for help" were of interest. Marie demonstrated a well-developed idea about her responsibility as a member of her study group as seen in her construct, *Doing your share/Not doing your share*. It is revealing that she ranks "Element 2. Asking the teacher for help" strongly as an aspect of *Not doing your share* and the "Element 3. Figure out on my own what to do" as strongly representing *Doing your share*. She ranks "Element (1) Watching the other kids to find out what to do" and "Element (5) Ask a student who usually knows what to do" as strongly representative of her construct, *Not really trying to answer on your own,* as well as *Not doing your share in the group.* She talks about using the strategy, "using my own mind to learn" and says that she feels "I am making progress when I try to figure things out on my own." Her view that she is "not doing her job" can be seen in her ranking of "Element (2) Ask the teacher for help." It is ranked as strongly consistent with her construct, *Not really trying to discover the answer on your own.* Marie's ratings of "Element 9. Doing nothing," generated the largest number of negative outcomes (as shown by the large number of 5s and one 4). Her constructs reveal a strongly developed sense of responsibility as a member of her learning community, "I try to help the other people in my group when I can because then we are all doing a good job."

Shenai

Shenai was nearly 9 years old at the time of the research and a Grade 3 student. Classroom observations and conversations with Shenai and her teacher reveals her struggle in the classroom with academic achievement. They also showed her intense interests in both achieving understanding in science being accepted and involved socially (Table 7.2). Shenai often does not appear to understand the requirements of learning tasks or what it is that she should do next. She seeks help from peers regularly and is always ready to give help to fellow students when asked, but is often ignored by peers when she asks for help. Rarely does she ask her teacher for assistance. She is identified by her teacher as a low achiever, with low interest in studying science and very low help-seeking skills. Her teacher rates her low in self-confidence in learning and with average acceptance among her peers and in social skills. Shenai identifies herself as a low achiever academically with low interest in science. Her repertory grid ratings and constructs show that she has a limited repertoire of strategies for seeking help when needed.

Table 7.2. Shenai, female, grade 3, age: 8 years, 10 months

	Teacher observations	Student self report
Academic achievement:	Low	Low
Interest in science:	Low	Low
Help-seeking skills:	Very Low	
Self-confidence:	Low	
Peer acceptance/social skills:	Average	

Researcher Observations/Themes

Shenai shows intense interest in being involved socially and in being involved with others in science study. She often does not know what to do or how to proceed but appears to keep working even when she has the wrong ideas about how to proceed;

PRIMARY SCHOOL STUDENTS' CONSTRUCTIONS OF HELP-SEEKING

solitary persistence in activities when she does not understand what to do; issues of low self esteem; low academic ability.

Shenai does not appear to know how to frame her concerns in order to ask for help effectively. Peers often ignore her questions and regular requests for help. She does not ask the teacher for help but waits for the teacher to come to her. Despite this she shows great interest in persisting in learning even when she is clearly working ineffectively.

DISPLAY: Shenai
Domain: Personal Constructs
Context: Help-seeking behavior, 9 elements, 6 constructs

Do something not sitting around	1 1 1 1 1 1 1 1 5	Not doing anything
You don't have to do reading	1 1 1 1 1 5 1 5 1	You have to do reading
Easy	1 1 3 1 3 5 3 5 1	Difficult
Is about asking someone	3 1 5 3 1 3 1 5 3	Is about working on your own
This is what you do before before you have trouble	1 5 3 1 3 5 5 5 3	This is what you do after you have trouble
Sometimes I do this	1 3 1 3 1 1 1 3 5	Don't usually do this

9. Do nothing
8. Re-read the directions on the worksheet or board to figure out what to do
7. Ask my parent or guardian for help
6. Look in a book for help
5. Ask another student who usually knows what to do
4. Ask a friend for help
3. Figure out on my own what to do
2. Ask the teacher for help
1. Watch the other kids to find out what to do

Figure 7.2. Shenai, display grid

Shenai's Display Grid (Figure 7.2)

Observations of Shenai during lessons and conversations with her teachers show that she is working with a very limited set of ideas and ideas about actions to take that might serve as a resource to guide her thoughts and actions when she needs help. In conversation Shenai is not able to express her specific personal goals or the strategies she uses in her approaches to seeking help. She is not able to express ideas about what she believes is important as she is working to complete tasks. Shenai's grid shows that she makes very few distinctions as she ranks the elements using her constructs indicating a very limited range of ideas about seeking help. When working with her construct, *Easy/Difficult,* she strongly ranks as *Easy*, "Element 1. Watching the other kids to find out what to do," "Element 2. Ask the teacher for help" and "Element 4. Ask a friend for help," and "Element 9. Do nothing." She ranks as *Difficult* "Element 6. Look in a book for help," and "Element 8. Re-read the directions on the worksheet or board to figure out what to do." Her construct, "You have to do reading/You don't have to do reading," shows that reading, as an action to take when she needs help is one of the greatest challenges she experiences in school. Her teacher indicates that reading is clearly at the heart of her difficulties in school learning. Conversations with Shenai show that although she is always ready to try, limited reading skills and a limited ability to identify and express her needs make up the complex repertoire of language skills that she needs yet struggles with in learning. Despite this, she continually makes regular and often courageous efforts to try to understand what is required in the task and despite their regular expressions of annoyance. She persistently strives to engage in positive ways primarily with her peers in learning. "Sometimes it is really hard to figure out what to do in science and I am not…it is not, my best subject. But I say to friends, what they are doing to get the answers… and sometimes that way I learn to do it."

Alan

Alan was also an 8-year-old Grade 3 student in the same classroom. Classroom observations and conversations with Alan and his teacher show that he is a thoughtful, careful, quiet student who always waits for others to respond before speaking up in class. He appears reluctant to ask for help even when it is clearly needed. During the research period we observed that when he does ask, he asks only his teacher for assistance. Alan's repertory grid and comments show that his major goal in his academic work is to "get the right answer," yet he also shows an interest in gaining deep understanding of content. He is very concerned with putting the correct responses in his notebook or on worksheets, yet shows a deep interest in understanding science concepts. Alan is described by his teacher as an average to high achiever with high interest in science and possessing high help-seeking skills. She believes that he has average self-confidence and average peer acceptance and social skills. Alan believes that he is a high academic achiever in science and states that he has high interest in science.

Table 7.3. Alan, male, grade 3, age: 8 years, 7 months

	Teacher observations	Student self report
Academic achievement:	Average-High	High
Interest in science:	High	High
Help-seeking skills:	High	
Self-confidence:	Average	
Peer acceptance/social skills:	Average	

Researcher Observations/Themes

Alan demonstrates a preference for working alone, even when in a group setting. He pauses and gives careful thought before responding to questions or when sharing ideas. Alan often seems reluctant to ask for help and when he does, he only from the teacher. He is a high achiever. In class work and in conversation with the researcher he expresses a strong desire to get the right answers and appears to seek deep and authentic understanding.

DISPLAY: Alan
Domain: Personal Constructs
Context: Help-seeking behavior, 9 elements, 6 constructs

Construct (left)	Ratings	Construct (right)
Finding someone who can give me an idea	3 1 4 2 2 3 1 5 3	Doing it on my own
Pretty confident they will know the answer	4 1 4 3 2 2 2 1 5	Not really doing anything not getting help. Might not get the answer
Asking someone	4 1 5 1 1 5 1 5 3	Looking in something
100% sure you're going to get the right answer	5 1 5 3 4 3 2 1 5	50% chance of figuring it out on your own
A higher percentage of figuring out the right answer	4 1 3 5 1 4 1 1 5	Pretty low percentage of figuring out
Won't make noise or disrupt class	1 2 1 5 5 1 4 1 1	May make noise and disrupt class

9. Do nothing
8. Re-read the directions on the worksheet or board to figure out what to do
7. Ask my parent or guardian for help
6. Look in a book for help
5. Ask another student who usually knows what to do
4. Ask a friend for help
3. Figure out on my own what to do
2. Ask the teacher for help
1. Watch the other kids to find out what to do

Figure 7.3. Alan, display grid

Alan's Display Grid (Figure 7.3)

Alan showed a strong, consistent pattern in his constructs and in his rankings of Elements. These ideas were clearly seen in his actions in the classroom. In both conversation and as represented in the constructs generated he describes his help-seeking strategies with an emphasis on the importance of achieving his goals: getting correct answers and the correct understanding. Secondary goals appear to be (1) Getting the right answers by disrupting the class as little as possible, and (2) Learning primarily on his own. Despite the success he achieves in classwork, Alan shows a very limited interest in working with fellow students in the classroom or in his study group either to request help from them when needed or to offer assistance to them. Four of his six constructs relate to his concern with interacting with someone who will help him to get the right idea. Although he is a strong achiever, like Shenai, his grid shows that he draws on a limited repertoire of constructions and ideas about help-seeking. His rankings for "Element 2. Ask the teacher for help," shows how this strategy strongly addresses his two major goals, but interestingly, his rankings for "Element 3. Figure it out on my own" show that he does not have a strong belief in his own ability to "get the right answers." He appears to have a high regard for knowledge that comes from his teacher. "I always ask the teacher because she is the one that will help me best." His teacher ranks his help-seeking skills as "High", perhaps because he approaches her so regularly with fairly precise questions that allow her to readily address his needs.

RESEARCH INSIGHTS FOR 21ST CENTURY LEARNING

Teachers will benefit from considering the ways they construct the social and cultural environments to support not only help-seeking, but help-giving in learning settings.

Rather than indicating dependent behaviour on the part of a student, this research is based on the view that development of the ability to reach out to others for help when needed should be seen as a valuable adaptive learning strategy. Development of the skill of seeking help can be effectively developed into an empowering self-regulating strategy not only in school learning, but also in life. To different degrees, the natural desire to help others is a valuable foundation upon which to build skills that make can make a powerful contribution to learning and to the realities of new learning experiences. Significant recent efforts to support peer mentoring in learning are just the beginning to help learners build and enhance the skill of help-giving, as well as for teachers. Engagement in this research to observe and converse with students and teachers and in the review of constructs and grid representations provides data that suggests strong potential for this work to contribute to new educational thinking about help-seeking in two ways: (1) Reconceptualising the meaning and value of asking for and giving help in learning for both teachers and students and (2) As a resource to suggest the design of structures in learning environments that support and encourage help-seeking and help-giving. Interviews and the conversations surrounding the grids with the researcher, teachers and research assistants helped identify, and in some cases initiate new ideas about why some students *may not* regularly seek help when needed in learning. Some of these include feelings of embarrassment at needing help, and avoiding a sense of indebtedness to the help giver, concerns about what may happen when reaching out for help, and a sense of the inappropriateness of asking for information and assistance when competing with fellow students for grades or speedy task completion. Many students report the significant social cost involved in asking for assistance that causes some, and in particular very capable students to be reluctant to reveal that they do not understand. In Marie's case, a considerable sense of responsibility to the group's learning is remarkable, and can be seen as a significant factor in the ease of sharing ideas, collaboration, cohesiveness and collegiality among group members. In contrast, although Alan achieves at a very high level in Science and in this STEM activity, he elects to work on his own and does not benefit from the work of the group nor does he contribute to the success of group members.

The research shows another highly significant finding: that many students both native English speakers and those new to English speaking culture do not know *how to begin* the conversation to ask for assistance.

As shown in Shenai's case report, one of the first and most difficult aspects of learning to seek assistance for students is learning to recognize when one is experiencing difficulty, and learning to frame one's needs into a request and directing questions about difficult material to those who may be able to provide assistance. Learners will benefit from the time taken to engage them in metacognitive conversations designed to help them consider the best ways to identify when they need help and how to most effectively seek help. The development of new language and interaction skills that enable the identification of social support networks one can access will help learners create features of a repertoire of skills that students can use to seek assistance to acquire needed information and competencies. Other capacities that can help students learn to help themselves include the development of the skills needed to access and evaluate library and online research resources and the creation of heuristic devices to organize information.

PEDOGOGICAL APPROACHES: DESIGNING SETTINGS TO SUPPORT HELP-SEEKING

This research, designed to understand and document individual learners' ideas and approaches reveals some of the successful strategies learners are using to get and give help, as well as unsuccessful approaches that may create obstacles to seeking help. The insights from this research will help teachers develop new ways to more effectively guide students to participate in their own learning and address features of learning environments that are disruptive to getting and giving help when needed.

One of the practical purposes of this research is to use insights and understandings shown in learner views and actions to create environments informed by learners' ideas and strategies that better support students' own efforts to seek assistance to learn. Carefully considering learner experiences and ideas about seeking help can suggest new ways to transform the design of learning settings to support and positively develop the help-seeking behaviour of children.

In addition to examining the individual strategies and constructs of children, the research program also investigates teachers' ideas and beliefs about help-seeking approaches and the ways social and cultural features in schools are organized to support help-seeking. Three example case reports are presented here to illustrate some successful teaching and organizational strategies. The examples show educators' efforts to design individual and institutional structures that encourage help-giving and receiving. These examples have been used in teacher preparation programs, and have been presented to professional conferences to inspire reflection, conversation, insights and creative new approaches to help students learn to access help when needed.

Engaging in Conversations with Students about the Hallmarks of an Effective Working Group

The acquisition of academic and technological content and literacy are skills identified as important for 21st century learning that also include communication and collaboration, initiative and self-direction, leadership and responsibility, flexibility and adaptability, social and cross-cultural skills and productivity and accountability. As much of our work in science and in STEM related activities takes place in a group, I have found great value in engaging classroom learners and student teachers in discussions about what it means to be a member of a group who are working on a task together. This metacognitive approach has been of great interest to students who are eager to learn strategies that will help them to become more involved in their own learning success. Our conversations began with a discussion about the roles and responsibilities as a teacher and their roles and responsibilities as learners. We discussed what it means to engage in effective collaboration and communication among group members. I share with group members my observations of engineers who speak about the value of "talking through and bouncing ideas off one another to solve a problem." What would that look like in our group work? We consider steps that might be taken to assure that all members of a group have a chance to take an active role in the work of the group, how the group might work to assure that each member has a chance to speak and make sure that all ideas are heard and valued as well as critiqued.

A Tool and Strategy to Support Student Participation in Their Own Learning in a Grade One Classroom

Students are deeply engaged in a writing assignment describing the ways they use senses in teacher Linnea Don.'s Grade 2 science class. Aurelia, a student in the class stops writing for a moment, looks at me and says, "Um, once. I want to spell, um, one, one, *once*. I *once* tasted, um, I got to taste lemon ice cream." Wha, wha, she speaks the sound at the beginning of the word and looks to the center of the table. She picks up a set of orange cards. She flips to the column labeled "W" and scans it carefully with her finger. No success. Marc, who sits at her table comments, "Sometime the "wha" sound is actually made with an o, like in "one." She flips over the card and looks up and down the "O" column. "Oh!" she exclaims, and puts her finger on the word. "It's right here. I found it!" Aurelia writes the word, in the sentence she is working on in her notebook and reads it: "I once got to eat lemon ice cream." In Ms. Don's class, copies of the card are available at the centre of every table in the classroom and a larger format version sits in a prominent place for additional reference on the classroom wall. The card is a resource created by primary teachers in the school for students seeking help to spell and use of commonly used words. Ms. Don has encouraged students to use the cards when writing.

Creating Social Capital—Learning the Language and Skills Needed to Take Action to Ask for Help

Teachers Liz McManus and Lindsey Bourgeois noticed that at some time all students encounter roadblocks in learning, but some students have a particularly difficult time recognizing the fact that they *need* help. These students benefit from guidance to organize their thinking and ways to ask for assistance when they need it. Some students may have learning challenges or may struggle with learning a new language. They often do not know where to start in the process of seeking assistance, a recognition that sometimes comes more readily to others. The teachers suggested several questions that students might ask to help them identify their specific needs and how to frame effectively request assistance. On a wall in their grade five classroom is a large poster that they created initially for one student in the classroom, but which has been valued by many others. It reads:

I feel like...	*I can say/ask*
I don't know how to begin.	Could you repeat the instructions, please?
I'm confused.	I'm confused. Can you help me understand?
I don't have everything I need.	What do I need to begin. I need to get a...
I've started, but have gone wrong somewhere.	Can you help me find my mistake?
I'm bored, frustrated. I don't want to do my work.	Is there a different way I can do this?
I don't have enough time.	May I have extra time to work?

By encouraging them to use the language and strategies suggested, students are given powerful tools that build social capital. Using this social capital allows learners to gain new access to practice communication structures and social networks to make their needs known. These strategies are reviewed regularly in the classroom. Students learn to identify what is behind their feelings of confusion and to see their need for help. Using this strategy, students learn to participate more effectively in their own learning.

Students Transitioning to High School Learn Take Responsibility for Their Own Learning by Asking for Help in Mathematics

Science area coordinator Jon Hoyt-Hallet described the ways teachers of grade nine students at Calgary Science School have shared ideas about ways they might work to develop students' help-seeking skills in several classes Teachers wanted to create opportunities to help students learn to take responsible action to address difficult topics in the curriculum that would translate into greater success when they leave the school in their transition to high school. They asked the school administration if they might pilot a project that set aside special periods to offer concentrated study of topics in science, mathematics and humanities, identified as being worthy of deeper study in the previous week. Students are guided to recognize their own areas of difficulty and to take action – "voting with their feet" – to attend the focused sessions they believe will benefit them most. Students identified and deepened understanding of difficult concepts in science, mathematics and humanities. They learned how they might take actions of their own to take responsibility for seeking help when encountering difficulty. In this way, students learned to frame useful questions to get the help they needed, and they built knowledge about how to take charge of their own learning.

HELP-GIVING AS A "WAY OF SOCIAL ACTION": THE VALUE OF THE RESEARCH

DeWaal (1996) argues that the desire to *provide* help is hard-wired in human beings and there is evidence of its existence in groups within the animal world. Das and Gorman (1985) wrote in their beautiful book, *How can I help?*, that asking the question, "How can I best help?" is a timeless and unceasing inquiry asked by all those in the helping professions (p. ix). On a social action scale, giving help may be conceptualized as a "way of social action." Social action approaches emerge to correct injustices, create inclusiveness, increase unity, and ease suffering. Pedagogy that concerns itself with this question can become a medium to transform individuals, learning communities and work environments in ways that promote equity and social justice. One of the most important outcomes of the continuous asking of the question, "How can I help?" may be the way that it provides new insight and information for educators interested in building stronger intellectual engagement and stronger social support networks in schools. Social support is usually defined as the range of interpersonal relationships or connections that have an impact on an individual's functioning, and generally includes support provided by individuals and by social institutions. Many organizations that provide social supports recognize that engagement to learn effective help-seeking skills and the ability to access support resources when needed are considered protective factors for many adolescent mental health and development outcomes. With the emergence of a wide and vibrant range of social networking technologies currently available, there is tremendous potential to more fully employ these resources to help students take actions of their own to acquire help.

As they work to help learners acquire science knowledge, one of the most important skills that teachers and others in the "helping professions" develop is the ability to provide effective help and encouragement to others. In order to do this, they must create environments that help students recognize when and how to ask for help and how to help others. When sharing the results of this research, I have found students and educators deeply interested in talking about ideas surrounding help-giving and help-seeking. They often describe valuing Vygotsky's (1978) discussion about the importance of the role of the caring adult who helps learners develop language and ways of acting that help them move towards achievable goals. A number of other research studies provide helpful ideas about the ways learners' help-seeking efforts can more effectively serve as adaptive responses to learning challenges (Gardner, 2007; Karabenick, 1998; Karabenick & Knapp, 1991; Karabenick & Newman, 2011), and the ways learning environments might be explicitly designed to support help-seeking, (Aleven et al., 2003; Shwalb & Sukemune, 1998; Ryan et al., 2001). While the research literature is extensive, missing from it are in depth descriptions of help-seeking *in action* in the naturalistic environments of classrooms. A goal of the present research is to add new insights through the observation of and discussions with young children in a school learning settings. The study looks at the ways individuals differ in their approaches to getting and receiving assistance when needed. In addition, research on help-giving in the literature is an activity often reported as conceptualized and undertaken primarily by teachers. Significant help may also be given by students to one another, and the development of skills to seek help when needed is an important life strategy. Information on learner thinking and actions to support of one another has not previously been reported as an important feature of environments created to support help-seeking and help-giving. As a learned strategy, the skills of seeking and giving help are built through social interaction. There are significant benefits that result from working with others in school and in life. There are occasions when students also give significant help to teachers and these instances have not been insufficiently documented or analysed. This research helps educators recognize that traditional architectural elements are powerful features in school settings may determine the ways we become culturally conditioned to think about them. The literature shows that the ways learning environments are built and organized to encourage peer assistance is an area that has not been sufficiently examined. With many emerging environments such as Maker Spaces and Learning Commons settings, there is much potential here for future work in this area.

Educators who were involved with this research study pointed to the new awareness they gained by more deeply considering this aspect of their practice. These discussions show the complexities, assumptions and challenges involved in organizing learning environments and the value of considering the ways learners' own concerns and voices inform the design of learning settings. I have used the results to engage in discussions with both students and teachers to help them reflect on the depth and complexity of their help-seeking strategies. Of considerable value in the conversations with student teachers have been discussions surrounding ways to guide students to build better positive mental habits such as self-discipline, development of an intrinsic interest in learning well and showing students how, when engaging in learning activities such as the tower building activity, to best perform at one's highest potential when working with others. This means understanding students' natural approaches to their work, particularly when they are deeply engaged, and assisting them to develop new strategies to work cooperatively with others in work and learning communities. The research techniques used in this study reveal the processes involved when seeking help, the ideas and kinds of language learners themselves contribute to understanding help-seeking as an overlooked strategic resource for learners and teachers in the elementary classroom.

There are other very important secondary outcomes for those engaged in the process, such as the development of the learner's sense of competence and view of self as successful in learning. Other skills and abilities are also developed, such as mental habits of self-discipline, the development of an intrinsic interest in learning what it means to learn well and to assure that one is learning for the purpose of gaining authentic, deep understanding of the subject of study. Students also recognize that in order to achieve at their highest potential there is value in learning to work cooperatively. Success in these areas can lead to the development of clear ideas about the real purposes of learning, and what it means to engage in learning for its own sake rather than completing tasks simply to receive a mark or grade. These outcomes are essential to help students develop the confidence to persist in and enjoy learning. They can also help learners develop the skills to take more responsibility to participate in their own learning and to see value in helping to support the work of others, developing this valuable skill not only for use in school, but as a resource for learning for living as a compassionate and giving human being.

REFERENCES

Aleven, V., Stahl, E., Schworm, S., Fischer, F., & Wallace, R. (2003). Help seeking and help design in interactive learning environments. *Review of Educational Research, 73*(3), 277–320.
Britzman, D. (2004). *Thinking about teacher education* (personal communication). Presentation to University of Calgary Faculty of Education, Calgary.
Danesi, M. (2007). *The quest for meaning: A guide to semiotic theory and practice*. Toronto: University of Toronto Press.
Das, R., & Gorman, P. (1985). *How can I help?* New York, NY: Alfred Knopf.
deWaal, F. (1996). *Good natured: The origins of right and wrong in humans and other animals*. Cambridge, MA: Harvard University Press.
Gardner, B. K. (2007). *Getting to "got it!": Helping struggling students learn how to learn*. Alexandria, VA: Association for Supervision and Curriculum Development.
Halliday, M. (1978). *Language as social semiotic*. London: Edward Arnold.
Karabenick, S. A. (1998). Help-seeking as a strategic resource. In S. Karabenick (Ed.), *Strategic help seeking: Implications for learning and teaching* (pp. 1–12). Mahwah, NJ: Lawrence Erlbaum Associates.
Karabenick, S. A., & Knapp, J. R. (1991). Relationship of academic help seeking to the use of learning strategies and other instrumental achievement behavior in college students. *Journal of Educational Psychology, 83*(2), 221–230.
Karabenick, S. A., & Newman, R. S. (2011). Seeking help as an adaptive response to learning difficulties: Person, situation and developmental influences. In S. Jarvela (Ed.), *Social and emotional aspects of learning* (pp. 244–250). Amsterdam: Elsevier.
Kelly, G. A. (1963). *A theory of personality: The psychology of personal constructs*. New York, NY: W. W. Norton.
Kelly, G. A. (2003). A brief introduction to personal construct theory. In F. Fransella (Ed.), *International handbook of personal construct psychology* (pp. 3–20). New York, NY: John Wiley & Sons Ltd. Retrieved from http://dx.doi.org/10.1002/0470013370.ch1
Lemke, J. (2003). Texts and discourses in the technologies of social organization. In G. Weiss & R. Wodak (Eds.), *Critical discourse analysis: Theory and interdisciplinarity* (pp. 130–149). Basingstoke: Palgrave Macmillan.
Luckin, R., & Hammerton, L. (2002). Getting to know me: Helping learners understand their own learning needs through metacognitive scaffolding. In S. A. Cerris, G. Gouarderes, & F. Paraguaco (Eds.), *Intelligent tutoring systems: Proceedings of the 6th international conference, ITS 2002*. Berlin: Springer.
Meichenbaum, D., & Biemiller, A. (1998). *Nurturing independent learners: Helping students take charge of their learning*. Cambridge, MA: Brookline Books.
Ryan, A., & Pintrich, P. (1998). Achievement and social motivation influences on help seeking in the classroom. In S. Karabenick (Ed.), *Strategic help seeking: Implications for learning and teaching* (pp. 117–139). Mahwah, NJ: Lawrence Erlbaum Associates.
Ryan, A., Pintrich, P., & Midgley, C. (2001). Avoiding seeking help in the classroom: Who and why? *Educational Psychology Review, 13*(2), 93–114.

Shapiro, B. L. (1994). *What children bring to light: A constructivist perspective on children's learning in science*. New York, NY: Teachers College Press.

Shapiro, B. L. (1998). Reading the furniture: The semiotic interpretation of science learning environments. In K. Tobin & B. Fraser (Eds.), *International handbook of science education* (pp. 600–621). Dordrecht: Kluwer Academic Publishers.

Shapiro, B. L. (2008, May 30-June 3). *Help and encouragement: A program of research to understand personal, social and culturally constructed features of help-seeking and help-giving in science and environmental education*. Paper presented at the Canadian Society for Studies in Education Annual Conference (Social Sciences and Humanities Research Council of Canada) Vancouver.

Shapiro, B. L. (2014). Engaging novice teachers in semiotic inquiry: Considering the environmental messages of school learning settings. *Cultural Studies of Science Education, 9*(4), 809–824. doi:10.1007/s11422-013-9565-9

Shapiro, B. L., & Kirby, D. (1998). An approach to consider the messages of science learning culture. *Journal of Science Teacher Education, 9*(3), 221–240.

Shwalb, D. W., & Sukemune, S. (1998). Help seeking in the Japanese college classroom: Cultural, developmental, and social-psychological influences. In S. Karabenick (Ed.), *Strategic help seeking: Implications for learning and teaching* (pp. 141–170). Mahwah, NJ: Lawrence Erlbaum Associates.

Vygotsky, L. S. (1978). *Mind in society: The development of higher psychological processes*. Cambridge, MA: Harvard University Press.

Bonnie Shapiro
Werklund School of Education
University of Calgary, Canada

ALISON PEACOCK

8. THE SCHOOL THAT LISTENS

Freedom to Learn without Labels

Children need space to develop independence within an environment where they are both supported and trusted. This chapter tells the story of a small English primary school where listening and responding to children is central to all aspects of school life; this enables our pupils to attain highly whilst becoming articulate, self-directed learners. The leadership dispositions of students and teachers uncovered by researchers working with the school from 2006–2010 are discussed, alongside some key organizational structures and routines in place at the School to ensure that children's voices are heard in all aspects of learning. This foundational view guides our work and efforts to create an learning environment where children take actions of their own needed for them to learn.

CONTEXT

The Wroxham School is a primary school with two hundred and forty pupils, situated on the outskirts of London, England. Children attend nursery from the age of three and leave at the end of Year Six when they are eleven years of age. All classes have thirty pupils. The Wroxham School is well known in England as a school that has been transformed through an ethos that places the uniqueness of children at the heart. The school was in the worst national inspection category in 2001 and moved to sustained and repeated judgements of 'outstanding' performance under new leadership from 2003 onwards. The story of The Wroxham School's dramatic improvement was the subject of *'Creating Learning without Limits'* (Swann et al., 2012) that I co-authored with a team from the University of Cambridge. This research case study has become highly influential in England even at ministerial level. The attention that our small school gets, in a building that was originally put up as a temporary over-spill solution, is surprising; and yet the energy and optimism that abounds there, gives small sparks of hope to many within the English school system.

The Wroxham School was designated as a Teaching School in 2011 and since that time has built a network alliance that comprises over two hundred and twenty primary schools. It has a reputation for inclusive creativity and high standards of attainment. Engagement with research and big ideas in education has been a key way of building professional skill and courage within the teaching team and in 2015 the school became an Educational Research Centre. Courses for teachers are held each week in the school gymnasium and hundreds of visitors are welcomed throughout the year. We work closely with the University of Hertfordshire to support initial teacher education inspired by the principles of Learning without Limits. Some of the visitors to our school are from governments and educational institutions from as far afield as Thailand, India, Australia and the United States of America. *Creating Learning without Limits* will be published in Japanese and Spanish during 2015, no doubt generating even greater attention on this small school in the future.

What is it like to be a child studying in this school? How are children encouraged and enabled to take actions of their own to learn? In preparation for this chapter, I worked with a small group of eleven year-old children to explore their views about learning and in particular their sense of agency as learners. I have set out to share their stories and to explain the structures in place to provide genuine choice for children and illustrate ways that teachers use their curricular freedom to respond to the children's interests. Throughout the chapter, Ezra, Abigail, Phoebe and Esin reflect on their experience of being eleven year-old members of The Wroxham School learning community. When I interviewed them they discussed many aspects of school life and the curriculum; for the purposes of this chapter I have particularly focused on their feedback about learning maths as a means of explaining our whole-school approach to teaching without ability-labelling that builds independence, ambition and agency.

THE VISION FOR A LISTENING SCHOOL

My vision for The Wroxham School was to build an ambitious, inclusive whole-school culture where no child or adult would ever be written off or limited by pre-determined assumptions about their capacity to learn. When I first arrived at the school it was evident that children did not expect to have any say about their own learning or to influence decisions taken at class-level, leave alone at a whole-school level. The culture amongst the oldest children at that time was one of apathy and low-level resistance. The 'cool' approach was one of disinterest and lack of engagement. Children were reluctant to answer questions or to engage in debate. Those who found learning difficult were skilled at sitting back and blaming their own inability to understand. The power of 'yet' as described by Dweck (2006) was not part of these children's thinking i.e "I don't know how to do this *yet*..." They were far more likely to give up, than to show that effort was needed.

At that time in English schools, the default expectation from external advisers and inspectors was that children would be seated in 'ability' groups and would receive differing work according to their perceived intelligence. At The Wroxham School this, in part, had led to children developing low self-esteem and limited self-expectation. Energy that could have been put into learning, was instead channelled into class-based disruption and fights on the playground. It was clear to me that these children needed to have their love of learning reignited and that the best way to achieve this would be to offer them curricular experiences that they would be unable to resist. Additionally it was important to establish from the outset that the school was a community and could only achieve excellence if everybody became involved.

THE JOURNEY

When I joined the school as a new head teacher I found a community that was exhausted by failure. Inspection visits occurred every few weeks and teachers were continually trying to adapt their teaching to the demands of visiting 'experts.' The pupils had been described by the inspection team in 2001, as 'unteachable' and as a consequence, strict behavior management routines had been put in place. However, this had resulted in a culture of passive resistance in lessons, punctuated with isolated incidents of extreme behavior such as chair-throwing, children running off site, windows smashed in anger. The first few months of my headship were dominated with incidents where children and teachers were upset or angry. It was clear that staff on the playground at lunchtime needed to change their approach, as the dominant, expectation of these adults was negative; with a deterministic expectation that conflict would occur on a daily basis. The final straw came one day early in my headship, when the lead playground supervisor marched to my office, leant on the door jamb and growled: "They've been at it again … those retards…" I was shocked to realize that she was referring to some of the children in such an abusive manner.

To summarise, the problem at the outset of my headship was one of massive underachievement during lessons, disenfranchised teachers and pupils, a lacklustre learning environment and unpredictable volatile behavior issues, sometimes exacerbated by adults with little empathy or patience. How could this school, labeled as a failure, turn its fortunes around? I believed that the answer could be found by listening to the children, re-energising and inspiring the teaching team and engaging everyone who was willing, in rapid school improvement through empowerment.

LEARNING TO LISTEN

Throughout my career as a teacher, I have found that organizing regular structures such as whole-class circle time, has huge benefits and allows everyone to learn from others. On my first day as head teacher, I invited every class to join me for a circle time meeting in the gymnasium. I wanted my first message to the children to be one of openness and generosity in seeking to listen and find out how the school could become happier. I asked children to tell me what was good about their school and what they enjoyed. We also collected lots of ideas about how we could begin to make the school a happier, safer place. At that stage, the children did not believe it was their role to comment on aspects of learning or classrooms and they focused all their comments on the time they considered to be their own – i.e., break and play time.

I asked them to draw plans of how we might improve the play facilities and promised to work with them to make changes as soon as possible. Their requests were often very simple such as asking for more footballs and asking for adults to play with them and help organize games such as group skipping. They wanted a rotational schedule so that spaces were fairly used and did not become dominated all week by the oldest children. I discovered that there was a small unspent grant and within weeks we had ordered new trim-trail equipment that was subsequently installed by the site manager with a group of willing parents. I introduced a 'witness' form that children were asked to complete if they were sent in from the playground following a behavior incident. This meant that everybody's side of any argument was listened to and followed up instead of the adults dealing out punishment with scant regard for causes of incidents. The message was loud and clear – 'we value you and want to hear your views.' I began to get to know the teachers individually and to work alongside them to build their confidence and to establish an ethos where 'listening' and co-agency was understood to be important for adults as well as children. The following year the school's results placed it in the top hundred most improved schools in the country. We were on our way!

CHOICE AND CHALLENGE

Clearly, all children are different and do not all learn at the same pace and at the same moment. As David aged nine, pointed out recently 'We're not robots ... we are going to make mistakes' (The Wroxham School, 2013). Common practice in English schools has been for teachers to pre-plan lessons comprising a range of activities and tasks for children according to ranked groupings of so-called 'ability.' The imperative for differentiation has led, too often, to classrooms where decisions have already been made about what children are capable of achieving. For many children this means that the likely outcome of their learning is pre-judged and limited.

My own practice was researched for the book, *Learning without limits* (Hart, Dixon, Drummond, & McIntyre, 2004) and I had become convinced of the value and core imperative of listening to children and engaging them in dialogue about their learning rather than ranking them according to test outcomes. As the school began to improve, so did the atmosphere of optimism and 'can-do.' I had talked with teaching colleagues about the way my classroom practice had been researched and teachers at Wroxham began to ask for more details about how I was able to organize my classroom without resorting to ability-labelling. I made it clear that if colleagues across our school wanted to move away from ability groups to offering structured learning choices of progressive complexity to children; I would support this move. However, it was never centrally mandated and we did not have staff meetings where as a school we agreed to stop ability grouping and labelling. Change began with a few teachers who were keen to trial a new way of teaching and to experience how this would work within their room. Essentially, we initiated a pedagogical approach that is becoming increasingly popular in English schools and is often referred to as 'choice and challenge' where children are free to choose which level of challenge they feel able to tackle within the lesson. The teacher introduces the subject to be learned and then presents a range of tasks for the children to engage with, beginning with the simplest option leading to more complex tasks. Instead of predetermining what each child will do, this approach offers choice to the children. This builds self-efficacy and self- awareness about learning within the day-to-day context of the classroom.

I talked to the group of Year 6 children about their response to this approach. They were universally enthusiastic advocates of any practice in the classroom that builds their capacity to be genuinely independent. Phoebe spoke about the way that her confidence had grown:

> Well from the start of Wroxham I felt really shy and not confident about my work, but from starting at Wroxham and coming up to Y6 I feel like I've improved massively, I've conquered a lot of fears and I am happy a lot.

Abigail, usually quiet and cautious, reflected that:

> I know what I need to do and I can get on with it without worrying about what other people are choosing. When I get things right I feel really good because I know I have tried my best. My parents say learning maths is really important and I think they are right (huge smile).

Esin recalled her experience of previous schools before she joined Wroxham when she was seven years old:

> At my other schools I was always stressed about what I'm supposed to do, what I'm not supposed to do, how I'm supposed to sit ... because they were always making us stressed and all that. I don't know ... just at Wroxham, you can just relax. This school just feels like home, compared to the other ones? It's a nice feeling.

Children throughout the school are given the opportunity to make decisions about their learning within lessons. Recently, I was watching a video recorded for the school website and was delighted to see that even our very youngest children can talk confidently about how important it is to choose tasks. Susie (six years old) answered a question about why children should be able to choose their own level of challenge:

> If you just got pushed to one challenge you could think this is very difficult ... you might need ... I might need a low challenge so I can um ...discover it a bit more

We can hear from Susie's comments that she feels in control of her learning. Taking control and making decisions about learning tasks enables genuine independence and flourishing; thereby ensuring a school culture where children can take actions of their own to learn.

OPPORTUNITIES TO ACHIEVE 'PERSONAL BEST'

The school encourages children to work towards individual 'personal best' achievement across the curriculum and to collaborate as a team where possible. This contrasts strongly with the prevailing educational approach in English schools of ranking and scoring one child against another. The philosophy of 'learning without limits' is one of working in supportive partnership. Helping a colleague or peer to achieve more highly does not diminish one's own achievements in an environment where collective endeavour is celebrated. Individual children are encouraged through coaching conversations with teachers and peers to take advantage of additional tuition offers that may be of benefit to them. The crucial aspect here is that children are free to make their own decisions about what they would find helpful in their learning. Additional classes or extension sessions are always optional and open to all.

Abigail has taken up the opportunity to work with a maths extension group each week. She has not always found this work easy and has sometimes cried in frustration at the complexity of tasks and assessments associated with this level of mathematics. When I interviewed her she explained:

> I really like doing maths and my mum and dad say maths is really lovely to do. I find algebra hard but if I keep on doing it, it will get easier and easier for me and that really makes me enjoy it a lot. Like in music, when I practice I get better and better. I really want to keep up with everybody else in maths but sometimes I just lag behind because I keep asking the teacher if the answer is right and that slows me down ...

Providing opportunities for children to self-select additional learning builds a culture of self regulation where instead of being chosen or 'pushed' by the teacher, each child is expected to become intrinsically motivated to make an effort. The school funds additional music lessons, art therapy, choir, sports clubs, maths clubs, karate, art and craft clubs as a means of ensuring that there is always a breadth of offer for any child to access should they wish to do so. The temptation to participate, rather than requirement to comply, builds agency and motivation amongst our children.

LEADERSHIP ROLES IN YEAR SIX

Throughout the school there are opportunities for children to take the lead in decision making. However, in the final year of school, the opportunities for leadership are greatest. There are a range of roles that children take on in their final year. Central to these, is to provide advocacy for younger children through leading regular mixed-age circle meetings. Building on this role as a lead mentor and example-giver for younger children; the Year Six class members are also able to opt to become peer mentors on the playground. They receive formal training for this role and are supervised by our therapeutic support teacher. Records of incidents between children that have been resolved by Year Six peer mediators are filed alongside behavior records in the Headteacher's office. 11-year-old Esin commented:

> Sometimes in peer-mediation you have to work with younger kids and it is hard because you might upset them easily because you're used to speaking to older kids so in peer mediation you just have to be a bit more careful. It is a good idea to do it because it gives all of us more confidence really

Ezra demonstrates his values and sense of justice:

> It is good to look after the younger children, but if there has been an argument and you're a peer mediator, you have to listen to both sides so you can't have a favourite child that's in the argument and then say um like "Oh I believe you and not you" – you have to listen to both sides, you have to respect what other people say. Also, when there is an argument, make sure that you don't get involved too much, so you stay your distance, so you help them but you don't get too much involved. If it's really serious get a teacher, but if it's not too serious as a peer mediator you should be able to sort it out and then write it up in the folder.

The school has pet guinea pigs that are housed in the open courtyard adjacent to the Year Six classroom. Caring for the guinea pigs and helping younger children to handle them with consideration, is a special role for the Year Six children. Some children become very attached to these school pets and they therefore hold great importance within the school community. Some children come back to visit the school regularly to see the guinea pigs even after they have left for Secondary School. The therapeutic role of caring for animals is an area that we seek to develop further as a school in the years ahead.

Ezra is very proud of the positive role model that he presents to the younger boys in particular. He observed:

> In Buddy Reading I'm with a boy called Tim and he picks out some very funny stories, actually … and another job for that is no matter what book it is you should read it, but if it is a long, long book or an information book, tell them nicely. Don't go "Oh you can't read that book because it's too long" just say to them "We can't read that book because the amount of time we have, we won't be able to finish it.

Play-leading on the playground at lunchtimes is another role assumed by the oldest children on a rotational basis. Phoebe says she loves being a play leader but 'you definitely have to be responsible' and Abigail explains:

> We do this so they can stay happy and enjoy their lunch and break so they don't get worried about anything else – that's what we try and do.

CIRCLE GROUP MEETINGS – A FORUM TO HELP PUPILS CONTRIBUTE TO DECISIONS ABOUT SCHOOL ACTIVITIES

Each week we hold Circle Group meetings on Tuesday mornings at 10.15am instead of gathering for a school assembly. These meetings give everyone in the school community a forum to discuss and debate ideas. The meetings are organized and led by the Year 6 children and attended by children aged six to eleven, with staff in attendance as group members. Year 6 gather together in class prior to the meeting to prepare and to decide on aspects of the session such as news of the week, areas for discussion and the warm-up and warm-down games that will be played. Each group is attended by on average twenty-five children from Year One to Year Five and is led by four Year Six children. Leadership tasks such as introducing the topic for discussion, note-taking and prompting participation are divided amongst the Year Six pupils. The groups are mixed age and provide an opportunity for the youngest children in the school to get to know their peers in other year groups and to observe modelling of democratic engagement.

Establishing Circle Groups has ensured that there is a regular formal opportunity for children to express their ideas and views and to learn empathy, dialogue and presentation skills. Esin believes that Circle Groups help children to become more confident and to believe in themselves:

> I have really loved leading our Circle Group. Sometimes it is difficult to get everyone to listen to each other because they are very keen and other times no-one says very much, so I have had to think how to help everyone to work together. The little ones in Year One and Two really seem to love being given a chance to speak and I make sure they have enough time to think. We all try really hard to encourage them. We make decisions about things like whether to build a tunnel on the playground, or whether we should have class pets and things like that. It feels really good to know everyone's ideas matter. I think it's good because you can work with all years, everyone gets a go at speaking. Sometimes we go round in a circle, sometimes we put our hands up … It's just different.

Phoebe reflected:

> I think with circle groups it is quite nice to lead because everyone in the school has a turn of leading circle groups in Year 6 and its nice to see everyone's views and in Circle Group we have challenges we might like to do like "Think of all the words you have learnt in maths" and we can see what all the younger children have learnt and come up with and its nice to see what they've learnt in their year. It's sometimes quite tricky to get their attention if they really want to put their idea forward and we have to make sure that everyone has their turn but sometimes we have a limit of time and we need to be quite quick before break so we make sure we do it systematically like we go round in a circle and

if they can't come up with an idea we come back to them so that everyone gets a turn.'

Building a culture of opportunity where children and staff know they can contribute to the whole organization means that everyone works together as a collective. The alternative in too many schools is to listen to the convenient minority. When I was first at Wroxham, one of the children who was prone to periodically losing his temper and causing mayhem around the school told me that he began to calm down once he knew he was being heard:

> If you don't get listened to you kind of end up having to take your own way if you are not given it and that means I get louder and angrier.

Behaviour is now judged by inspectors to be 'outstanding' at Wroxham as a result of a democratic inclusive culture where children are trusted, and feel trusted.

PUPIL LED LEARNING REVIEW MEETINGS

In Year Five and in Year Six every child meets twice a year with the head teacher, the class teacher and their parents to discuss their challenges and successes. The children lead these meetings and prepare for them with a PowerPoint presentation. The meetings are very positive occasions where everyone gathers together to share strategies to ensure that optimum teaching and learning is provided with support from home.

Phoebe's learning review meeting in February demonstrated just how much her confidence and charisma has grown. She prepared a presentation and described many successes, particularly her love of sport ('I DO love running') she described her successes and challenges in relation to maths:

> I do love maths and I find it something that is sometimes challenging but I usually understand it and I go to maths club that helps me after school – I just feel a bit more confident. I am happy with my times tables. I usually find problem solving a bit tricky – just to find out which operation to use and to help myself to remember how to solve it. We have something called RUCSAC time which stands for: Read, Understand, Choose, Solve, Answer, Check and that helps me to understand and to see where I could go wrong in a problem, so that helps me a lot.

We then looked at Phoebe's maths books and we discussed the progress being made and the teacher used her mark book to feed back about specific aspects of Phoebe's work. Phoebe's family were then able to see where they could help her with practicing skills at home and the suggestion of attending 'toast club' each morning for additional study time before school was made. Each meeting takes fifteen minutes and is either held during the day or the evening. We ensure that every family attends as each child is keen to share their presentation. In other year groups, family consultations are held twice a year and children are encouraged to attend where possible in order that the conversations about learning engage the child as an active participant. The process of Learning Review meetings is rigorous but enabling. Meetings reinforce the message and philosophy of the school that opportunities are carefully designed to allow each child to determine their own future success through making careful decisions about how much challenge they can embrace. It is the role of the family and school to support the child as much as possible in enabling them to achieve success. Children will almost always recognize areas for development with regard to their attitude to learning. For example, in Ezra's Review meeting he reflected that he has a tendency to rush '*and then I make silly mistakes – very silly mistakes.*' This honest appraisal helps everyone to support the child with their endeavor to improve.

PROVIDING REGULAR WRITTEN FEEDBACK TO PUPILS

The Year Six class teachers provide detailed written feedback for the children each day in their English and maths books. They also record the challenge task chosen by each child as another means of tracking progress. The school does not provide graded feedback and avoids discussion of test results and grades wherever possible. The standpoint taken by our school is that the children are best informed by formative feedback related to learning rather than summative grades. Instead of the teacher issuing targets, children are guided to select key points from the marking feedback and use these to add to a list at the end of their exercise book. When errors are noted by the teacher in the child's book, time is provided during the next lesson for corrections and editing by the child in green pen. This ensures that the marking is acted upon by the child and that feedback given has been understood as a learning point. Abigail was very clear that the teacher's marking is helpful:

> When I get my book back I look straight away to see how I can improve and what to do next.

Feedback comes in other forms apart from written marking and with regard to literature the most helpful feedback is from the audience. Ezra was very proud of the picture book he made for the Reception Class (five year olds). He recalls:

> My picture story book that I created was called 'Tiny Tony Gets a Snow Board' and it's about this boy that gets a snow board and he keeps crashing and eventually he gets it right. Year 6 had to read it to Reception (big grin) and I ended up reading it to almost all of the whole class.

PUPILS WRITE THEIR OWN END-OF-YEAR PERFORMANCE REPORTS

At The Wroxham School, children write their own end-of-year Performance Reports electronically. These reports are then saved on the school server and form the basis of a written dialogue between the child and the teacher. The youngest children from age six upwards are helped by older children to formulate their comments and to type them up. Photographs of assignments and project work are included and the head teacher adds a comment to every document. The reports are proudly taken home at the end of the summer term and parents are encouraged to add their comments to the document. Summaries of key points are then compiled by the head teacher during the summer to inform the next teacher. The children know that these documents form summative assessment summaries of their progress throughout the year. In English schools statutory test outcomes are also reported to families at the end of Year One, Year Two and Year Six. The Wroxham School does not provide assessment grades at the end of Years Three, Four and Five although this information is collected through teacher assessment and is used by the school to closely monitor progress and performance. The decision to focus on formative, qualitative feedback rather than numerical grades is a deliberate move by the school to encourage continuous ambitious development of every child rather than ranking by numbers.

Phoebe's end of Year Six report begins with a summary of how she is feeling:

My time has been amazing in the school from being really shy and not that confident with subjects to then wanting to learn more and more each day. My friendships are great and I love having new friends. I have gone from having a small group to having the whole class in my friendship group. Year Six has been really good because I have covered all the things I wasn't too sure about over the years and now I can write all about it. I have enjoyed every moment of Wroxham and it has really inspired me to do all the things I wanted to do. Secondary School … I am feeling really nervous at the same time I am happy to share all the things I have learned from Wroxham at my new school.

It is encouraging to note Phoebe's growing sense of agency and independence about her school that '*has really inspired me to do all the things I wanted to do*' she writes with confidence about her own interests and learning agenda rather than one of compliance, focused on attainment grades. Phoebe is keen to show how she has become more confident in her own capacity to learn. It is important to consider what she does *not* say. No-where in her report does she comment on the expectation of her teacher or her peers, or a desire to chase grades; she believes that the harder she works the more she will achieve. However, alongside Phoebe's report, her family also receive her standardized national test results. These test results are issued for all children in Year 6 but rarely present any surprises as the children understand their achievements and 'next steps' very well.

Ezra talks about writing his last ever Wroxham report and attending his final Learning Review meeting:

What was intense was writing out last reports ever in Wroxham and our last Learning Reviews which was quite scary, knowing that we are leaving primary school and going up to secondary school which is quite a big challenge for some people …. Every week we will get around ten hours of homework, which is quite a lot, but we will get a lot of learning out of it which is good. It is very scary ….

The end of year reports build an important record of progress achieved over time. Subject leaders for maths and English cut and paste the children's comments into new record documents for transition purposes. It is very helpful to review each child's self-evaluation of learning before the new academic year begins and also ensures that every opportunity to listen and act accordingly, is taken.

LEADERSHIP DISPOSITIONS FOR GUIDING INDEPENDENT LEARNERS

A foundational perspective in all of our work at The Wroxham School is the view that in order for children to gain independence in their school-based learning they need to exist within a leadership culture that celebrates and welcomes individual voice and autonomy within a democratic community. Too often schools in England are dominated by routines, practices and structures that seek to control rather than to enable.

As a school seeking to listen to children and adults, The Wroxham School has developed a culture where individual opportunity is in harmony with a collective endeavor to learn. The vision of 'learning without limits' is a relentless pursuit of excellence for every child that extends to adults too. Lifelong learning and the continuous, restless, quest to improve, is a strong part of the school culture. Research that took place at The Wroxham School between 2006–2010 identified seven leadership dispositions underpin the ethos and culture that permeates the school (Swann et al., 2012). As head teacher, I kept a leadership journal each week during the research period and this was analysed alongside interview data from children, teachers and families. The seven dispositions are summarized below:

Openness

Openness to new ways of thinking is a foundational dispositional quality and underpins the following six dispositions. If teachers are to lift limits from children and reject ability labels they need to be open to *possibility*. This means that classroom practices that may unintentionally prevent children from making progress are avoided. Restrictive practice and ranking will not take place in a school that is constantly open to possibility. Open pedagogy casts out fixed thinking. The Wroxham School prides itself on a leadership of learning that is continually open to the 'art of the possible.' This is symbolized powerfully through the innovative, creative learning environment of the school and through pride in the school's capacity to achieve more than is expected.

Empathy

Empathy involves looking through the child's eyes to understand their thinking and understanding in order to help them. Empathy transforms relationships in school, as children know that they are being listened to and taken seriously. Empathetic relationships between staff ensure that mutual supportiveness will enable the community to be stronger and will foster a culture of ideas and opportunity. Mutual supportiveness also enables everyone to feel safe in the knowledge that asking questions or seeking help will be responded to with kindness borne out of a collective endeavour to lift limits on learning. This disposition reminds us of the importance of resisting quick judgements. For example, many families at the school are under pressure for a variety of reasons. Empathy helps teachers to understand when occasionally parents lose their temper and blame the school for matters that are beyond their control. This means that relationships can be built and sustained over time, with tolerance and mutual respect.

Generosity

A generous view of learning trusts that everybody has capacity to learn. Open acceptance of individuals means that everybody has a rightful place within the learning community. This leads to collective responsibility for finding ways forward when problems arise. It also means that difference is welcomed. A generous learning community never gives up on people and takes responsibility to keep searching for 'a way through' for each individual, no matter how challenging or complex their needs may be. This approach enables our school to provide a warm, welcoming environment to children with additional needs. Supporting children to develop independence, whilst having access to specific support, is a balancing act. Recently, one of our children in Year Four has begun to play independently outside at break-times for the first time since joining us in Reception. This is a huge breakthrough and is celebrated by many of us who have tried so hard to help her take this step towards independent outdoor play.

Emotional Stability

At The Wroxham School, teachers know that they are trusted to use their own judgement. This stability creates conditions where teachers are able to make decisions that feel right to them, as opposed to doing what is expected by others, or to follow the group. This enables a culture of risk-taking and innovation to flourish. It generates the strength to resist popular notions of ability and norms of practice, and nurtures the capacity to take risks, thereby providing freedom to learn. Emotional stability means the readiness to both challenge and be challenged, to resist new orthodoxies, to stay close to the vision and not be knocked off course. The leadership disposition of emotional stability is exemplified through investment in professional learning and support for families and children. The school funds an art therapist who spends two days a week at the school to provide therapeutic appointments for children and staff. This resource enables all staff to have additional support in helping to find a way through for children who may have encountered extremely difficult situations in their home lives. There is also an opportunity in a culture of trust, for staff members to request confidential support for themselves.

Inventiveness

The capacity to imagine and do something new is essential if teachers are to lift constraints on learning. Removing ability labels and notions of fixed ability means thinking differently and liberating children from limited pre-determined outcomes.

Creative leadership throughout the school builds a culture of ideas where there is a sense that anything can happen. Outside on the playground there is a double-decker bus that has been transformed into a library and nurture space; a music garden formed from junk metal such as saucepans, car doors and a kitchen sink; a thatched Celtic roundhouse with fire-pit and wooden seating-circles in the forest . The art of the imagination is fostered amongst every member of the school and this almost feels tangible within classrooms where children know they are trusted.

Persistence

In a culture where persistence is at the centre, there is capacity to keep on trying and a refusal to give up on people. This means holding onto the view that there is always more that can be done to free children to learn; the belief that however challenging a situation, change is always possible. Courage and humility are needed in order to constantly seek a way to transform learning; as answers will always need to be individual and flexible. Persistence is a necessary quality if we are to be liberated from fixed thinking. Recognition of this leadership disposition gives colleagues the courage to be patient. This is particularly helpful when trying to 'find a way through' for a child that is finding learning difficult. Last year one of the Year 6 boys left school with an excellent maths grade and the expected level of literacy despite having battled for years with learning to read and write. The school simply refused to give up on him and he became increasingly determined and resilient as a result.

Questioning and Humility

We believe it is important to constantly ask oneself whether what worked yesterday is still the correct solution for today. Teachers need the confidence to question their practice and to make space to hear what the children are telling them. Humility allows us to constantly seek other ways of understanding how we can help children learn. It is humility that enables The Wroxham School to constantly strive for further success. There is a restless ambition within a humble learning environment that always accepts that there is more to do.

THE WROXHAM TRANSFORMATIVE LEARNING ALLIANCE: SHARING OUR PHILOSOPHY AND EXPERIENCES WITH COLLEAGUES AND THROUGH PROFESSIONAL DEVELOPMENT

A core finding of *Creating Learning without Limits* was that professional learning opportunities for all staff are an important and necessary means of securing school improvement. Since 2011 our school has become increasingly outward-facing and has developed an extensive network of schools that choose to join with us because of our ethical, inclusive approach to building trust and co-agency amongst colleagues. Increasingly, the school is engaged in research and has a national voice through membership of highly influential bodies such as the Royal Society Education Committee. The school now trains teachers and engages hundreds more in continuing professional development.

The seven leadership dispositions underpin our whole-school approach to openness. It is my belief that children flourish when adults around them enable them to act upon their own learning through making meaningful choices and decisions. Abigail's surprisingly passionate reflections at the end of Year Six summarize the impact of a school environment that builds intrinsic motivation:

> Don't be scared of what you can do ... you can show the whole world if you want to, you can show your teachers if you want to, go for it! There is nothing to be scared of ... There is nothing you can't do in life.

REFERENCES

Dweck, C. S. (2006). *Mindset: The new psychology of success*. New York, NY: Random House.
Hart, S., Dixon, A., Drummond, M. J., & McIntyre, D. (2004). *Learning without limits*. Maidenhead: Open University Press.
Peacock, A. M. (2012). Developing outward-facing schools where citizenship is a lived experience. In J. Brown (Ed.), *Democratic citizenship in schools* (pp. 120–133). Edinburgh: Dunedin Press.
Swann, M., Peacock, A., Hart, S., & Drummond, M. J. (2012). *Creating learning without limits*. Maidenhead: Open University Press.
The Wroxham School. (2013). *Year 4 – We challenge ourselves*. Retrieved from http://thewroxham.org.uk/for-parents/school-videos/ and https://vimeo.com/69709930

Alison Peacock
Educational Research Centre
The Wroxham School, United Kingdom

SHERRI MELROSE

9. UNDERSTANDING AND SUPPORTING PROFESSIONALS' OWN EFFORTS TO LEARN IN ONLINE HEALTH DISCIPLINES COURSES

INTRODUCTION

When health professionals upgrade their education by attending online programs in higher education, their studies can be impacted by family and employer responsibilities. In the Faculty of Health Disciplines at Canada's Open University, Athabasca University (AU), nurses, psychologists and professionals from a variety of different health disciplines have opportunities to earn post-basic undergraduate and graduate degrees in predominantly online classrooms. These practising professionals bring experience, wisdom and passion to their learning. In response, faculty seek to implement teaching approaches that affirm students' own efforts to learn and to support them towards constructing relevant, meaningful new knowledge. In this chapter I share a selection of approaches faculty have found effective in understanding students own efforts to learn and then creating responsive supportive online learning environments.

HOW CAN HEALTH PROFESSIONALS LEARN ONLINE?

An Approach to Understand Online Learners' Efforts

Members of the lay public often have questions about how health professionals could possibly learn the knowledge they need to practice competently in their discipline in online classrooms. How could nurses, dental hygienists, physical therapists and occupational therapists master hands on skills? How could psychologists master counselling skills? And beyond skill development, how could online environments provide health care professionals with opportunities to integrate the knowledge, skills and attitudes they need to provide safe care to their patients and clients?

Through a process of seeking answers to these and other questions, colleagues and I from the Faculty of Health Disciplines at Canada's Open University, Athabasca University (http://www.athabascau.ca/) have worked to establish and re-vitalize post-basic programs for health professionals who were already qualified in their discipline, but who wanted to upgrade their education. For example, one program provides nurses previously educated at college or vocational institutes with opportunities to earn a baccalaureate degree in nursing. This degree allows candidates to write national Registered Nurse qualifying examinations.

Similarly, another program provides nurses, dental hygienists, physical therapists, occupational therapists, dietitians and other university educated health professionals with opportunities to earn a master's degree. Professional counsellors and counselling psychologists have opportunities to earn graduate degrees in counselling. While some of the Athabasca University programs require students to attend face-to-face practicums in clinical settings, others are offered entirely online.

A common thread that our faculty group weaves throughout the programs and courses is our belief that our students are self-directed, reflexive practitioners who can already think critically. Our goals include extending and building on these strengths. As we designed and implemented different levels of learning experiences, we were guided by our university's mission statement. As Canada's Open University, Athabasca University's mission is dedicated to removing the educational, geographical, financial, social, cultural and other barriers that often limit access to post-secondary achievement. In doing so, AU guarantees access to university-level study to a broad range of non-traditional students (Athabasca University, n.d.).

We also grounded our thinking in our university's mandate, which highlights how Athabasca University, as a distance education university, provides seamless and responsive advanced education, flexibility for lifelong learners who cannot or choose not to undertake residential post-secondary education and offers learners the opportunity to interact with students across Canada and around the world (Athabasca University, n.d.).

Given the commitment to understand and support learners' own efforts inherent in the university's mission and mandate, taking advantage of university wide opportunities already in place was an important consideration as we designed programs for health professionals. Athabasca University implements ongoing research with current and former students. For example, a recent survey indicated that over 90 per cent of AU students study year round, balancing their studies with work, family or community responsibilities; 81 per cent work while they study and 63 per cent support dependents (AU at a Glance, n.d.). The average undergraduate student is 29; the average graduate student is 37 and 67 per cent are women (AU at a Glance, n.d.). 74 per cent of AU graduates are the first in their family to earn a university degree.

Knowing that AU students are generally working adults who could find it difficult to accommodate traditional university terms and class schedules, the university makes every effort to incorporate this understanding of student needs with unique learning opportunities. Many Athabasca University courses are self-paced and students are not limited to typical university term registration times. They can register at the beginning of any month and may take a year or longer to complete courses. Transfer credit is given whenever possible.

Students also have opportunities to take the initiative to challenge non-required courses. They are invited to reflect on and document the valuable experiential learning they already bring to their courses with a Prior Learning Assessment and Recognition PLAR submission (Centre for Learning Accreditation, n.d.). To assist students at either the program or course level, PLAR applicants are mentored through a process of creating a portfolio that demonstrates their mastery of a topic area. Successful applicants are granted course credits.

Online classrooms at Athabasca University use a variety of learning management systems to facilitate interaction among faculty and students. For example, the Faculty of Health Disciplines currently use the moodle learning platform (moodle, n.d.). Moodle allows faculty and students to interact asynchronously in secure discussion forums and to exchange e-mail within their courses. Conferencing software such as Adobe Connect (Adobe connect, n.d.) is also used to provide opportunities for synchronous interaction and the real-time sessions can be recorded for later use by students.

Courses are instructed by both full time continuing faculty and tutors who are employed on a contract basis. Both groups of instructors maintain toll free telephones. Students can log in to their courses on their computers or Smartphones anytime or anywhere and faculty are only a telephone call away. Students are encouraged to engage faculty in their learning by emailing or calling them throughout their program.

Autonomy Support

As faculty at AU consider approaches that can support online students' own efforts to learn and autonomy, existing research provides important guidance. Autonomy support is defined as "the interpersonal behaviour one person provides to involve and nurture another person's internally locused, volitional intentions to act, such as when a teacher supports a student's psychological needs (e.g., autonomy, competency, relatedness), interests, preferences and values" (Reeve & Jang, 2006, P. 210). In online learning environments, the construct of autonomy support involves teaching actions that support students' towards becoming more self-determined, independent, intrinsically motivated and engaged (Lee, Pate & Cozart, 2015).

Self-regulation is essential for student success in online learning environments, and autonomy support can make an important difference in students' feelings of ownership and responsibility for their work (Chen & Jang, 2010). Autonomy support can help students feel more emotionally connected to their teachers (Ryan, LaGuardia, Solky-Butzel, Chirkov, & Kim, 2005). When students' feel that their own efforts to learn are supported, their engagement, concentration, time management and self-regulation can improve (Reeve, Jang, Carrell, Jeon, & Barch, 2004).

Lee, Pate and Cozart (2015) summarized three overarching guidelines for providing autonomy support to online students. First, provide choices; second, provide rationale; and third, provide opportunities for personalization. Providing choices, such as inviting students to choose among several options for assignments and activities offers a variety of different ways for students to demonstrate expected learning outcomes. Choices should be limited to a finite list and include clear structure and parameters that specify what students are expected to do (Lee, Pate, & Cozart). Providing rationale, or why students are required to complete a task, even when the task may seem uninteresting can increase student engagement and autonomous motivation (Jang, 2008). When students are provided with opportunities to customize required activities and make them personally relevant, they become more invested in their learning (Lee, Pate, & Cozart). As faculty at Athabasca University seek to provide autonomy support to our students, who are practicing health professionals, strategies for providing choices, rationale and opportunities for personalization are intentionally woven throughout the curriculum.

Understanding the Learning Needs of Three Health Professions Students

Life circumstances of the health professionals who upgrade their education through online courses at Athabasca University can be expected to be different than those of traditional university students. A traditional university student, particularly at the undergraduate level, could be single without dependents; live at home or in lower cost student housing; and could work in a non-professional job. However, an AU student typically supports children, elders or other family members; lives in a home with significant associated costs; and works at least one professional job. As adult learners, AU students juggle family and work responsibilities in addition to their studies. Many are the first in their family to earn a university degree. In the Faculty of Health Disciplines, the majority of students are women with children.

Learning online can be a lifeline for health professionals. Shift work, unpredictable employment schedules, children's activities, family commitments and unexpected events make attending brick-and mortar classrooms challenging. In this section, I share the stories of three students from the Faculty of Health Disciplines (without using their real names) as a way of illustrating how health professionals can learn online.

Kim

Kim is a Licensed Practical Nurse LPN (known in other jurisdictions as Licensed Vocational Nurse LVN, Enrolled Nurse EN, or Registered Practical Nurse RPN) who began her career as a Nursing Assistant. Kim did not graduate from high school. After completing six weeks of Nursing Assistant training, Kim worked in a care home for the elderly and later bridged into an LPN program. She continued working in the care home and completed the needed upgrades to gain admission into the Athabasca University Post Basic LPN to BN program. Earning a Bachelor of Nursing (BN) degree will allow Kim to write the qualifying examinations required to practice as a Registered Nurse RN in Canada.

I met Kim, as a student during a two-week required clinical practicum I instructed. To complete this practicum, students and faculty travel to a specified clinical setting and are billeted in local homes. As students come from all across Canada, many leave their spouses and children and may travel hundreds of miles across the country. They are responsible for all travel and accommodation costs. In some instances, employers do not grant leave and students must terminate their employment to attend the practicum. Required practicums in the program range from two-weeks through to four-weeks.

One of the most poignant memories I have of learning with Kim throughout her practicum was her tenacity. Kim's newborn baby was just two months old and she was still breastfeeding. In order to complete her practicum within the timeframe she set for herself, Kim's mother and her baby travelled with her to the practicum site and stayed with the billet family as well. Kim's mother took unpaid leave from her own job. Kim attended the clinical course each day and her mother brought the baby in every three hours to feed.

After completing her practicum, Kim returned home and continued with the online portion of her program. If and when she needed extra help understanding concepts or perhaps an extension for an assignment, faculty and tutors were there to help and accommodate her needs.

Kim received ongoing support for the actions she was taking on her own to learn. For example, one of the assignment choices Kim selected in her public health course required students to create a health teaching plan for a new mother. Kim's tutor listened carefully to Kim's recent experiences as a new mother and then customized the assignment to include some of the non-assigned readings and experiential learning Kim had been doing on her own to understand her new role. In another instance, during a telephone call with Kim, her tutor became aware that Kim's verbal skills seemed stronger than her written work, and that her practice background was working in a care home for the elderly. In response, this tutor invited Kim to create an audio-recording explaining a topic she had experience with in her workplace. This recording was used as a foundation and Kim's tutor helped her build and extend the assignment to also include written work that integrated reviews of relevant literature.

Anna

Anna is a health professional earning a graduate degree. Under difficult conditions, she left an Asian country and arrived in Canada as a young girl with her parents. Learning English as a second language posed a continuing challenge for her.

The scholarly writing requirements of graduate study seemed overwhelming. Despite working two part-time jobs in busy clinical agencies and caring for young children and aging parents, Anna attended supplemental writing workshops offered by both Athabasca University and a community college in her area. She sought help from one of her children's school teachers and employed a freelance editor to review her assignments before submitting them.

Anna made a point of devoting one hour on work days and at least four hours on each of her days off to the time she needed for completing assignments. When illness in the family required her attention during the day, she worked well past midnight.

Kelly

Kelly is also a health professional earning a graduate degree. His practice is in the military and online learning provided the flexibility he needed to further his career whether he was stationed at home or deployed abroad. During one period of his studies, Kelly was on active duty in a war zone. For security reasons, at times he was unable to access the internet and complete required assignments. He worked around this hurdle by letting his instructors know about times he might not be available and made every effort to complete and submit his assignments well before they were due. In many instances, without contact with his instructors, this self-directed approach increased the difficulty of course requirements for him, but despite this, he succeeded in completing his degree.

Online faculty and tutors became aware of Kim, Anna and Kelly's unique circumstances through posts they made in the 'Introduction' forums of their classes. All courses in the Faculty of Health Disciplines at Athabasca University provide 'Introduction' forums where students are invited to post thoughtful introductions. Reading students' introductions carefully and gently probing for further information at the beginning of online courses can encourage students to share relevant information about their learning strengths, needs and barriers.

From her posts in the course introductory forum, Kim's tutor learned that she had a new baby. Further discussion revealed that Kim had been reading about the role and responsibilities of new mothers. So, her tutor used this knowledge to help Kim integrate her personal experiences into an assignment. Similarly, Anna's introductory posts revealed that she was struggling with English as a second language and scholarly writing. She hoped attending supplemental writing workshops would help. Knowing this, Anna's tutor could build on what Anna was learning in activities beyond the classroom. Finally, Kelly's introductory posts explained how he was in the military and could suddenly be denied access to the internet. In response, Kelly's tutor was more than willing to be flexible with deadlines. Programs that consistently provide introductory forums, where teachers and students can get to know one another, are an important tool for teachers seeking to understand and support online students' own efforts to learn.

INSTRUCTORS' STRATEGIES TO UNDERSTAND STUDENTS' OWN EFFORTS TO LEARN

In the Faculty of Health Disciplines, most instructors ground their teaching approaches in the belief that students themselves are making efforts to learn. While instructors may be aware of some of the kinds of efforts students are making, striving to understand those they may not be aware of is also critically important. Kim, Anna and Kelly's stories are special, but they are not unique. Like Kim, many students must go to great lengths just to be present and available to learn. Even when students' online courses are accessible anytime and anywhere online, they still must carve out time away from family and employment responsibilities to sit quietly and focus. Like Anna, many students must seek help from additional resources to attain competencies and complete rigorous scholarly writing requirements. As Kelly did, many need to work around uncompromising employer requirements.

When students introduce themselves to their instructors, some details of their circumstances become apparent. However, it is also likely that instructors are unaware of many of the less obvious learning efforts students are undertaking. One effective way to consider some of the actions learners themselves are taking to learn is to ask them directly. Inviting learners to share their experiences opens the door to recognizing and supporting their work.

Strategies That Support Learners' Efforts

Research exploring students' online learning experiences offers direction and helps instructors begin to recognize learners' own efforts. In Kim's program, for example, recognizing her efforts was particularly useful to successfully support her in her studies. A qualitative descriptive study with Post LPN to BN students revealed that they valued affirmation of both the unique challenges they faced and the strategies they were implementing to overcome these challenges (Melrose & Gordon, 2008). A longitudinal study exploring LPN to BN transitions revealed that this group of students set their own personal learning goals and that it was these self-determined goals that sustained and motivated them when learning became difficult (Melrose & Gordon, 2011).

One strategy that this non-traditional group of adult learners found useful was turning to workplace mentors for help applying what they were learning online (Melrose & Gordon, 2011). As a way of recognizing and supporting these efforts, course designers developed assignments that involved discussing course concepts in learners' own workplaces and then reporting on these discussions.

In Anna and Kelly's graduate program, an action research project highlighted how learners were seeking help from their family, friends and co-workers (Melrose, Shapiro, & LaVallie, 2005). Course designers recognized this important source of help by building in assignments that invited learners to adapt coursework for immediate use in learners' lives and workplaces.

This research has also shown that another effective help-seeking strategy used by online learners is asking for help from fellow students in their classes (Melrose, 2008). Instructors can therefore build in opportunities for this kind of interaction to take place. In Open University settings, interactions and relationships with fellow students are increasingly being found valuable to student retention and progression (Baxter, 2012). Here, course designers recognized and supported this effort by ensuring that coffee lounges as well as private group forums and email functions were available in the courses so students could readily connect with one another.

CREATING SUPPORTIVE ONLINE LEARNING ENVIRONMENTS

As the above discussion illustrated, at the university, program and course design levels, Athabasca University provides opportunities for faculty and tutors to recognize and support what learners themselves are doing to strengthen their upgrading experiences. However, the heart of creating genuinely supportive learning environments occurs at the instructional level in online classrooms. In order to understand the efforts Kim, Anna, and Kelly were putting into their studies, their classroom teachers needed to take special care to establish positive relationships with them and communicate genuine interest in their individual learning.

Developing Positive Relationships with and between Students

Affirming, supportive learning environments are grounded in strong relationships between students and teachers. In online classrooms, engaged supportive relationships with teachers have consistently been found to be critically important to online learners (Fedynich, Bradley, & Bradley, 2015; Marin, Martinez, Pecino, Rodriguez, & Melero, 2011; Wright, 2014). Positive teacher-student relationships set the stage for creating supportive environments where students are more willing to take responsibility for their own learning. Students can feel emotionally connected to teachers who support their autonomy and the actions they are taking on their own to learn (Ryan et al., 2005). Understanding the construct of instructional immediacy can help online teachers establish supportive relationships with their students.

Engaging in Instructional Immediacy

Instructional immediacy involves communicating availability, friendliness, and a willingness to connect in personal ways with students. The construct of immediacy was introduced in the 1960s by social psychologist Albert Mehrabian, who defined immediacy as an affective expression of emotional attachment, feelings of liking and being close to another person (Mehrabian, 1967, 1971; Wiener & Mehrabian, 1968). Thus, immediacy is a sense of psychological closeness.

In traditional face to face university classrooms, instructors express immediacy through nonverbal communication such as maintaining eye contact, leaning in closer, touching, smiling, maintaining a relaxed body posture, and attending to voice inflection (Andersen, 1979). They express immediacy verbally by using personal examples, engaging in humour, asking questions, initiating conversations, addressing students by name, praising students' work, and encouraging students to express their opinions (Gorham, 1988). These high affect expressions of immediacy have been found to decrease anxiety (Kelly, Rice, Wyatt, Ducking, & Denton, 2015) and positively impact motivation among higher education students (Baker, 2010; Gitin, Niemi, & Levin, 2012).

In online learning environments, the experience of liking and feeling close to instructors also leads to positive effects in the classrooms (Chakraborty & Nafukho, 2015), higher interactivity (Fahara & Castro, 2015) and greater student satisfaction (Ghamdi, Samarji, & Watt, 2016; Woods & Baker, 2004) In essence, instructional immediacy online refers to the extent to which teachers are able to project a feeling of warmth and likeability in their communication with students (Melrose, 2009). During real-time synchronous conferencing sessions, instructors can demonstrate immediacy verbally and non-verbally in the same way instructors do in traditional classrooms. This process of modeling of immediacy can include invitations to students to imagine new ways of learning that extend beyond course requirements.

On the other hand, during asynchronous interactions, intentional word choices can be an effective way of expressing immediacy. For example, messages and posts with words that refer to "*our*" class and indications that an instructor is willing to work "*with*" learners project interest in understanding students' circumstances, their goals and their own efforts. Words that communicate a genuine interest in getting to know each class member as a unique individual can create a feeling of safety within the teacher-student relationship. Learning in health professions programs can be expected to be a high stakes endeavour and feeling safe can make it easier to take risks and try integrating new ways of thinking.

Research exploring online graduate students' perceptions of instructional immediacy highlighted that learners value instructional behaviours that model engaging and personal ways of connecting; that maintain collegial relationships; and that honour individual learning accomplishments (Melrose & Bergeron, 2006). Examples include instructors posting self-introductions that include pictures and appropriate personal and professional information, creating a course document incorporating biographical information for each member of the class, and choosing words with gentle connotations (Melrose & Bergeron, 2006).

Instructional immediacy can help establish instructor-student relationships that encourage students to share their circumstances, their goals and the learning activities they are initiating on their own. Modelling immediacy during interactions with students can help emphasize the value of autonomy, self-regulation and taking responsibility for one's own learning. In turn, knowing what students themselves are tackling and the risks they are taking, instructors can respond to these efforts and offer further guidance and suggestions. Additionally, instructors can create affirming supportive online environments by connecting students with one another and establishing expressions of immediacy in class groups.

Encouraging Peer Engagement and Support

Valuable affirmation of how students are reaching out and taking responsibility for their own learning can also come from their peers. Peer learning can be defined as "the acquisition of knowledge and skill through active helping and supporting among status equals or matched companions. It involves people from similar social groupings who are not professional teachers helping each other to learn and learning themselves by so doing" (Topping, 2005, p. 631). When higher education students learn with and from each other, their experiences are enriched and they gain useful skills in discerning the accuracy of information (Kauffman, 2015; Boud, Cohen, & Sampson, 2001). Learning through connections with peers has been an established practice in health care education programs, particularly in clinical practicum settings. As programs move online, instructional approaches that invite peer connections are becoming more common and they have been well received (Janssen, Robinson, & Shaw, 2014; Rosenau, Lisella, Clancy, & Nowell, 2014). In most online programs for health professionals, opportunities for peer collaborations are available.

Creating and Using Innovative Podcasts

At AU, faculty embrace traditional activities for peer connections such as partnering during assignments and including peer evaluations whenever possible. Additionally, innovations such podcasts created by students are also being used to encourage student autonomy. In online classrooms, where most interaction is text-based, podcasts can be used to create opportunities for peers to literally "hear from" others in their program. For example, in some asynchronous self-paced courses in the undergraduate LPN to BN program, junior students work alone rather than in class groups. In an effort to decrease their feelings of isolation, senior students were asked to record brief podcasts that offered mentorship and advice. The podcasts were embedded in the moodle learning platform where their course was hosted (Gordon & Melrose, 2011). With the podcasts so readily available, students could click on the MP3 audio file any time of day or night and hear a mentoring tip from a peer who had successfully completed the course. Although the students did not know one another and no further interaction occurred, a connection was made. Senior students felt the process affirmed that actions they were taking on their own were important and worthwhile enough to record and share with others.

Podcasts created by students have also been used in the graduate programs at AU. Once again students further along in their programs were invited to share messages of encouragement with less experienced peers. The messages were collected on a telephone answering machine as MP3 files and then embedded in the moodle learning platform (Melrose & Swettenham, 2012). In this instance, the messages were not just available in a particular course, rather they were included in a graduate student orientation manual that students access throughout their program.

The podcasts illustrated practical examples of strategies students could use to take responsibility for their own learning.

Organizing Group Work and Networking as Integral to the Course Experience

Group work can also provide opportunities where the actions students are taking on their own to learn can be affirmed and supported. All students in the Faculty of Health Disciplines at AU do have access to groups where they can interact with other students. For self-paced courses, participation in the groups may be optional. In paced courses, participation in class groups is required and graded. Just as in traditional learning situations, group work in online classes can foster supportive relationships among students and their teachers. Examples of group work include completing projects with peers, facilitating online seminars with others in a class and offering feedback on student papers.

In a three year qualitative research project AU faculty found that students believed meaningful learning in their online group work occurred for them in three different stages (Melrose & Bergeron, 2007). First, a, beginning/engagement stage; second, a middle/encouragement stage; and third, an ending/closure stage. Viewing the experience of group work through the eyes of the students, we heard our students say that in the beginning/engagement stage, they valued knowing their instructors were available "if you need me" and that it was "safe" to contact them. When they felt that their instructors were present, they could risk sharing their concerns and any strategies they were implementing to overcome these concerns.

In the middle/encouragement stage, students said they appreciated personal help with networking. Again simply knowing their instructors were present and would help them manage any conflict that might emerge was helpful as they worked through issues. During this middle time of needing encouragement, students appreciated private feedback and prompt responses.

Lastly, in the ending/closing stage, students needed opportunities to debrief and reflect. Knowing about the needs that students can be expected to have at different stages of their group work can help instructors offer timely and meaningful support. As instructors model immediacy and recognition of student strengths and efforts in their discussions with student groups, the students are likely to extend this affirming way of interacting to their conversations with one another. For health professionals, who often interact with patients and clients from a strengths based approach, dialogue where individuals are recognized for their efforts can be expected to be a familiar and comfortable way of relating.

Creating Virtual Gathering Spaces for Students

Another innovation for establishing peer connections that faculty at AU implemented was creating program-wide virtual gathering spaces (Getzlaf et al., 2012). Here, graduate students from different health disciplines and programs were invited to gather together in forums not associated with their classes. The forums were named according to clinical interests that students shared. For example, one forum, the *Mental Health Clinical Interest Group* was of interest to students involved in or hoping to become involved in mental health care.

Access to these forums was not limited to course terms, so students could drop in throughout their program. Faculty members were welcome to attend and join any conversations underway, but they did not provide leadership or initiate activities. Participants in the virtual gathering spaces were free to share their experiences, seek and receive help from one another and exchange information about issues of common interest. The process of creating a space where students could gather and connect beyond their classes was another way faculty could indicate to students that their ideas and the actions they were taking to strengthen their learning were important and should be communicated.

Developing an E-Textbook for Online Health Professions Educators

In an effort to disseminate the innovative activities (such as those mentioned in the preceding discussion) that faculty and tutors at Athabasca University have been using with their students to create affirming environments, colleagues and I have collected these activities and presented them in an e-textbook. The e-textbook is titled: *Teaching Health Professionals Online: Frameworks and Strategies* (Melrose, Park, & Perry, 2013). Each chapter suggests creative challenging activities that educators in the health professions can readily implement in their online classes.

The activities were developed by the experienced faculty and tutors at AU. As these instructors come from various disciplines within the health professions, and live in different jurisdictions in Canada and internationally, a wide scope of perspectives is represented. As many health professionals begin their teaching career with strong clinical knowledge but limited understanding of educational theory, we felt it was beneficial to link the activities to established theories. Each activity is therefore presented within the grounding context of a particular theory of learning. As an Open Education Resources or OER, the e-textbook is available for free at http://www.aupress.ca/index.php/books/120234. It is available online, on Smartphones or in print (for a small printing charge).

CONCLUSION

In this chapter I illustrated a selection of approaches that faculty and tutors in the Faculty of Health Disciplines at Athabasca University, Canada's Open University have successfully implemented with online undergraduate and graduate students. The approaches are grounded in a view that post basic health professions students are passionate about upgrading their education and are actively engaged in their own efforts to learn. They are supported by literature exploring the construct of autonomy support.

The chapter began with a discussion of how health professionals can learn online and described Athabasca's unique approach to providing services, programs and courses that invite students to demonstrate what they already know. Next, three health professions students, Kim, Anna and Kelly were introduced. These students' stories illustrate how profoundly family and employer demands can impact students' efforts to learn. They also show the extreme challenges many students are overcoming to achieve the goals they set for themselves.

This discussion is followed by a presentation of a range of strategies instructors can use as they begin to recognize and support students' own efforts to learn. I explained how instructors can demonstrate instructional immediacy in online classes. The chapter concluded with a suggestion that podcasts, group work and virtual gathering spaces can be used to establish the kinds of peer connections that also affirm learners' own efforts. For those who are interested in reading about additional approaches that AU instructors use, a free e-textbook is available.

In closing, although understanding and supporting students' efforts to learn may not always be straightforward, the ongoing process of continually encouraging students to share the ways they are engaging with course material and the actions they are taking to integrate the new knowledge is critically important. This is both a challenge and an opportunity for online educators in health professions programs.

REFERENCES

Adobe Connect. (n.d.). *Adobe connect* [website]. Retrieved from http://www.adobe.com/sea/products/adobeconnect.html

Andersen, J. F. (1979). Teacher immediacy as a predictor of teaching effectiveness. *Communication Yearbook, 3*, 543–559.

Athabasca University. (n.d.). *Mission and mandate* [website]. Retrieved from http://www.athabascau.ca/aboutau/mission.php

Athabasca University. (n.d.). *AU at a glance* [brochure]. Retrieved from http://www.athabascau.ca/content/aboutau/media/documents/AUbrochure.pdf

Baker, C. (2010). The impact of instructor immediacy and presence for online student affective learning, cognition, and motivation. *The Journal of Educators Online, 7*(1), 1–30. Retrieved from http://www.thejeo.com/Archives/Volume7Number1/BakerPaper.pdf

Bates, A. W. (2015). *Teaching in a digital age.* Victoria: British Columbia Campus. Retrieved from http://opentextbc.ca/teachinginadigitalage/

Baxter, J. (2012). Who am I and what keeps me going? Profiling the distance learning student in higher education. *International Review of Research in Open and Distributed Learning, 13*(4), 107–129. Retrieved from http://www.irrodl.org/index.php/irrodl/article/view/1283/2292

Boud, D., Cohen, R., & Sampson, J. (2001). *Peer learning in higher education: Learning with and from each other*. London: Kogan Page.

Centre for Learning Accreditation. (n.d.). *Prior learning assessment and recognition PLAR* [website]. Retrieved from http://priorlearning.athabascau.ca/

Chakraborty, M., & Nafukho, F. (2015). Strategies for virtual learning environments: Focus on teaching presence and teaching immediacy. *Internet Learning Journal, 4*(1), Article 2. Retrieved from http://digitalcommons.apus.edu/cgi/viewcontent.cgi?article=1046&context=internetlearning

Chen, K., & Jang, S. (2010). Motivation in online learning: Testing a model of self-determination theory. *Computers in Human Behavior, 26*(4), 741–752.

Fahara, M., & Castro, A. (2015). Teaching strategies to promote immediacy in online graduate courses. *Open Praxis, 7*(4), 363–376.

Fedynich, L., Bradley, K., & Bradley, J. (2015). Graduate students' perceptions of online learning. *Research in Higher Education Journal, 27*, 1–30. Retrieved from http://www.aabri.com/manuscripts/142108.pdf

Getzlaf. B, Melrose, S., Moore, S., Ewing, H., Fedorchuk, J., & Troute-Wood, T. (2012). Online interest groups: Virtual gathering spaces to promote graduate student interaction. *International Journal of Online Pedagogy and Course Design, 2*(4), 63–76.

Ghamdi, A., Samarji, A., & Watt, A. (2016). Essential considerations in distance education in KSA: Teacher immediacy in a virtual teaching and learning environment. *International Journal of Information and Education Technology, 6*(1), 17–22.

Gitin, E., Niemi, D., & Levin, J. (2012). Effects of online faculty immediacy behaviors on student performance. In *Proceedings of Global TIME 2012* (pp. 89–94). Association for the Advancement of Computing in Education.

Gordon, K., & Melrose, S. (2011). Peer e-mentoring podcasts in a self-paced course. *Academic Exchange Quarterly, 15*(3), 145–149.

Gorham, J. (1988). The relationship between verbal teacher immediacy behaviors and student learning. *Communication Education, 37*(1), 40–53.

Jang, H. (2008). Supporting students' motivation, engagement, and learning during an uninteresting activity. *Journal of Educational Psychology, 100*(4), 798–811.

Janssen, A., Robinson, T., & Shaw, T. (2014). The evolution of a professional practice forum: Balancing peer-to-peer learning with course objectives. *JMIR Research Protocols, 3*(4), e58. Retrieved from http://www.researchprotocols.org/2014/4/e58/

Kauffman, H. (2015). A review of predictive factors of student success in and satisfaction with learning. *Research in Learning Technology, 23*, 26507. Retrieved from http://dx.doi.org/10.3402/rlt.v23.26507

Kelly, S., Rice, C., Wyatt, B., Ducking, J., & Denton, Z (2015). Teacher immediacy and decreased student quantitative reasoning anxiety: The mediating effect of perception. *Communication Education, 64*(2), 171–186.

Lee, E., Pate, J., & Cozart, D. (2015). Autonomy support for online students. *TechTrends, 59*(4), 54–61.

Marin Sánchez, M., Martinez-Pecino, R., Rodriguez, Y. T., & Melero, P. T. (2011). Student perspectives on the university professor role. *Social Behavior & Personality: An International Journal, 39*(4), 491–496.

Mehrabian, A. (1967). Attitudes inferred from nonimmediacy of verbal communication. *Journal of Verbal Learning and Verbal Behavior, 6*(2), 294–295.

Mehrabian, A. (1971). *Silent messages*. Belmont, CA: Wadsworth.

Melrose, S. (2006). Facilitating help-seeking through student interactions in a WebCT online graduate study program. *Nursing and Health Sciences, 8*(3), 175–178.

Melrose, S. (2009). Instructional immediacy online. In P. Rogers, G. Berg, J. Boettcher, C. Howard, L. Justice, & K. Schenk (Eds.), *Encyclopedia of distance learning* (2nd ed., Vol. 3, pp. P1212–P1215). Hershey, PA: Information Science Reference.

Melrose, S., & Bergeron, K. (2006). Online healthcare graduate study learners' perceptions of instructional immediacy. *International Review of Research in Open and Distance Learning, 7*(1), 1–13. Retrieved from http://www.irrodl.org/index.php/irrodl/article/viewArticle/255/477

Melrose, S., & Bergeron, K. (2007). Instructor immediacy strategies to facilitate group work in online graduate study. *Australasian Journal of Educational Technology, 23*(1), 132–148.

Melrose, S., & Gordon, K. (2008). Online post LPN to BN students' views of transitioning to a new nursing role. *International Journal of Nursing Education Scholarship, 5*(1), Article 14.

Melrose, S., & Gordon, K. (2011). Overcoming barriers to role transition during an online post LPN to BN program. *Nurse Education in Practice, 11*(1), 31–35.

Melrose, S., & Swettenham, S. (2012) Asynchronous online peer assistance: Telephone messages of encouragement in post licensure nursing programs. *Journal of Peer Learning, 5*(1), 1–5.

Melrose , S., Shapiro, B., & LaVallie, C. (2005). Help seeking experiences of health care learners in a WebCT online graduate study program. *Canadian Journal of Learning and Technology, 31*(2), 5–21.

Melrose, S., Park, C., & Perry, B. (2013). *Teaching health professionals online: Frameworks and strategies*. Athabasca: Athabasca University Press. Retrieved from http://www.aupress.ca/index.php/books/120234

Moodle. (n.d.). *moodle* [website]. Retrieved from https://moodle.org/
Reeve, J., & Jang, H. (2006). What teachers say and do to support students' autonomy during a learning activity. *Journal of Educational Psychology, 98*(1), 209–218.
Reeve, J., Jang, H., Carrell, D., Jeon, S., & Barch, J. (2004). Enhancing students' engagement by increasing teachers' autonomy support. *Motivation and Emotion, 28*(2), 147–169.
Rosenau, P., Lisella, R., Clancy, T., & Nowell, L. (2014). Developing future nurse educators through peer mentoring. *Nursing Research and Reviews, 5*, 13–21.
Ryan, R., LaGuardia, J,. Solky-Butzel, J. Chirkov, V., & Kim, Y. (2005). On the interpersonal regulation of emotions: Emotional reliance across gender, relationships and cultures. *Personal Relationships, 12*(1), 145–163.
Topping, K. (2005). Trends in peer learning. *Educational Psychology, 25*(6), 631–645.
Wiener, M., & Mehrabian, A. (1968). *Language within language: Immediacy, a channel in verbal communication.* New York, NY: Appleton-Century-Crofts.
Woods, R. H., & Baker, J. D. (2004). Interaction and immediacy in online learning. *International Review of Research in Open and Distance Learning, 5*(2). Retrieved from http://www.irrodl.org/content/v5.2/woods-baker.html
Wright, R. (2014). *Student-teacher interaction in online learning environments.* Hershey, PA: IGI Global. doi:10.4018/978-1-4666-6461-6

Sherri Melrose
Faculty of Health Disciplines
Athabasca University, Canada

PART III

PARTICIPATIVE RESEARCH, TEACHING, AND LEARNING: DISRUPTING SOCIAL AND POLITICAL DISCOURSES

J. LAWRENCE BENCZE

10. STUDENT-LED LEARNING FOR 'ALTRUISTIC' SOCIO-POLITICAL ACTIONS

INTRODUCTION

Preamble

Throughout my nearly 40-year career as a science educator, I have been promoting students' actions of their own to learn. More specifically, with reference to the schema in Figure 10.1, I have been promoting *student-directed* (SD) and *open-ended* (OE) science inquiry and technology design projects and related communications. Such approaches to inquiry promote knowledge-building and dissemination activities in which students control decisions about procedures, including those for experiments and technology design projects. They also allow for many different conclusions, depending on emergent data and available theory (Lock, 1990). In this way, research project conclusions are effectively, student-controlled and they may or may not align with those of mainstream professional scientists and/or engineers.

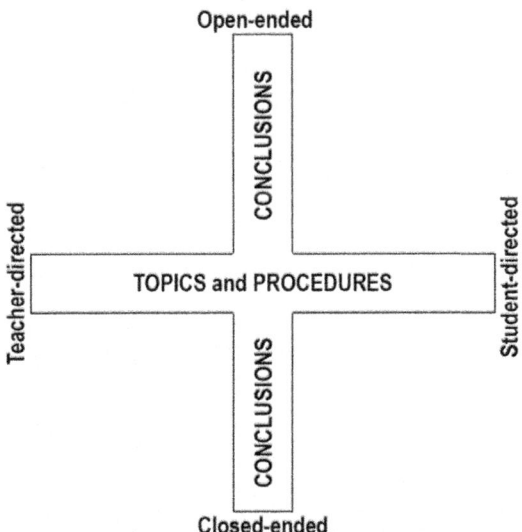

Figure 10.1. Control-of-learning framework

B. Shapiro (Ed.), Actions of Their Own to Learn, 177–198.
© 2018 Koninklijke Brill NV. All rights reserved.

My orientation to encourage students' science and technology projects seems to have arisen from my experiences conducting research for my Masters of Science degree (1977). I thoroughly enjoyed this investigative work. Afterwards, while studying to become a science teacher (B.Ed., 1977), my interests in student-led inquiry were reinforced when one of my instructors (Bert Horwood) congratulated me on a unit of study I had prepared that featured lessons and activities to help students develop skills, strategies and habits of mind enabling them to be self-directing in primary research projects.

The goal of promoting student-initiated science and technology projects, became a cornerstone of my 11-year career as a teacher and subsequent 4-year career as a science consultant for my school district. Throughout that fifteen year period, I implemented revised versions of the unit I had prepared in teacher's college – frequently spurred on by the wonderful projects students were able to complete. I was particularly enamoured with the observation that students who often did not receive high grades in their work in other aspects of science education often thrived when allowed to self-determine their study topics and methods and to self-determine conclusions based, along with theory, on data they had collected during their science inquiry and/or technology design projects.

Especially in my work as a secondary school teacher and consultant, I noticed that many teachers resisted encouraging students to conduct SD/OE science inquiry and/or technology design projects. It seemed more common for teachers to engage students in teacher-guided empirical activities – often called 'labs' – that provided students with support for well-established claims about the world (e.g., 'opposite magnetic charges attract') from fields of science. Indeed, others have suggested that school science focuses "almost exclusively on the well-established products of science [e.g., laws & theories] and cookbook approaches to laboratory exercises, using authoritarian teaching modes" (Bell, 2006, p. 430). In these experiences, emphases appear to be on *teacher-directed* and *closed-ended* activities (Figure 10.1) – antithetical to the kinds of projects I was promoting.

In this chapter, my purpose is to review progress in my career surrounding work to help students take actions of their own to learn—and more specifically, my developing thought and actions to help students engage in research to build projects that contribute new knowledge that may address social/environmental issues and concerns associated with fields of science and technology.

Empirical Inquiries Supporting Pre-Specified Knowledge Claims

I was puzzled by many school science teachers' resistance to encourage students to conduct science inquiry/technology design projects, prompting me to develop a PhD research project in Science Education to address this concern. Through my secondary research (e.g., reading of published works), it became apparent that there has been a long tradition, with some exceptions, of teacher control of students' decision-making in science education. For the most part, empirical activities have been primarily used to support claims of professional science and technology – a focus possibly designed to portray these fields as highly-successful; and, therefore, perhaps worth pursuing as careers (Hodson, 1993). A major goal of such approaches appears to be to deepen students' commitments to abstract claims from the sciences by matching them with examples demonstrating physical phenomena (White, 1991). Generally, this can be accomplished using one of two reciprocal approaches: (i) *induction*[1] (specific observations → generalizations) and (ii) *deduction* (generalizations → specific observations). The former is said to be the context of *discovery*, while the latter is presented as a context of *confirmation*. Curiously, it is apparent that, despite strong suggestions that scientists mainly engage in confirmation activities (e.g., as 'hypothetico-deductivist' approaches) (Lawson, 2005), school science, includes confirmation activities but tends to prioritize discovery learning (Hodson, 1993). A discovery orientation towards inquiry activities can be seen, for instance, in some science teaching curriculum documents – such as one in my jurisdiction: "Research and successful classroom practice have shown that an inquiry approach, with emphasis on learning through concrete, hands-on experiences, best enables students to develop the conceptual foundation they need" (MoE, 2008, p. 30).

While students may gain some sense of 'being scientists' through inquiry-based empirical activities, as elaborated in Bencze and Alsop (2009), there appear to be at least three major problems associated with them:

- *Exclusion*: Expecting students to discover pre-determined (closed-ended) conclusions from 'actions of their own to learn' has long been known to be *discriminatory* – mainly because students lacking cultural capital (Bourdieu, 1986) often struggle to 'discover' abstractions expected of them from inquiry experiences (Welch et al., 1981). Consequently, teachers commonly support (or 'scaffold') such actions of their own to learn. In principle, this could reduce the discriminatory effects of being left on their own to learn pre-specified knowledge claims. However, it seems that largely because of the great 'mass' of knowledge claims in curricula, students must make their 'discoveries' very quickly (Hodson, 1986), making it difficult for some students to develop expected conclusions. Consequently, discovery activities may largely represent a kind of 'survival of the richest'—apparently perpetuating inequities in student learning.
- *Subjectification*: As suggested above, it seems that inquiry-based activities often, if not always, are teacher-guided and closed-ended. This practice is described by prominent science educators who promote inquiry-based learning in the USA:

> Within a classroom, scientific inquiry involves student-centered projects, with students actively engaged in inquiry processes and meaning construction, *with teacher guidance*, to achieve meaningful understanding of scientifically accepted ideas targeted by the curriculum. (Schwartz, Lederman, & Crawford, 2004, p. 612)

Although such guidance may enable more students to learn science products, it also may contribute to a sense of dependency among them. With teachers ultimately controlling tasks and conclusions, students' development of inquiry skills can be significantly compromised (Hodson, 1993). Moreover, prescriptiveness of teacher guidance for both procedures and conclusions (Figure 10.1) can *subjectify* them. It can, in other words, condition them, to varying degrees, into accepting pre-determined science perspectives and practices.

- *Idealization*: By guiding students through appropriate methods to reach widely-accepted conclusions, teachers may be making progress in the sciences seem much more logical and systematic than is apparent by studies of scientists in action (Hodson, 2008). Perhaps science is practised, to a great extent, instead, somewhere within in the Naturalist-Antirealist quadrant of Loving's (1991) *Scientific Theory Profile*[2] (see Figure 10.2). School science, meanwhile, tends to portray science as being practised somewhere within the Rationalist-Realist quadrant—implying, instead, that scientists are unaffected by non-logical factors, such as, psychological (e.g., stress, theoretical biases), sociological (e.g., preferences of prestigious scientists), political (e.g., priorities of elected officials) and/or economic (e.g., corporate priorities) influences. Congruent with this claim, Carter (2005) notes that school science tends to omit reference to government-sanctioned business-science partnerships, which may sometimes compromise the integrity of knowledge generation and dissemination practices in the sciences (Mirowski, 2011). References to problematic business-science partnerships may be avoided to keep from casting fields of science in a bad light. But this practice may leave students/citizens poorly prepared to judge the merits of companies' products and services.

Overall, if teachers want students to develop deep understanding and commitments to 'products' (e.g., laws, theories & innovations) of science and technology, then a main focus on inductive, inquiry-based, empirical activities may not be the best choice. In these cases, students' actions of their own to learn may be inappropriate.

If guided discovery activities are as problematic as suggested above, then it would be natural to wonder what kinds of empirical activities, if any, might be used to help support widely-accepted claims in the major fields of science and technology. An alternative might be to engage students in more *deductive* empirical activities; that is, those in which students conduct empirical tests to confirm 'products' from the sciences previously taught by the teacher, rather than those needing 'discovery' by students. Such tests could be conceived as either *deductive science investigations* or *evaluations of technology designs*, which are considered quite comparable (Lewis, 2006). A simple example of the former would be for students to be taught the law of reflection for plane mirrors and then asked to evaluate this law by using it to predict angles of resultant rays from different angles of incidence. Regarding tests of invention or innovation, after being taught various principles of heat transfer, students could design a model home that would

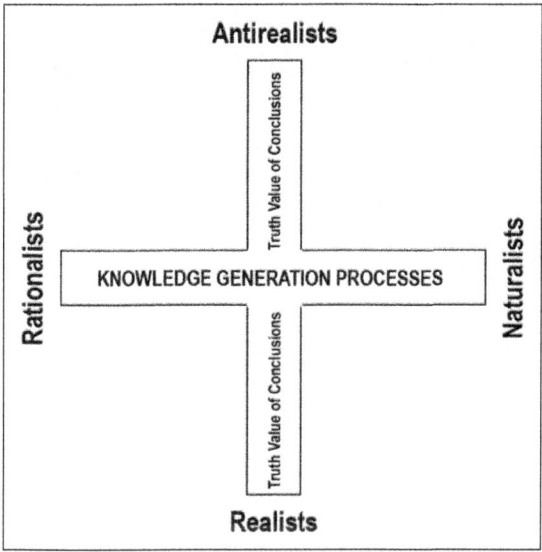

Figure 10.2. Scientific theory profile

be highly efficient in heat conservation. They could test its heat conservation under various environmental conditions, such as through documenting variations in light and wind exposure.

On the one hand, use of guided deductive inquiries might help alleviate problems with exclusion of some learners, as discussed above, since more direct teaching of 'products' of science and technology would minimize risks of students not 'discovering' the expected results/conclusions. On the other hand, problems of subjectification and idealization may remain with deductivist approaches. Inevitably, some students' results will not match their predictions or those of accepted science. Rather than making them 'closed-ended' (Figure 10.1) and insisting on a particular set of results and conclusions, the teacher could allow for more open-ended conclusions, using these situations to teach students about the nature of science. This process would help students to see that scientists often get unexpected results, as well as results that differ from those of other scientists performing similar tests (Hodson, 2008). Depending on ages and developmental stages of students, the teacher might also present and discuss aspects of sociology of science, pointing out that decisions about data meaning among scientists may be based on their participation in particular research paradigms (Kuhn, 1970). Discussions along these lines can bring some authenticity to students' deductive activities. To enhance such experiences, the teacher can urge students to make choices about methods and conclusions in groups. Group work simulates decision-making by teams of scientists. Such simulations of scientists' work could also be extended to include considerations of competition within and among research groups. An example that might be used is an instance where data have been co-opted by others for personal gain, as in the case of James Watson, who reportedly used Rosalind Franklin's X-ray crystallographic image of DNA without her consent to 'discover' its helical structure (Sayre, 1987). To help students see political dimensions and issues raised when doing science, teachers could provide students with examples of government-sponsored business-science partnerships (Angell, 2004). They could then be asked to conduct simulated drug tests (e.g., nicotine effects on mealworm larvae) that are time and profit dependent. Associated with such tests, they might also be encouraged to debate merits of releasing negative results of drug uses to the public.

Student-Directed and Open-Ended Empirical Science Inquiry

Although teachers can use various strategies to address problems of exclusion, subjectification and idealization associated with guided empirical activities intended to teach 'products' of science and technology, these three concerns might be best addressed using student-directed and open-ended science inquiries and technology design projects (Figure 10.1). Through opportunities that help students learn to plan and conduct actions of their own to learn, students may be subjected to less judgment and exclusion from success based on their social/economic backgrounds and linguistic abilities. As students are offered greater freedom of choice, they may resist subjectification through opportunities for greater *self-determination* in learning. When students identify their own research questions, they may become situated in contexts that have greater meaning for them. Experiences of identifying variables and procedures needed to collect information may provide them with more *authentic* (less idealized) conceptions of the nature of science. When students design their own questions and research approaches, they experience complexities and uncertainties that promote authentic understanding of the nature of science (Shapiro, 1996). With such perspectives in mind, for my doctoral thesis primary research, I set out to explore the extent to which and factors affecting secondary school science teachers' successes in enabling and motivating students to self-direct open-ended science inquiry and technology design projects (Bencze, 1995). Working with two teachers over two school years, we developed 'apprenticeship' lessons and activities that appeared to be successful in this regard (Bencze, 2000). Students' successes with and enjoyment of such investigations continually impressed me, serving as further motivation to promote them as I progressed throughout my career and to this day.

I found through my experiences as a teacher, and teachers I worked with also noted that such project work seemed more inclusive. Some students who otherwise had struggled in their science education experienced successes with SD/OE projects. Much of this success seemed attributable to self-determination associated with such projects. Students often chose research topics unfamiliar to teachers, for instance, frequently relating them to their personal experiences. Examples of topics selected by students reported in my thesis include:

- "*The effects of age on the occurrence of the common cold.* Thirty people between the ages of 5 and 76 were asked how often they get a cold in a year. The results suggested that it occurs in the very young (ages 0–10) and the progressively older (ages 30–80) [Louis' student, 12Mar94]".
- "*The effect of temperature on the mass of melted snow.* One hundred measurements of the temperature and mass of varying quantities of melted snow collected by a class of students was sampled. The student concluded that there was no relationship between the two variables, based on her widely-scattered plot [Michael's student, 7Mar94]" (Bencze, 1995, p. 190).

Students noted their appreciation of the opportunity for self-determination during project work, as indicated by comments like: "It's a lot more interesting than reading the textbook, and doing questions [from the book], and him having that hour lecture" (Louis' student, 29Apr93) and "Working it out yourself is better than book learning; you can find out things that are not in the book' (Louis' student, 4May93)" (Bencze, 1995, p. 197).

Finally, there was evidence that students developed more authentic conceptions of the nature of science: "I always thought [scientists] wore pocket protectors with glasses, and were bald with lab coats. [Now] … if you look at [my teacher], they are not like that. They are just regular people who know a lot about science' (Michael's student, 14May93)" and "I will listen to everyone else's point, and I will take it into consideration, but I really like my ideas! … To a degree, some scientists, if they come up with something and they really like the way it sounds, they tend to want to work on their own' (Louis' student, 11May93)" (Bencze, 1995, p. 194).

It was a joy to witness students' learning and enthusiasm for learning when it was under their control. On the other hand, in the 'discovery' of laws and theories approach, students may not be able to discover all aspects of the nature of science, such as government and business-science partnerships through actions of their own to learn. As a colleague and I later found in research with teachers who were learning about science in 'authentic' contexts, one approach is to teach them—using more teacher-directed and closed-ended approaches—aspects of the nature of science that they may or may not 'discover' and then encourage them to evaluate such claims in the contexts of their student-led investigations with no pre-set conclusions (Bencze & Elshof, 2004).

Although many teachers with whom I have worked over the years have had successes like those above in encouraging and enabling young people to self-direct open-ended science inquiry and technology design projects, promoting such project work with secondary school teachers of science, especially, continued to be difficult after my doctoral work and on into my professorial career. Teachers often exclaim, for instance, that 'with all of the "content" (laws, theories & inventions) to teach, there is little time to allow students to self-direct open-ended projects.' This continues to be highly frustrating for me. I believe strongly in students' actions of their own to learn and to arrive at open-ended conclusions, but it seems as though there has been an 'invisible hand' preventing such critical and creative activities from happening in schools. A major focus of my research and writing has been, accordingly, founded in efforts to understand the nature of this force. This involves examining ways that larger political and social contexts may impact schooling.

STUDENTS ACTING ON THEIR OWN TO LEARN AND GIVE

Neoliberal Capitalism and Science and Technology

Although there are likely numerous factors affecting human thoughts and actions, not the least of which are religious, cultural and gender-related, chief among them in many places in the world are *economic* considerations. More specifically, the world seems under the grip of a network of mutually-supporting entities ('actants') promoting *neoliberal* capitalism (Harvey, 2010; McMurtry, 2013). Briefly, although definitions are debated, neoliberal capitalism appears to be an ideology encouraging orchestration of a vast (global) network of living (e.g., financiers, think tanks & corporations), non-living entities (e.g., computer and transportation networks) and symbolic actants (competitiveness, entrepreneurialism & growth). Such entities seem largely facilitated by interventions in markets and in the broader society by governments and transnational actants, like the World Trade Organization, in ways that favour private sector gains over public goods.

Particularly important to for-profit activities of this capitalist network are fields of science and technology. Since about the 1980s, companies have not only hired their own scientists and engineers, but they also have been allowed to enter into financial agreements with university-based 'academic' scientists and engineers (Ziman, 2000). Although it does not appear to be a universal problem, some evidence suggests that the integrity of topic choice, methods and dissemination of findings within fields of commercial and academic science and engineering funded by private sector interests have sometimes been compromised (Krimsky, 2003; Mirowski, 2011). Such compromises have, in turn, been associated with numerous realized and/or potential problems for the wellbeing of individuals, societies and environments. The power of companies to direct the nature of science and technology inquiry raises concerns about relatively immediate health and social justice risks linked to various commercial products and services. These include fast foods and other processed foods (e.g., Weber, 2009), pharmaceuticals (e.g., Angell, 2004), biotechnologies (e.g., Krimsky, 2003), toxic chemicals in everyday things (e.g., Vasil, 2007) and agricultural research and practices (e.g., Kleinman, 2003). Perhaps most worrisome, however, is climate change, that is often associated with 'greenhouse gas' emissions from factories, modes of transportation, energy generation stations and other sources. According to the Intergovernmental Panel on Climate Change, for example, Earth is on course for catastrophic loss of life, unless immediate significant actions are taken to reduce emissions (Klein, 2014). There is an urgent need to include these topics in work that helps learners identify and address issues through their own science learning.

STSE/SSI Education

In about the last 40 years, governments have included science curricular opportunities to help students address potential social and environmental problems associated with fields of science and technology (Pedretti & Nazir, 2013). Although various approaches have been advocated, there has been an ongoing tendency to treat potential problems as *controversies*. Often called *socio-scientific issues*[3] (SSIs), a common curricular approach is to provide students with data and conflicting claims from different 'stakeholders' that may include scientists and/or government versus company officials. They are then asked to develop with classmates logical argumentation-based defenses of their personal positions on issues (Levinson, 2013). Zeidler et al. (2009), who have significantly influenced the nature and progress of SSI education, suggest that the approach presents students with opportunities to "reflect on issues in order to evaluate claims, analyze evidence, and assess multiple viewpoints regarding ethical issues on scientific topics through social interaction and discourse" (p. 75). These approaches appear to have generated some important learning gains, including improved socioscientific reasoning skills (Sadler, Barab, & Scott, 2007) and learning of science laws and theories (Castano, 2008). On the other hand, one wonders if the intense focus on *controversy* may be limiting the extent to which potential harms are addressed. Indeed, it has been suggested that many SSI approaches cast students/citizens as either passive recipients of professional science knowledge ('Deficit' citizenship roles) or as subservient negotiators ('Deliberative' citizenship roles) of professional science knowledge (Levinson, 2010). In light of government-sanctioned compromises to the integrity of fields of science and technology that appear to be compromising the wellbeing of individuals, societies and environments, several scholars have suggested that science education systems need to educate students about such problems and prepare them to engage in socio-political actions[4] to try to bring about a better world (Bencze & Alsop, 2014; Hodson, 2011; Pierce, 2013). This seems particularly necessary, given the degree to which the economic elite appear to have profound influences on larger populations' discourse, identities and public and private lives through their vast and complex networks of transnational and national actants (Ball, 2012; McMurtry, 2013; Pierce, 2013) – often using fields of science and technology for such control (Krimsky, 2003; Mirowski, 2011; Ziman, 2000). Perhaps especially pertinent to education is the phenomena of intense and widespread advertising that encourages cycles of consumption and disposal of commodities by progressively younger and younger children (Bakan, 2011).

Altruistic Science and Technology Education

Acknowledging calls for more activism in science education, in 2006, I developed the 'STEPWISE'[5] curricular and pedagogical framework. This framework arranges teaching/learning domains, such as 'Products Education' (i.e., learning of products of science, such as laws & theories), in ways that encourage students to 'spend' at least some of their literacy (e.g., knowledge and skills) on actions to bring about a better world (Bencze, 2017). A central feature of STEPWISE is to encourage and enable students to develop and carry out student-directed and open-ended research-informed and negotiated action (RiNA) projects to address STSE relationships that are of concern to them. Mainly through Internet searches of the nature and extent of climate change and possible factors contributing to it, students in an 'academic' (university-bound) grade 10 class then designed and conducted a correlational study to determine gender effects on peers' shower durations. Based on findings, they then produced an educational brochure that reviewed the nature and extent of and contributions to climate change (including peers' shower durations) – which they made available to peers in their school in various strategic locations (Bencze & Krstovic, 2017a).

Figure 10.3. Schema for RiNA projects.
Copyright Springer 2017. From L. Bencze (2017), Science & technology education promoting wellbeing for individuals, societies & environments *(p. 27),* Springer, Dordrecht. Reproduced here with permission of Springer

The nature of such RiNA projects to address problematic STSE relationships can be conceived in terms of the schema in Figure 10.3.[6] This schema depicts reciprocal translations between the 'World' (e.g., objects and events) and 'Signs' (e.g. symbols) representing them. Translations[7] from World (e.g., 'showering') to Sign (e.g., graphs of showering), commonly considered a major focus of 'science,' may be considered the *research* in RiNA; while translations from Sign (e.g., brochure) to World (e.g., water-conserving shower head), commonly-associated with technology design (engineering), would be the *actions* in RiNA to bring about a better world.

The schema in Figure 10.3 also seems to have important implications for concepts surrounding the purpose of this book; that is, *students' actions of their own to learn.* Because World ←→ Sign relationships are reciprocal, it follows that 'World' and 'Sign' would have some of each other in them.[8] For example, making a drawing (Sign) of a cell (World) will affect future drawings of cells (new Signs) and, perhaps, engineering changes to cells (new World). Consequently, while 'science' (World → Sign) often is considered related to 'learning,' we can say that 'learning' also occurs in Sign → World translations ('technology'). We might learn what and how inventions/innovations work. So, when students are allowed to control (SD/OE) RiNA projects, they can be said to take 'actions of their own to learn' in *both directions*. They can, in other words, take actions of their own to learn (representations) about the World and actions of their own to learn about changes to (actions on) the World. Moreover, by giving them control over such translations, it is claimed their attachments/affinities to both translations may be deepened—largely because personal control increases learners' sense of personal identity and belonging (Wenger, 1998).

Over the decade of use of the STEPWISE framework in science and technology education, teachers have indicated that students may – particularly, as described below, after helpful lessons and activities – develop significant expertise, confidence and motivation for self-directing such critical and activist projects (Bencze, 2017). A group of four tenth-grade students chose, for example, to study potential problems and solutions regarding automobile idling at 'drive-thru' facilities of common fast food outlets (e.g., Tim Horton's™, Wendy's™, McDonalds™). Their study involved counting the number of cars passing through various drive-thru restaurants in an hour, while also noting the driver's gender and the hour of the day for each visit. They also counted customers' average wait-times in the morning, afternoon and evening, then calculated how much petroleum is not only being wasted but, through combustion, is contributing to greenhouse gas emissions. They used an idling calculator from a government website that relates greenhouse gas emissions to the number of trees needed to be planted to capture the gases. Using findings from their research, they produced a series of posters they then placed at strategic locations around fast-food outlets. They chose to get customers' attention by pointing out the financial savings associated with avoiding use of the drive-thru facilities, with statements like, "Want to Save Over $100? Avoid Drive-Thrus!" They described how they chose such appeals to economic interests for practical reasons:

> When people are driving through, they are not going to have a lot of time to read all the stuff that we need to get across to them. So, we just grabbed their attention with the money claim, but then they go to our website [taken off-line] and see all the information that we put there. We also give them an idling calculator, which allows them to calculate how much money they would save with each minute of less idling. (STSE Action Fair interview, January 14, 2013)

With students developing and conducting research to inform decisions about appropriate actions regarding perceived problems in STSE relationships, societies may be moving along a trajectory from more representative to more participatory forms of democracy. In Levinson's (2010) schema, their self-led research aligns with his 'Praxis' (reflective practice) level of citizenship – which he suggests would help move citizenship into greater levels of participation. In cases where students have used their research to 'speak truth to power,' such as in writing letters to people in power, like school principals, local government officials and company representatives, they may take steps towards achieving Levinson's (2010) 'Dissent and Conflict' level of citizenship – which, as described above, he suggests may be necessary in societies where those with power are perhaps not adequately representing interests of all societal members or environments.

Apprenticeships for Student-Led RiNA Projects

While students' actions of their own to learn through self-directed and open-ended RiNA projects can engender numerous benefits to students and, indeed, the wellbeing of individuals, societies and environments, students often struggle with such projects without teacher support. Often, this appears to be the case because of the extent to which science education systems often prioritize, as noted above, more

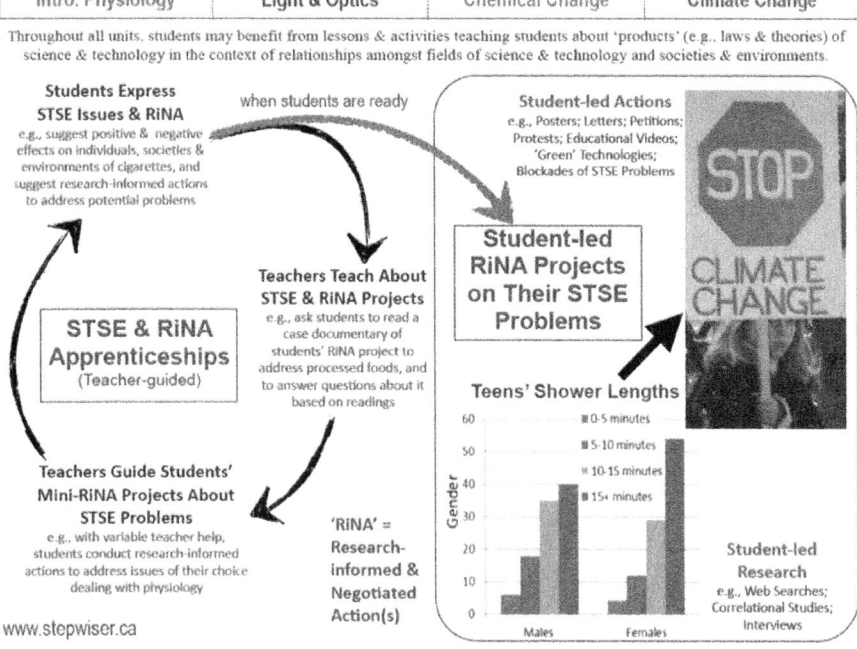

Figure 10.4. STEPWISE pedagogical approach.
Copyright Springer 2017. From L. Bencze (2017), Science & technology education promoting wellbeing for individuals, societies & environments *(pp. 27 & 664), Springer, Dordrecht. Reproduced here with permission of Springer*

teacher-directed and closed-ended instructional activities (Bencze & Alsop, 2009). Indeed, during my work with teachers attempting to implement STEPWISE since 2006, it seems clear that students often need one or more sets of 'apprenticeship' lessons and activities, as depicted in Figure 10.4, before they may self-direct projects. Although elaborated in Bencze (2017), some major approaches for preparing students for actions of their own to learn and to act for the common good, may include the following:

- *Students express STSE issues & RiNA.* Because learners often have pre-conceived attitudes, skills and knowledge ('ASK') relating to those teachers intend to address, and because many of these are *subconscious*, it can be helpful to encourage students to 'express' them in various ways (e.g., through speech, writing, drawing) prior to teacher instruction. A simple approach we have used for encouraging students to express pre-instructional conceptions of STSE issues, research and actions is to ask them to evaluate a range of for-profit commodities associated with fields of science and technology in terms of possible harms for the wellbeing of individuals, societies and environments (WISE). In doing so, students are commonly asked to name various individuals and/or groups who would defend opposing positions about the commodity's effects on WISE. They often also are asked to propose actions they might take to address any problems they perceive, including 'preparation' (e.g., research) they might conduct prior to taking actions. Regarding cell phones, for instance, students might suggest that groups like Greenpeace™ would advise people of environmental hazards of chemicals in old phones, while companies making the phones might deny such effects. Students might suggest that people need to be educated, perhaps through Facebook™ posts, of environmental problems with cell phones – perhaps adding that they feel they need to do more research, perhaps via the Internet, to make the best recommendations about cell phones. As with many school science activities, there is considerable variation in students' reactions and, perhaps more importantly, details of their analyses of and recommendations for actions regarding purchase and uses of commodities. Teachers could take advantage of such variation by encouraging students to share their perspectives and recommended practices, acknowledging that such differences of opinion are characteristic of STSE issues.
- *Teachers teach about STSE & RiNA projects.* Although some students may have relatively sophisticated views about STSE relationships and RiNA projects, my work suggests that many students can benefit[9] from relatively teacher-led lessons and activities aimed at providing them with additional relevant ASK. Although there are many possible approaches in this regard, *case methods* have been very successful. These involve providing students with descriptions ('cases'), in varying detail, of STSE issues, research and actions. These can be given to students in different forms, including as descriptions on paper or as multimedia documentaries. The activist videos from *The Story of Stuff* project,

such as *The Story of Bottled Water*,[10] are excellent; but, there are numerous others available through YouTube™. During or after students' reading/viewing of cases, they can be asked to complete various assignments—including to discuss their current positions on the issues, to conduct some secondary research (e.g., Internet searches) to learn more about the issues and to answer questions about them. After reading a brief description of controversies surrounding snack food, for instance, a 10th-grade student searched the Internet and wrote the following:

> Advertisements for snack foods are usually advertised with famous and powerful people that will influence young teenagers. It is all done for profit and tricks teenagers thinking that if my favourite actor or my idol eats all these snack food I should eat them to [sic]. Sports people that play soccer, for example, David Beckham are shown in commercials for Burger King). (Excerpt from student's secondary research report, June 22, 2012)

Although students can learn a great deal about STSE issues, research and actions through such teacher-managed case methods, students often are limited in their conceptions of issues, research and actions without significant further teacher input. Pierce (2013), for example, suggests students can broaden their perspectives of STSE issues (and research and actions) through instruction in and use of actor networks—which can expose them to perhaps a more realistic range of living, non-living and semiotic (symbolic) actants. After such instruction and their secondary research on hairspray, students produced, for example, the actor network drawing reproduced in Figure 10.5. Enlightened by harms associated with often-hidden actants, such as workers in poor contexts, these students then designed an environmentally-sound hairspray that also would be manufactured using fair labour practices (Bencze & Krstovic, 2017b).

- *Teachers guide students' mini-RiNA projects about STSE problems.* Although students can learn much about STSE issues, research and actions from teachers' lessons, as described above, including with some teacher-guided secondary research, it seems clear that deep, committed, learning best occurs when students have increasing control over decisions about research and actions on issues. Accordingly, in this third phase of the apprenticeship (see Figure 10.4), students would be given control over both types of translation processes in RiNA projects (see Figure 10.3); that is, for 'research' (e.g., cigarette smoking → graphs of cigarette smoking) and for 'actions' (e.g., anti-smoking posters, videos, letters to government, etc. → reduced cigarette smoking).

Depending on students' background experiences, the teacher may have to provide supplementary lessons and activities regarding various skills for RiNA projects to address problematic STSE relationships. An aspect of research that

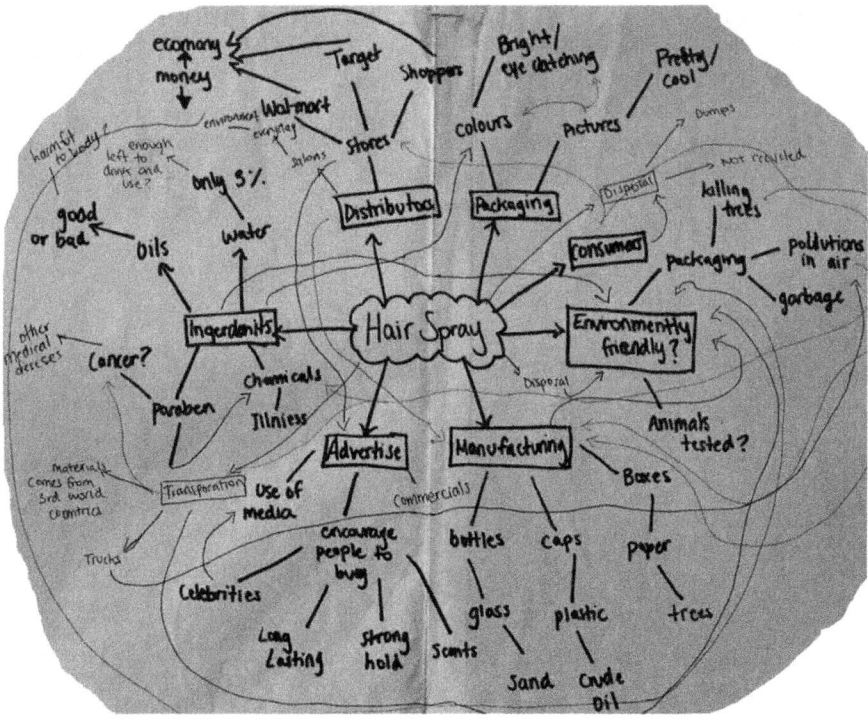

Figure 10.5. Student's actor network drawing about hairspray. Copyright Springer 2017. From L. Bencze (2017), Science & technology education promoting wellbeing for individuals, societies & environments *(p. 242), Springer, Dordrecht. Reproduced here with permission of Springer*

is often not addressed in schools, for instance, is uses of correlational studies (Bencze, 1996). These are empirical investigations in which researchers compare possible associations between pairs of naturally-changing variables, rather than forcing changes in independent variables, as in experimentation. Correlational studies are a good choice, along with qualitative studies, for STSE inquiries because harmful dependent variables in living things (e.g., cancer in smokers) would not be brought about by the investigator, as in experimentation.

To help students develop expertise, confidence and motivation for conducting studies that may generate findings that could inform decisions about socio-political actions, teachers may choose a range of apprenticeship activities. So that the teacher does not interfere with methods and conclusions for studies students would use for their actual RiNA project topics, however, teachers may choose to provide students with lessons and activities on relatively simple, perhaps unrelated, topics to help them become familiar and proficient with studies (Bencze, 2000). With reference to the excerpt from such an activity illustrated in

Figure 10.6, for example, students may gain familiarity with distinctions between studies with experiments.

2) How would you conduct the following investigations? Would you perform an **experiment** or conduct a **study**? Identify independent and dependent variables in each case (IV/DV). *Also, think about what you would have to control!*

a) The effect of cigarette smoking on the amount of coughing

Study	Experiment	I.V:	D.V:

b) Solubility of salt at various temperatures

Study	Experiment	I.V:	D.V:

c) Amount of time spent in front of the computer and quality of sleep

Study	Experiment	I.V:	D.V:

d) The effect of pH on corrosion of metal

Study	Experiment	I.V:	D.V:

e) Time you spend playing video games and your grades in school

Study	Experiment	I.V:	D.V:

Figure 10.6. Excerpt from student activity about correlational studies

After skills apprenticeship activities like those above, the teacher may then feel confident that students have sufficient expertise to conduct RiNA projects involving studies with relatively minimal teacher guidance (depending on the students, etc.). Students may then 'target' their actions, based on findings from their studies. Among tenth-grade students' findings regarding birth control, for instance, was that teenaged girls attending Roman Catholic schools tended not to be as well informed about them as their public high school counterparts. Recognizing the power of popular magazines, these students then chose to lobby the editors of Vogue™ magazine, which often is read by teenaged girls, to include articles about birth control in future issues.

By the end of one three-phase cycle of apprenticeship lessons and activities (see Figure 10.4), teachers may, depending on their judgements of students' expertise, confidence and motivation for self-directing RiNA projects, engage students in one or more of the RiNA apprenticeship activities described in the above three sub-sections. When they feel it is appropriate, teachers can then ask students to take actions of their own to learn about STSE issues that may lead to socio-political actions promoting a better world.

SUMMARY AND CONCLUSIONS

As an educator, watching students take *actions of their own to learn* can be a wonderful thing. In democracies, a teacher's job should involve efforts to make their work with students *obsolete* – to bring students to the point that they don't need a teacher (at least at a certain level of expertise). It also is wonderful to observe what students can achieve when given resources and guidance they can use to design significant aspects of their own learning. They can develop ideas and inventions/innovations not imagined by their teachers. It is particularly rewarding to see students who were previously not successful in traditional teacher-led learning do outstanding work when given the chance to select their own topics to research and, where they feel necessary, take actions of their own to improve the world around them.

In this chapter, I have suggested that, if it is the educational intention to have students learn particular pre-determined science 'products' (e.g., laws, theories & inventions) of science and technology through their engagement in empirical activities, it seems that it is best *not* to require students to act on their own to learn. This form of learning seems associated, to varying degrees, with such problems as: *exclusion*, *subjectification* and *idealization*. To overcome problems like these, it may be that student-directed and open-ended science inquiry and/or technology design projects – supplemented with directed instruction in the nature of science – are appropriate for helping students take 'actions of their own to learn.' While actions of one's own to learn for its own sake is, clearly, a worthy goal, it seems that an essential goal of student-led learning must be to serve as a source of information and motivation to address personal, social and environmental harms associated with fields of science and technology. Particularly in light of adverse effects of neoliberal capitalism on fields of science and technology and many other entities, it seems clear that we need more citizens ready and willing to investigate potential problems faced by all humanity and to act on them for the benefit of all. I suggest that educators recognizing this need may turn to perspectives and practices based on the 'STEPWISE' educational framework. I have learned, through many years of working with the framework, that through use of its apprenticeships, students have been able to take actions of their to learn more about problematic STSE relationships and actions of their own to learn what actions may be appropriate and feasible to address such problems.

Although students can act on their own to learn more about STSE problems concerning them and use findings to enact socio-political actions that may contribute to positive personal, social and environmental changes. My work suggests characteristics of such student-led activities are largely antithetical to current perspectives and practices in many science education contexts. School science *systems*, comprised, for example, of governments, international comparative tests, transnational organizations like the Organisation for Economic Co-operation and Development, textbook publishers, testing agencies, school district officials, parents, teachers, news agencies, etc., tend to prioritize teacher or text controlled celebratory instruction of 'products' (e.g., laws & theories) of science and technology. This preoccupation tends to compromise achievements in other worthwhile components, such as realistic conceptions of the nature of these fields and their relationships with powerful members of societies and development of expertise and confidence with self-directed knowledge production for purposes students/citizens deem important. As Stephen Ball (2012) describes in his book, *Global Education Inc.*, such systems that surround the globe are detached from nation states like a vast spider web and infiltrate into nation states in support of wealth concentration. Such a vast, complex and malleable network seems highly resistant to change—as its comfortable adaption to the 2007–2008 global financial crisis attests (Harvey, 2010). Instead, it seems more like 'The Borg' from the Star Trek™ television and movie series—threatening to assimilate anything in its path, declaring, 'Resistance is futile!' Arising, for example, from and supporting the global capitalist network appear to be many 'STEM' (Science, Technology, Engineering, Mathematics) education initiatives. These seem to be encircling the globe and infiltrating into nation states, claiming 'salvation' in global economic competition while focusing on identifying and educating relatively few students who will work in STEM fields, largely on behalf of private sector entities (Pierce, 2012). In doing so, they seem to minimize attention to student-led investigations and, perhaps more importantly, problematic aspects of relationships between STEM fields and powerful societal members (Gough, 2015; Zeidler, in press).

As Naomi Klein (2014) suggests with regards to predicted crises for much of the globe's people and living and non-living environments, due to dramatic and devastating climate change, little will change in the apparent trajectory of destruction without fundamental transformation of our global economic system – changes that essentially, would prioritize social justice and environmental sustainability. While she offers hope in achievements of various large-scale social movements, like enlightenment about 'The 1%' from the Occupy Wall Street movement, she acknowledges that capitalists have traditionally survived well under a range of threats and crises. Consequently, it is difficult to know exactly what course of action education must take to address problems stemming from neoliberal capitalism in light of 'its' success in rallying a great range of living, non-living and symbolic entities to its causes. However, perhaps those wanting greater social justice and environmental sustainability can learn from capitalists' uses of networks and, accordingly, work to rally many and varied actants to support each other. Among the rallying 'cries' may be calls for coordinated efforts to promote actions of their own to *critically* learn about the world and, where potential harms are perceived, actions of their own to *altruistically* bring about a better world for all individuals, societies and environments.

ACKNOWLEDGEMENTS

Much of the research reported here was funded by a generous grant from the Social Sciences and Humanities Research Council of Canada. I would also like to thank Mr.

Mirjan Krstovic, a secondary school teacher of science who has had considerable success engaging students in self-directed research-informed and negotiated actions to address socioscientific problems of their concern. He provided me with numerous samples of students' project work in this regard. Much of the research also would not have been possible without contributions of several other teachers of science working with me, along with several graduate students who assisted me in data collection and analyses over the years. All of these people exhibited considerable actions of their own to learn and act.

NOTES

[1] There is the argument that pure induction is impossible, in the sense that we can only make sense of observations based on our existing cognitive conceptions. Thus, development of generalizations from specific observations may best be thought of in terms of *abduction*; that is, finding best conceptions to fit specific observations (Lawson, 2005).

[2] The horizontal axis spans a continuum regarding the nature of theory negotiation in the sciences. Rationalists tend to believe in highly systematic methods of science, including rational judgments about theory. Naturalists, by contrast, assume that the conduct of science is highly situational and idiosyncratic, depending on various factors, including psychological, social, cultural and political influences. The vertical axis, meanwhile, depicts a continuum reflecting the truth-value of knowledge. Realists believe that scientific knowledge corresponds to reality, while (extreme) Antirealists claim that each person's constructions are valid. These continua have 'ordinal' scales. On the horizontal axis, for example, placing a mark close to the 'Rationalist' end indicates a 'strong' Naturalist view about science. A mark about mid-way between the two poles, by contrast, indicates that science has moderately Rationalist and Naturalist features.

[3] This term is one of several used to describe controversies regarding potential problems associated with fields of science and technology. In Canada, the site of this research, such issues are addressed in terms of 'STSE' (Science, Technology, Society & Environment) relationships.

[4] Forms of action students might take include: *educating others* (e.g., via posters and pamphlets), *lobbying power-brokers* (e.g., via petitions and letters to politicians), developing potentially-improved products and systems (e.g., a cell phone with recyclable components) and/or *making personal improvements* (e.g., using a travel mug) (Bencze et al., 2012).

[5] 'STEPWISE' is the acronym for Science & Technology Education Promoting Wellbeing for Individuals, Societies & Environments. Details of the STEPWISE framework and related resources are available at: www.stepwiser.ca

[6] Elaboration of this schema is provided in Bencze and Carter (2015). Briefly, it is adapted from a schema provided by Roth (2001), who used semiotics (study of signs & symbols) to discuss relationships between conduct of science and technology.

[7] Translations in both directions may have 'ontological' gaps' i.e., inconsistencies in translating from one kind of thing (e.g., cell) into another kind of thing (e.g., drawing of cell) due to differences in forms of representation between the two entities. 'Ideological' gaps may be considered *purposeful* inconsistencies in such translations—such as intentional mis-representations of commodities (e.g., manufactured food) and advertisements for them (e.g., 'organic').

[8] Because of the reciprocal nature of these translations, we can think of 'science' and 'technology' as co-affecting each other and, thus, having some of the other in them—leading some scholars to consider the two processes as one entity, perhaps called 'technoscience' (Sismondo, 2008).

[9] Reasons for such needs are, undoubtedly, complex; but, it seems that a major factor is school science systems' tendencies – as discussed above – to emphasize teacher-directed and closed-ended instruction in products of science and technology (Hodson, 2011).

[10] http://storyofstuff.org/movies/story-of-bottled-water/

REFERENCES

Angell, M. (2004). *The truth about the drug companies: How they deceive us and what to do about it.* New York, NY: Random House.
Bakan, J. (2011). *Childhood under siege: How big business targets children.* Toronto: Allen Lane.
Ball, S. J. (2012). *Global education inc.: New policy networks and the neo-liberal imaginary.* Abingdon: Routledge.
Bell, R. L. (2006). Perusing pandora's box: Exploring the what, when, and how of nature of science instruction. In L. B. Flick & N. G. Lederman (Eds.), *Scientific inquiry and nature of science: Implications for teaching, learning, and teacher education* (pp. 427–446). Dordrecht: Springer.
Bencze, J. L. (1995). *Towards a more authentic and feasible science curriculum for secondary schools* (Unpublished PhD thesis). The Ontario Institute for Studies in Education, University of Toronto, Toronto.
Bencze, J. L. (1996). Correlational studies in school science: Breaking the science-experiment-certainty connection. *School Science Review, 78*(282), 95–101.
Bencze, J. L. (2000). Procedural apprenticeship in school science: Constructivist enabling of connoisseurship. *Science Education, 84*(6), 727–739.
Bencze, J. L. (Ed.). (2017). *Science and technology education promoting wellbeing for individuals, societies and environments.* Dordrecht: Springer.
Bencze, J. L., & Alsop, S. (2009). A critical and creative inquiry into school science inquiry. In W.-M. Roth & K. Tobin (Eds.), *The world of science education: North America* (pp. 27–47). Rotterdam: Sense Publishers.
Bencze, J. L., & Alsop, S. (Eds.). (2014). *Activist science & technology education.* Dordrecht: Springer.
Bencze, J. L., & Carter, L. (2015). Capitalists' profitable virtual worlds: Roles for science & technology education. In P. P. Trifonas (Ed.), *International handbook of semiotics* (Vol. 1–2, pp. 1197–1212). Dordrecht: Springer.
Bencze, L., & Elshof, L. (2004). Science teachers as metascientists: An inductive-deductive dialectic immersion in northern alpine field ecology. *International Journal of Science Education, 26*(12), 1507–1526.
Bencze, L., & Krstovic, M. (2017a). Students' social studies influences on their socioscientific actions. In J. L. Bencze (Ed.), *Science & technology education promoting wellbeing for individuals, societies & environments* (pp. 115–140). Dordrecht: Springer.
Bencze, L., & Krstovic, M. (2017b). Science students' ethical technology designs as solutions to socio-scientific problems. In J. L. Bencze (Ed.), *Science & technology education promoting wellbeing for individuals, societies & environments* (pp. 201–226). Dordrecht: Springer.
Bourdieu, P. (1986). The forms of capital. In J. G. Richardson (Ed.), *The handbook of theory: Research for the sociology of education* (pp. 241–258). New York, NY: Greenwood Press.
Carter, L. (2005). Globalisation and science education: Rethinking science education reforms. *Journal of Research in Science Teaching, 42*(5), 561–580.
Castano, C. (2008). Socio-scientific discussions as a way to improve the comprehension of science and the understanding of the interrelation between species and the environment. *Research in Science Education, 38*(5), 565–587.
Gough, A. (2015). STEM policy and science education: Scientistic curriculum and sociopolitical silences. *Cultural Studies of Science Education, 10*(2), 445–458.
Harvey, D. (2010). *The enigma of capital and the crises of capitalism.* Oxford: Oxford University Press.
Hodson, D. (1986). The nature of scientific observation. *School Science Review, 68*, 17–29.
Hodson, D. (1993). Re-thinking old ways: Towards a more critical approach to practical work in school science. *Studies in Science Education, 22*(1), 85–142.
Hodson, D. (2008). *Towards scientific literacy: A teachers' guide to the history, philosophy and sociology of science.* Rotterdam: Sense Publishers.
Hodson, D. (2011). *Looking to the future: Building a curriculum for social activism.* Rotterdam: Sense Publishers.
Klein, N. (2014). *This changes everything: Capitalism and the climate.* Toronto: Simon & Schuster.

Kleinman, D. L. (2003). *Impure cultures: University biology and the world of commerce*. Madison, WI: University of Wisconsin Press.
Krimsky, S. (2003). *Science in the private interest: Has the lure of profits corrupted biomedical research?* Lanham, MD: Rowman & Littlefield.
Kuhn, T. S. (1970). *The structure of scientific revolutions* (2nd ed.). Chicago, IL: University of Chicago Press.
Latour, B. (2005). *Reassembling the social: An introduction to actor-network-theory*. Oxford: Oxford University Press.
Lawson, A. E. (2005). What is the role of induction and deduction in reasoning and scientific inquiry? *Journal of Research in Science Teaching, 42*(6), 716–740.
Levinson, R. (2010). Science education and democratic participation: An uneasy congruence? *Studies in Science Education, 46*(1), 69–119.
Levinson, R. (2013). Practice and theory of socio-scientific issues: An authentic model? *Studies in Science Education, 49*(10), 99–116.
Lewis, T. (2006). Design and inquiry: Bases for an accommodation between science and technology education in the curriculum? *Journal of Research in Science Teaching, 43*(3), 255–281.
Lock, R. (1990). Open-ended, problem-solving investigations—What do we mean and how can we use them? *School Science Review, 71*(256), 63–72.
Loving, C. C. (1991). The scientific theory profile: A philosophy of science model for science teachers. *Journal of Research in Science Teaching, 28*(9), 823–838.
McMurtry, J. (2013). *The cancer stage of capitalism: From crisis to cure*. London: Pluto.
Ministry of Education. (2008). *The Ontario curriculum, grades 9 and 10: Science*. Toronto: Queen's Printer for Ontario.
Mirowski, P. (2011). *Science-mart: Privatizing American science*. Cambridge, MA: Harvard University Press.
Pedretti, E., & Nazir, J. (2011). Currents in STSE education: Mapping a complex field, 40 years on. *Science Education, 95*(4), 601–626.
Pierce, C. (2012). The promissory future(s) of education: Rethinking scientific literacy in the era of biocapitalism. *Educational Philosophy and Theory, 44*(7), 721–745.
Pierce, C. (2013). *Education in the age of biocapitalism: Optimizing educational life for a flat world*. New York, NY: Palgrave Macmillan.
Roth, W. M. (2001). Learning science through technological design. *Journal of Research in Science Teaching, 38*(7), 768–790.
Sadler, T. D., Barab, S. A., & Scott, B. (2007). What do students gain by engaging in socioscientific inquiry? *Research in Science Education, 37*(4), 371–391.
Sayre, A. (1987). *Rosalind Franklin and DNA*. London: Norton.
Schwartz, R. S., Lederman, N. G., & Crawford, B. A. (2004). Developing views of nature of science in an authentic context: An explicit approach to bridging the gap between nature of science and scientific inquiry. *Science Education, 88*(4), 610–645.
Shapiro, B. (1996). A case study of change in elementary student teacher thinking during an independent investigation in science: Turning to the 'face of science that does not yet know.' *Science Education, 80*(5), 535–560.
Sismondo, S. (2008). Science and technology studies and an engaged program. In E. J. Hackett, O. Amsterdamska, M. Lynch, & J. Wajcman (Eds.), *The handbook of science and technology studies* (3rd ed., pp. 13–31). Cambridge, MA: The MIT Press.
Vasil, A. (2007). *Ecoholic: Your guide to the most environmentally friendly information, products and services in Canada*. Toronto: Vintage.
Watson, J. (1968). *The double helix: A personal account of the discovery of the structure of DNA*. New York, NY: Atheneum.
Weber, K. (Ed.). (2009). *Food inc.: How industrial food is making us sicker, fatter, and poorer – and what you can do about it, A participant media guide*. New York, NY: Public Affairs.
Welch, W. W., Klopfer, L. E., Robinson, J., & Aikenhead, G. S. (1981). Inquiry and school science: Analysis and recommendations. *Science Education, 65*(1), 33–50.

Wenger, E. (1998). *Communities of practice*. Cambridge: Cambridge University Press.
White, R. T. (1991). Episodes, and the purpose and conduct of practical work. In B. E. Woolnough (Ed.), *Practical science: The role and reality of practical work in school science* (pp. 78–86). Milton Keynes: Open University Press.
Zeidler, D. L. (2016). STEM education: A deficit framework for the twenty first century?: A sociocultural socioscientific response. *Cultural Studies of Science Education, 11*(1), 11–26.
Zeidler, D. L., Sadler, T. D., Applebaum, S., & Callahan, B. E. (2009). Advancing reflective judgement through socioscientific issues. *Journal of Research in Science Teaching, 46*(1), 74–101.
Ziman, J. (2000). *Real science: What it is, and what it means*. Cambridge: Cambridge University Press.

J. Lawrence Bencze
Ontario Institute for Studies in Education
University of Toronto, Canada

KATHLEEN C. SITTER

11. LEARNING TO ENGAGE IN SOCIAL ACTION USING PHOTOVOICE

A Participatory Action Engagement to Transform Learning

INTRODUCTION

This chapter focuses on the methodology of photovoice as a form of participatory action engagement and considers the ways in which learners in both formal and informal settings take action to address social justice issues through photography. The chapter begins with locating photovoice within the context of participatory visual media. It follows with a brief historical trajectory of the development and uses of documentary and community photography in efforts to listen to previously unheard voices and raise awareness of social justice issues. The final section explores photovoice as a form of participatory action engagement, with examples of how this creative methodology supports individuals in both community and classroom settings as active participants in their own learning. The chapter concludes with further considerations associated with ethics and distribution.

PARTICIPATORY VISUAL MEDIA

As a filmmaker and arts-based researcher, I have had the privilege of working in community-based projects using multiple forms of participant-generated visual media. These experiences have led me to reflect on the creative process of developing visual media that both honour and amplify previously unheard voices, and the role images can play to promote critical thought, raise awareness, and engage in social action. I agree with Deborah Barndt's claim that this form of media "is always part of a broader, ongoing process, linked to critical education and collective organizing for change" (2001, p. 35).

The creative process behind the camera involves an intersection of listening, watching, and discussing images. I have found that it is in the midst of these pedagogical spaces where critical moments of consciousness occur and where individuals also become active participants in transformational learning. My interest in participatory visual media, where people come together and create film and photographs for the purposes of education, awareness, and political action, is further influenced by theories of grass-roots organizing (see Alinsky, 1971; Pyles, 2009), the histories of documentary and community photography (see Braden, 1983;

de Cuyper, 1997; Rosler, 1989/2003), and participatory video and the Fogo process (Crocker, 2003). This work is also informed by many applications of visual media that bring to light social justice and human rights issues through the use of cameras as pedagogical tools in storytelling to help learners take actions in their own learning (de Lange et al., 2007; Edwards, Perry, Janzen, & Menzies, 2012).

While exploring the literature on visual media and social change, I found examples that held certain commonalities in both academic and community settings. Unlike traditional approaches such as documentary photography where communities were typically presented as objects of the camera, these examples cited community groups' uses of photography as a means to communicate their own lived experiences and perspectives around a topic or issue of concern. The visual stories produced by community members were subsequently shown in different community forums in efforts to inspire action and raise awareness of social justice issues (see Braden, 1983; de Lange, Mitchell, & Stuart, 2007).

Over the last 30 years, there has been a growing interest in participant-generated visual media (Guillemin & Drew, 2010; Li, 2008). These methodologies often involve community members using visual media to learn to communicate their own perspectives (Li, 2008). These methods have been used to honour local knowledge (Insight, n.d.), to explore lived experiences (Bery, 2003), and as a means of emancipatory praxis (White, 2003). Examples of collaborative visual methodologies include participatory video (White, 2003), digital storytelling (Walsh, Shier, Sitter, & Sieppert, 2010), and photovoice (Guillemin & Drew, 2010).

The following section considers the historical trajectory of documentary traditions during the social reform era and the community photography movement that gained momentum during the 1960s. These earlier trends provide further insight into the evolution of photography as a tool to help community members raise awareness of social justice issues and concerns.

TAKING ACTION THROUGH THE USE OF IMAGES

Social Reform, the FSA and the Early Traditions of Documentary Photography

In 1926, Scottish filmmaker John Grierson coined the term 'documentary' to describe work based on "interpretations of reality" (Wells, 2003, p. 252). Although Grierson was referring to the use of film, the phrase 'documentary photography' was soon adopted in reference to early photographers who used their photographic images in social change efforts. Early methods of the documentary tradition are often defined within the framework of the Progressive Era (1880–1920) in the United States (Solomon-Godeau, 1991). The work of early documentary photographers was intended to effect social change through the power of the image (Szto, 2008). Documentary photography gained significant influence and exposure during this period, as middle-class reformers often desired objective and rational approaches to describe and examine social problems (Szto, 2008).

Early documentary photographers often sought improvements to the conditions of exploited communities (Blyton, 1987). Through the publication of photographic work that captured the degradations of urban and rural poverty, many documentary photographers successfully used their pictures to affect changes in social policy and reform (Blyton, 1987). Jacoob Riis is widely acknowledged as the first American reformer to use a camera and his work contributed to improving the living and working conditions of New York immigrants (Blyton, 1987). Another prominent documentary photographer during this period was Lewis Hine. Hine photographed working conditions of child labour, and his photographs were instrumental in persuading the American Congress to stop the exploitation of child labour in the United States (Seixas, 1987; Szto, 2008).

Photographers covering the Great Depression during the 1930s also adopted a similar approach (Szto, 2008). During this period, the United States government initiated a New Deal legislation with its goals to insure social security for all Americans by way of relief and reform (Szto, 2008). In 1934, the photo division of the Farm Security Administration (FSA) was created as a means of fostering support of the New Deal Relief program. Under the direction of Roy Emerson Styker, photographers documented the social impact of the Great Depression between 1935–1943. These photographs were often published in magazines and journals as a means of educating the public on the New Deal project whilst challenging public perceptions of America's social well being (Szto, 2008). When the FSA documentary project finally ended, over 270,000 photographs had been taken that represented various aspects of rural poverty (Szto, 2008, p. 106).

Several people who were photographed in the FSA project also evolved into cultural symbolic icons. An example is Dorthea Lange's 1936 photograph '*Migrant Mother*' which is one of the most reproduced documentary photographs in history and has become an archetypical representation of suffering (Curtis, 1986). Wells (2003) notes that the position of the mother, the absence of the father, and the exclusion of details anchoring the photograph to a particular place and time reflected universal similarities in the condition of human kind. It was through these aesthetics that Lange made it possible "for the picture to be seen as a universal symbol of motherhood, poverty, and survival" (Wells, 2003, p. 39).

However, these early documentary traditions are also criticized for appropriating a paternalistic approach to addressing social issues (Burgin, 1982; Rosler, 1989/2003; Sekula, 1984). The methods used reflected the power of the privileged to define the experiences of the oppressed. The act of photographing those who did not have access to a means of representing themselves further reinforced dominant social relations (Rosler, 1989/2003). Braden (1983) notes that documentary photographers such as Hine, Riis, and those of the FSA appealed to pitying those presented as helpless victims of misfortune, and in choosing to appeal to that emotion the audiences for these pictures were not the people experiencing the issues but were reform-minded individuals. Thus, the documentary photographer acted as an interpreter of people's experiences (Braden, 1983).

Community Photography

In contrast to early approaches to documentary photography, community photography took a different approach where photographers were also members of the working class and underprivileged communities they photographed. People who were directly impacted by social injustices began to take photographs to visually represent topics and issues of concern, based on their perspectives and experiences (Braden, 1983). The genesis of this community approach to photography occurred during the early part of the 19th Century. During this period, community photography was defined as a practice with a political basis that aligned with socialist ideologies (de Cuyper, 1998). The worker-photography movement in Germany photographed the rise of Fascism whereas the Workers' Film and Photo League (WFPL) in the United States provided militant workers with the skills to create photographic records of class struggle (Braden, 1983). Community groups began to use photographs to reinforce political messages and raise community consciousness and solidarity (Braden, 1983). Although the worker-photography movement in Europe ultimately disappeared in the 1930s and the American League dispersed in the 1950s under pressure from the federal government, these early photographic methods capture the historical precedent of communities intervening in the professional mass media's domination of public information (Braden, 1983).

Community photography was revived during the 1960s as a result of changes in Western societies that were heavily influenced by the American Civil Rights movement, second wave feminism, and protests against the Vietnam War (de Cuyper, 1998). The process involved blending visual images with other artistic forms, and was considered art that was created by non-professionals, with a recognition that the content was relevant to the respective artists (Braden, 1983). These projects were often set up in low-income industrial areas of urban cities, and aimed to encourage people on the margins of society to learn about and articulate their own histories and experiences through creative visual methods such as photography, posters, photomontages, and photo stories (de Cuyper, 1998). These projects often emphasized collaborative efforts and collective involvement by community groups (Braden, 1983; de Cuyper, 1998; Wells, 2003).

Community photography involved learning to create images to explore experiences and connections with others. As one of the main goals was to counter hegemonic conceptions of gender, class, and race, a plan for the distribution of these images was central to the social change goals of these projects (Braden, 1983; de Cuyper, 1998). In efforts to develop solidarity and to support learning to engage in social action, these methods predominantly targeted local communities experiencing similar issues. Community photography exhibits were often used to alert people to issues of immediate concern, and provided a focus for community meetings and discussion groups (de Cuyper, 1998).

Whereas Tagg (1998) asserts that amateur photography "will rarely be seen as impacting social change to any degree" (p. 18), Braden contends that groups such as the social feminist *Hackney Flashers Collective* proves it is possible for community photography "to move from the local context to the wider social and political area without losing impact" (1983, p. 33). In their project, "*Who's holding the baby?*," the group combined photographs, text, and cartoon images to raise issues of class and the need for child-care facilities. The exhibition was distributed throughout the U.K. in various community centres, and through university courses, conferences, and art and museum locations.

The photovoice process shares many aspects of community photography as a pedagogical practice that aims to be both an emancipatory and social transformative endeavour. And similar to the early methods of documentary photography, photovoice involves the use of images as a tool to learn about and communicate societal issues, and advocate for social change. The following sections explore the goals and theories informing the photovoice methodology.

THE EMERGENCE OF PHOTOVOICE: AN ACTIVE COLLABORATION
BETWEEN RESEARCHER AND PARTICIPANT

Visual Research and Participant-Generated Photography

Visual research refers to both the study of the visual as a topic of inquiry and the use of visual-oriented tools as methods of collecting and analyzing data (Wagner, 2006). Examples of the visual as a topic of inquiry include the investigation of social behaviour and cultural ways in which images are appropriated and read in everyday life. The examination of different forms of representation and interpretation occur through content analysis and semiology of an image and the exploration of the ways in which photographs convey meaning, to whom, and for what purposes (Rose, 2007; Wagner, 2006). Visual oriented methods such as photographic pictures, drawings, and videos are also applied by researchers using approaches to describe, portray, or analyze a social phenomena (Harper, 1988; Rose, 2007).

Photography is amongst the most widely recognized forms of visual social scientific data (Wagner, 2006). During the 1990s, scholars in the fields of anthropology and sociology began advocating for a collaborative approach between researcher and participant in the use of photography, beginning with the notion that photographs are not simply a mode to record data, but a medium through which new knowledge can be created (Chaplin, 1994; Harper, 1998). A method that evolved out of this period was "photo-elicitation" (Harper, 1988). Photo-elicitation describes the process of using photographs to stimulate dialogue during individual and focus group interviews (Harper, 2003). There are primarily two dominant approaches to this process. The first involves the researcher taking photographs and showing the participants pictures of themselves or aspects of their environment, and asking them to talk about what they see (Frohmann, 2005). The second approach involves the *participant* taking the photographs. This is based on the assumption that the process of engaging in image production will reveal what the participant considers most critical to the topic of inquiry (Harrison, 2002). However, both forms of photo-elicitation reflect significant learning taking place for both the participant and the researcher. In both instances, the participant is encouraged to consider elements internal to the picture as well as socio-cultural content external to the images in order for the researcher to develop deeper insights into participant's social interaction, social relations, and cultural norms (Harper, 2003).

The Emergence of Photovoice

During the 1990s, when new approaches were developed, image-based tools quickly evolved into participant-generated visual media methods due to the focus of community-based research and participatory approaches that grew in popularity and focus, especially within cross-cultural research (Brooks, Poudrier, & Thomas-MacLean, 2008; Castleden, Garvin, & Huuayaht First Nation, 2008; de Lange et al., 2007; Gotschi, Freyer, & Delve, 2008; Reason & Bradbury, 2006; Wang, 1999; Wang & Redwood-Jones, 2001; White, 2003).

It was Public Health scholar, Dr. Caroline Wang, who first developed a participatory approach to photography, which is often referred to as "participatory photography" or "photovoice" (Molloy, 2007). Photovoice guides participants to use cameras to capture aspects of their life and community, and photos are then used to stimulate discussion and gain deeper insights into people's lived experiences (Singhal, Harter, Chitnis, & Sharma 2007). However, a distinguishing feature of photovoice is the display of photographs in public venues in order to raise awareness in the community about the social issues raised, and to encourage community dialogue aimed at social change (Wang & Redwood-Jones, 2001). Photovoice emerged from Drs. Wang and Burris' work in teaching language and literacy skills to women in the Chinese province of Yunnan. The women were guided to take photographs and combined them with their personal narrative to represent their lived experiences (Wang & Burris, 1997). These photographs and written texts were presented in a book titled Visual Voices: 100 Photographs of Village China by the Woman of Yunnan Province (Wang & Burris, 1997). Wang has since written extensively on the overall process, methodology, and ethics of photovoice (see: Wang, 1999; Wang, 2000; Wang, Burris, & Ping, 1996; Wang & Redwood-Jones, 2001).

Changing Learning Culture Using Photovoice as an Emancipatory Learning and Teaching Resource

The literature describing photovoice often refers to documentary photography, feminism, and Freirean pedagogy as the main underlying philosophies (Wang, 1999; Wang & Burris, 1997; Wang & Redwood-Jones, 2001). All three theories support participatory, dialogical, arts-based methods that privilege different ways of knowing the creative representation of lived experiences. Documentary photography suggests a grassroots approach to representation and democratic ways individuals and groups can use photos to share their personal meanings (Wang & Pies, 2004). Feminist theory informing this approach is based on the notion that "power accrues to those who have voice, set language, make history and participate in decision making" (Wang & Pies, 2004, p. 96). Its methods value tacit knowledge while taking into account power, representation, and voice (Wang & Burris, 1997). Using photovoice, participants communicate their embodied knowledge through photography. Collective knowledge arises as participants discuss their shared experiences in relation to the images (Wang & Burris, 1997) and choose how to communicate their knowledge through photographs. Freire's theory recognizes that people are experts in their own lives, and emphasizes that their role in research involves active participation (1970/2008).

Freirean pedagogy aims for transformative education through the interdependent concepts of community-led learning, participation, critical consciousness, and praxis (Fleuri, 2008; Wallerstein & Duran, 2003). This approach to critical consciousness involves reflecting critically about self in relation to the everyday socio-political conditions that impact personal circumstances. Freire argued that images are also tools for people to see their reality from a new perspective and to think about the circumstances that influence thir experiences. In this process, group dialogue further reveals themes that are embedded in the images, where participants interrogate these themes through the ongoing cycles of reflection – dialogue – action (Wallerstein & Duran, 2003).

Freire's theory of dialogue provides a foundation to guide dialogical approaches that allow understanding of the ways images can be used to stimulate group discussion. By providing learners the opportunity to create photographs that represent their own experiences, images can be used to communicate their own knowledge, not only to others, but also to themselves. With regards to photography, using the camera can contribute in the transformative process of education and self-awareness.

PHOTOVOICE AND COMMUNITY-BASED RESEARCH

Community-based research projects that use photovoice in efforts to transform conditions and address significant social issues, at the same time makes the research process an important pedagogical practice (Daniels, 2008). According to Banks (2003), participatory methods start with the assumption that community members are experts in their situations, thus the role of the community should involve active participation (p. 103). By valuing the knowledge and experiences of people, and through dialectical encounters with others, groups begin to find solutions and address the types of social change that must occur at the macro level in order to achieve a more just and equitable society.

There are three main goals that guide photovoice: (1) to enable people to record and reflect on their particular community's strengths, needs and concerns; (2) to promote critical dialogue and knowledge about important issues through large and small group discussion of photographs; and (3) to reach policymakers, health planners, and community leaders, who can be mobilized to make change (Wang, 1999; Wang, Cash, & Powers, 2000; Wang & Redwood-Jones, 2001). In the process, participants are also responsible for identifying themes by analyzing and codifying the photographs. Subsequently, the photos are displayed in public venues to raise awareness in the community about the issues and concerns identified by the participants (Wang, 1999; Wang & Pies, 2004; Wang & Redwood-Jones, 2001).

The overall process of employing photovoice varies from project to project, but usually involves a discussion with participants on the use of consent forms and training on how to use the camera. Individuals are given several weeks or months to take photographs, then the group comes back together to collectively analyze the photographic meanings. Wang and Burris (1997) also developed a reflexive process to support participants to take further action in their own learning to identify connections and comment on experiences in the photographs. This is demonstrated using the acronym SHOWED. (*W*hat do you *S*ee here? *H*ow does this relate to *O*ur Lives? *W*hy does this problem, concern, or strength exist? What can we *D*o about it?) The final aspect of the method is a public exhibit of the photographs, where policy makers and community members are invited to view the display.

Photovoice as a participatory research methodology is often used when working with marginalized populations (Gotschi, Freyer, & Delve, 2008; Wang, 1999, 2000; Wang & Burris, 1997; Wang & Pies, 2004). Some examples include: youth (de Lange, Mitchell, Moletsane, Stuart, & Buthelezi, 2006); people who are homeless (Wang, Cash, & Powers, 2000); Aboriginal women (Brooks, Poudrier, Thomas, & MacLean, 2008); rural African American breast cancer survivors (Lopez, Eng, Randall-David, & Robinson, 2005); and people with disabilities (Jurkowski & Paul-Ward, 2007).

Molloy (2007) notes that photovoice "allows diverse populations of oppressed individuals the opportunity to take social action by raising awareness in the community and among policy-makers" (p. 40). The use of photovoice offer researchers opportunities to gain deeper insights into people's lived experiences, which may have been previously overlooked, rejected, or silenced (Singhal et al., 2007, p. 217). Researchers note that the this methods increases participants' overall self-esteem (Molloly, 2007; Wang, 1999); builds rapport and trust within the group (Brooks et al., 2008), promotes critical consciousness (LeClerc et al., 2002; Wang et al., 2000), and honours different ways of knowing through artistic expression whilst removing the privileging of the written word (Castleden et al., 2008; Daniels, 2008). Photovoice also offers marginalized communities the opportunity for participation, collaboration, and a forum and space to document their concerns, issues and community assets through the use of photography. Wang and colleagues note that in sharing these photographs with the broader community, the method fosters social support, raises awareness of social issues, and enables community members to rethink issues from the perspective of marginalized groups, and thus serves as a catalyst for broader social change (Wang & Pies, 2004; Wang & Redwood-Jones, 2001).

Photovoice has also been blended with other media in a participatory framework. For instance, Barlow and Hurlock (2014) describe a participatory action research study that explored the lived experiences of sex trade workers in Western Canada. In this study, a group of women who were former sex trade workers were guided through the photovoice process. They used their photographs to create a series of short personal videos about their experiences. Through creating the videos, participants integrated music, personal narrative, and visual effects, which afforded another pathway for exploration and critical reflection. The final videos also provided another medium to visually articulate and raise awareness about the lives of sex trade workers (Barlow & Hurlock, 2014).

A Participatory Action Engagement of Transformative Learning: The Right to Love Project

Both still and moving images in research and social action initiatives can be taken-up in the context of emancipatory learning. Engaging in the process of participatory video involves learners in the production of moving images to document and explore a topic of concern. This approach is also informed by the same theoretical framework as collaborative photography. One example of this is the *The Right to Love: A Participatory Video Project* (Sitter, 2012). This 12-month study involved adults with developmental disabilities creating a series of short videos on the barriers and supports of sexual rights for persons with disabilities. In this research, participants engaged in new forms of learning while also creating new resources for the learning of others. Participants did this through (1) the use of videos to position themselves in advocacy; (2) learning to strengthen community bridges; (3) developing new communication skills; and (4) providing new learning for others by presenting their visual stories.

In the *Right to Love* project, participants led their advocacy efforts by sharing their visual stories. Participants entered into these public spaces as educators and film-collaborators. These roles afforded participants a level of recognition as experts in their lived experiences. By approaching these interactions from a place of authority, participants extended and enhanced their community connections. They also recognized that audiences truly wanted to hear what they had to say. As one participant explained: "It really stands out what we're all about and that *we give the education* to the public and we act on it. We say: Yes, we have the right to love, and we will act on it." The comment also reflects the importance of power arrangements in the process of sharing knowledge and how images as media become more than an educational tool solely for the people who create and use them. As another participant described the process of distribution, "Our voices become louder and stronger. We're also developing relationships with others inside and outside our group."

Participants learned to build bridges within and beyond the community. Advocacy as storytelling further captivates the broader community as the visual stories personalized how people take up their cause. As one participant from the *Right to Love* study further explained: "Through our stories, there's a human piece that comes out, and a lot of times that's hidden by statistics, or other people's voices." Another participant emphasized that it raises awareness "It's about building bridges so communities know who we are. And they can help us tackle these issues. The issues have a lot more meaning when you put a face on them."

At a practical level, learners also developed new skills. This contributed to building self confidence. One participant described his experience: "I got to hold the camera and do interviews and I was scared because I never did that before, but [it] was the best thing I ever did...I tried my best. I thought maybe I did a bad job, but we all did a really good job."

The visual images were also also tools for others to learn. In the *Right to Love* project, participants indicated that showing the visual stories to family members presented an opportunity for parents to understand how denying their sexual rights had an impact on their overall wellbeing. For one participant, the videos served as a pathway to have difficult conversations with her parents. Before the project, she was unable to talk with her parents about love and sexuality, but the videos gave her the space and courage to open up the channels of communication: "The films have helped me create a safe space to talk about sexuality with my parents. We may not see eye-to-eye, but the films act as a springboard to talk about it."

PHOTOVOICE: HELPING LEARNERS BECOME MORE ACTIVE PARTICIPANTS IN THEIR OWN LEARNING

More recently, educators have also engaged in different applications of photovoice in efforts for learners to be active participants in their own learning (Chio & Fandt, 2007; Cook, 2014; Edwards, Perry, Janzen, & Menzies, 2012; Warne, Snyder, & Gillander Gadin, 2012). As experiential learning requires greater involvement from students, students can apply their own knowledge and expertise to their learning, which can facilitate an increased sense of ownership associated with the overall process (Mulder & Dull, 2014). Through the engagement of photovoice, students are not passive recipients of education, but are actively involved in the concepts being explored which according to Lichty (2013) results in developing a deeper connection with course content.

Using photography to explore and reflect on topics in collaboration with other learners can also support the creation of environments that stimulate critical education while recognizing participants as active learners. For example, Warne et al. (2012) used photovoice to engage high school students in shaping healthy school environments. Unlike community-based photovoice projects, in this study photovoice was conducted in a classroom setting.

Photovoice as a pedagogical tool for self-reflection has been used in higher education. For example, Mulder and Dull (2014) integrated the photovoice process in a graduate social work course to encourage self-awareness through discussing and exploring lived histories through photographs. In this process, learners were asked to explore their own thoughts about their values and perceptions about social work.

These authors also stress that adopting photovoice requires flexibility on behalf of the educator, as various styles of learning need to be considered. Thus blending photovoice with various other pedagogical tools can further support learners in their various approaches to learning. Edwards et al. (2012) further stress that creative forms of engagement facilitate a stronger connection with course content while supporting different learning styles. When artistic and creative methods such as photovoice are the blended into the foundation of teaching strategies, there is greater potential for deeper reflection amongst learners as the process moves people to consider multiple concepts, "in thinking broadly, deeply and holistically, learners are stimulated to think creatively, critically and analytically about course content" (p. 34).

FURTHER CONSIDERATIONS OF THE PHOTOVOICE PROCESS

Although photovoice continues to gain attention in both research and classroom settings, there are opportunities to further consider the ethical complexities associated with the process (Daniels, 2008; de Lange et al., 2006; Packard, 2008; Sinding, Gray, & Nisker, 2008). To date, the majority of the literature on ethics in photovoice has focused on issues such as privacy, copyright, and consent forms (Wang & Redwood-Jones, 2001). Although these are important contributions in understanding the process, these discussions predominantly focus on the requirements of Institutional Review Boards, with limited information on dealing with issues that transcend the legal aspects. There is also a paucity of literature that explores the perceptions and experiences of the participants when their photographs are publicly distributed. As noted by Sinding et al. (2008, p. 459), when this type of research is presented as art in the public arena, access to the work is deliberately arranged, and the recontextualizations of the research and participants' stories become audible, visible, and felt by them in visceral and potentially lasting ways.

One of the three main goals of photovoice involves publicly displaying projects that are targeted to community members who hold various levels of decision making power, such as policymakers, health planners, and community leaders (Wang, 1999; Wang, Cash, & Powers, 2000; Wang & Redwood-Jones, 2001). However, by targeting distribution efforts aimed at 'privileged' groups within the community, the process risks reiterating dominant social relations, which also supports the earlier critiques inherent in documentary photography. To address these issues, it is worthwhile to explore other distribution opportunities that include community members and groups who can be mobilized for social action. There are many interesting and creative distribution methods that can be explored that include communities beyond the physical locality. Webpages and social media platforms such as Twitter also afford new ways of engaging online audiences. It is worthwhile to discuss these potential tactics with participants, as the methods should be guided by the needs and wants of the group.

What I have noticed in my community-based research is the value of ensuring the ongoing involvement of participants throughout the distribution phase. In many of the presentations, participants are often the keynote presenters of the research, and have been involved in panel discussions and workshop facilitations whilst often leading discussions on how the photographs should be disseminated, and which audiences to target. Although there may be many participants who chose not to be part of this phase of the research, for the individuals who want to be continually involved, their presence provides immense support in translating this research into social and community action. As these approaches to distribution also require consideration with anonymity, developing a shared understanding of how distribution practices is essential.

As noted earlier in the chapter, there are also blended and adapted forms of photovoice taking shape, in particular in the classroom setting that indicate adopting different goals associated with the photovoice methodology. As the process of photovoice continues to gain attention in both research and educational settings, researchers and educators must critically reflect and continue to document the ways in which images are used, presented, and distributed. In doing so, we develop a deeper understanding of the methodology and how it can be blended and adapted with other pedagogical tools in order to further develop photovoice as a form of participatory action engagement.

REFERENCES

Alinsky, S. D. (1971). *Rules for radicals*. New York, NY: Vintage Books.
Banks, K. (2003). Community social work practice across Canada. In F. J. Turner (Ed.), *Social work practice: A Canadian perspective* (pp. 301–314). Toronto: Prentice Hall.
Barlow, C. A., & Hurlock, D. (2013). Group meeting dynamics in a community-based participatory research project with exited sex trade workers. *International Journal of Qualitative Methods, 12*(1), 132–151.
Barndt, D. (2001). Naming, making, and connecting–Reclaiming lost arts: The pedagogical possibilities of photo-story production. In P. Campbell & B. Burnaby (Eds.), *Participatory practice in adult education* (pp. 31–54). Mahwah, NJ: Lawrence Erlbaum.
Bery, R. (2003). Participatory video that empowers. In S. A. White (Ed.), *Participatory video: Images that transform and empower* (pp. 102–121). New Delhi: Sage Publishers.
Blyton, P. (1987). The image of work: Documentary photography and the production of 'reality'. *International Social Science Journal, 39*(2), 415–424.
Braden, S. (1983). *Committing photography*. London: Pluto Press.
Brooks, C., Poudrier, J., & Thomas-MacLean, R. (2008). Creating collaborative visions with Aboriginal women: A photovoice project. In L. Liamputtong (Ed.), *Doing cross-cultural research: Ethical and methodological perspectives* (pp. 193–211). Dordrecht: Springer.
Burgin, V. (1982). Introduction. In V. Burgin (Ed.), *Thinking photography* (pp. 1–14). London: MacMillan.
Castleden, H., Garvin, T., & Huuayaht First Nation. (2008). Modifying photovoice for community-based participatory Indigenous research. *Social Sciences and Medicine, 66*(6), 1393–1405. doi:10.1016/j.socscimed.2007.11.030
Chaplin, E. (1994). *Sociology and visual representation*. London: Routledge.
Chio, V. C., & Fandt, P. M. (2007). Photovoice in the diversity classroom: Engagement, voice, and the "eye/I" of the camera. *Journal of Management Education, 31*(4), 484–504. doi:10.1177/1052562906288124
Cook, K. L. (2014). Beginning a classroom inquiry: Using photovoice to connect college students to community science. *Journal of College Science Teaching, 43*(6), 28–33.

Crocker, S. (2003). The Fogo process: Participatory communication in a globalizing world. In S. A. White (Ed.), *Participatory video: Images that transform and empower* (pp. 122–144). New Delhi: Sage Publishers.

Curtis, J. C. (1986). Dorthea Lange, migrant mother, and the culture of the great depression. *Winterthur Portfolio, 21*(1), 1–20.

Daniels, D. (2008). Exploring ethical issues when using visual tools in education research. In L. Liamputtong (Ed.), *Doing cross-cultural research: Ethical and methodological perspectives* (pp. 119–133). Dordrecht: Springer.

de Cuyper, S. (1997). On the future of photographic representation in anthropology: Lessons from the practice of community photography in Britain. *Visual Anthropology Review, 13*(2), 1–18. doi:10.1525/var.1997.13.2.2

de Lange, N., Mitchell, C., & Stuart, J. (2007). An introduction to putting people in the picture: Visual methodologies for social change. In N. De Lange, C. Mitchell, & J. Stuart (Eds.), *Putting people in the picture: Visual methodologies for social change* (pp. 1–9). Rotterdam: Sense Publishers.

Edwards, M., Perry, B., Janzen, K., & Menzies, C. (2012). Using the artistic pedagogical technology of photovoice to promote interaction in the online post-secondary classroom: The students' perspective. *Electronic Journal of e-Learning, 10*(1), 32–43.

Fals-Borda, O. (1991). Some basic ingredients. In O. Fals-Borda & M. H. Rahman (Eds.), *Action and knowledge: Breaking the monopoly with participatory action research*. New York, NY: The Apex Press.

Fleuri, R. M. (2008). Can rebelliousness bear democracy? In D. E. Lund & P. R. Carr (Eds.), *Doing democracy: Striving for political literacy and social justice* (pp. 103–117). New York, NY: Peter Lang.

Freire, P. (1973). *Education for critical consciousness*. London: Sheed & Ward.

Freire, P. (2008). *Pedagogy of the oppressed* (M. B. Ramos, Trans.). New York, NY: Continuum. (Original work published 1970)

Freire, P., & Faundez, A. (1989). *Learning to question: A pedagogy of liberation*. New York, NY: Continuum.

Frohmann, L. (2005). The framing safety project: Photographs and narratives by battered women. *Violence Against Women, 11*(11), 1396–1419.

Gotschi, E., Freyer, B., & Delve, R. (2008). Participatory photography in cross-cultural research: A case study of investigating farmer groups in rural Mozambique. In L. Liamputtong (Ed.), *Doing cross-cultural research: Ethical and methodological perspectives* (pp. 213–231). Dordrecht: Springer.

Guillemin, M., & Drew, S. (2010). Questions of process in participant-generated visual methodologies. *Visual Studies, 25*(2), 175–188. doi:10.1080/1472586x.2010.502676

Harper, D. (1988). Visual sociology: Expanding sociological vision. *The American Sociologist, 19*(1), 54–70.

Harper, D. (1998). An argument for visual sociology. In J. Prosser (Ed.), *Image-based research* (pp. 24–41). London: Falmer.

Harper, D. (2003). Framing photographic ethnography: A case study. *Ethnography, 4*(2), 241–266.

Harrison, B. (2002). Seeing health and illness worlds – using visual methodologies in a sociology of health and illness: A methodological review. *Sociology of Health and Illness, 24*(6), 856–872.

hooks, b. (1993). Bell Hooks speaking about Paulo Freire – the man, his work. In P. McLaren & P. Leonard (Eds.), *Paulo Freire: A critical encounter* (pp. 146–154). New York, NY: Routledge.

Insight. (n.d.). *Insight small world action projects*. Retrieved from http://www.insightshare.org

Jurkowski, J. M., & Paul-Ward, A. (2007). Photovoice with vulnerable populations: Addressing disparities in health promotion among people with intellectual disabilities. *Health Promotion Practice, 8*(4), 358–365. doi:10.1177/1524839906292181

LeClerc, C., Wells, D., Craig, D., & Wilson, J. (2002). Falling short of the mark: Tales of life after hospital discharge. *Clinical Nursing Research, 11*(3), 242–263.

Li, Y. (2008, May). *Towards a conceptual framework for participation and empowerment in digital storytelling and participatory video*. Paper presented at the annual meeting of the International Communication Association, Montreal. Retrieved from http://www.allacademic.com/meta/p232576_index.html

Lichty, L. F. (2013). Photovoice as a pedagogical tool in the community psychology classroom. *Journal of Prevention & Intervention in the Community, 41*(2), 89–96. doi:10.1080/10852352.2013.757984

Lopez, E. D., Eng, E., Randall-David, E., & Robertson, N. (2005). Quality-of-life concerns of African American breast cancer survivors within rural North Carolina: Blending the techniques of photovoice and grounded theory. *Qualitative Health Research, 15*(1), 99–115.

Molloy, J. K. (2007). Photovoice as a tool for social justice workers. *Journal of Progressive Human Services, 18*(2), 39–55.

Mulder, C., & Dull, A. (2014). Facilitating self-reflection: The integration of photovoice in graduate social work education. *Social Work Education, 33*(8), 1017–1036. doi:10.1080/02615479.2014.937416

Packard, J. (2008). 'I'm gonna show you what it's really like out here': The power and limitation of participatory visual methods. *Visual Studies, 23*(1) 63–76.

Park, P. (2006). Knowledge and participatory research. In P. Reason & H. Bradbury (Eds.), *Handbook of action research* (pp. 83–93). London: Sage Publications.

Pyles, L. (2009). *Progressive community organizing: A critical approach for a globalizing world.* New York, NY: Routledge.

Reason, P. (1994). Three approaches to participative inquiry. In N. K. Denzin & Y. S. Lincoln (Eds.), *Handbook of qualitative research* (pp. 324–339). Thousand Oaks, CA: Sage Publications.

Reason, P., & Bradbury, H. (2006). Introduction: Inquiry and participation in search of a world worthy of human aspiration. In P. Reason & H. Bradbury (Eds.), *Handbook of action research.* London: Sage Publications.

Rose, G. (2007). *Visual methodologies: An introduction to the interpretation of visual materials* (2nd ed.). London: Sage Publications.

Rosler, M. (2003). In, around, and afterthoughts (on documentary photography). In L. Wells (Ed.), *The photography reader* (pp. 261–274). London: Routledge. (Reprinted from *The contest of meaning*, by R. Bolton, Ed., 1989, Cambridge: MIT Press).

Seixas, P. (1987). Lewis Hine: From 'social' to 'interpretive' photographer. *American Quarterly, 39*(3), 381–409.

Sekula, A. (1984). *Photography against the grain: Essays and photo works 1973–1983.* Halifax: Press of the Nova Scotia College of Art and Design.

Sinding, C., Gray, R., & Nisker, J. (2008). Ethical issues and issues of ethics. In J. G. Knowles & A. L. Cole (Eds.). *Handbook of the arts in qualitative research* (pp. 459–468). Los Angeles, CA: Sage Publications.

Singhal, A., Harter, L. M., Chitnis, K., & Sharma, D. (2007). Participatory photographs as theory, method and praxis: Analyzing an entertainment-education project in India. *Critical Arts, 21*(1), 212–227.

Solomon-Godeau, A. (1991). *Photography at the dock: Essays on photographic history, institutions, and practices.* Minneapolis, MN: University of Minnesota Press.

Szto, P. (2008). Documentary photography in American social welfare history: 1887–1943. *Journal of Sociology & Social Welfare, 35*(2), 91–110.

Tagg, J. (1988). *The burden of representation: Essays on photographies and histories.* Amherst, MA: The University of Massachusetts Press.

Wagner, J. (2006). Visible materials, visualized theory and images in social research. *Visual Studies, 21*(1), 55–69.

Wallerstein, N. B., & Duran, B. (2003). The conceptual, historical and practice roots of community based participatory research and related participatory traditions. In M. Minkler & N. B. Wallerstein (Eds.), *Community based participatory research in health* (pp. 27–52). San Francisco, CA: Jossey-Bass.

Walsh, C., Shier, M. L., Sitter, K. C., & Sieppert, J. D. (2010). Applied methods of teaching about oppression and diversity to graduate social work students: A case example of digital stories. *The Canadian Journal for the Scholarship of Teaching and Learning, 1*(2), 1–15. Retrieved from http://ir.lib.uwo.ca/cjsotl_rcacea/vol1/iss2/3

Wang, C. (1999). Photovoice: A participatory action research strategy applied to women's health. *Journal of Women's Health, 8*(2), 185–192. doi:10.1089/jwh.1999.8.185

Wang, C. C. (2000). The future of health promotion: Talkin' technology blues. *Health Promotion Practice, 1*(1), 78–81.
Wang, C. C., & Burris, M. A. (1997). Photovoice: Concept, methodology, and use for participatory needs assessment. *Health Education & Behavior, 24*(3), 369–387. doi:10.1177/109019819702400309
Wang, C. C., & Pies, C. A. (2004). Family, maternal, and child health through photovoice. *Maternal and Child Health Journal, 8*(2), 95–102.
Wang, C. C., & Redwood-Jones, Y. A. (2001). Photovoice ethics: Perspectives from Flint photovoice. *Health Education & Behavior, 28*(5), 560–572. doi:10.1177/109019810102800504
Wang, C., Burris, M. A., & Ping, X. Y. (1996). Chinese village women as visual anthropologists: A participatory approach to research policy makers. *Social Science & Medicine, 42*(10), 1391–1400. doi:10.1016/0277-9536(95)00287-1
Wang, C. C., Cash, J. L., & Powers, L. S. (2000). Who knows the streets as well as the homeless? Promoting personal and community action through photovoice. *Health Promotion Practice, 1*(1), 81–89. doi:10.1177/152483990000100113
Warne, M., Snyder, K., & Gillander Gadin, K. (2013). Photovoice: An opportunity and challenge for students' genuine participation. *Health Promotion International, 28*(3), 299–310. doi:10.1093/heapro/das011
Weber, S. (2008). Visual images in research. In J. G. Knowles, & A. L. Cole (Eds.), *Handbook of the arts in qualitative research* (pp. 41–54). Los Angeles, CA: Sage Publications.
Wells, L. (2003). *The photography reader*. London: Routledge.
White, S. A. (Ed.). (2003). *Participatory video: Images that transform and empower*. New Delhi: Sage Publications.

Kathleen C. Sitter
Faculty of Social Work
University of Calgary, Canada

KATHLEEN C. SITTER

12. ADAPTING PHOTOVOICE IN THE CLASSROOM

Guiding Students in the Creation of a Photovoice Project

INTRODUCTION

In this chapter, I describe an approach that I used to engage learners in a photovoice project in a classroom setting. Strategies are provided that educators might use to introduce a photovoice approach to support students in taking action to represent their own learning. This example shows how I thought about and used photovoice to help students create a project in an undergraduate course, "Communities and Societies." The task for students was to share their thoughts and experiences related to places that 'build community among university students'.

PHOTOVOICE: A CATALYST FOR CONVERSATION

First, I share the purposes of using photovoice with the students. Participatory visual media engages individuals and groups who have an important message to present. Using a collaborative process, participants create photographs, short videos, and/or artistic forms of representation and discuss their images in a group setting. Examples of participatory visual media include digital storytelling, participatory video, and photovoice.

The process involves the selection of a topic that is considered important to the group, taking photographs about the topic and discussing the photographs in both small and large group settings. While photographs record visual content, images can also be used as a tool to facilitate discussions. The participants' visual interpretations and the meaning they give to the photographs are considered a key part of the photovoice process. I share with students that this form of group-based storytelling allows them to explore the multiple experiences that contribute to the collective effort to build understanding of a topic. Learners will enhance their reflexive skills while learning how to articulate and represent their views, their concerns, and insights in visual and narrative form. When presenting an image for the first time, students are also asked to reflect on not only what is in the photograph, but what are the reasons for including a particular photo. Narrative captions that accompany the images place a photograph in further context for the viewer.

The images created through the photovoice process also invite learners to take a lead in their own learning. As noted by Hagedorn (1994), photographs "invite people to take the lead in inquiry, facilitating their discussions of an experience" (p. 47).

B. Shapiro (Ed.), Actions of Their Own to Learn, 215–223.
© 2018 Koninklijke Brill NV. All rights reserved.

As part of the initial process, learners discuss the images they elect to include in relation to their own lived experiences. In this way, the images serve as a *catalyst for conversations* in both small and large group settings in the classroom.

However, adapting the photovoice process requires more than simply introducing visual applications into a classroom setting; while images serve as a pathway to discuss topics and reflect on one's own experiences, not all images resonate with everyone. Consequently, it is not enough to merely let images "speak for themselves." Part of the educator's role also involves providing support to help learners think about and convey the contextual elements associated with selected images.

AN APPROACH TO HELP STUDENTS TAKE ACTION TO LEARN PHOTOVOICE

The following section provides an example of how photovoice can be adapted in an undergraduate course as a blended pedagogical tool to encourage learners to take action in their learning.

Setting the Stage—Guiding Students Using a Collaborative Group Activity

For a number of years, I have a applied a photovoice activity in an undergraduate course entitled "Communities and Societies." This is an elective undergraduate course and is offered through the Department of General Education. Based on the university curriculum framework, any undergraduate student has the option to enrol in this course. Thus cohorts are often comprised of interdisciplinary students across various fields such as Communications, English, Sociology, and so on. The purpose of the course is for students to develop a rich awareness of the various communities and societies students live and participate in at the micro and macro/systems level.

During two weeks of the term, there is a focus on the "sense of place" in communities and societies that we are part of. A sense of place considers how geographical, physical, and virtual spaces influence our sense of connection. At this point in the course, we also explore the concept of "Third Places," a term coined by Ray Oldenburg (1989), which refers to the importance of informal gathering places and why they are essential to community and public life. The student experience at this university is a shared experience that connected with everyone in the class. To explore this topic as it relates to student's experiences, I introduce an activity that is based on an adapted version of photovoice.

In the initiating process, students must consider the physical nature of spaces in their learning environment, and what these spaces reveal to them about the nature of post-secondary institutions and experiences. One of the key concepts of the course builds on a semiotic interpretative approach to interpreting learning spaces described by Shapiro (2012). According to Shapiro, "physical features of learning environments function as a form of curriculum text" where "text" refers to the interwoven messages that are read as "cultural rules about how communication and learning will proceed" (p. 2).

For this activity, students are asked to walk around the university campus in small groups and pay particular attention to their environment. During this process, students must take photographs of places that reveal something about the university as it relates to Third Places and their sense of place. They are then expected to explore these concepts in more depth amongst each other, and with the entire class. This activity is designed for approximately 30–35 students, although it can be adapted to fit for larger or smaller group sizes. The activity takes place during two 3-hour classes, and involves online group discussions that continue throughout the semester. The photovoice activity is purposefully located in the middle of the term. This timing also provides me, as instructor, with an opportunity to understand how the class dynamics are unfolding that might suggest the need to make ongoing adjustments to the assignment. It also gives students a chance to become more comfortable with one another.

Typically we dedicate only two classes to the photovoice process. Creating a safe space for students to contribute and share their voices is also very important. This is also one of the main reasons for choosing a topic that is broad enough to allow students to draw from diverse and multiple experiences. Students can then also together determine how they feel most comfortable sharing ideas with one another.

INTRODUCING PHOTOVOICE

Prior to the class, students read three articles:

- Banning, J. H., Clemons, S., McKelfresh, D., & Gibbs, R. W. (2010). Special places for students: Third place and restorative place. *College Student Journal, 44*(4), 906–912.
- Wang, C. C., & Redwood-Jones, Y. A. (2001). Photovoice ethics: Perspectives from Flint photovoice. *Health Education & Behavior, 28*(5), 560–572.
- Wang, C. C., Cash, J. L., & Powers, L. S. (2000). Who knows the streets as well as the homeless? Promoting personal and community action through photovoice. *Health Promotion Practice, 1*(1), 81–89.

The first is on formal/informal learning spaces that touch on notions of exclusion and inclusion for students. Students are asked to reflect on their own experiences and make connections to concepts developed in the article (i.e., "what do these spaces tell us about post-secondary institutions from a student's perspective?")

The second and third assigned readings are about photovoice, so the class becomes familiar with the concept. I ensure that one of the readings focuses on ethics and photovoice. A favourite is Wang and Redwood-Jones' 2001 article "photovoice ethics." I use this article as a pathway to discuss ethics in the context of photovoice and in particular the activity students will engage in.

When introducing photovoice to the class, I share examples from previous projects I've been part of that relate to the topic of "communities and societies." Often I model the procedure of briefly introducing the topic, sharing a photo image on a screen without the text, and then asking the group what they see and what the image means to them. Then I post the text that was created to accompany the image, reading it out loud. I then go back to the same image, and let the students look at it again in silence considering what the photo caption text meant to them.

Following Shapiro's (2012) approach, students are invited to explore the university and reflect on what campus environments explicitly and implicitly reveal about 'building community' in their university experience. In class, I highlight some of the concepts discussed from the Banning, Clemons, McKelfresh, and Gibbs (2010) article associated with "Third Places," however I stress that learners will be taking photographs of spaces that resonate with them personally.

Activity details such as the timeline for the activity are provided. It is important to ensure each group has at least one person with a cell phone who will take photographs and email them to the instructor. Learners are then randomly placed into groups of 3–4. At this point, each group takes a few minutes to decide on a group name. A group member from each group writes their group name on the board, along with the names of the other members. While this is done to encourage interaction within the small group and can be fun, this group name is also included in their e-mail subject line when they email me their chosen photos. The groups have approximately 30–45 minutes to explore the campus and take photographs. Each group determines how they will use their time.

Creating Photographs

Before students leave the classroom to take photographs, we discuss ethical considerations. Drawing on Wang and Redwood-Jones' (2001) article, we discuss some of the challenges and issues that must be considered when taking photographs such as safety, anonymity, and consent. I present a scenario that involves a person taking a photograph of the Student Counselling Service Center, while a student is walking in the door. The student is captured in the photograph, but hasn't given consent. We then explore potential unintended consequences of sharing this photograph with the larger group while considering approaches that might eliminate encountering these types of situations (e.g., taking photographs without people in the picture, or having class group members pose in the photographs).

Small Group Discussions

Small group dialogue begins in the classroom and continues when learners are "in the field" and negotiate which photographs they choose to take. These discussions continue when they return. They have the remainder of the class to carry on in their small groups. Students often share this small group dialogue within the larger class discussion that happens in the following week. To guide these small group conversations about the photographs, I provide the students with questions based on the acronym **SHOWeD**.

S- what do you **S**ee here? **H**- **H**ow does this relate to our lives as students? How does this relate to **O**- **O**ur notions of community? **W**- **W**hy does this problem, concern, or strength exist? What can we **D**- **D**o about it?). In their small groups, students then write brief descriptions and create titles for 2–3 of their photos. They are invited to reflect on the following questions when writing their descriptions: Why did your group take this particular picture? What do you see in the photo about places that build community? What might it represent to those who inhabit the setting? How does it relate to your own experience of being a student on campus?

Each group sends their photos by email with titles and descriptions to the instructor. Before the next class, these photographs and descriptors are placed on PowerPoint slides for each group to share with the entire class.

Second Class: Large Group Dialogue

In the following class, students are given 10–15 minutes to review their photos and decide how they wish to present their selected photographs with the larger class. This short amount of time is given so that the messages will be thoughtfully constructed yet spontaneous. The group presentations are also a form of celebrating knowledge and the learner's own efforts to learn. Often these larger group discussions that unfold from the presentations deepen the conversation and meaning of the topic as viewers share how they make connections with or perhaps do not connect with the images. During class discussion, I introduce the **LENS** acronym so learners can move into deeper and more critical discussions. Exploring a topic through photovoice involves more than exploring what is merely "inside" or "outside" the visual frame; it calls for learners to consider ideas and discourses tethered to the selected image itself. To facilitate this process, I often use a series of questions that captured in the acronym **LENS:** How is this photograph **L**- **L**inked to historical, cultural, political and social contexts? How does this photo relate to our **E**- **E**xperiences? What is **N**- **N**ot in the photograph, but vacillates between the topic and the visual frame? What **S**- **S**ilenced stories are revealed in relation the photograph? Using the questions from **LENS** sparks further dialogue as students continue to learn with one another.

Helping Students Engage in Critical Framality

This approach to the process of photovoice brings it into a space of arts-based pedagogy and draws on what I refer to as critical framality. If we consider that photographs are constituted by what is outside the frame (Butler, 2009), the primary focus is not to solely examine what is captured in an image. In photovoice activities, I encourage learners to consider what is implied by the image itself. As learners become curious about what may be outside of the frame, yet connected to the photographic image, stories and experiences that are visibly left out of a photograph can be revealed. Learners begin to consider the social, political, cultural and historical aspects tethered to the photographic frame, and how these concepts may provide a deeper meaning from what is explicitly depicted in the photograph itself.

The notion of critical framality is based on the need to ensure the transitive aspect of the visual is not inadvertently suppressed – which can occur if discussions solely focus on the visual contents – by supporting learners to consider the embedded relationships associated with the participatory images. Critical framality in this way, carries with it an explicit analysis into the ongoing influences of the image and how it is taken up; it aims to extend the notion of the visual frame by rejecting the inside/outside dichotomy through looking at both the hidden and explicit discourses surrounding the image in the context of viewing. In this way, interconnected themes associated with the act of seeing and bearing witness to different social, political, historical, and cultural influences that are at play. As such, these visual methods enhance reflexive conversations amongst learners as well as enhancing their capacity to visually communicate, interpret and critically explore topics and issues important to them.

Continuing the Discussion Online

At the end of the class, I upload the images and descriptions onto the course Blackboard site, where students are invited to continue their discussion. The online interactive component provides another communication forum for learners who may not be comfortable with large-group discussions, and are more at ease expressing their views and thoughts in writing. In the forum, I post the LENS questions again, where students are also asked to juxtapose the themes and ideas brought forth in this activity with the academic literature on the topic. Through this adapted photovoice format, students reflect on their relationships to systems, structures, and environments by giving them opportunities to consider these ideas in relation to their personal experiences.

Addressing Learning Outcomes

Through this assignment, learners are encouraged to make connections across student experiences and further reflect on "Third Places" as they relate to post-secondary communities. From this activity, students have identified a number of themes associated with a sense of place, including formal and informal learning environments. For instance, several learners have indicated the library being a life-line and a "go-to place" for students in the academic careers. Learners have also highlighted informal learning spaces such as the financial aid office, where students compared bank machines to "slot machines" and the challenges of economically navigating life as a student over a four-year period which was an unexpected experience for a number of students.

The activity also reiterates core learning outcomes that are part of the course offering that related to students developing the skills to critically assess foundational concepts of communities and societies and how they apply to our lives. This was facilitated through the adapted photovoice activity by reflecting on the course readings and the images students create in class. Students must also consider how they relate to their experiences of being a student. In this exercise, students are also asked to apply the "Third Place" concept and articulate this connection to their own student experiences in both visual and written text (i.e., their photo and description). In doing so, students engage in the creative process of using photographic records tools to explore and facilitate their own learning.

It is also worth sharing the meaning of this experience for students enrolled in the course. The positive depth of thinking that resulted when students have both choice and voice in their learning was powerful. While a few students were sceptical of the approach at first, they found that the process offered a way to explore a number of complexities associated with places on campus that build communities. Creating, engaging, and sharing the photographs afforded a unique opportunity to communicate and reflect on their own community connections. Students also appreciated being able to see the photographs taken from the other groups and to learn reasons why those locations were selected. Students also said they valued the alternative forms of participation offered in the assignment (photography, small group discussions, large group dialogue, online posts) in reading and analysing the images. They appreciated the structure provided by the **SHOWeD** and **LENS** acronyms as a guide to thoughtfully engage in conversation. For many students, the photovoice process presented the opportunity to use media in different ways that deeply contributed to their own learning and that allowed them the opportunity to think about community spaces and social processes in unique and interesting new ways.

ADAPTING PHOTOVOICE: SUMMARY	
Preparation	1. Relevant readings on the topic under investigation 2. Photovoice articles, one focusing on ethics (e.g., Wang & Redwood-Jones, 2001) 3. Handouts for *SHOWeD* and *LENS* questions
Resources Needed	1. To conduct the activity in "real time" students must have phones, with the ability to take photos and email. 2. An e-mail account 3. An online discussion platform for students and where you could facilitate discussions when needed (e.g., Blackboard, wiki page, a closed Facebook site, or use Twitter where the group can use a shared hashtag to follow the conversation, etc.)
Time:	Two 3-hour classes, followed with online discussions Based on a class-size of 30–40 students

First Class (approximately 3 hours)
Introduction – Ethics: 1 hour
In the Field: 45 minutes
Small group discussions: Reminder of class

Introduce Photovoice Instructions	1. Share and discuss visual photovoice examples 2. Review the topic Provide outline instructions on 1-page (or one slide that learners can continuously refer to when needed). Instructions should include: Topic focus/guiding question Timeline/schedule over the 2 classes Online discussion details ***SHOWeD*** acronym questions
Groups	1. Create small groups of 3–4 (ensure at least one person has a cell with email and camera capabilities) 2. Groups create and write a group name on the board with their respective members. They use this name in the subject line for all email communication.
Ethics	1. Review ethical considerations before going into the field. 2. Provide a scenario and discuss potential unintended consequences and ways to be proactive with ethical concerns. Use photovoice ethics article as a pathway for discussions
In the Field	Learners take photographs (30–45 minutes)
Small Group Discussions	1. Discuss photographs using ***SHOWeD*** as a guide 2. Decide on 2–3 to share with larger group. Create caption and description. 3. Before the end of the class, groups email educator the above details. The educator puts these on individual slides (e.g., PPT, JPEGS, PDFs) that can be viewed via a projector or printed out and shared.

Second Class (approximately 3 hours)
Overview of the activity and last class: 10 minutes
Learners review/prepare: 10–20 minutes
Large-group discussions: approx. 2 hours (depending on number of groups)
Online discussion overview: 15–20 minutes

Overview	1. Briefly review last class topic and process for the large-group discussions 2. Review ***SHOWeD*** with group and provide handout 3. Review ***LENS*** with group and provide handout
Preparation	Learners have 10–20 minutes to review their images, discuss how they'll share their photographs and ideas. Keep this brief as the focus is on the group dialogue
Large-group discussions	Each group shares their respective images. If needed, the educator invites learners who are viewing the photographs for the first time to consider ***LENS*** and facilitates these conversations.

Online discussion overview	1. The educator puts the images on the respective discussion forum, along with the ***LENS*** questions. 2. Review instructions that will be online. Instructions should include: Timeline for online discussion Questions encouraging learners to juxtapose the photovoice themes discussed in class and in the photographs with academic literature on the topic.
Online discussion	Discussion forum remains open for the remainder of the course or as identified

REFERENCES

Baldwin, R. G. (1996). Faculty career stages and implications for professional development. In D. Finnegan, D. Webster, & Z. F. Gamson (Eds.), *Faculty and faculty issues in colleges and universities* (2nd ed.). Boston, MA: Pearson Custom Publishing.

Banning, J. H., Clemons, S., McKelfresh, D., & Gibbs, R. W. (2010). Special places for students: Third place and restorative place. *College Student Journal, 44*(4), 906–912.

Butler, J. (2009). *Frames of war: When is life grievable?* London: Verso.

Hagedorn, M. (1994). Hermeneutic photography: An innovative esthetic technique for generating data in nursing research. *Advances in Nursing Sciences, 17*(1), 44–50.

Oldenburg, R. (1989). *The great good place*. New York, NY: Marlowe.

Shapiro, B. (2012). Structures that teach: Using a semiotic framework to study the environmental messages of learning settings. *Eco-Thinking, 1*(1), 1–13. Retrieved from http://www.eco-thinking.org/index.php/journal/article/view/7

Wang, C. C., & Redwood-Jones, Y. A. (2001). Photovoice ethics: Perspectives from flint photovoice. *Health Education & Behavior, 28*(5), 560–572. doi:10.1177/109019810102800504

Wang, C. C., Cash, J. L., & Powers, L. S. (2000). Who knows the streets as well as the homeless? Promoting personal and community action through photovoice. *Health Promotion Practice, 1*(1), 81–89. doi:10.1177/152483990000100113

Kathleen C. Sitter
Faculty of Social Work
University of Calgary, Canada

EUGENE G. KOWCH

13. A NEW PARADIGM FOR TEACHING, LEADING AND LEARNING IN PARTICIPATORY LEARNING ENVIRONMENTS

> Digital and social technologies have changed how people of all ages learn, collaborate, play, socialize, access resources and services, and connect... Participatory learning designs require teachers to balance both structure and openness, to offer flexible boundaries that support and guide learners as they undertake meaningful, challenging and complex collaborative inquiries into enduring ideas and complex problems and issues.
> (Jacobsen et al., 2016, p. 6)

INTRODUCTION

I have studied education systems for almost 20 years, working with interdisciplinary research teams bridging the traditional gap between education administration and education technology disciplines. Two persistent, surprising research findings have emerged after studying institutions involving well over 300,000 teachers, leaders and communities. First, we find that contemporary education professionals use abundant language describing an ideal – better student learning outcomes by transforming schools into more social, participatory technology-enhanced learning environments. The second and more troubling theme is that the vast majority of these same school leaders, teachers and educational technologists are falling short of their ideals. Educators are failing to imagine, to lead and to sustain truly participatory schools and school districts.

This chapter is a response to those findings. To fill a knowledge gap, this chapter provides some theory and several sets of practical guidelines for participatory teachers, leaders, learners and the educational technologists who must work together to sustain meaningful Participatory Teaching and Learning (PTL) environments in the information age. Grounded by research findings from large studies of entire school districts and built from a complexivist, post structural approach, this chapter concludes with sets of *practical guidelines* for educators reconceptualizing an integration of teaching, supports and leadership across our schools and districts. This is an initial guide for school districts that want to explore and reconceptualize education so that we can lead, teach, build and learn together within more robust PTL environments.

First, this chapter examines a *paradigm shift* that is necessary for sustainable PTL in school districts. Next, we survey important lessons from complexity theory to help educators understand the essential *patterns* of interconnected relationships that are essential for participatory teachers, learners and leaders. Following a brief overview of *network* and cluster theory for readers we suggest that participatory learning is better in a garden environment than in a tight flower box. Next, we examine the enabling role of educational technology and not just tools found within well-*designed* participatory environments. Finally, we conclude by offering guidelines for future school and district PTL teachers and leaders:

- Five design principles for project based, enabling LMS environments
- Seven principles for high capacity participatory network teams
- Four principles for leading innovation in participatory schools & districts
- Three principles for leading change in participatory schools & districts

The complicated nature of schooling today can make school teachers and school leaders feel that the constraints of procedures, policies and structures severely limit some of our most innovative new pedagogical practices (Shirky, 2008). Traditional practices sometimes represent more independent or closed 'boxes' for teaching and learning rather than the 'open garden' that is necessary for more liberated, meaningful participatory learning praxis. Our historical disciplinary or subject-based professional preparation for teaching very often separates contemporary education professionals at a time when *interdisciplinary* mindsets are required to design and enact, in particular, *sustainable, PTL practices*. Participatory education systems need new thinking to reconceptualise the complex interplay of disciplines, pedagogy and changing system structures to support sustainable collaboration in the education project.

We know that no single subject expert, school administrator or educational technologist can sustain meaningful participatory learning designs alone so to support PTL educators, this chapter suggests new ways that education professionals can open up pedagogical spaces by shifting to an information age paradigm where collaborative learning in education systems integrates within an education technology (not tool based) ecosystem. I argue that with this collection of new ideas and approaches educators can create more flexible administrative approaches and teaching supports to sustain *genuinely social* classes, schools, districts and communities. I suggest that this work must be done collaboratively and collegially by shedding old disciplinary and epistemological baggage brought from an outdated idea that technology is a tool, teaching is art and collaboration is piecemeal (polite) delegation. A failure to support and to co-create participatory learning designs, instruction and resources *together* in context, will result in more beautiful but unsustainable PTL efforts. This would be a recognizable but sad reality.

PTL: An Imperative for Shifting to an Information Age Paradigm

PTL is a learning environment where a teacher is a learning facilitator for student-driven inquiry and knowledge-building (Barab et al., 1998). In this constructionist and often technology-laden environment, well-engaged students make choices about what they learn and they negotiate how they learn by *choosing* meaningful, challenging and complex collaborative inquiries into problems and issues (Jacobsen, Lock, & Friesen, 2016). Such an empowering environment must be designed for students and teachers to learn together in an environment that could involve the world (via the internet) and each other. But how? Such environments, well designed, require students to have the autonomy and freedom to *learn* and to *choose* what they need to learn over time – in projects that do not need to be bounded within a prescribed 'period' of time where content mastery occurs (Reigeluth & Duffy, 2008). New pedagogies informing PTL designs in information age schools include discovery and inquiry-based learning, differentiated instruction, inclusive education, design based research informed by constructivist pedagogies (Barab, 1999). Experienced PTL scholars know that a strong focus on social learning (Shapiro, 2011, 2014) demands that PTL teachers, administrators and support systems in school districts also embrace more open and flexible systems thinking so that learners can indeed choose both learning problems and learning content to make meaning from effortful inquiry. *Collaboration* is key in this environment where leaders, teachers and learners are all learning together. Genuine collaboration means that the role of a participatory learning team is not limited to '*instructional leadership*' and that school leaders are part of the learning team (Heck & Hallinger, 2005). By supporting both the teacher and the learner, leaders collaborate to design a changing environment with supporting policies to enable robust teamwork and their own learning too. This means school leaders are actively managing innovation, change and learning networks – but they'll need some new principles to lead dynamic teams that are faster, better and more nimble than the piecemeal, labor-sorted learning teams of the past.

Education is benefitting from an evolution of a leadership field that has paralleled PTL thinking to such an extent that school leadership, policy and governance models today implicitly embrace the creation of flexible models for participatory learning environments as a high order priority. These nascent approaches to whole-environment support are emerging to include distributed leadership, decentralized leadership and shared governance models capable of empowering, not over-structuring, participatory learning (Kowch, 2016; Hazy & Uhl-Bein, 2015). Teamwork is essential.

At the same time, developments in the educational technology field have evolved in parallel with similar impulses, epistemologies, theories and practices to support truly co-connected teachers, learners and administrators. Too often a convenient ideal rather than a reality, we find that effective PTL supports work to create more open and flexible teaching (Kowch, 2007). Sustainable PTL will require a network of cooperating leadership, curriculum, instruction and educational technology thinkers to support and to empower the visions of participatory teachers across classes, schools and school districts (Hargreaves et al., 2009) as well. *Teamwork* among professional colleagues and learners in learning environment *design* is critical to success. Design thinking must replace input-process-output thinking embedded in lesson and unit plans (Tracey & Boling, 2014).

An integrated approach across classes, schools and school districts really does represent a newer paradigm that could hold out a promise for teachers, researchers and school leaders. Interweaving school organization and teaching is an imperative for professionals creating a new set of supportive, less theoretical social and interactive teaching and learning models. This approach helps them to design much more dynamic, co-connected and co-creative learning processes where the very culture of an institution environment helps shape important learner outcomes (Shapiro, 2014) and vice-versa. First, we need to explore why educator paradigm shift is an essential first step in designing and leading PTL school systems. Next, we explore how *participation* by everyone can happen well in complex networks of participatory relationships with a post structural (more flexible) systems approach to learning, leading and schooling (Reigeluth & Duffy, 2008). If we can think beyond the dominant linear, rigid bureaucratic structures and processes binding education today we can come to understand collaboration beyond cooperation (Bourdieu, 1972).

Shifting industrial mindsets to an information age paradigm. While society evolved from agrarian to industrial to information age societal systems our education system is failing to meet the needs of society in the information age (Reigeluth & Karnapp, 2013). Educators blame this lag on our collective inability to develop the mindsets and practices necessary for embracing the new connectivity offered by the information age. As we will explore, stark differences between industrial and information age thinking illustrate why participatory teachers, learners, administrators and educational technologists need to adopt a new paradigm that helps us move beyond the often unseen, powerful constraints that participatory learning teachers and school leaders face every day. Some of us are fully aware of these constraints while others remain locked up in the industrial age without knowing it.

Industrial age or factory models of education met the needs of a labour oriented society when:

- Manual labour was the predominant form of labour
- We did not need to educate many learners to high levels
- We could not afford to educate many learners to high levels and
- Few learners would be content with assembly line/agrarian work if we educated them to high levels (Reigeluth & Duffy, 2008).

To further the goals of industrial age societies we organized our classes, schools and school districts to create productive workers. We delivered education by teaching a fixed amount of content and curriculum in a specific pedagogical manner within a fixed amount of time via the pre-kindergarten to grade 12 system, for example. We filled up flower pots with competencies. We also held time constant for every learner and we forced achievement to vary. Then we used norm-based assessment to measure that variance (p. 45). This system was not designed for learning as much as it was designed for sorting students into time slices with fixed spaces and fixed resources (grades/classrooms), assuming a static environment overall. The result was the creation of stacked, inflexible bureaucratic and technocratic administrative processes with instructor-centred classroom practices rather independent from teacher and learner curiosities and needs (Hargreaves & Shirley, 2009). From this mindset we created teaching and learning boxes to produce labour, not flourishing gardens affording knowledge building. We also created labourers that were not prepared to be knowledge workers – learners who absorbed content for a productive purpose while ignoring the methods and meaning for their learning. Administrators were prepared to stock the factory with content, teachers and resources to keep the learning machines going and in fact, technologists even produced learning machines to accelerate the process. Teaching machines were a disaster as much as rigid bureaucracies have hobbled creative teaching, learning and leadership. These mechanistic processes allow us to hide behind disciplinary walls, technological determinism and leader power functionalism to create an unpleasant machine where we talk transformation but we create exhaustion.

In my research I am always surprised at how one can walk down most school hallways in any country and find examples of industrial age paradigms in action from room to room, floor to floor. This is causing unnecessary, degenerative tensions among *everyone* in systems that really want to work together well for learning while still thinking of learning as a collection of students in boxes (classes) rather disconnected from their environments in a day when any child can find any fact on the internet.

Information age education serves the knowledge worker and builders of knowledge as well as the labourer who builds with objects. Because information technologies have afforded learners far higher levels of education in more complex, interconnected learning contexts, educators today needs an expanded mindset that is more *learning*-focused, not *sorting*-focused. To help, a emerging new generation of complexity and systems change thinkers in the educational technology discipline have conceptualized information age education for the information age using *design* thinking – a cornerstone of educational technology work (Merrill, 2012). Design thinking means that educational technologies are included only to enhance robust participatory learning where time and lesson content structures can be conceptualized differently:

> So rather than holding time constant, which forces achievement to vary, we need a paradigm that holds achievement constant-at some level of mastery of each standard – which means we must not force a student to move on before attaining the standard, and we must allow each student to move on to the next standard as soon as it is attained. (Reigeluth & Duffy, 2008, p. 46)

The Information age paradigm helps us to imagine a co-connected, more dynamic participatory learning garden as opposed to imagining a collection of atomistic learning flower boxes that simply offer 'containers' for sorted teaching and learning activity. This new mindset empowers interdisciplinary education professionals to share deep disciplinary knowledge (teaching, leadership, educational technologists, and other supports) who are less attracted to sorting students in for time-sequenced grade level placements that are so very content and curriculum centred. Learning process matters as much as learning outputs (Bransford, Brown, & Cocking, 2000). So the focus for new professionals is changed to new ways to imagine, design and create learning environments along with administrative environments that are negotiated, flexible and student centred. That is a *big* leap for many teachers, educational technologists and school leaders keeping industrial age paradigms dear. As we will explore later in the educational technology section of this chapter, student-led *participatory* learning projects can be supported in any well-designed collaborative teaching and learning setting created with careful designs for problem based, constructivist technology-enhanced learning environments where everyone is involved in learning with a learning environment design mindset (Merrill, 2012; Anderson & Dron, 2010).

Working from this newer paradigm, information age systems thinkers assert that educators will also shift toward more self-directed, customized learning technologies enhanced by artificial intelligence. In these immersive environments learners can more self-direct their inquiries in attainment-based systems designed to be far less bound by time-sorting and traditional teacher/learner relationships. Such an approach empowers teams of teachers and learners who build more collaborative relationships to leverage self-directed, evidence-informed teaching and learning designs – hallmarks for new ways of thinking and learning that underlie the approach of information age schools (Reigeluth & Karnapp, 2013). This approach also means that integrated school leaders must understand both learning and technology as part of a carefully designed, but not prescriptive process involving people, disciplines and learning goals well beyond mere skill creation formed by the tools of industrial age technocracies. Outdated education leadership has, for too long led to bureaucracies and technocracies that hold PTL ideas hostage to old linear systems thinking promoting even older ideas of schools and districts as cogs in a wheel, sadly.

Industrial age educators engaged in piecemeal education system change in a top-down fashion by sifting and sorting learners, teachers, supports and resources resulting in inflexible, overspecialized and highly disconnected education environments bound by institutions empowered by isolationist policy thinking (Kowch, 2016; Thompson-Klein, 2010). Industrial age education leaders spent decades creating linear leadership models and hierarchical organizations conceived using steady state presumptions (linear) and not unsteady state (constant flux) principles that far better characterize the real world of information age learning. As a result, leadership practice and theory fell far, far short of describing or predicting the complex reality of education (Willower & Forsythe, 1999). In the information age, education teaching, technology and administration scholars realize that flexible programs, resourcing, professional network teams and less rigid policy and governance will empower the next generation of social learning, and complexity theory is helping us reconceptualise these more co-connected information age environments (McKelvey & Lichtenstein, 2007).

Lessons from complexity theory. Systems thinkers take a complexity stance to conceptualize thriving educational ecosystems as interconnected, nested and complex subsystems (Sumara & L'Amour, 2012). Working in nested, co-dependent systems means true inclusion among teachers, administrators and educational technologists working in an information age in vastly different ways than they worked in the industrial age. Everyone and everything impacts all other things in such systems where knowledge not production occurs.

Part of the problem with this paradigm shift is that when busy educators and scholars imagine truly participatory teaching, leadership and supporting educational technologies from more holistic standpoints, we can quickly become overwhelmed if we try to reduce the 'whole' to its incompressible elements (Stacey, 2009). There's just too much going on. Reductionism creates complication, not complexity – machine-like systems, not ecosystems (Capra, 2010).

Complexity thinking is part of the information age paradigm essential for PTL ecosystems of the future. This perspective allows us to consider simple rules and powerful computer programs to help us understand how and why many elements in a school, for example are connected to one another and how they/we are impacting one another constantly (Stacey, 2009). Complexity thinking is a more appropriate lens for information-age paradigm participatory teachers, learners, administrators and educational technologists when we understand that our work occurs within *patterns of relationships* among many people and ideas at once. Instead of 'cutting up' or reducing the system to its parts, complexity thinking allows us to look for patterns among the intricate relationships found in the *whole* (Cilliers, 1998) so as to design cultivate highly capable patterns of relations (Kowch, 2013). In education systems we know that our interactions are usually non-linear, guaranteeing a chance that small causes can have large impacts on entire (school, district) and vice versa (p. 6). Another helpful characteristic of complex systems is that they exist in *environments that are far from equilibrium* – in constant states of change (p. 6). Education settings, especially flexible social situation are constantly changing (Fullan, 2010).

Deep explanation of complex systems design and analysis is beyond the scope of this chapter so here we explore my work showing that certain kinds or patterns of relationship is leading (or can lead) to information age education principles for relationship-building. This is to help teachers, leaders and others engaged in highly social professional activity essential for PTL in constantly changing education spaces. In fact, the final section of the chapter, offers a practical list research-based principles for creating and for leading patterns (networks) of professional and learner relations in and among schools so that highly capable teams can innovate to change and shape the work of PLT groups in healthy learning ecosystems.

I have built a body of work tracing complex relationships among people, ideas and institutions influencing one another in complex education settings to also find principles for *leading* complex adaptive collectives like PTL. At its core this work offers a set of modified social and policy network analysis constructs to help educators describe, interpret, lead and design highly capable relationship patterns or networks that are the essential 'oxygen' and 'respiratory systems' in robust information age education ecosystems (Kowch, 2005, 2007, 2013). We have also found that the most capable professional and community-integrated teams seem to get the work done well together from a set of principles offered in the conclusion of this chapter. These principles for robust PTL systems emerge from social network theory (Scott, 2012) and policy network theory (Pal, 2013) that allow us to understand a whole set of interacting people, ideas or organizations by mapping and analysing the patterns of connections and the contents of their relationships. By using advanced software to account for the complex interconnections of many people and ideas we have found that network structures *can* describe relationships well beyond organization prescribed role functions, and that helps us to create the best patterns and principles for designing collaborative and participatory teaching and learning networks or teams. In fact, the work has found ample evidence that the connections found in a garden are much more accurate metaphors for the dynamics of highly capable education teams than the older industrial age depictions of teams (organization charts). Industrial age thinking is better aligned with 'flower box' metaphors describing people who with mandated, specialized functions connected by vertical power lines (Kowch, 2016).

Why use complexity thinking to characterize sustainable PTLs? It is one thing to simply name a collaboration as a community of practice (COP), as a team, or a to use 'network' as a convenient metaphor with no precise qualities. It is entirely another matter to *become* a resonant team or network. My research finds that COPs are a good intention, but mostly a myth that does not help us understand collaborative work as it is happening in schools. In fact, studies of many education teams, groups and systems by this author find, overall that most communities of practice do not by the Wenger & Lave (2000) criteria, and that the term 'COP' is a convenient, loose way of advocating togetherness in bureaucratic systems (Kowch, 2013a, 2013c, 2016). By contrast, a network approach to understanding interconnected effort does help us see more complexity as co-creative relationships – so that by using a few simple principles we can work more effectively in partnered educational settings with school leaders who share our zeal for better learning with more autonomy to teach, to learn and to lead (Harris, 2008). So if educators finally embrace the idea that we're not educating in the industrial age anymore we need some theory that allows us to describe and to cultivate learning gardens instead of learning flower boxes. *Complexity thinking* is one such holistic perspective that has been developed for educators with exactly this need – to go beyond isolated thinking about parts and processes in education to see the interconnectedness of it all without getting lost in the complication of the parts. The principles for leading and teaching PTL emerge from this complexity theory and distributed leadership theory.

Sustainable education efforts change constantly and they require participatory, complexivist thinking because a 'one shot' change impacts classes, schools or systems that are far from stable. The only stable ecosystems are dead ecosystems (Capra, 2010). We have found that information age – oriented teachers and school leaders need guidelines for sustaining participatory teams that need new kinds of education ecosystem resources like time, money, policy and political support.

There is no time to lose. Education publics are pushing a global imperative forcing educators to 'get it together' with teachers and for children in the information age so that learning technology-supported environments return more to us than the 50 Billion dollar global investments we sink into them annually (OECD, 2010). Leaders and teachers alike are constantly challenged to imagine more coherent education student experiences where every student is accommodated *uniquely* rather than by a 'one size fits all' public education system experience (Cuban, 2011) – much as PTL proposes. At a same time, there is a global imperative demanding that education leaders improve and innovate our education institutions to become more change capable through more open and more innovative processes (Hargreaves & Shirley, 2012; Willower & Forsythe, 1999). Once again the intertwined nature of teaching and leading school must be recognized in information age social learning – demanding that teachers and leaders learn and perform well as key actors among a network of students, teachers, leaders and learners. We must understand and accept that these are people engaged in a rich learning project where everyone can change roles in a participatory learning network where teacher becomes learner for a while, for example, and where leader becomes teacher at times (Bransford et al., 2000). Our roles will change in the information age and we need principles for helping us out in that complex world.

My research finds over and over what many education administration, learning science and educational technology graduate student researchers are also finding from large system level research projects: *relatively few education stakeholders possess both the necessary theoretical* and *practical knowledge necessary for bridging educational technology disciplines and educational leadership disciplines in sustainable, impactful participatory education contexts* (Humby, 2009; Winkelmans, 2014; Hull, 2012; Krause, 2009; Warren, 2008). This chapter is an attempt toward filling that knowledge gap for education professionals stuck in industrial age paradigms and practices while they are well into the information age.

While education leadership and education technology fields have identical epistemological and ontological developmental trajectories in the humanities (Kowch, 2013) they tend to attract people who can conceptualize a plan for change via *design thinking* (Nelson & Stolterman, 2012) as well. We've been overspecializing in the educational technology field for some time – breaking into new subfields like learning science, human performance, instructional science, instructional systems technology, instructional design, etc. for the last decade. But as a group, people in the educational technology have moved toward information age paradigm thinking with *design thinking processes* that involve designing instruction and learning experiences with technologies. Their models, techniques, theory and designs are more aimed today to enhance and support the entire changing learner process – while the technology tools themselves are the last things to be selected and employed for learning (Merrill, 2012; Januszewski & Molenda, 2008). The field hasn't been about the toys since 1970, because the toys change weekly. All educational technologists and learning scientists also possess, by their graduate degree requirements a good stock of pedagogical knowledge for designing participatory or other learning environments with technology and networks of people. Still, we often find that school teachers are more attracted to their K-12 *subject* teaching areas or to a tech *tool* than they are to leadership or to educational technology thinking. Too frequently (over 80% of the time) our research finds that school leaders are attracted more to tools than to collaborative learning environment designs as well (Kowch, 2007). This is a problem for information age education because all of our work actually involves leading, following, design and instruction in the same 'space.' PTL is a good example. Newer thinking about flexible schools and administration tells us what we already feel in their bones – that *teachers* can and must play with learners in both education administration and leadership disciplines (Hargreaves & Shirley, 2009). In this chapter we consider the role of 'leader' taken interchangeably by teachers, students and education technologists who work and will work more with changing clusters of relationships connecting people who come and go in PTL learning contexts.

The idea of relational patterns has informed this research and I have found that most effective school leaders, school teachers and educational technologists attract to one another primarily by connecting from their own disciplinary interests first, then by 'entertaining' other disciplines – sometimes – in a curriculum or subject/oriented profession like K-12 education (Kowch, 2005). In my research teams go beyond using the convenient metaphor of 'community' and 'teamwork' to describe our changing work as *patterns* of relations rather than describing our work as teaching, leading and learning from the bounded layers of specialized labor (bureaucracies) so often found in leadership study (Kowch, 2005, 2013b). The results from studying interconnection in this way allows us to map and study both formal and informal professional activities among people with weak or strong relationships and patterns. Because we know about the features of strong and weak relational patterns from social and policy network analysis rules, we can describe, interpret and *design* teams and clusters of professionals better than every today (Kowch, 2007).

One surprising finding from studying our post-modern world is that even when educators are given total freedom in education work, *education professionals most often tend to organize themselves as top-down bureaucratic teams* (Kowch, 2007, 2016). So organizing participatory or PTL networks isn't just a problem for principals and superintendents, it's a challenge for everyone in the information age With more design thinking, the more open and flexible spaces necessary for sustainable PTL could afford teachers and leaders more freedom to make exactly the same mistakes we have found in our research when self-organizing teams have freedom. We

A NEW PARADIGM FOR TEACHING, LEADING AND LEARNING

need these new approaches and guidelines for leading information age networked, changing teams, and we can't just use these descriptive words to believe we've achieved this as we have done with 'communities of practice' (Kowch, 2007). This means that in a robust PTL-capable school and district environment *everyone* needs to understand something about team dynamics, change leadership and partnering to gain good habits for work in high capacity networks of *reciprocal* relationships – so that we do not fall back into the weaker top-down patters that are the least flexible patterns of relations found in nature (Scott, 2012). The final section in this chapter offers 7 principles for designing, leading and living well in highly capable, flexible participatory education clusters, networks or teams. On our way to that we explore next the essential characteristics of healthy, networked collaborations in general.

UNDERSTANDING PARTICIPATORY EDUCATION TEAMS AS NETWORKS OF RELATIONSHIPS

We are a lot smarter as collectives than we are as individuals (Stacey, 2009). Given our earlier argument that 21st century skills, communication technology and ICTs in the classroom will characterize the school of the future, we know that the PTL school will be a lot less bounded by bricks, mortar and isolationism. Similarly, the rigid top-down industrial age education structures we have in our minds will eventually fade and be replaced by softer, more open relational patterns of healthy, flexible learning environments nested within in other environments. While our research repeatedly finds that teachers and leaders *talk* continuously about doing just that, we're not quite there yet in education. We need simple guidelines to imagine and create these participatory, flexible structures. What does it mean to lead more autonomous learning groups? How can we avoid descending into chaos and still embrace constant change in PTL environments? In this section we lay out some of the important, very basic characteristics of diverse and strong participatory education teams so that educators can use these guidelines for designing and leading flexible, effective PTL teams in our constant-flux world.

Diversity defines today's schools and diversity is an essential feature in healthy ecosystems. *Classroom* populations in Calgary, Alberta schools for example range in size from 1 to 50 learners per teacher. These classrooms coexist in public, chartered and private *schools* whose populations range from 50 to 2,000 learners. As nested subsystems Calgary schools also belong to overlapping school *district* jurisdictions serving from 4,000 to 100,000+ learners serviced by tens of thousands of teachers (Calgary Board of Education, 2015). In large systems a classroom teacher, student or a school leader can be quite isolated from the relationships that make things happen – but in general, all teachers work with the school in some way.

In my work as a professor serving both preservice teachers and educational leadership graduate students for over 15 years, I notice that my undergraduate and graduate students in the learning sciences and in leadership disciplines are attracted to *specialized* theory and practice that helping them learning to a manageable flower

235

box fixed on the deck of a ship in rolling seas. They choose to focus either on teaching, education technology or on leadership disciplines almost to the exclusion of *learning* principles found across all three areas (Ashbough & Pina, 2014; Kowch, 2013a). Too often our brightest education university students become professional practitioners who quickly adopt a quiet isolationism that can manifest in a less incoherent, fractured education community experiences where professionals *cluster together* within the complicated, closed machinery of education praxis rather than by connecting to what attracts them in the education garden (Kowch & Gereluk, 2015). This is a regrettable and consistent finding in my research. We cannot 'do' participative teaching and learning like that. Our overspecializations are pulling us towards atomism while we find coping mechanisms to handle the complicated overloads resulting from adapting industrial era contexts to information age learning chances.

Those small isolated clusters of people form smaller, tighter and less flexible 'spaces' for professional practice. In network theory, clusters are strong when they are connected to other clusters by key individuals across an ecosystem – but when clusters (or teams) are separate from others they are far more weak than organizations that tend to turn inward, to reduce their diversity and they resist change. These isolated clusters weaken any participatory team capacity and it weakens the school organization and school district capacity to change ideas or to respond to external shocks – much like a cluster of English class teachers in a high school may feel excluded when the school decides to engage interdisciplinary teaching, and isolate from the others. When funding is cut, system – wide change occurs and the English teachers, for example are are less able to adjust when they are not well connected. For them, it's tougher to know, learn or to lead their way forward as co-connected partners in the school and district. If education professionals and learners want to create complex adaptive participatory learning networks, we need to know at least some of the features of high capacity networks mentioned next to design our PTL work with these features in mind.

Networks, Clusters and Patterns of Relationships: An Overview

Researchers have learned a lot about networked collaboration (Borgatti et al., 2014) from research grounded in a complexity mindset. We can describe collective leadership, teaching and learning dynamics without the old boundaries of organization structure. We can describe (and design) who matters to whom, who attracts to what idea, and which relation types and patterns help genuine partnerships develop simultaneously at micro (individual), meso (school) and macro (district, ecosystem) levels. We have found that *certain patterns* of connections among teachers, learners, leaders and communities are far more adaptable than others (Kowch, 2013c). We have learned that some relational patterns are flexible and open decentralized networks while some networks patterns are found to be more closed and rigid centralized networks. PTL *requires* social, technical and personal interaction that is flexible and open, like the decentralized (B) in Figure 13.1. Such a figure could represent clusters of learner groups solving different problems in a high school social studies class who are connected by different teachers and content experts, for example.

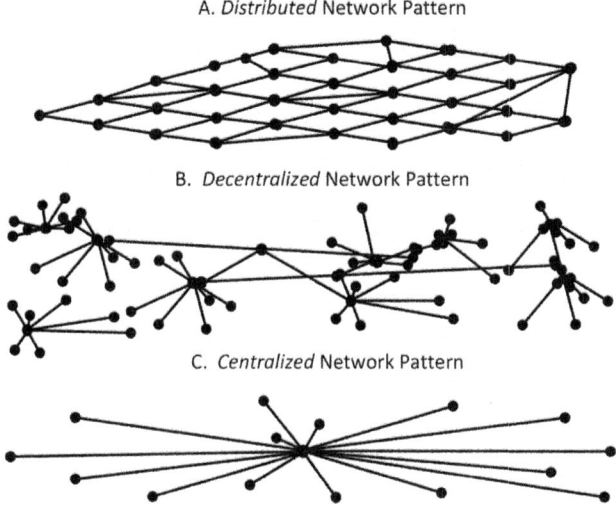

Figure 13.1. Distributed, decentralized and centralized participatory teacher, learner and leader network patterns

A decentralized pattern of people and relationships (B) is the most flexible and open structure/pattern because some groups can finish their work and 'disappear' and different people can come and go from 'connecting' points to work with different teams – even at the same time. The fact that parts of a decentralized network have enough diversity and redundancy (Kowch, 2013c) means people can come and go without severely impacting the entire system. Network type A is overly connected – impacts in any one point of the system impact every other part of the system. In a participatory learning situation this would mean if one teacher leaves the network, all other people are significantly affected and learning changes (Burke, 2011). In other words, different clusters can finish their work and disband without impacting other groups – a concept teachers know well from classrooms.

Teaching and leadership work can be similarly understood. In an industrial age school like the centralized network (C), knowledge gatekeepers at the centre (or top) regulate all discourse between teachers or learners, usually with one-directional and rather static power relationships that are unreciprocated. See Kowch (2005, 2013b) for more on patterns for participatory leading and learning. Can we re-imagine a network of school leaders, learners and communities in this way so that participatory, social technology-enabled learning and knowledge building (Scardamalia & Bereiter, 2006) can be sustained? Imagine that one cluster in (B) describes a terrific participatory learning project. To *sustain* the great learning in that cluster, say in a great participatory learning inquiry STEM project, the right *kinds* of connections between resources and knowledge builders has to exist between clusters of people with the right kinds of capacity or capability to work in teams (Kowch, 2005). We can educate and shape the kinds of people, expertise, technologies we connect for learners and we can design interactivities with our learners if we involve information age colleagues and school leaders. Knowledge building in a problem-solving space requires no less than this expansive thinking. To help participatory teachers, leaders and support systems to support, lead or to design highly capable network teams, the author provides principles for that leadership later in this chapter.

So *interconnected clusters* of teachers can be strong and vibrant within a school (network) but when the entire school faces change the less connected professional clusters of people usually cannot form a flexible enough network of relations to accommodate 'the space of the possible' in our contemporary our teaching/learning dynamics. Like pickets in a fence we need to be connected to one another for our 'fence' to sustain strong winds. In a participatory learning or PTL classroom with a good distributed team pattern we can better sustain clusters of learners in context – even if certain people or connections change, or when technology or resources (funds) run out for one of the project clusters. Centralized and decentralized patterned participatory learning networks are much harder to maintain because leaders need to do too much and a resource change (say lab fund shortages) impact the entire system. In a recent study of a large school system in Alberta we found that the entire system of schools in a district were quite unable to adapt to environmental change because leaders clustered together in schools without connecting to one another (Thompson et al., 2015). This means that while successful participatory learning is occurring in some schools and among leadership at the school level, the system itself is relatively weak in terms of responding to environmental issues impacting all schools at once. A strong team does not make a strong league or the best play. Teams and schools are, together, much smarter than we are as independents or as subgroups (Hargreaves et al., 2009).

Just as it is with learners within a classroom, when we separate from each other as teaching colleagues in closed classrooms our professional learning slows and we lose the power of being in an organizational collective – 1 so we cannot expect the participatory leadership benefits in a school running in a democratic mode, for example (Aslan, Reigeluth, & Thomas, 2003). When we are isolated from others the sum of different perspectives among us only adds to differences and away from essential diversity in schools and districts (Kowch, 2013c). That pattern makes teachers and leaders particularly vulnerable to conflicting preferences found among different teaching specializations (Science, Art, Phys. Ed) and leadership specializations (Human Resources, Instructional Leaders, Economists) too. Collegiality is back in the information age meaning that all of our relationships will morph into more flexible, capable learning PTL learning networks focused on learning results (Tyack & Tobin, 1994). PTL requires that nimbleness in a system that can support innovative pedagogy.

By reconceptualising professional relationships as *reciprocal patterns* of people with relationships and attractive ideas found in connected clusters, we access systems theory to find that a pattern of relations need not necessarily be hierarchical (bureaucratic), but rather that our relation patterns can be based on more lateral common attractions and reciprocal relations among us (Miller & Scott, 2007). What a liberating idea! There are good examples of this impulse or attraction in the global re-emergence of STEM and STEAM programming, for example. STEM is an aggregation of traditionally separate disciplinary clusters from science, teaching and pedagogy, engineering, arts and mathematics coming together to offer an advantage for teachers and learners who practice and learn as collectives, most often. Preventing STEM from isolation in a school or district will help assure its sustainability as an attractor so that it's not just another 'fad' among educators in schools. The same is true for any powerful idea that coalesces educators from merely 'interested others' into networks of action-takers. That is something to ponder the next time you must decide between attractors and fashionable ideas when building a PTL team, for example. You can't build a sustainable team around fashion or dogma.

The right kinds of PTL relational network can also 'connect' to support from technologists, designers, psychologists, accountants and content experts using today's technology – if – the network is open and flexible in a learning garden. Well-designed networks are incompressible – that is, that these collectives cannot be reduced to the sum of their parts and we know that sustainable teaching and learning classes and schools are that kind of entity more than they are vertical systems of authority and skill with 'clients' at the bottom of the pyramid. And we will argue more. For example, new information is showing that STEM education programs in higher education are also much more expensive than traditional programs and this will strain the relationships of STEM pedagogues and their administration (Lenovo, 2016). From just this one example we see an opportunity stemming from an imperative to better connect school leaders with teachers and educational technologists so that together we can imagine a larger and perhaps more sustainable 'space of the possible.' Next, we explore the nature of educational technology as an empowering actor in a robust participatory teaching, leading and learning networks dependent upon connectivity.

ENABLING PTL ENVIRONMENTS WITH EDUCATIONAL TECHNOLOGY

The Systems Thinking and Change Division at the Association of Education Technology and Communications (AECT) is a cluster of educational technology and education leadership scholars (www.aect.org) in the world's premier learning technology professional society. They represent thousands of university graduate programs, schools and industries in 13 countries pioneering information age concepts and designs for leading and learning. From teamwork creating a major reference work that is updating the field we are finding (Kowch, 2017) that project based, problem based and collaborative learning beg us to evolve new skill sets and mindsets so necessary for information age school teachers, leaders and learners

(Trilling & Fadel, 2009; Gronn, 2002). Research-based guidelines for practice are needed to make these ideas useful.

Participatory-oriented educators will continue to see an increase in self-directed, interdisciplinary project-based participatory learning happening with educational games and more robust learning simulations containing on-board assessments in student/teacher project learning spaces (Aslan & Reigeluth, 2013). Some fitting methods of instruction are also evolving for PTL so that better educational support systems can be more powerful, yet invisible scaffolds for the self-directed learner (Aslan et al., 2003). This trend in learning environment design is impacting school level shared services and school leaders while they strive to resource and to properly sustain effective practices in our learner centred schools (EdVisions Schools, 2013). As we have shown, technology (tools or processes) exist that can use big data about participatory student learning activities to help PTL teams set their own goals, find problems to solve, connect with other learners and teachers and set their own attainment pace and progression (Reigeluth et al., 2008). A combination of Teaching, leading and learning with technology expertise will be a silent enabler in successful, agile PTL learning networks of the future. Next, we explore how a shift of mindset from 'tools' to 'process' will help you use the principles at the end of this chapter to realize lasting technology-enhanced PTL in classes, schools and districts.

Shifting from Industrial Age to Information Age Conceptions of Educational Technology and Design Thinking

Long ago, ancient Greek plays sometimes presented unsolvable dichotomies or 'wicked problems' for actors to solve on the stage. To help the storyline, playwrights created the 'Deus ex Machina' which in Latin means 'God from the machine.' At a point of actor confusion stage hands would lift a pedestal that would rise slowly from a hole in the stage floor to reveal a 'God' into audience view. Shortly, this entity would offer wisdom to solve the most vexing problems in the story and all would be well. Postman (1992) uses Deus ex Machina as a fine example of current *technological determinism* I find in most schools and education faculties – a naive perspective where people employ a positivistic, reductionist mindset based on beliefs that there is an answer for all problems, and that where technology is concerned the answer is just a matter of finding the right 'magic box' or tool for a quick solution. This is great for tool vendors but it harms PTL education. Reflecting on the earlier garden metaphor for a participatory learning environment, the Deus Ex Machina represents another form of a black 'window' box that prohibits our understanding of the integrative role of educational environment designers or educational technologists who not only know how to choose tools for learning, but who also take a design mindset to the complex interplay of technology when supporting PTL and the many dimensions a the learning environment we have explored. Leadership professionals need to take a design thinker stance as well – for the team of teacher, leader and technologist will only become more prevalent in successful PTL contexts.

Technology itself has been called a reflection of man's best wishes – and we have known for 50 years that educational technology is of no value in teaching and learning unless it is supported by good pedagogy, good learning environment design and good system leadership teamwork. The magic is not in the educational technology 'box' and if it is used effectively a technology can open up the classroom and the school to a wider range of learning 'spaces' as we see in well-designed distributed education, for example (Keegan, 2013). This is an example of technology as is own end. A *participatory* classroom, by contrast requires a well-connected team also connected by communications and information technology to extend the relational network. In the education technology field, design thinking assures that generative constraints are placed on teaching and learning conduct afforded by machines so that predators and harm stays out of the environment. So information age thinking is not a technology tool issue – it's a combined teacher, leader and learner *design* issue dependent on everyone's ability to partner with network, change and PTL thinking. Technocrats, your day is done – unless bureaucrats reign supreme in education ecosystems.

Beyond the education field, technology has completely restructured society by changing the way we understand our world (Castells & Cordoso, 2005). Within our professional practices, the internet and online communication technologies have added enormous complexity along with a new opportunity for professional learners to engage content and *each other* in more contemporary participatory learning settings – like from their homes (Keegan, 2013). Oddly, more than a few education leadership specialists know almost much about the educational technology discipline beyond a surface understanding of these professionals as 'technicians.' This excludes an important PTL team member in the information age.

Educational technologists know how to put technology in place after careful environmental analyses, learner analyses, instructional design, instructor preparation, learning assessments and, finally, tech tool selection (Merrill, 2012). Their research tells them not to produce a Deus ex Machina or 'black boxes.' These education professionals know that tools or IT/technology machinery is selected as the final step in a long learning environment analysis and design process.

Sadly, *education leadership* team members do not yet know well enough the connectivity, context and impact of those learning designs within the sphere of school administration (Kowch, 2013a). Unfortunately, this misunderstanding-from-isolation reduces the potential for learning environment designers to 'put technology in its place' for even the most holistic participatory learning designs and implementations. Instead, PTL teachers are faced with political arguments about the evil of tools without understanding the value of the educational technology discipline in a PTL team setting (McRae, 2014). IT technicians, by contrast have college educations to install tools and software while possessing none of the extensive education educational technologists gain in university designing educational (learning) technology integrated learning and performance environments (Januszewski & Molenda, 2008). *Educational technologists* make good nodes in a PTL network.

Some *teachers* take up technology as "champions" of tools without an educational technology background. Often, without the principles at the end of this chapter to guide their PTL teamwork they wind up as technocrats – promoting vendors or fads (games) without linking the instruction tool to the learning team or school/division learning ecosystem. As we inch toward better designed technology-enhanced participatory learning environments (Friesen, 2009) with embedded internet connectivity, our leaders and teachers can afford classrooms and schools opportunities to 'break through' classic brick-and-mortar bound schools and classrooms to engage *each other* better. This includes our communities and many nested subsystems in a global ecosystem of learning and being that will be essential for more self-directed learners (Anderson & Dron, 2010). Teachers can't be tech determinists any more than leaders can be bureaucrats if we want to create truly sustainable PTL teams.

By taking holistic approaches to the common project of connecting people and resources our PTL teams can create more possibilities for flexible school or organization transformation through innovation (Goldstein et al., 2010). For example, Clayton Christensen is right that education technology has become the next great disruptor in education (Christensen, Horn, & Johnson, 2008). He pointed out that distance learning would likely offer the education 'market' alternatives where poor education might exist, causing a stir that remains. So when we lead PTL teams we'll also have to lead disruptive innovation. The final sections of this chapter help PTL teams lead change, innovation and robust networks that can be sustained in schools and school districts. Without a design approach for information age learning we end up adopting technology as a commodity or a tool that we don't critically understand well enough beyond our own mind (Nelson & Stolterman, 2012).

Case Example: Principles for Designing Technology-Enabled PTL Schools

By taking a *design thinking* approach (Nelson & Stolterman, 2012) and a few guidelines provided at the end of this chapter we can design more relational PTL environments so that technology amplifies teaching and learning outcomes.

In a study of the Minnesota New Country School, for example (Aslan et al., 2003) found that (an entire) successful decentralized participatory learning school can be designed well by using *4 whole-school design principles*, each embodying instructional design, teaching community, pedagogy, assessment and leadership ideas enhanced by educational technology. The successful PTL information age school can be designed by creating:

1. Small learning communities
2. Self-directed project based learning
3. Authentic assessment
4. Teacher ownership and democratic governance

Reigeluth et al. (2008) further identified specific *roles* for connective and supporting educational technologies to support this kind of more adaptable school:

1. Recordkeeping (standards, attainments, leaner characteristics inventories
2. Planning (goal setting, projects, teams, roles, contract parameters)
3. Instruction (initiation, instruction, support)
4. Assessment for students learning (authentic tasks, performance evaluation, immediate feedback, and certification of learning attainments)

Beyond the scope of this chapter, we can easily imagine that a participatory learning class context implies the eventual *integration* of big data, integrated learning management systems, cloud based computing and the best in mobile learning tools. These are already supported by artificial intelligence-assisted software to let students set goals, find projects, share results, connect to people, self and peer assess, engage teachers and to know when they can move to higher learning. Almost impossible to imagine years ago, today we can see this augmentation already emerging for teachers and learners in pilot form today. What is missing is teacher and leader paradigm changes enabling us all to collaborate as PTL teams that can integrate technology in much more open network learning environments. We have seen it done and we know this change is possible. In the next and final section of the chapter we offer evidence-based principles for leading *highly capable participatory network teams* affecting change and innovation in education contexts. These research-based principles are intended as guidelines for PTL team development and sustainability where resources, relations and ideas flow freely.

PUTTING IT ALL TOGETHER: PRINCIPLES FOR TEACHING, LEADING AND LEARNING IN ROBUST PTL ENVIRONMENTS

Contemporary educators aim for student-centred discovery learning, distributed leadership with truly collegial community-engaged governance paints a bright and hopeful foreground for us. We now have ways to open up school praxis by using complexity thinking, design thinking and post structural leadership ideas to help PTL teams thrive. Society and even some education systems are emerging from an outdated industrial view of education towards a more social teaching, leading and learning ecosystem with a generative perspective (Goldstein et al., 2010), so we need guidelines on how to lead more social learning forward despite one cautionary note: This brighter praxis stands in the foreground against a much darker background where at the same time educators survive in highly bureaucratic, vertical power organizations necessitated by overspecialized, overcomplicated processes, policies and education structures that have evolved over the centuries of the industrial age. They're everywhere today.

This context means that by the very nature of PTL work, you will be creating new education 'products and processes' (Goldstein et al., 2010) defining whole-system innovations as networked teams change class work and the learning environments bridging schools and communities. This is the new kind of organization where leaders can sustain complex, constant flux efforts like PTL. We need practical ideas to make it happen. So this chapter ends with a first set of guides for leading PTL network teams (Kowch, 2016), for designing PTL schools, and for designing supporting technologies. We also offer some research-informed principles for handling change and innovation so that PTL team members create sustainable and adaptive PTL in the context of our ever-changing schools and school districts.

We conclude the chapter with guiding principles to help PTL professional teams for imagining and sustaining robust PTL environments:

- Four design principles for creating information age schools
- Four design principles for project based, self-directed learner management supported environments
- Seven principles for leading high capacity networks of people in PTL schools
- Five principles for leading innovation in participatory learning schools and Districts
- Three principles for leading change in participatory learning schools and Districts

Four Design Principles for Creating Information Age Schools

Research using *design thinking* has recently uncovered 4 school design principles for information age schools. Note that most of the learning designs employ teams including other learners, teachers, school leaders and IT systems. Aslan and Reigeluth (2013) and Joseph and Reigeluth (2005) studied a number of learner centred, project based schools to find 4 principles for teachers and leader teams designing effective school leaders use when designing these learners centred schools:

1. Create a small learner community.
2. Employ self-directed project based learning.
3. Use authentic assessment.
4. Actualize teacher/leader and leader/teacher relational governance models in the school (Aslan et al., 2003).

Again you will notice that older bureaucratic organizational models won't work for the technology enabled, information age learner centred school and we see that more relational leadership teams matter. These researchers also found design parameters for creating and using learning management systems based on evidence from some more open, participatory learning schools, summarized below.

Four Design Principles for Project Based, Self-Directed Learner Management Supported Environments

We have begun to explore some of the most advanced models informing today's learning management systems (LMSs) in information age schools, identifying major roles for these supra-systems designed to support more self-directed learner. Such systems include continuously evolving Blackboard, Desire to Learn, Moodle and others. Given what we have proposed for robust PTL environments as products of highly capable PTL network teamwork, professionals will need some guiding principles for assuring whatever LMS they have available can fit their paradigm, practice and teamwork as well as the needs of the system purchasing the tools.

Reigeluth et al. (2008) posit that technology supported, distributed and relational school/community connections will occur between students, teachers, student families and the school (p. 32). These more open schools will need LMSs designed with 4 primary and 3 secondary features to support everyone in the student's network (including the school and the district) in this evidence-based, just-in-time learner driven/timed environment.

The following LMS elements presently exist in their infancy only – tested and published but a few times – but PTL readers can imagine how they could empower students, families, teachers and the school with automatic reporting and AI (artificial intelligence) level analytics in the school:

1. *Record keeping* will be important as student attainments and material usage will occur on the student's timeline. General records of learning goals set by students and participatory learning teams, a personal record of student learning and analytic information about student learning methods, progress and resource needs will help teachers and the school organize support for participatory learners. A standards inventory will be needed to inform teacher/student/parent teams in planning the learning with the learner will likely be necessary with personal inventories of attainments and learner characteristics as well.
2. *Planning for student learning* systems will assist a participatory student in setting long term personal and even group learning goals, particularly incolleges or universities. Planning systems will help students and the learning team when selecting project topics and learning attainments, setting short term goals (interests, opportunities, and content areas) and defining team information (students will work in small project teams for social learning). Learning contract information in the system will hold the ideal attainments and actual participatory learning attainment data for students, parents, teachers and the school to help the student support learning network know how well the student is doing (p. 34). All of this would be visible as part of the instructional learning environment, not at all as 'rules' or 'constraints.' For example, when a participatory learner decides on a problem to solve and chooses from a (minimum) set of learning attainments, the system will monitor incremental attainments, provide formative feedback and scaffold learning experiences until attainments set (by the student) are reached.
3. *Instruction for student learning* will focus on the projects constructed by the learner and the team. The system might help the student with project initiation and identification, offline attainment activities (and online ones) and debriefing and reflection communications systems between teachers, the school administration and the learner (and between other learners). Once the learner has the attainments needed to proceed forward, the learner tool will notify the team and begin next project identification. Instructional development tools supporting participatory

teachers will work from a widening open repository of instructional tools and methods but this will never be powerful enough for self-directed learners in different contexts. Here, teacher work with students will be essential. Much as future drivers will negotiate self-driving vehicle system information to get to Aunty Betty's house safely and quickly, teachers and learners will negotiate evidence-based alternatives for scaffolding learning so that students attain what is needed and planned.

4. *Assessment for (and of) learning* will involve systems (1) presenting authentic tasks for PBL assessment, (2) evaluating subsequent student performance, (3) providing immediate feedback to team members, (4) certification and rewards, (5) developing new student assessments, and (6) improving instruction using the evidence from this system. Using big data, AI informed LMS systems can quietly scaffold teacher, learner, parent and school administrator decision making about the learning process and student learning attainments before students are presented with the next 'level' of learning options/attainments.

In the information age, large system learning management technologies are an increasing part of school districts engaged in more and more distance learning. These principles indicate how we can guide our networks and teams toward using them well for PTL. Teams, as we explored in earlier sections are networks, and distributed networks allow the most flexible PTL collectives. The following 7 principles help PTL professionals guide the setup and operation of network team individuals and their relationships so that the collective or network is flexible and adaptable (Kowch, 2005, 2016).

Seven Principles for Leading High Capacity Networks of People in PTL Schools

1. Assure that every network member has a clear *concept of their role*.
2. Develop a common, supporting *value system* among all participants.
3. A unique, *professional ethos* among everyone helps (in professional teams, a duty of care ethos is prominent, for example).
4. As a collective, the network should have the will and capability to *generate information* internally.
5. As a network, people should all possess a capability and a will to maintain *cohesion*.
6. As a network, people should, overall possess a capability to *organize and manage complex tasks*, leading toward the creation of a response.
7. Perhaps most importantly, all network participants need a capacity to *raise above self-interest* in the context of the organization goals in the context.

Creating highly capable teams that get work done well matters as much as sustaining those teams in diverse and ever changing networks of classes, schools, personnel, ideas and teachers in information age school districts. The following 5 principles summarize the best guides for leading innovations – new processes and learning results that are the goal of PTL teams.

A NEW PARADIGM FOR TEACHING, LEADING AND LEARNING

Five Principles for Leading Innovation in Participatory Learning Schools and Districts

1. Information age education professionals engaged in PTL will inevitably be leading innovation in schools. The following guidelines are adapted from (Kowch, 2016) for PTL networks facing innovation leadership. Learners in nested subsystems extending well beyond a class, school or district jurisdiction boundaries appreciate the value of an innovation in a learning environment (Christensen et al., 2008).
2. The community or network of people valuing a critical innovation may at first be very small (Rogers, 2003).
3. An innovation can disrupt or displace the existing processes and purposes of any organization unpredictably. Education organization ecosystems must have the capacity to innovate. Learning leaders cannot manage non-consumption of their services (Christensen et al., 2008).
4. Complex adaptive systems (education organizations) transform or emerge via innovations (Goldstein et al., 2010; Kowch, 2013c). At the cusp of change, generative tensions can drive complex experimentation, generating innovation.
5. Learning leader networks will develop new ways and common understandings to identify critical novelty and experimentation in their primary processes and products to seize the opportunity for complete organizational emergence (Hazy, 2011).

Finally, our PTL teams will need to manage the change that comes from introducing participatory learning teamwork in schools, particularly if the dominant paradigm is industrial. Grounded by the thinking in the earlier parts of this chapter, the following three principles help teams to lead change in the context of a school and school district so that the work we do isn't rejected or unable to sustain in a 'garden' of learning:

Three Principles for Leading Change in Participatory Learning Schools and Districts

1. Change may happen across a *distributed authority/disaggregated influence network* (Atkinson & Coleman, 1996). Change may not impact the entire organization, innovation can – so change means a shift or a gesture to an outcome that is planned (or not) at the operational level of leadership (getting things done) (Hazy, 2011).
2. Inspired and engaged people and *resources* interplay across the organization and beyond it. Classical top-down, specialized leaders may need to lead systemic change 'steps' on the way to leading organizational change. Those steps are: paradigm change; envisioning; networking; sustaining and evaluating effortful change (Reigeluth & Duffy, 2008).

3. Interconnected, co-dependent, shifting professional and non-professional *partnerships* will likely be a constant factor for next generation organization change leaders. Collegiality is back (Hargreaves & Shirley, 2009).

CONCLUSION

We have shown that educators are using language about transformation and participatory learning, and that teachers and leaders need new guidelines, mindsets and skills to make participatory learning happen. This chapter is designed to offer grounded principles for mindsets and network PTL team design features to fill that knowledge-builder gap.

We have explored the tremendous importance of educators *moving to an information age paradigm* so that we can use guiding principles for PTL dynamics that are an essential part of well-designed, healthy *patterns of professional relationship networks* linking clusters of people and resources well beyond a single classroom. We demonstrated the importance of PTL team networks informed by design thinking principles to create, manage and to lead flexible teams and the enabling technologies, policies and resources with leaders in schools. Finally, we offered *design principles* for creating *highly capable participatory teams*, and schools with tips for *leading the change* and *innovations* that will inevitably come from robust, flexible PTL environments. These principles open a discussion space and some beginning guidelines to help educators realize their participatory learning ideals through good old genuinely collaborative professional teamwork in an information age context.

REFERENCES

Anderson, T., & Dron, J. (2010). Three generations of distance education pedagogy. *The International Review of Research in Open and Distance Learning, 12*(3), 80–97. Retrieved from http://www.irrodl.org/index.php/irrodl/article/view/890/1663

Ashbough, M. L., & Pina, A. A. (2014). Improving instructional design processes through leaders participatory learning teamwork hip-thinking and modeling. In B. Hokanson & A. Gibbons (Eds.), *Design in educational technology: Design thinking, design process, and the design studio* (pp. 223–247). Switzerland: Springer.

Aslan, S., & Reigeluth, C. (2013). Leading a new paradigm of education. *TechTrends, 57*(5), 18–24.

Aslan, S., Reigeluth, C., & Thomas, D. (2003). Transforming education with self-directed project-based learning: The Minnesota New Country School. *Educational Technology, 54*(3), 39–42.

Atkinson, M., & Coleman, W. (1996). Policy networks, policy communities and the problems of governance. In L. Dobuzinskis, M. Howlett, & D. Laycock (Eds.), *Policy studies in Canada: The state of the art* (pp. 193–213). Toronto: University of Toronto Press.

Barab, S. A. (1999). Ecologizing instruction through integrated units. *Middle School Journal, 30*(1), 21–28.

Bourdieu, P. (1972). *The logic of practice* (R. Nice, Trans.). Stanford, CA: Stanford University Press.

Bransford, J. D., Brown, A. L., & Cocking, R. R. (Eds.). (2000). *How people learn: Brain, mind, experience, and school*. Washington, DC: National Academy Press.

Burke, W. (2011). *Organizational change theory and practice* (3rd ed.). Thousand Oaks, CA: Sage Publications.

Calgary Board of Education. (2015). *CBE school enrolment report*. Retrieved from http://www.cbe.ab.ca/FormsManuals/School-Enrolment-Report-2015-2016.pdf

Capra, F. (2010). *The web of life*. New York, NY: Anchor Books.

Castells, M., & Cordoso, G. (2005). *The networked society: From knowledge to policy*. Washington, DC: Johns Hopkins University Press.

Christensen, C., Horn, M., & Johnson, W. (2008). *Disrupting class*. New York, NY: McGraw-Hill.

Cilliers, P. (1998). *Complexity and postmodernism: Understanding complex systems*. New York, NY: Routledge.

Cuban, L. (2011). Teacher, superintendent, scholar: The gift of multiple careers. *Leaders in Educational Studies, 3*, 45–54.

Duffy, F. M. (2008, July). The School System Transformation (SST) protocol. *Educational Technology, 48*(4), 41–48.

EdVisions Schools. (2013). *Report on the innovation*. Retrieved from http:www.edvisions.com/custom/Splashpage.asp

Friesen, S. (2009). Teaching effectiveness: Framework and rubric. *What did you do in school today?* Toronto: Canadian Education Association.

Fullan, M. (2010). Positive pressure. In A. Hargreaves, A. Lieberman, M. Fullan, & D. Hopkins (Eds.), *Second handbook of educational change* (Vol. 1, pp. 119–131). London: Springer.

Goldstein, J., Hazy, J., & Lichtenstein, B. (2010). *Complexity and the nexus of leadership*. New York, NY: Palgrave Macmillan.

Goldstein, J., Hazy, J., & Lichtenstein, B. (2010). *Complexity and the nexus of leadership: Leveraging nonlinear science to create ccologies of innovation*. New York, NY: Palgrave MacMillan. (ISBN 978-0-230-62227-2)

Gronn, P. (2002). Distributed leadership. In K. Liethwood & P. Hallinger (Eds.), *Second international handbook of educational leadership administration* (pp. 653–697). Boston, MA: Kluwer.

Hargreaves, A., & Shirley, D. (2009). *The fourth way: The inspiring future for educational change*. Thousand Oaks, CA: Corwin.

Hargreaves, A., & Shirley, D. (2012). *The global fourth way*. Thousand Oaks, CA: Corwin.

Hargreaves, A., Crocker, R., Davis, B., McEwan, L., Sahlberg, P., Shirley, D., & Sumara, D. (2009). *The learning mosaic: Multiple perspectives of the Alberta Initiative for School Improvement (AISI)*. Edmonton: Alberta Learning.

Harris, A. (2008). *Distributed school leadership*. London: Routledge.

Hazy, J. K. (2011). Parsing the 'influential increment' in the language of complexity: Uncovering systemic mechanisms of leadership influence. *Journal of Complexity in Leadership and Management, 1*(2), 116–132.

Hazy, J., & Uhl-Bein, M. (2015). Towards operationalizing complexity leadership. *Leadership, 11*(1), 79–104.

Heck, R., & Hallinger, P. (2005). The study of educational leadership and management: Where does the field stand today? *Educational Management Administration & Leadership, 33*(1), 229–244.

Hull, P. (2012). *Canadian university nursing deanship* (Unpublished Doctoral Dissertation). University of Calgary, Calgary.

Humby, R. (2009). *Leading decision making and planning for online HRD in a national health and wellness NGO* (Unpublished Masters Thesis Dissertation). University of Calgary, Calgary.

Jacobsen, M., Lock, J., & Friesen, S. (2016). Strategies for engagement: Knowledge building and intellectual engagement in participatory learning environments. *Education Canada, 56*(2), 17–26.

Januszewski, A., & Molenda, M. (Eds.). (2008). *Educational technology: A definition with commentary*. New York, NY: Routledge.

Joseph, R., & Reigeluth, C. (2005). Formative research on an early stage of the systemic change process in a smaller school district. *British Journal of Educational Technology, 36*(6), 937–956.

Keegan, D. (2013). *Theoretical principles of distance education*. New York, NY: Routledge.

Kowch, E. (2005). The knowledge network: A fundamentally new (relational) approach to knowledge management & the study of dependent organizations. *Journal of Knowledge Management Practice, 6*, 13–37.

Kowch, E. (2007). *Alberta shared services/thin client innovation. System leadership study #2.* Edmonton: Alberta Education Publication.

Kowch, E. (2013). Conceptualizing the essential qualities of complex adaptive leadership: Networks that organize and learn. *International Journal of Complexity in Leadership and Management, 2*(3), 162–184.

Kowch, E. G. (2013a) Wither thee, educational technology? Suggesting a critical expansion of our epistemology for emerging leaders. *TechTrends, 57*(5), 11–27.

Kowch, E. G. (2013b). 21st century citizen networks in complex states: Shall we dance or play tug-of-war? In J. Arvanitakis & I. Matthews (Eds.), *The 21st century citizen: Global, interdisciplinary perspectives* (pp. 11–27). Oxford: Interdisciplinary Press.

Kowch, E. G. (2013c). Towards leading diverse, smarter and more adaptable organizations that learn. In J. Lewis, A. Green, & D. Surry (Eds.), *Technology as a tool for diversity leadership: Implementation* (pp. 11–34). Hershey, PA: IGI Global.

Kowch, E. (2016). Surviving the next generation of organizations as leaders. In N. Rushby & D. Surry (Eds.), *Wiley handbook of learning technology* (pp. 484–508). London: Wiley-Blackwell.

Kowch, E. (Ed.). (2017). Systems thinking and change. In M. Spector, B. Lockee, & M. Childress (Eds.), *Learning, design and technology: An international compenduim of theory, research, practice and policy* (Vol. 7, pp. 400–600). London: Springer.

Kowch, E., & Gereluk, D. (2015). *Increasing charter school innovation and impact.* Paper presented at the 2015 AERA Annual Meeting, Chicago, IL.

Krause, F. (2009). *Designer decision-making for newcomer orientation training and on-boarding programs* (Unpublished Doctoral Dissertation). University of Calgary, Calgary.

Lenovo. (2016). *Four trends to watch for in higher education* (report). Retrieved from http://iKlion.solutions.lenovo.com/higher-education/connected-campus-infographic

McKelvey, B., & Lichtenstein, B. (2007). Leadership in the four stages of emergence. In J. Hazy, J. Goldstein, & B. Lichtenstein (Eds.), *Complex systems leadership theory* (pp. 93–107). Mansfield, MA: ISCE Publishing.

McRae, P. (2014). Myth: Blended learning is the next ed-tech revolution – Hype, harm and hope. *Alberta Teachers Association Magazine, 95*(4), 11–17.

Merrill, D. (2012). *First principles of instruction.* New York, NY: Wiley.

Miller, J., & Scott, P. (2007). *Complex adaptive systems.* Princeton, NJ: Princeton University Press.

Nelson, H., & Stolterman, E. (2012). Composing and connecting. In H. Nelson & E. Stolterman (Eds.), *The design way: Intentional change in an unpredictable world.* Boston, MA: MIT Press.

OECD. (2010). The policy debate about technology in education: Are the new millennium learners making the grade? *Technology use and educational performance in PISA 2006.* Paris: OECD Publishing.

Pal, L. A. (2013). *Beyond policy analysis: Public issue management in turbulent times* (5th ed.). Toronto: Nelson.

Postman, N. (1992). *Technopoly.* New York, NY: Knopf.

Reigeluth, C. M., & Duffy, F. M. (2008). The AECT FutureMinds initiative: Transforming America's school systems. *Educational Technology, 48*(3), 45–49.

Reigeluth, C. M., & Karnapp, J. R. (2013, November). *Reinventing schools.* Boston, MA: R&L Education.

Reigeluth, C. M., Watson, B., Watson, S., Dutta, P., Zengguan, C., & Powell, N. (2008). Roles for techology in the infomration-age paradigm of education: Learning management systems. *Educational Technology, 48*(6), 32–39.

Rogers, E. M. (2003). *Diffusion of innovations* (5th ed.). New York, NY: Free Press.

Scardamalia, M., & Bereiter, C. (2006). Knowledge building: Theory, pedagogy, and technology. In K. Sawyer (Ed.), *Cambridge handbook of the learning sciences* (pp. 97–118). New York, NY: Cambridge University Press.

Scott, J. (2012). *Social network analysis* (3rd ed.). London: Sage Publications.

Shapiro, B. (2011). Towards a transforming constructivism: Understanding learners' meanings and messages of learning environments. *Journal of Educational Thought, 45*(2), 165–202.

Shapiro, B. (2014). Engaging novice teachers in semiotic inquiry: Considering the environmental messages of school learning settings. *Cultural Studies of Science Education, 9*(4), 809–824.

Shirky, C. (2008). *Here comes everybody: The power of organizing without organizations.* New York, NY: Penguin.

Stacey, R. (2009). *Complexity and organizational reality: Uncertainty and the need to rethink management after the collapse of investment capitalism.* London: Routledge.

Sumara, D., & D'Amour, L. (2012). Understanding school districts as learning systems: Some lessons from three cases of complex transformation. *Journal of Educational Change, 13*(3), 373–399.

Thompson, M., Gereluk, D., & Kowch, E. (2015). School identity in the context of Alberta chartered schools. *Journal of School Choice, 10*(1), 1–24.

Thompson-Klein, J. (2010). *Creating interdisciplinary campus cultures: A model for strength and sustainability.* San Francisco, CA: Jossey-Bass.

Tracey, M., & Boling, E. (2014). Preparing instructional designers: Traditional and emerging perspectives. In M. Spector, D. Merrill, J. Elen, & M. Bishop (Eds.), *Handbook of research on educational communications and technology* (4th ed., pp. 373–383). New York, NY: Springer.

Trilling, B., & Fadel, C. (2009). *21st century skills. Learning for life in our times.* San Francisco, CA: Jossey-Bass.

Tyack, D., & Tobin, W. (1994). The "grammar" of schooling: Why has it been so hard to change? *American Educational Research Journal, 31*(3), 453–459.

Warren, W. (2008). *How do rural schools respond to system wide policy interventions? A study of the nature of decision making networks* (Unpublished Doctoral Dissertation). University of Calgary, Calgary.

Wenger, E., McDermott, R., & Snyder, W. (2002). *Cultivating communities of practice.* Boston, MA: Harvard University Press.

Willower, D. J., & Forsythe, B. (1999). A brief history of scholarship on educational administration. In J. Murphy & K. Louis (Eds.), *Handbook of research on educational administration* (pp. 1–25). San Francisco, CA: Jossey-Bass.

Winkelmans, T. (2014). *High school principal and student power relationships when students choose distance education courses* (Unpublished Doctoral Dissertation). University of Calgary, Calgary.

Eugene Kowch
Werklund School of Education
University of Calgary, Canada

BONNIE SHAPIRO

14. DESIGNING SUPPORT FOR ACTIVE PARTICIPATION IN LEARNING AND RESEARCH

HELPING LEARNERS FIND THEIR PLACE AS AGENTS
IN THEIR OWN LEARNING

My first experience as a student with a teacher who truly understood what it meant to create structures to help students participate more effectively in their own learning was in Mr Don's Language Arts class. I was a 14-year-old junior high school student. Mr Don wore pastel coloured suits and a perpetual smile. We loved him for the ways he showed genuine interest in our lives and in our learning. He would often talk about the ideas behind his teaching philosophy, and shared with us that he spoke regularly with his fellow teacher colleagues in our school. He frequently told us what he learned in those conversations and how interested he was in the ways we were learning in other classes. One day Mr Don described how he had discovered that in Social Studies class we were being asked to write reports. He said that our Social Studies teacher told him that many students seemed to know very little about writing reports, most students were simply copying and turning in material from encyclopaedia articles. I recall Mr Don telling us,

> I understand why many are doing this. I want you to know that copying someone else's work is always plagiarism. Plagiarism is presenting someone else's work as your own. I realize that you do not know what else to do – and that is not your fault. You have not been given the tools and experiences you need to understand what it means to do research and write a report using more than one source. So here is where we are going with this: We are going to learn how to write an original report over the next two months, and the topic of this assignment is something that you will decide. You are going to be asking a *question of your own*. If it is your own question, it should be a question that really interests you. We are going to learn how to do the research needed to address your question using multiple research resources.

I was enchanted by the opportunity Mr Don presented to participate in an experience that connected work in his class to learning in other course disciplines. He told us that he had created a curriculum experience to give his students tools to learn how to take actions, take notes and organize a research paper of our own. His efforts and the concern and caring for our learning that was behind it stand out so vividly in my memory of that year. He provided experiences that enlivened my thinking about learning and created a truly authentic learning experience. What I did not realize at the time was the way Mr Don was involved in changing, even challenging the established curriculum and established ways of working in the classroom. He was also altering the design of the culture of the learning setting. I was aware that not every student enthusiastically took up this new approach to work in period 4 Language Arts. In conversations with students, parents and school administrators, Mr Don was asked to defend how spending time on independent research addressed curriculum goals. I admired his courage and realized over the years the ways he ignited a spark that year that gave me the courage to embrace my own deeply held views about learning and try new directions in my future work as an educator and researcher.

This book reflects research and teaching themes that originated in these experiences. These themes have permeated my lifework in Education as a student teacher, elementary/junior high school teacher, teacher educator and researcher. Like my teacher Mr Don, colleagues and I have worked to help change aspects of the culture of learning. These new learning structures and routines of engagement are designed to help students develop the experiences and skills needed to ask and answer questions of their own in learning. It has also meant the need for new and appropriate research approaches and frameworks such as those described by the authors of this volume. My own research goals are organized to build understanding of how learners engage in and contribute to their own learning. This work also explores the ways their teachers strive to impact the social and cultural structures of learning settings ((Shapiro, 1996, 2015; Shapiro & Kirby, 1998).

The first opportunity to work with some of the ideas Mr Don presented, emerged during my student teaching experience. I requested permission from my partner teacher to organize a series of lessons to guide the work of the 11–12 year old children I was working with. The goal was to help them learn to gather and organize information using three different sources as they created reports during their studies of animal families. My partner teacher strongly voiced her scepticism, saying, "I don't think this will work. *These kids* will not be able to understand what you are asking them to do. You can try, but I don't believe this will work with them." The school, located in an economically impoverished area, was well known for its generally poor results on standardized tests administered annually in the school systems. I felt so fortunate that she was willing to allow me to try something new. I found the children bright, interested in learning and excited to be working with a student teacher. They were receptive yet it was indeed, very challenging at first for them to learn to take notes as they read about their animals using a variety of sources. It was a completely new way of engaging in learning in the classroom, as it would have been for any class of 11–12 year olds. I began by sharing my own project, a study of Elephants, showing them how I used many reference resources and the steps I followed to bring the project to completion. During the experience, I found that the children did grasp the value of changing the ways they had been previously writing reports by moving away from copying from encyclopaedia articles. Their greatest challenge was in organizing the information, something that takes practice. I learned that it was in this area that it would be best to focus attention. I gathered examples from the children to create a report for my partner teacher and university supervisor. I believe that these results were a wonderful first step.

As a teacher in my own grade 5 classroom (ages 11–12), I involved students in original research during our studies of insect life cycles. Following extensive observations of mealworms, students posed questions of their own. They gathered data to answer their questions and shared their results during our Classroom Scientist Roundtable afternoons. What emerged for me was recognition and admiration of the remarkable levels of competency in some of the youngest of learners. Engaging in their own research meant creating new routines and structures for learning in Science. This way of learning in science was completely new to them. One day, as I went around the room asking students to share their questions with me, one of my students, Raylie, asked, "Which surfaces do mealworms prefer to walk on, rough or smooth surfaces?" 'What a wonderful question!' I exclaimed. She looked at me quizzically for a moment, then asked, "But you *do know the answer*... don't you?" I replied, "No, I don't know the answer – I have never studied this particular problem before. I am looking forward to hearing what you find out!" Clearly, for Raylie, the idea that her teacher did not know the answer to all of the questions the students were about to pursue was something very new to many of the children. I hoped that my response represented me as a learner, to be the same kind of learner I hoped they would be. Suddenly I was not the teacher-as-fount-of-all-information. I became teacher-the-inquirer, one who posed interesting, testable questions. This broke unspoken rules about the expectation many children had about their teacher, as someone who held all of the information. I was curious and learning along with them. They learned that I was trying to help them have greater control over aspects of their own learning. I included information about our project and the outcomes of the children's learning in our regular classroom newsletter to parents. This was a teaching approach that was new to parents also, and many expressed the same surprise as Raylie. Encouraging the children to learn to ask their own questions was met with excitement and many more questions! How far would I be taking this experience? Would all of my teaching for all subjects in the curriculum be addressed in the same way? A description of this project and some of its successes and challenges became the subject of my first academic article for the profession, titled, *Science: Learn with them* (Shapiro, 1979).

Later, during university research studies, I continued to pursue understanding of how children take action to build knowledge of their own. My book, *What children bring to light* explores patterns of individual children's natural actions to learn during study of the topic, *Light* in their elementary science class (Shapiro, 1994). The research approach was based on extended engagement in the classroom and involved regular conversation with children as collaborators to build understanding of their learning processes. As a professor of Science Education, I continue to share this work with teachers and teachers in preparation to stimulate discussions about the kinds of learning structures that may facilitate or constrain students' efforts to actively participate in their own learning. I engage student teachers in a foundational assignment to help them reflect on the nature of science knowledge and what it means to participate in the process of building knowledge in science. Working in teams of two, they prepare a simple, testable question, one that truly interests them. They are encouraged to propose a simple question, the kind of question that might be posed in an Elementary School Science Fair project. They then design an approach to gather and analyse data to answer their question. When I first introduced this assignment, I learned that most student teachers have had over their school careers, very little opportunity to engage in any form of original research. The task turned out to be very challenging to many student teachers at first. I was able to document the project using an action research approach. The process of engaging the student teachers in the research assisted them to reflect on their research processes and also, how they felt about working in this new way to understand the nature of scientific investigation. A personal construct research approach showed that many made significant shifts in their thinking about the intellectual and instructional value of engaging in the experience. Many stated that they built new understandings of the ways knowledge in science is constructed and evaluated. Many also commented on the value of organizing learning structures in their own classrooms to help their students learn to design their own research (Shapiro, 1996).

Creating Environments to Support Help-Seeking and Help-Giving in Learning

Working with children and student teachers demonstrated the need to create new ways to assist my students to engage in their own research. I discovered the vital importance of providing opportunities to allow students to speak regularly with me and with one another about their research. This inspired a new direction in the Program of Research described in Chapter 7 in this volume – a focus on the ways learners take action to seek help in learning, when needed, and the ways educators create environments that support help-seeking and help-giving (Shapiro, 2016). This line of research explores the ways culturally constructed features of learning settings, define and structure the ways learners behave in and experience those learning settings. The physical and social structures of learning environments provide supports that help students take action to seek help in learning. On the other hand, institutional structures may also create obstacles that keep students silent when they need help, or discourage students from taking an active role in their learning. The restrictions of such settings must be researched, understood and challenged (Shapiro, 2011, 2014a, 2014b, 2015, 2016; Shapiro, Richards, Ross, & Kendal-Knitter, 1999).

There have been many wonderful educators like Mr Don, who often with little structural or system support, have worked to change the rules to help learners develop greater understanding of their abilities and the confidence to engage in their own efforts to take actions to learn. Stories of the devoted work and successes of such educators are presented in the chapters in this volume. It is our hope that this book supports the efforts of those seeking to understand what it is that educators can do, and how institutions might continue to engage in changes that offer environments where learners are building meaningful knowledge in this new world with all of its opportunities and great challenges.

PERSPECTIVES ON ACTIONS OF THEIR OWN IN LEARNING AND RESEARCH

Current research designed to understand the contributions learners make to their own learning is having an influence on the construction of many new learning environments worldwide. Emerging understandings of researchers' connections and commitments to the concerns of the subjects of their research have also inspired new ways of thinking about research engagement, in particular, the development of more agentic ways of working with research participants. In this volume we explore the potential for the design of research and learning environments rooted in a conception of learning that embraces ideas about the vital connections between knowledge, agency, personal meaning and identity. Five perspectives about what it means to *take actions of our own to learn* run through our chapters:

1. Taking Actions to Build Knowledge Involves the Whole Person in Specific Contexts

Each individual engages in his or her own unique and highly individual ways of moving through the world in an effort to understand it and their place in it. Knowledge-building involves the whole person. Individuals use the mind and also the body to learn. Engagement in the process of building knowledge also involves acting within specific relationships and in specific contexts. Each person does so with resources that they bring to the experience of knowledge-building such as: prior knowledge and life experiences; natural inclinations and habits; unique abilities; physical, intellectual and emotional states; economic, social, religious and cultural backgrounds; personal interests and questions; feelings, hopes and desires; widely ranging political views; and differing social and communication skills.

2. Students, Teachers and Researchers, as Individuals, Are Learning Persons Who Take Actions of Their Own in Ways Similar to Those Involved in Formal Research Activities

Researchers identify questions about a topic of study, then gather information to build understanding about the subject they are studying. In these ways, researchers are acting as learners. They make their research processes explicit, presenting them to a community of others interested in the same questions. Learners engage in knowledge-building using strategies that are individual and unique. In many ways their strategies are similar to those of researchers. They pose questions about a topic of interest, gather data and make conclusions based on their findings. They incorporate new ideas into their evolving understandings of the world and they develop ideas about their place in the world. And, like many researchers, they take actions in the world based on their new understandings.

3. The Construction of New Knowledge Takes Place Both Individually and Within Communities

This perspective extends the view that just as knowledge-building relies on unique and individual efforts and contexts, it also develops through the emergence of meanings as participants engage as members of a community. Knowledge-building is therefore both unique and individual, and it is also constructed communally. Learners often engage collaboratively with others, exploring and testing ideas using all of the skills and resources at their disposal. Similarly, researchers pursue sense-making in unique and individual ways, constantly developing new skills and approaches to gathering knowledge. They share insights with the research community, and in many cases, also with their research subjects. Research subjects can often be effectively engaged in collaborative research efforts to build understanding as noted by Sarah Pink (2009).

4. Structures and Settings for Learning and Research Are Influenced by Cultural, Social and Political Values and Discourses.

One of the most important tasks of education must be to create structures and environments that help educators offer opportunities for learners to frame and ask questions about the world in ways that reflect the relevant and authentic interests of the asker. Learning environments, curriculum materials and routines of interaction should be thoughtfully constructed to provide the kind of assistance needed to develop research skills and information gathering activities. These structures and environments should also be informed by recognition that the physical environments within which we work represent deeply rooted, and sometimes traditional social and cultural values that may present obstacles and constraints that must be addressed and disrupted. Researchers, educators, curriculum leaders and learners are the products of learning environments. They are also producers of social and cultural environments offered to learners (Shapiro, 2014b, 2015). We will benefit from striving to more deeply understand the social and cultural environments we inhabit and how they influence our knowledge-building practices. Recognition of the traditional values and perspectives that are embodied in the practices and physical structures we create helps consider which structures must be challenged and changed as we create new and more relevant settings and practices.

5. Greater Attention Is Needed at Institutional Levels to Create Environments That Build Experiences That Develop Learner/Researchers' Skills and Views of Themselves as Capable and Effective Knowledge Builders

Along with opportunities to develop higher levels of self-direction, experiences must be developed to help learners discover and express what they need and want to know. Educators are learning to use new strategies to help learners develop and reflect on their capabilities as agents of their own learning. Increasingly, new efforts at institutional levels are building environments that support such experiences. An example at the university level is the introduction of programs that engage students in studies of global issues that are identified by learners and studied collaboratively. At the workplace level and in elementary classrooms, programs such as "The Genius Hour", promote setting aside time for learners to engage in independent inquiry studies based on topics that individuals identify as important and interesting to them. Inspired by Daniel Pink's book, *Drive* (2009), Krebs and Zvi's (2016) book, *The Genius Hour Guidebook* is a resource for educators who are introducing schools and children to structures to help learners develop the skills needed to propose and research questions reflecting their own deep interests. Steinberg and Kinchloe's (1998) edited volume, *Students as researchers: creating classrooms that matter,* is also a valuable resource for the design of new learning environments.

SELF-KNOWLEDGE, SELF-CONFIDENCE AND THE DEVELOPMENT OF LEARNER AGENCY

As noted above, the research and writing in the present volume is rooted in the view that human beings engage in knowledge-building using prior knowledge, life experience, unique abilities, widely ranging personal and political views, social and cultural backgrounds, ideas, curiosities, questions, feelings, hopes and desires, and emerging social and communication skills. These are resources used by individuals to engage in learning in their social world. Learners also build emerging understandings of the extent of their abilities to serve as active agents in their own learning. These views influence the development of self-confidence and interest in taking actions to persist as agents in their own learning.

Social cognition theorist, Albert Bandura (2001), describes the social and structural influences that impact the psychological mechanisms of human agency. He defines human agency as the capacity to act in the world and exercise control over the nature and quality of one's life (p. 3). Bandura argues that human beings are able to exert control when engaging in experiences that offer opportunities to make choices and build action plans. He asserts that "monitoring one's pattern of behaviour and awareness of the cognitive and environmental conditions under which it occurs is the first step toward doing something to affect it" (p. 8). Further, human beings are "not only agents of action, they are also self-examiners of their own functioning" (p. 10). This kind of self-examination can help learners build positive images of themselves as effective agents in the quest to acquire knowledge. They learn to recognize that they can take actions that lead to achieving their own success. These insights can usefully inform the design of learning settings that help teach learners how to develop the skills needed to learn how to gather and analyse information. Bandura identifies four core agentic features: forethought, intentionality, self-regulation, and self-reflection, and also three modes of human agency: personal, proxy, and collective. Additional factors of learner autonomy described by others include desire (Meyer, 2001), resourcefulness and initiative (Ponton & Carr, 2000), and persistence (Derrick, 2001). Vygotsky's (1986) investigations into the importance of paying attention to learners' self-talk when engaged in knowledge-building activities shows how human beings naturally take an active role in their own learning development. A focus on metacognition in the form of self-monitoring and reflection suggests new ways that educators might guide and deepen self-awareness and learners' recognition of the possibilities for self-direction in learning.

Dweck's (1999, 2006, 2012) research on self-theories suggests how people develop ideas about themselves and their abilities to make decisions about their learning. Self-theories reveal ideas about personal abilities that can either encourage learners to work harder or that may contribute to the development of discouraging views of self as incapable of learning well. Ideas about the self as learner are often rooted in socially constructed ideas and metaphors that characterize human qualities such as intelligence. Dweck points to two very different socially constructed perspectives relating to intelligence: a "fixed" versus a "growth mindset" view. The "fixed mindset" perspective sees human traits like ability, intelligence, or talent as innate and unchangeable. High intelligence is possessed only by some individuals. Dweck suggests that a "growth mindset" or incremental view of intelligence, in contrast, asserts that most basic abilities and skills are malleable. They can be developed by anyone who has the dedication to achieve, energy and passion for learning, and the motivation to work hard. These qualities combined with a deep interest in the topic of study can lead to unexpected accomplishment. Dweck (2006) notes how traditional learning environments often perpetuate a fixed mindset perspective, and because of this, many students come to believe that when they do not succeed it is because they lack innate intelligence or are not "smart enough." She suggests that students instead be encouraged to develop a growth mindset view, so that they might develop the personal theory perspective that with persistent strong effort, they can accomplish any task undertaken. Hart et al.'s (2004), resource, "*Learning without limits*", suggests approaches for the creation of learning environments that help children build more positive self-theories. Their recommendations support the creation of environments that allow children to be involved as co-agents in learning. Dweck's work is foundational to Peacock's (2010) award-winning work with teacher colleagues to bring dramatic change to a school previously known for its poor academic and social ranking. With colleagues she created a school built on the growth mindset view where both children and the adults who guided them successfully worked together to build the confidence "to challenge themselves." Their well-known success at Wroxham

School provides a new, positive environment that supports the work of students and teachers based on philosophy of "excellence achieved through equity, empowerment and expertise" (Peacock, 2010, pp. 374–378).

A significant feature of research on child agency in learning that emerges in the environmental education research literature and research on transformational thinking relates to the importance of believing in one's own ability to learn (Malone, 2013; Percy-Smith & Burns, 2013). Confidence in one's own ability leads to a sense of agency in learning, development of the ability to articulate one's point of view, and ultimately, the confidence to take a stand to argue for one's position. Blanchet-Cohen's (2008) research describes six dimensions of child agency: connectedness, engagement with the environment, questioning, belief in capacity, taking a stance, and strategic action (p. 257). My colleague, Laura Istead and I studied the nature of the influence of a small group of 10–12 year old children as agents of intergenerational learning in environmental studies (Istead & Shapiro, 2014). This study looked at knowledge that children attempted to share with their families following a school environmental education experience. We investigated the variety of ways that parents, and children themselves consider children as valuable learning catalysts and influencers of family knowledge. We discovered that acceptance of the view that children may offer authentic new knowledge may disrupt traditional organizational structures and power relationships in family settings. Children and their parents did not always report the extent of influence in the same way. The reasons for these differences present new and complex insights. Parents' views of the child's status in the family appeared to be a significant factor as to whether they were considered a significant source of knowledge or in the case of our study whether they would be listened to as encouragers of ecologically sound behaviours in the family. Individual parents reported that they often considered other children in the family to have more valuable knowledge than the children in the study group. Some parents revealed that they were not interested in listening to or accepting their child as a source of new knowledge. They were not interested in relinquishing their role as holding the most authoritative source of knowledge in the family. The research suggests that whether a child will attempt to share information depends on factors relating to the child's self-confidence and decisions about whether they believe their knowledge and views will be accepted and appreciated by family members. Other parents considered their children as outstanding knowledge resources when asked if they considered their children as reliable sources of new information. As one parent stated,

> Absolutely. All the time. They have the most current information about everything, whether it's computers or what's going on in new environmental science discoveries. Every time they come home and say, 'This is what we learned at school today,' it influences us in some way or another. They are bringing home the most current information.

Interviews with both children and their parents showed insight into the complex set of social and personal factors that impact the extent of parents' willingness to accept knowledge that children might offer to parents and families based on their school and informal learning activities.

Toshalis and Nakkula (2012 propose a developmental framework to describe the language and information organizing skills learners exhibit as they progress in their abilities to become problem solvers and take actions of their own to learn. The framework presents a set of categories of "learner-voiced activities." In their view, one of the most important foundations to facilitate academic achievement is helping students feel that they have a stake in their own learning. They believe that youth, like adults, perform best in an activity when they "have a voice in how it is conducted and an impact on how it concludes." This means that learners should be helped to articulate their positions as stakeholders in their learning, then develop skills and the autonomy needed to participate in data gathering activities that allow them to participate in higher level conversations. By beginning with support for the abilities to articulate and express ideas, learners can be guided to move to "partnership, activism and leadership roles." Toshalis and Nakkula's framework may be useful for curriculum designers interested in creating experiences to provide developmentally appropriate experiences to help build agency and voice in learning. As Wilson, Winkler, Dasho, Wallerstein and Martin (2008) also suggest, students can learn to take on the challenges involved in making decisions and ultimately to engage in responsible social action. Educators will find this work useful to guide the design of curricula and programs to help learners and researchers build higher level skills that lead to becoming problem solvers, decision makers and activists for change.

Helping Learners Design Research to Explore Their Own Questions and Present their Research Findings – Opportunities and Challenges

Von Duyke (2013) points to the importance of understanding the variety of ways educators employ conceptions of student autonomy, personal agency, and research. Much of this work is inspired by a concern for the loss of personal agency in traditional and dominantly outcomes-based, standardization-oriented learning programs. She points out that simply increasing learner autonomy by giving students the opportunity to learn independently does not automatically lead to an increase in the development of personal agency, the ability to make choices, and the ability to take control of one's learning. Kellett (2005a, 2005b) writes that considerations of children taking action of their own to conduct research requires the development of a "new research paradigm for the 21st century" (p. 1).

Many authors note that just as there is significant value in learners' engagement in independent and collaborative research activities, there are obstacles to their full participation that must be addressed (Bucknall, 2012; Kellett, 2010; Shapiro, 1996). Learners must develop knowledge about the strategies of research. New teaching approaches are needed to help learners identify a question or problem that is of deep interest. Teachers must also create new organizational structures to help learners develop strategies to gather preliminary information to provide insight into the problem. Students will then benefit from learning how to access resources to understand how the topic may have already been previously studied by others. Good models of research practice are needed to identify and planning to use appropriate data gathering approaches. Students need time to develop and practice data collection techniques such as interviewing skills, taking photographs, making video records and note-taking. They require guidance in how to organize and preserve data, and how to consider the ethical implications of their work. Adults regularly develop these skills in work environments and in graduate programs geared to their academic level. Kellett also notes the importance of considering the power dynamics involved in working with children. She suggests that when working with children as knowledge producers, educators should take care not to raise the unrealistic expectation for children that their research is going to necessarily "change the world" (Kellett, 2010, p. 116). In her view, managing child researchers' outcome expectations is an important responsibility of the adults who support their work. She also points out that children, like adults, must expect their research and findings to be critically scrutinized. And for these reasons, she states: "It is so important to give children quality research training and help them develop valid research methods that will stand up to independent scrutiny" (Kellett, 2010). Bucknall (2012) also emphasizes the crucial need to create age appropriate strategies to help students develop the skills needed to engage in research.

SEMIOTIC UNDERSTANDINGS AND THE DESIGN OF STRUCTURES TO SUPPORT ACTIVE PARTICIPATION IN LEARNING AND RESEARCH

Designing Learning Settings That Teach

The research and writing in this volume advocates for greater support for the kinds of personal and collective agency needed to disrupt traditional structures that have focused on 'pre-formed' or formal, static views of knowledge. As Hopkins (2010) notes, traditional educational structures present learning goals that are typically prescribed and pre-determined. Structures for learning and research designed to build skills to help individuals *take actions of their own to learn* must incorporate learning goals and build meanings that are also dynamic and emerging. Research questions may be developed and explored with fellow students or in collaboration with research subjects who may also become co-authors. Space, time, and a conception of research must be in place in a way that allows research questions to evolve and change. Research projects may require ongoing modification and should allow learners the kind of intellectual space needed to present unexpected outcomes that challenge existing knowledge.

B. SHAPIRO

Semiotic Readings of Learning Environments

All of the physical and social features of a learning environment are available as potential resources to help learners to take a more active role in learning. Learning environments are constructed to support and perpetuate the cultural values of those who designed them. For example, the date of construction means that the educational values of a particular era are embodied in a building's architectural design and used for many years thereafter. These design features reflect views about how education during a particular time period was expected to proceed. Learners, and all who inhabit a learning setting, read their school buildings as a form of text. These structures contain messages that reflect the educational goals and aspirations of the culture that created them. They are read as text forms by all who inhabit and visit the learning communities.

Semiotics is the study of these sign and symbol systems. Like a golden key, semiotics reveals the ways cultural values are embodied in physical and social structures (Shapiro, 2014a, 2014b, 2015). These messages are also represented in the "unwritten rules" of classroom communication and behavior. This is particularly relevant for the kinds of structures available to support self-directed learning. Lemke (1990) noted that such cultural views and values are available for study in two ways: (1) through activity structures that portray sequences of actions and expected behavior in learning settings and (2) through an examination of the functions of these patterns of actions (p. 49). Learners experience the ways the physical and social structures of learning settings, free or constrain their movements. They learn the social rules of the classroom that direct the kinds of interactions that are possible and acceptable in the learning setting. They learn how learning will proceed, what is rewarded during the classroom session and what is not, what kinds of questions may be asked, who may ask the questions and how they may be asked. Individuals interact with others as they build new knowledge within communities and cultures. Learning how to learn is dictated by the values and rules of one's environment and the ways those who guide learning interpret those values. When educators begin to view such everyday cultural practices as learning resources, they can engage in critical reflection on the ideas and messages they convey, and consider how to introduce new ideas about how learning will proceed. This points to opportunities for the creation of new physical and social structures and new curriculum materials. It also shows the importance of teacher professional development and the design of resources to specifically support learner agency and the skills needed to engage in self-directed work (Shapiro, 2015; Vaugh, 2014).

Personal agency operates within a broad network of social and cultural and structures. Semiotic interpretive studies help build understanding of the ways learners read the messages of these structures. Armed with knowledge of their impacts, educators may disrupt discourses that represent obstacles to learning and environments that work against the development of the skills needed to build the confidence and ability to take self-directed actions to learn (Shapiro, 2014a, 2015). Involving learners in research, for example, requires deep engagement and the allotment of extensive time periods. Shapiro, Richards, Ross, and Kendall (1999) show how semiotic readings of the organization of educational timetables, which structures the organization of time in learning settings, sends messages about the importance of subject area topics relative to one another revealed by the amount of time devoted to each in the school day. Messages about the rules of communication are revealed in the daily rituals of interaction in learning environments. They tell participants who may speak in the environment and when, who asks the questions in the classroom and who is expected to answer the questions asked. The messages are understood by all who share the common everyday culture of the learning environment. Maturana and Varela (1987) showed how the environment holds a dynamic and reciprocal quality that is specific to the setting one participates in. We are affected by the environment and we also have an impact on it. We build new knowledge individually, and also through interaction with others who are members of our social community. As with language, knowledge of one's culture serves as an everyday and ever ready resource for the ideas and actions shared in learning settings. When educators build semiotic understandings they are able to engage in thoughtful reflection on the ways learning and research environments represent cultural values. This can lead to the confidence to create new learning structures. Educational environments can be changed to offer more powerful messages about the value of offering learners greater degrees of control and responsibility for their own learning.

MOVING IN EMANCIPATORY NEW DIRECTIONS IN RESEARCH AND LEARNING

Awareness of the cultural messages also conveyed in research approaches can lead to the design research strategies that allow more authentic collaborative engagements with research participants. The chapters in our book describe our work and thinking to create structures that support fresh new values to guide learning and research. Authors have explored possibilities using a wide range of theoretical frameworks and foundations:

- Activist and agentic emphases in research in environmental education (Paul Hart & Catherine Hart)
- Ethno-autobiographical studies in environmental education (Peta White)
- Transformative learning in parks education settings (Don Carruthers den Hoed)
- Enactivist studies in mathematics education (Jo Towers and Lyndon Martin)
- Guiding the design of research on original questions asked by physics education students (Emily Hanke Van Zee)
- A personal construct theory approach to understand the help-seeking strategies of children in science education (Bonnie Shapiro)
- Building theoretical foundations to support student led learning for altruistic actions (Larry Bencze)
- Creating a new school culture built on trust, equity, empowerment and expertise for students and teachers (Dame Alison Peacock)

- Online learning experiences built on knowledge of the lives and needs of learners in a nursing and health education program (Sherri Melrose)
- Using photovoice to engage social work students in social action research (Kathy Sitter)
- Exploring features of a new educational paradigm to support the creation of participatory learning environments (Eugene Kowch)
- Helping educators build semiotic interpretive understandings as a resource for the design of learning environments that support active participation in learning and research (Bonnie Shapiro)

To move in new emancipatory directions means helping individuals build the skills of self-direction while at the same time developing the collaborative skills needed to make contributions as a member of a learning community. The concept at the heart of this book, '*actions of their own to learn*' with its focus on the central role of agency, expands ideas about traditional definitions of learning and research, valuing both as components of knowledge-building processes. In this way, learning is a form of engagement in research and research is viewed as a form of learning.

There have been some excellent efforts to describe innovative new practices, settings and their implications worldwide (Wolner, Hall, Higgins, McCaughey, & Wall, 2007; Hampson, Patton, & Shanks, 2013). Learner outcomes in many cases are still reported in terms of achievement scores on standardized tests, grades, or other objective measures of performance. Such measures compare student achievements to those of students who are learning in traditional settings. They do not necessarily assess the stated goals and achievements of innovative programs designed to teach more than subject matter content. Measures are also needed to understand the extent to which educational practices are also helping learners develop autonomy, voice, choice, and confidence in their own learning abilities. More collaborative research and evaluation approaches are needed that build insight into aspects of the nature of the experience for the learner that are not typically captured, such as (1) the development of connections between cognitive and emotional growth, (2) the ways new programs build habits of mind that sustain learning effort and achievement, and (3) the extent to which such programs nurture focused and enduring interests that go beyond school to impact learning in everyday life. Other questions about learning and research that support self direction and taking action to learn must also be asked:

- What are and learners' and educators' experiences in these settings?
- How might educators be best supported as they learn to place control of learning in the hands of learners?
- How effective are programs created to provide guidance for learners as they engage in open-ended, sustained actions to learn?
- How well do these opportunities enable learners to have a voice in and control over important aspects of their own learning?
- What new criteria are needed to define effective learning in these settings?

- How might we best evaluate and improve the design of structures created to offer such environments for learners?
- How might the design of collaborative research studies more fully involve learners, educators and other stake-holders in the design of research?

There is a dramatic increase worldwide in new kinds of learning settings that seek to offer innovative new structures and experiences that support learners' efforts to take actions of their own to learn. These include traditional, formal settings such as those found in school classrooms, learning commons and learning communities, as well as informal learning environments such as Maker spaces, Science Centres, Nature and Conservation Centres, Parks, Zoos, University Camps, Pre-schools and Community Activity Centres. New curriculum and resources are being created for use in these settings as educators strive to build new understandings about learner capacities that in turn, require rethinking the nature and purposes of learning spaces (Jonassen & Land, 2012). We need to know more about how learners, educators and researchers are incorporating knowledge about learning as they create these settings (Marquez-Zenkov, 2007; Wang, Cash, & Powers, 2000). There are many wonderful teachers who, often with little support, strive to help learners develop their creative and intellectual capacities in their learning. The stories of the devoted work, deep thinking and successes of such educators are represented in many of the chapters in this volume. This work is about striving to understand what it is that educators do to create environments for those who are learning in this new world with all of its opportunities and great challenges.

Recent collaborative research designed to support these new goals provides accounts of teacher efforts and activities to engage students in new ways as they are given voice and learn to make choices in their learning (Drummond, Hart, & Swann, 2013; Hart, Dixon, Drummond, & McIntyre, 2004; Lowe, 2005; Peacock, 2010). New approaches to the reporting of insights are contained in the comprehensive and influential Organization for Economic Co-operation and Development (2013) document, *Innovative Learning Environments*. The Innovative Learning Environments document also describes the "vital importance" of including youth voice as part of the ongoing formative cycle to more deeply understand what happens "when learners are engaged in decision-making" (pp. 124–128). What is needed are continuing studies such as these that generate rich accounts of learner experiences in environments where students are given the tools and resources to take greater control of and therefore more responsibility for their own learning.

Our book is designed to offer insights for researchers, educators and institutions who seek to design new spaces and structures that provide greater support for knowledge-building work. We believe that planning to help people come to know should be a transformative experience, one that gives learners and researchers fresh new opportunities as actors in their own knowledge-building work. The chapters in this volume are intended to inspire conversations and further explorations into what it means to take action in knowing and learning, as well as the kinds of institutional structures needed to support collaborative and participative research. It is our hope that our accounts of researcher and learner experiences will continue to support the creation of new structures and opportunities to help researchers and learners develop the skills needed *to take actions of their own to learn.*

REFERENCES

Bandura, A. (2001). Social cognitive theory: An agentic perspective. *Annual Review of Psychology, 52,* 1–26.
Blanchet-Cohen, N. (2008). Taking a stance: Child agency across the dimensions of early adolescents' environmental involvement. *Environmental Education Research, 14,* 257–272. doi:10.1080/13504620802156496
Bucknall, S. (2012). *Children as researchers in primary schools: Choice, voice and participation.* New York, NY: Routledge.
Derrick, M. G. (2001). *The measurement of an adult's intention to exhibit persistence in autonomous learning* (Unpublished doctoral dissertation). The George Washington University, Washington, DC.
Drummond, M. J., Hart, S., & Swann, M. (2013). An alternative approach to school development: The children are the evidence. *Forum, 55,* 121–132. Retrieved from http://learningwithoutlimits.educ.cam.ac.uk/downloads/creatinglwl_forumarticle.pdf
Dweck, C. (1999). *Self-theories: Their role in motivation, personality and development.* Philadelphia, PA: Psychology Press.
Dweck, C. (2006). *Mindset: The new psychology of success.* New York, NY: Random House.
Dweck, C. (2012). *Mindset: How you can fulfil your potential.* London: Constable & Robinson.
Hampson, M., Patton, A., & Shanks, L. (2013). *10 schools for the 21st century.* Retrieved from http://www.innovationunit.org/sites/default/files/10 Schools for the 21st Century_0.pdf
Hart, S., Dixon, A., Drummond, J. J., & McIntyre, D. (2004). *Learning without limits.* Maidenhead: Open University Press.
Hopkins, K. R. (2010). *Teaching how to learn in a what-to-learn culture.* San Francisco, CA: Jossey-Bass.
Istead, L., & Shapiro, B. (2014). Recognizing the child as knowledgeable other: Intergenerational learning research to consider child-to-adult influence on parent and family eco-knowledge. *Journal of Research in Childhood Education, 28*(1), 115–127.
Jonassen, D., & Land, S. (Eds.). (2012). *Theoretical foundations of learning environments.* New York, NY: Routledge. Retrieved from http://www.ebrary.com
Kellet, M. (2005a). *Children as active researchers: A new research paradigm for the 21st century?* ERSC National Centre for Research Methods, Economic and Social Research Council, Swindon. Retrieved from http://eprints.ncrm.ac.uk/87/1/MethodsReviewPaperNCRM-003.pdf
Kellet, M. (2005b). *How to develop children as researchers.* London: Paul Chapman.
Kellett, M. (2010). *Rethinking children and research: Attitudes in contemporary society series.* New York, NY: Continuum International Publishing Group.
Krebs, D., & Zvi, G. (2016). *The genius hour guidebook: Fostering passion, wonder and inquiry in the classroom.* London: Routledge.
Lemke, J. (1990). *Talking science: Language, learning, and values.* New York, NY: Ablex Publishing Corporation.
Lowe, H. (2005). Review of the book learning without limits, by S. Hart, A. Dixon, J. J. Drummond & D. McIntyre. *British Journal of Educational Studies, 53*(1), 102–103. Retrieved from http://www.jstor.org/stable/1556027
Malone, K. (2013). The future lies in our hands: Children as researchers and environmental change agents in designing a child-friendly neighbourhood. *Local Environment: The International Journal of Justice and Sustainability, 18,* 372–395.

Marquez-Zenkov, K. (2007). Through city students' eyes: Urban students' beliefs about school's purposes, supports and impediments. *Visual Studies, 22*, 138–154. doi:10.1080/14725860701507099

Maturana, H. R., & Varela, F. J. (1987). *The tree of knowledge: The biological roots of human understanding.* Boston, MA: Shambala.

Meyer, D. T. (2001). *The measurement of intentional behaviour as a prerequisite to autonomous learning* (Unpublished doctoral dissertation). The George Washington University, Washington, DC.

OECD. (2013). *Innovative learning environments, centre for educational research and innovation.* Paris: OECD Publishing. doi:10.1787/9789264203488-en

Peacock, A. (2010). The Cambridge primary review: A voice for the future. *Forum, 52*, 373–380.

Percy-Smith, B., & Burns, D. (2013). Exploring the role of children and young people as agents of change in sustainable community development. *Local Environment: The International Journal of Justice and Sustainability, 18*, 323–339. Retrieved from http://www.uiowa.edu/~grpproc

Pink, D. (2009). *Drive: The surprising truth about what motivates us.* New York, NY: Riverhead Books.

Pink, S. (2009). *Doing sensory ethnography* (2nd ed.). Los Angeles, CA: Sage Publications Ltd.

Ponton, M. K., & Carr, P. B. (2000). Understanding and promoting autonomy in self-directed learning. *Current Research in Social Psychology, 5*(19), 271–284.

Shapiro, B. (1979, November). Science-learn with them. *Elements-Translating Theory into Practice, 3*(11), 1–5.

Shapiro, B. (1994). *What children bring to light: A constructivist perspective on children's learning in science.* New York, NY: Teachers College Press.

Shapiro, B. (1996). A case study of change in elementary student teacher thinking during an independent investigation in science: Learning about the face of science that does not yet know. *Science Education, 80*(5), 535–560.

Shapiro, B. (2011). Towards a transforming constructivism: Understanding learners' meanings and messages of learning environments. *Journal of Educational Thought, 45*(2), 165–202.

Shapiro, B. (2014a, July 24–27). *Personal constructions of STEM learning.* First Congress on the Construction of Personal Meaning, The Constructivist Psychology Network, Coast Plaza Hotel, Vancouver.

Shapiro, B. (2014b). Engaging novice teachers in semiotic inquiry: Considering the environmental messages of school learning settings. *Cultural Studies in Science Education, 9*, 809–824.

Shapiro, B. (2015). Structures that teach: Using a semiotic framework to study the environmental messages of learning settings. *Journal of Eco-Thinking, 1*, 1–15.

Shapiro, B. (2016, January 31–February 2). *Children's constructions of help-seeking in learning: A resource for the design of science learning experiences.* Presentation to the 28th Annual Ethnographic & Qualitative and AABSS Research Conference and Pre-Conference Workshops, University of Las Vegas College of Education, Las Vegas, NV.

Shapiro, B., & Kirby, D. (1998). An approach the to consider messages of science learning culture. *Journal of Science Teacher Education, 9*(3), 221–240.

Shapiro, B., Richards, L., Ross, N., & Kendal-Knitter, K. (1999). Time and the environments of schooling. *Learning Environments Research, 2*, 1–19.

Steinberg, S., & Kincheloe, J. (Eds.). (1998). *Students as researchers: Creating classrooms that matter.* London: Falmer Press, Taylor & Francis Inc.

Toshalis, E., & Nakkula, M. (2012). *Motivation, engagement, and student voice.* Retrieved from http://studentsatthecenterhub.org/wp-content/uploads/2012/04/Exec-Toshalis-Nakkula-032312.pdf

Vaughn, C. (2014). Participatory research with youth: Idealising safe social spaces or building transformative links in difficult environments? *Journal of Health Psychology, 19*, 184–192.

von Duyke, K. S. (2013). *Students' autonomy, agency and emergent learning interests in two open democratic schools* (Doctoral dissertation). University of Delaware, Newark, DE. Retrieved from ProQuest Digital Dissertations. (AAT 3105626551).

Vygotsky, L. S. (1986). *Thought and language* (revised and expanded ed.). Cambridge, MA: MIT Press.

Wang, C., Cash, J., & Powers, L. (2000). Who knows the streets as well as the homeless? Promoting personal and community action through photo voice. *Health Promotion Practice, 1*, 81–89.

Wilson, N., Winkler, M., Dasho, S., Wallerstein, N., & Martin, A. C. (2008). Getting to social action: The Youth Empowerment Strategies (YES!) project. *Health Promotion Practice, 9,* 395–403.
Wolner, P., Hall, E., Higgins, S., McCaughey, C., & Wall, K. (2007). A sound foundation? What we know about the impact of environments on learning and the implications for building schools for the future. *Oxford Review of Education, 33,* 47–70.

Bonnie Shapiro
Werklund School of Education
University of Calgary, Canada

ABOUT THE CONTRIBUTORS

Larry Bencze, I am an Associate Professor in Science Education at the Ontario Institute for Studies in Education, University of Toronto, Canada, where I teach in the graduate studies programme. In addition to the PhD (U. Toronto, 1995) and BEd (Queen's U., 1977) in education, I hold BSc (Queen's U., 1974) and MSc (Queen's U., 1977) degrees in biology. Prior to work as a professor, I worked as a teacher of science in elementary and secondary schools and as a science education consultant in Ontario, Canada. My teaching and research emphasize history, philosophy and sociology of science and technology, along with student-led research-informed and negotiated socio-political actions to address personal, social and environmental harms associated with fields of science and technology. I have recently edited (or co-edited) two books about activism and am co-editor of the open-source, non-refereed, journal on activism at: goo.gl/cvO2TA

Don Carruthers Den Hoed, I am currently a PhD candidate at the University of Calgary, Canada. I grew up on a wooded acreage in the Alberta foothills, close to Kananaskis Country in the Canadian Rockies. This influenced my early career in park information and interpretation and offered me opportunities for camping, hiking, and playing outdoors. My desire to help people understand these wild places led to acquisition of a BA in Communications in rhetoric and geography. Later, my desire to help include persons with disabilities in parks (inspired by my mother's work in special education) lead to my MA in Education. My experience as a graduate of, and host of, the Canadian Parks Council Leadership Course and a growing desire to lead organizational change drove me to pursue the Interdisciplinary PhD in Environmental Design, Social Work, Education, and Health. My wife is smarter than me. Our children know where their food and heat comes from. A red fox lives in our yard.

Catherine Hart, I am currently a doctoral candidate at the University of Regina, Regina, Canada and am preparing to defend my dissertation about environmental subjectivity among environmental education researchers. I have a BSc in Biology and an MSc in Paleoecology. My research interests include environmental subjectivity and discourse, environmental justice and gender issues in environmental education research. I am also interested in qualitative approaches to research at onto-epistemic, theoretical and methodological levels. My teaching experience includes courses in biology, science methods and environmental education. I am a Consulting Editor for the *Journal of Environmental Education* and regular reviewer for *Environmental Education Research, Environmental Studies and Science,* the *Canadian Journal of Environmental Education* and the *Australian Journal of Environmental Education.* I have been a participant and presenter at AERA for the EE SIG and at the NAAEE

ABOUT THE CONTRIBUTORS

Research Symposium since 2012 and have recently completed an article for the *Journal of Environmental Education* Special Issue on Gender in Environmental Education Research.

Paul Hart, As a Professor of Science and Environmental Education at the University of Regina, Regina, Canada. I currently teach graduate courses in research methodology and curriculum inquiry. My research work has focused on teachers' identities as environmentally oriented educators. More recently, I have explored the potential of post-critically informed ideas for research practice across social-environmental boundaries. A current focus is grounded in applications of emerging qualitative research approaches. These may be useful, it seems to me, in extending conceptualizations of learning that implicate new perspectives on the subjectification of values and worldviews. I serve as an Executive Editor of the *Journal of Environmental Education* and as a consulting editor/editorial board member for several journals including *Environmental Education Research* and the *Canadian Journal of Environmental Education*.

Eugene Kowch, I am an Associate Professor in the Leadership, Policy and Governance area in the Werklund School of Education at the University of Calgary, Canada. My research program focuses on developing human and organizational capabilities in concert, so that innovative teaching and learning processes in the information age can be engaging, fun, sustainable and flexible. In my first career as a petroleum engineer I held progressive positions in multinational energy companies, culminating in senior corporate development leadership positions where I learned that human capability and happiness was a function of learning and leadership. Obtaining degrees in undergraduate and graduate education, I realized the incredible potential for computing and technologies with a new generation of teachers and learners looking for new ways to learn. As a professor in a research institution, my graduate students conceptualize and develop ideas and processes for designing education organizations in concert with student learning taking complexivist and post-structural systems approaches. My research focuses on developing senior leaders in organizations who are able to learn their way forward with the design and development of more flexible participatory and technology-enhanced learning environments.

Lyndon Martin, I am Dean, and Associate Professor of Mathematics Education, in the Faculty of Education at York University, Canada. My research is broadly situated in the field of mathematical thinking, learning and teaching. More specifically, I am interested in the notion of mathematical understanding and in how we might improve mathematics teaching to promote this.

Sherri Melrose, I am an Associate Professor in the Faculty of Health Disciplines at Athabasca University, Canada's Open University. It is my privilege to teach healthcare professionals who are upgrading their education in both undergraduate and graduate programs. I am a Registered Nurse and my clinical expertise is in the area of psychiatric mental health. Inspired by my doctoral studies supervisor, Dr. Bonnie Shapiro, I am committed to understanding who my students are, how they construct the knowledge they need and how I can best support their own efforts to learn. My program of research centers on how health professionals learn in online environments. Insights and findings from my work have been disseminated in peer reviewed articles and e-textbooks and many of these are available at http://auspace.athabascau.ca/handle/2149/1357

Alison Peacock, For fourteen wonderful years I was the headteacher of The Wroxham Primary School in Hertfordshire, England. During that time I engaged in research with the University of Cambridge to explore ways of teaching and leading that resisted notions that 'ability' is fixed. Our mission was to ensure that we always gave children (and adults) the opportunity to surprise us. I am the author of *Assessment for Learning without Limits* (2016) McGrawHill Education, and co-author of *Creating Learning without Limits* (2012) Open University Press. These books seek to tell the stories of individual children, teachers and schools where limits have been lifted on learning. I was honoured to be given the title of Dame by the Queen in 2014 and now also have a visiting Professorial role at the Universities of Hertfordshire, England, and Wrexham Glyndwr, Wales. My current role is as Chief Operating Officer of the newly established Chartered College of Teaching in England. This is a new professional body for the teaching profession that aims to re-empower teachers' authoritative voice through engagement with research.

Bonnie Shapiro, I am a Professor in the Werklund School of Education at the University of Calgary, Canada working with teachers-in-preparation and graduate students from a wide range of backgrounds and experiences. I first entered the profession as an elementary/junior high school teacher. Over many years, I have contributed to the curriculum and research literature in Education, with an ongoing passion for work in Science and Environmental Education. It has been a privilege to serve as an Editorial Advisory Board Member/Consulting Editor for several journals in these fields. The conceptualization of *Actions of Their Own to Learn* represents a career-long interest in in creating more authentic educational and research environments based on understanding the ways learners, teachers, and researchers contribute to, and are impacted by their work. I strive to develop research approaches that deepen insight into the social/cultural features that lie at the heart of the issues and challenges in Education that we all seek to address. This book has been a wonderful opportunity to present the research and thinking of outstanding, internationally recognized colleagues from a range of fields, who share these interests.

Kathleen C. Sitter, I am an Assistant Professor in the field of Social Work, having served at Memorial University and currently, the University of Calgary, Canada.

I have 12 years of teaching experience in education, social work, and business. My areas of interest include disability studies and human rights, accessibility and inclusion, and the theoretical and practical implications of collaborative visual methodologies. My research and scholarship primarily focus on the role of visual and social media in adult education and community engagement. My dissertation, titled "Participatory Video as Radical Incrementalism: Exploring the Right to Love Among Adults with Disabilities," won the 2012 AERA Disability Studies in Education Special Interest Group Outstanding Dissertation Award. My work has been published in venues such as Disability & Society, Social Work Education, Critical Questions in Education, and Intercultural Education.

Jo Towers, I am a Werklund Research Professor in the Werklund School of Education at the University of Calgary, Canada. My research interests include students' mathematical understanding, student experience and identity in relation to learning mathematics, and inquiry-oriented approaches to teaching and teacher education.

Emily Hanke van Zee, I am an Associate Professor of science education and senior researcher in the Department of Physics at Oregon State University, USA. My research has focused upon ways of speaking in which students express their own ideas while engaging one another in discussing what they think. For the past decade, I have designed and taught a laboratory-centered physics course for prospective elementary and middle school teachers. Details about this course are available through a wiki (http://physics.oregonstate.edu/coursewikis/ph111) and drafts of an open source textbook, Exploring Physical Phenomena. With funding from the US National Science Foundation, I explored ways to integrate science and literacy learning in this course. With support from the Spencer Foundation, I sponsored a Science Inquiry Group for teachers and teacher educators interested in sharing their inquiries and findings and served as co-organizer of Teacher Researcher Day at National Science Teachers Association conferences. I can be reached at Emily.vanZee@science.oregonstate.edu.

Peta White, I am a Lecturer in Science and Environmental Education at Deakin University, Australia, joining the team in 2014. I have worked in several jurisdictions across Canada and Australia in primary and secondary classrooms, as a curriculum consultant and manager, and as a teacher educator in under/post graduate programs. I gained my PhD at the University of Regina in Saskatchewan, Canada where I lived for 8 years, focusing on living sustainably and using this as a platform from which to educate future teachers. I continue with a strong commitment to sustainability practices, living with an agenda of responsible consumer choice, learning to live with enough, and practicing Education for Sustainability. Where possible, I take up leadership roles in state and national environmental education organisations, valuing the opportunity to work cross-sectorally with diverse colleagues. I have a background in zoology and I'm currently working on a number of exciting projects with students, teachers, and fellow academics including: developing biology education multi-media resources, researching in school-based contexts around teacher professional learning, and reflexively working on my own scholarship and teaching practice, bringing contemporary science into my teaching and learning. My passion for initial teacher education, activist environmental education, and action-orientated research methodologies drives my current teaching/research scholarship.

CPSIA information can be obtained
at www.ICGtesting.com
Printed in the USA
LVOW03s0219081217
558933LV00003B/41/P